Debates in Geography Educ

Debates in Geography Education encourages early career teachers, experienced teachers and teacher educators to engage with and reflect on key issues, concepts and debates. It aims to enable readers to reach their own informed judgements with deeper theoretical knowledge and understanding.

The second edition is fully updated in light of the latest research, policy and practice in the field, as well as key changes to the curriculum and examination specifications. Expert contributors provide a range of perspectives on international, historical and policy contexts in order to deepen our understanding of significant debates in geography education.

Key debates include:

- geography's identity as an academic discipline;
- what constitutes knowledge in geography;
- places and regional geography;
- what it means to think geographically;
- constructing the curriculum;
- how we link assessment to making progress in geography;
- the contribution of fieldwork and outdoor experiences;
- technology and the use of Geographical Information;
- school geography and employability;
- understanding the gap between school and university geography;
- evidence-based practice and research in geography education.

The comprehensive, rigorous coverage of these key issues, together with carefully annotated selected further reading, will help support and shape further research and writing. *Debates in Geography Education* is a key resource that is essential reading for all teachers and researchers who wish to extend their grasp of the place of geography in education.

Mark Jones is Senior Lecturer in Education at the University of the West of England, Bristol, UK.

David Lambert is Professor of Geography Education at UCL Institute of Education, London, UK.

Debates in Subject Teaching Series

www.routledge.com/Debates-in-Subject-Teaching/book-series/DIST

Series edited by: Susan Capel, Jon Davison, James Arthur, John Moss

The **Debates in Subject Teaching Series** is a sequel to the popular **Issues in Subject Teaching Series**, originally published by Routledge between 1999 and 2003. Each title presents high-quality material, specially commissioned to stimulate teachers engaged in initial training, continuing professional development and Masters level study to think more deeply about their practice, and link research and evidence to what they have observed in schools. By providing up-to-date, comprehensive coverage the titles in the **Debates in Subject Teaching Series** support teachers in reaching their own informed judgements, enabling them to discuss and argue their point of view with deeper theoretical knowledge and understanding.

Titles in the series:

Debates in Geography Education, 2nd edition
Edited by David Lambert and Mark Jones

Debates in History Teaching, 2nd edition
Edited by Ian Davies

Debates in Mathematics Education
Edited by Dawn Leslie and Heather Mendick

Debates in Modern Languages Education
Edited by Patricia Driscoll, Ernesto Macaro and Ann Swarbrick

Debates in Music Teaching
Edited by Chris Philpott and Gary Spruce

Debates in Physical Education
Edited by Susan Capel and Margaret Whitehead

Debates in Religious Education
Edited by L. Philip Barnes

Debates in Science Education
Edited by Matt Watts

Debates in Geography Education

Second Edition

Edited by Mark Jones and
David Lambert

Routledge
Taylor & Francis Group

LONDON AND NEW YORK

Second edition published 2018
by Routledge
2 Park Square, Milton Park, Abingdon, Oxon OX14 4RN

and by Routledge
711 Third Avenue, New York, NY 10017

Routledge is an imprint of the Taylor & Francis Group, an informa business

First edition published by Routledge 2012

British Library Cataloguing in Publication Data
A catalogue record for this book is available from the British Library

Library of Congress Cataloging in Publication Data
Names: Lambert, David, 1952- | Jones, Mark (Mark Stephen)
Title: Debates in geography education / edited by Mark Jones & David Lambert.
Description: Second edition. | Milton Park, Abingdon, Oxon; New York, NY: Routledge, 2017. | Includes index.
Identifiers: LCCN 2017003084 | ISBN 9781138672574 (hardback) | ISBN 9781138672581 (pbk.) | ISBN 9781315562452 (ebook)
Subjects: LCSH: Geography–Study and teaching
Classification: LCC G73 .D283 2017 | DDC 910.71–dc23
LC record available at https://lccn.loc.gov/2017003084

ISBN: 978-1-138-67257-4 (hbk)
ISBN: 978-1-138-67258-1 (pbk)
ISBN: 978-1-315-56245-2 (ebk)

Typeset in Galliard
by Deanta Global Publishing Services, Chennai, India

Printed in the United Kingdom
by Henry Ling Limited

Contents

Figures

Tables

Abbreviations

AB	Awarding Bodies
AfL	Assessment for Learning
ALCAB	A Level Content Advisory Board
AO	Assessment Objective
APG	Action Plan for Geography
BECTA	British Educational Communications and Technology Agency
BERA	British Educational Research Association
BTEC	Business and Technician Education Council
CPD	Continuing Professional Development
DCSF	Department for Children, Schools and Families
DES	Department of Education and Science
DfE	Department for Education
DfEE	Department for Education and Employment
DfES	Department for Education and Skills
EBacc	English Baccalaureate
GA	Geographical Association
GEReCo	Geography Education Research Collective
GIS	Geographic Information Systems
GNC	Geography National Curriculum
GNVQ	General National Vocational Qualification
GTCE	General Teaching Council for England
HEI	Higher Education Institution
HMCI	Her Majesty's Chief Inspector (English and Welsh Schools)
HMI	Her Majesty's Inspectorate
HMSO	Her Majesty's Stationery Office
ICT	Information and Communication Technology
ITE	Initial Teacher Education
ITT	Initial Teacher Training
IBG	Institute of British Geographers
KS	Key Stage
MAT	Multi Academy Trust
MGH	'Making Geography Happen'

NCTL   National College for Teaching and Leadership
Ofsted   Office for Standards in Education
PGCE   Postgraduate Certificate in Education
POS   Programme of Study
QCA   Qualifications and Curriculum Authority
QCDA   Qualifications and Curriculum Development Agency
RCT   Randomised Control Trials
RGS   Royal Geographical Society
RSA   Royal Society for the Encouragement of Arts, Manufactures and Commerce
SCAA   Schools Curriculum and Assessment Authority
SAT   Standard Assessment Task
SLE   Specialist Leader of Education
SLN   Staffordshire Learning Network
SOLO   Structure of Observed Learning Outcomes
TVEI   Technical and Vocational Education Initiative
VCE   Vocational Certificates of Education
YPG   Young People's Geographies

Contributors

Mary Biddulph is Lecturer in Geography Education at the University of Nottingham and is a member of the Geography Education Research Collective. She has written widely on the subject of young people's geographies, student agency and curriculum development in geography and with Roger Firth (Oxford) led the Young People's Geographies project. Mary is also lead author of the third edition of *Learning to Teach Geography in the Secondary School*.

Clare Brooks is Reader in Geography Education at UCL Institute of Education. A former London secondary school teacher, and Subject Leader for the Geography PGCE and Programme leader for the MA in Geography Education, Clare is now Head of Academic Department, and Co-Director of Initial Teacher Education. She has recently written *Teacher Subject Identity in Professional Practice: Teaching with a Professional Compass*, published by Routledge.

Graham Butt is Professor in Education and Co-Director of Research at the School of Education, Oxford Brookes University. He is a member of the Geography Education Research Collective (GEReCo) although he has also published on assessment, teacher workload, and modernisation of the teaching workforce. His books include *Geography, Education and the Future* (2011), *MasterClass in Geography Education* (2015) and *The Power of Geographical Thinking* (2017) (with Clare Brooks and Mary Fargher).

Nick Clifford is Professor of Geography and Dean, Social, Political and Geographical Sciences at Loughborough University. He is a physical geographer and geomorphologist by training. He has published widely in the field of river science and the history, philosophy and methodology of geography, and he is the lead editor of two popular foundation texts, *Key Methods*, and *Key Concepts in Geography*. He is a member of the editorial collective of the GA's flagship journal, *Geography*.

Gemma Collins is a Lecturer in Geography Education at the University of Birmingham. A former secondary school teacher, Gemma is now a teacher trainer. She has also worked with the Ministry of Education in Tanzania, in the areas of curriculum, pedagogy and CPD for teachers.

Mary Fargher is the Programme Leader for the Geography Education MA at UCL Institute of Education. A former secondary school teacher and school manager, she works on both the MA and the PGCE at the Institute. Mary's recent PhD was on the role of GIS in teaching and learning place in geography education. Having recently co-led a research project on online GIS in geography teacher education, Mary's current research interest is on the role of webGIS in teaching and learning geography in schools.

Jane Ferretti taught geography in secondary schools in Sheffield until 2003 and is now at the University of Sheffield where she is responsible for Geography PGDE and also works on Master's courses. She is an active member of the Geographical Association and sits on both the Publications Committee and the Editorial group for *Teaching Geography*. She edited *Meeting the Needs of Your Most Able Pupils: Geography* and has written for *Teaching Geography*.

Roger Firth is an Associate Professor and Fellow of St Anne's College at the University of Oxford. He is a member of the Geography Education Research Collective (GEReCo) and has research interests that include disciplined knowledge and its relation to curriculum and pedagogy, the school curriculum and subject pedagogy, and disadvantaged pupils. Recent research has focused on Robert Brandom's philosophical work on inferentialism and its applicability to education.

David Gardner is Lecturer in Geography Education at UCL Institute of Education. He was formerly geography adviser at QCDA from 2005 to 2011, before working in geography education at Goldsmiths and the Open University. David was a secondary school teacher for 28 years, and a deputy headteacher. He is also a freelance educational consultant, author of a range of successful geography textbooks, and an active member of the Geographical Association.

Lauren Hammond is Lecturer in Geography Education at UCL Institute of Education. A former secondary school teacher in the UK and Singapore, she worked as Subject Lead in a London school prior to working in Initial Teacher Education. Lauren is the geography subject lead for Teach First, and her PhD research is focused on exploring young people's geographies of London.

Duncan Hawley is a geography and geoscience educator with teaching experience spanning state and independent schools, a field studies centre and as

PGCE Tutor in Secondary Geography (Swansea Metropolitan University). He is Chair of the Geographical Association's Physical Geography Special Interest Group and a member of the Earth Science Education Forum. He was presented the Geographical Association's Award for Excellence 2012.

John Hopkin began his teaching career in Birmingham, teaching in a variety of comprehensive schools before becoming School Effectiveness Advisor. He currently works as Head of Accreditation at the Geographical Association, where he is also a longstanding member and past president. His particular interests include the teaching of places in geography, curriculum planning and assessment, and he is author and editor of a wide range of successful textbooks and other resources.

Mark Jones is a Senior Lecturer in Geography Education at the University of the West of England, Bristol. A former curriculum leader with 18 years' teaching experience in secondary schools in Bristol and South Gloucestershire, he leads the PGCE Secondary Geography course. His interests and publications focus on student participation, cross-curricular creativity and connecting university and school geography. His most recent edited volume is *The Handbook of Secondary Geography*, published in 2017 by the Geographical Association.

David Lambert is Professor of Geography Education at UCL Institute of Education. He was Chief Executive of the Geographical Association from 2002–2012. A former secondary school teacher and teacher educator, he has written widely on geography education, and recently completed the EU-funded GeoCapabilities project. He collaborated with Michael Young to produce *Knowledge and the Future School* (Bloomsbury) in 2014, and in 2015 produced the third edition of *Learning to Teach Geography in the Secondary School* (Routledge) with Mary Biddulph and David Balderstone.

John Lyon recently retired from the post of Programme Manager at the Geographical Association (GA), which he held for 10 years. He was formally an Assistant Headteacher at a large 11–18 comprehensive school in Rotherham, teaching geography for almost 30 years. He is a GA consultant, Chartered Geographer, Fellow of the RGS and holds an NPQH qualification.

Fran Martin is Senior Lecturer in Education at the University of Exeter. Her PhD investigated PGCE primary students' conceptions of geography, pedagogy and epistemology, leading to her description of primary geography as 'Ethnogeography'. Fran was president of the Geographical Association 2011–12, and is a member of the *Primary Geography* editorial board. Fran's other research interests are in development education and intercultural learning.

David Mitchell taught geography in a range of secondary schools and 16–19 colleges before moving into teacher education at UCL Institute of Education. He has been a tutor for student geography teachers for several years and currently leads the secondary PGCE programme. He also contributes to the MA in Geography Education and is completing a PhD exploring the influences on geography teachers' curriculum choices.

John Morgan currently works at the University of Auckland. He taught geography in schools before working in geography education at the University of Bristol and the Institute of Education, University of London. His most recent book is *Teaching Secondary Geography as if the Planet Matters* published by Routledge in 2011 and is currently writing a reference work on Human Geography (ABC-CLIO).

Alan Parkinson is an experienced teacher and author. He previously spent three years working as Secondary Curriculum Development Leader for the Geographical Association. He is currently Head of Geography at King's Ely Junior, and works as a freelance geographer and author. He co-creates the Mission:Explore books, and is a prominent geography blogger and online networker.

Charles Rawding is Senior Lecturer in Geography Education at Edge Hill University, Lancashire. Prior to becoming involved in teacher training, he was Head of Geography in a large comprehensive school on Humberside. His most recent book was *Effective Innovation in the Secondary Geography Curriculum* published by Routledge in 2013. He currently chairs the Teacher Education Special Interest Group of the Geographical Association.

Eleanor Rawling is an independent consultant and a research fellow at the University of Oxford's Department of Education. Formerly a school teacher, GA President (1991–92) and Geography Officer at the QCA (1993–2005), she was lead writer for changes to National Curriculum, GCSE and A level in England, 2012–16. Eleanor's main research interests are in curriculum matters, but she is also interested in changing approaches to the study of place and landscape. Recent publications include *Changing the Subject: The Impact of National Policy on School Geography 1980–2000* (2001).

Michael Simmons is a consultant to the Geographical Association and is a member of the Teacher Education and Secretary for the Assessment and Examinations Special Interest Groups. He is Deputy Director of The Arthur Terry National Teaching School, one of the first SCITT providers in the UK, where he is the Geography PGCE tutor. Michael has also worked in a diverse group of schools across Birmingham offering bespoke consultancy through work as a Specialist Leader of Education.

Alex Standish is a Senior Lecturer in Geography Education at UCL Institute of
Education, where he leads the PGCE geography programme and runs the
London Geography Alliance (www.londongeography.org) for teachers. His
research interests are in geography education, especially teacher education.
He previously taught at Western Connecticut State University and completed his PhD at Rutgers University, New Jersey. He is author of two
books, including *Global Perspectives in the Geography Curriculum: Reviewing
the Moral Case for Geography.*

Liz Taylor is a Senior Lecturer at the Faculty of Education, University of
Cambridge. She manages the undergraduate education degree and teaches
on the geography PGCE as well as supervising students for further degrees.
Her research interests include young people's understandings of space and
place, key ideas in geography education, and rural schooling.

Paul Weeden was Lecturer in Geography Education at the University of
Birmingham from 1999 until he retired in 2010, and at the University of
Bristol from 1993–1999. Previously he was a secondary school teacher and
an advisory teacher. He is a member of the Assessment and Examinations
Special Interest Group of the Geographical Association, and has written on
geography and assessment.

Introduction to the series

This book, *Debates in Geography Education*, is one of a series of books entitled *Debates in Subject Teaching*. The series has been designed to engage with a wide range of debates related to subject teaching. Unquestionably, debates vary among the subjects, but may include, for example, issues that:

- impact on Initial Teacher Education in the subject;
- are addressed in the classroom through the teaching of the subject;
- are related to the content of the subject and its definition;
- are related to subject pedagogy;
- are connected with the relationship between the subject and broader educational aims and objectives in society, and the philosophy and sociology of education;
- are related to the development of the subject and its future in the twenty-first century.

Consequently, each book presents key debates that subject teachers should understand, reflect on and engage in as part of their professional development. Chapters have been designed to highlight major questions, and to consider the evidence from research and practice in order to find possible answers. Some subject books or chapters offer at least one solution or a view of the ways forward, whereas others provide alternative views and leave readers to identify their own solution or view of the ways forward. The editors expect that readers will want to pursue the issues raised, and so chapters include questions for further debate and suggestions for further reading. Debates covered in the series will provide the basis for discussion in university subject seminars or as topics for assignments or classroom research. The books have been written for all those with a professional interest in their subject and, in particular, student teachers learning to teach the subject in secondary or primary school; newly qualified teachers; teachers undertaking study at Masters level; teachers with a subject coordination or leadership role; and those preparing for such responsibility; as well as mentors, university tutors, CPD organisers and advisers of the aforementioned groups.

Books in the series have a cross-phase dimension, because the editors believe that it is important for teachers in the primary, secondary and post-16 phases to look at subject teaching holistically, particularly in order to provide for continuity and progression, but also to increase their understanding of how children and young people learn. The balance of chapters that have a cross-phase relevance varies according to the issues relevant to different subjects. However, no matter where the emphasis is, the authors have drawn out the relevance of their topic to the whole of each book's intended audience.

Because of the range of the series, both in terms of the issues covered and its cross-phase concern, each book is an edited collection. Editors have commissioned new writing from experts on particular issues, who, collectively, represent many different perspectives on subject teaching. Readers should not expect a book in this series to cover the entire range of debates relevant to the subject, or to offer a completely unified view of subject teaching, or that every debate will be dealt with discretely, or that all aspects of a debate will be covered. Part of what each book in this series offers to readers is the opportunity to explore the interrelationships between positions in debates and, indeed, among the debates themselves, by identifying the overlapping concerns and competing arguments that are woven through the text.

The editors are aware that many initiatives in subject teaching continue to originate from the centre, and that teachers have decreasing control of subject content, pedagogy and assessment strategies. The editors strongly believe that for teaching to remain properly a vocation and a profession, teachers must be invited to be part of a creative and critical dialogue about subject teaching, and should be encouraged to reflect, criticise, problem-solve and innovate. This series is intended to provide teachers with a stimulus for democratic involvement in the development of the discourse of subject teaching.

Susan Capel, Jon Davison, James Arthur and
John Moss, December 2010

Introduction

The significance of continuing debates

Mark Jones and David Lambert

> In the absence of an institutional basis for debate, parents, teachers and the public at large must do what they can. One recourse is to write books ... but for this to be effective it must grow from a renewed habit of debate, in schools, higher and further education and particularly in places where teachers are trained and educated.
>
> (Burgess, 2004, p. 217)

Introduction

The ethos guiding both editions of this book is to provide a collective response to what Dennis Hayes (2004) has called a 'culture of compliance' (p. 3) where 'informed' debate in schools has become marginalised and 'out of fashion' (ibid., p. 1). And, as Burgess (2004) notes, the 'places' where geography teachers begin their formal training have become increasingly diverse in recent years through the rapid expansion of alternative routes and numbers of school-led providers. This makes certain kinds of debates very difficult to engage in Thus, where the single trainee model exists in schools, the focus on generic skills and competences at the expense of collegiate subject debates is difficult to avoid (see GA, 2015, p. 3). The importance given to geography in the challenging process of learning to teach can depend on whether or not individuals involved have the opportunity to collaborate with external subject experts and the wider geography community.

Furthermore, for those beginning their careers entirely in school settings where the professional environment is strongly shaped by accountability and performativity constraints, it can mean 'day-to-day practice is flooded with a baffling array of figures, indicators, comparisons and forms of competition' (Ball, 2003, p. 220). In such environments finding the space for teachers to discuss the very nature and purpose of the specialist teaching can be challenging, not least in terms of justifying such discussions in terms of outcomes and impact. However, in preparing the second edition of *Debates in Geography Education* we refuse to blink. The aim is to produce a collection of comparatively short, sharp and rigorous chapters to further debates concerning geography's spirit and purpose and particularly what teachers' subject expertise means in relation to this. These are, to be sure, not new debates (see Wooldridge and East, 1951; Bailey and Binns, 1986; Marsden, 1997; Walford, 2001) but recent educational policy shifts including the opportunities and challenges provided by academisation, the diversification of routes into initial teacher education and the increased interest in 'what works' require us *all* in the geography community to make a renewed habit of engaging in subject debates.

Authors have avoided polemics and instead offer narratives and explanatory accounts aiming to deepen our understanding of important debates in contemporary geography education in the UK. Sometimes the purpose of a chapter is to inform – to ensure that some fault lines and conflicts in the field are properly anchored and located in policy and historical perspective. Sometimes the purpose is to provoke, or at least to stimulate thought and reflection. The former may encourage us to see that things are not always what they seem (and that things come around!), whilst the latter may impel us to re-examine current orthodoxies and habitual practices.

In this chapter we remind you of the rich legacy of debates in geography education and, in support of this, provide an updated summary of the changing policy setting (Figure 0.1 on pages 3–5). In engaging in current debates it is, we argue, important to understand and acknowledge 'where we have come from' as well as 'where we might be going'.

Individual choices and challenges

An individual's subject identity and the moral and ethical values they hold are a key part of what Brooks (2016) calls a teacher's 'professional compass'. Like a traditional compass it helps us to navigate our way through existing and new challenges, and informs our decisions about how to respond to obstacles (or not). As we have seen in recent years, changes to government education policy, driven by underlying ideological concerns, have resulted in significant challenges but also opportunities for those in the subject community. We believe that teachers should be expected to take a view on such policy matters, because although we have to operate within a system, one that the democratically elected politicians have made for us, this does not mean that we simply 'obey orders'. Teachers, arguably more than any other professional group, need to do their work *responsibly*, which means with a sense of moral purpose. This is why we argue that teachers of geography need two things: a concept of geography and, equally important, a concept of education (see Lambert 2009 for an elaboration of this argument[1]). There is a sense in which these matters override and sit above mere policy debates.

One of the consequences of accepting that school teaching occupies such a moral space is that it demands reasoning on the part of the teacher. That is to say, we should not expect teachers to behave habitually, as compliant technocrats – delivering the curriculum and fulfilling Ofsted 'requirements' or whatever – without subjecting this activity to some questioning. Thus, in teacher education circles it has become *de rigueur* to conceptualise learning to teach as a critically reflective process, demanding the explicit articulation of theoretical frameworks which guide or shape classroom practices. Although not without its critics, this approach has become commonplace and a sort of modern orthodoxy. But it has in some ways, ironically, undermined an especially important core value of the teacher – at least in the secondary school. This is the value of subject specialism and the belief that young people can be inspired, dig deep and be 'initiated' into intellectual enquiry and the world of ideas. Education under this rubric cannot be reduced to reflecting on the effectiveness of teaching, just as learning cannot be reduced to the acquisition of a neutral set of generic 'skills'. The problem with reflective practice is that it can leave us very much trapped with a stripped-down concept of education, and with an attitude to the subject that it is nothing more than a vehicle for 'teaching and learning'. We are saying that to be a teacher of course one needs to 'know stuff': after all, it is obvious that teachers need something to teach. But much more importantly, subject specialist teachers also need a reasonably clear but dynamic grasp of the subject as a system of thought – as a discipline, or in our subject what used to be called the 'spirit and purpose' of geography (Wooldridge and East, 1951).

Policy challenges and choices

Educational policy and priorities under New Labour (1997–2010), which seemed to see education as a key plank of economic policy, were swiftly replaced when the Liberal-Conservative Coalition (2010–2015) took office. National Strategy materials and their messages extoling the virtues of 'effective' pedagogies were archived and teacher support agencies and bodies simply abolished for example BECTA and QCDA. Instead, the DfE (2010) White Paper *The Importance of Teaching* heralded:

- a radical departure from the previous government's orthodoxy of skills, competences and 'personalisation';
- a revised national curriculum to state 'core' and 'essential' knowledge in traditional established subjects;
- more emphasis on effort and motivation, and whole cohort achievement, rather than differentiation (personalisation) by 'ability'.

The role of the subject specialism in 'excellent teaching' remains a key debate, one which has assumed increased urgency. All apparently agree with the virtues of subject specialist teaching, including government ministers (see DfES 2003; DFE, 2010; DFE, 2016). But despite ministerial exhortation, and the importance placed on teachers' subject knowledge in the teaching standards, in practice little attention is given to the quality of subject teaching as distinct from general teaching skills. In the early 2010s, concerns about the 'geography' in geography education were being raised by a number of teacher educators. Margaret Roberts raised concerns about what we might call the strange disappearance of geography from the planning of geography lessons and more worryingly in feedback on beginning teachers' geography lessons (see Roberts, 2010, 2011). In addition, Alex Standish (2011) accused – we think rather harshly, but he has a point – geography teachers in England of turning their backs on the subject discipline. This echoes (but does not cite) the earlier measured and penetrating analysis of Bill Marsden (1997) 'on taking the geography out of geography education'.

Possible reasons for this reduced emphasis on subject (despite the rhetoric) include the steady erosion of infrastructure to nourish and support subject specialist teachers and curriculum development. At a policy level, despite the warm ministerial words, and in some cases more than that, such as the five year Action Plan for Geography (2006–11)[2], the fact is that Local Authorities, emptied of geography advisers/geography expertise, are now virtually irrelevant when it comes to nurturing, supporting and challenging geography teachers. In addition, after 2010 the number of academies, outside of local authority control, rose significantly with approximately 60 per cent of all secondary schools converted by 2016[3]. The rise of federations of academies, academy chains and Multi Academy Trusts (MATs) while offering the potential for more schools to work together, the activities promoted through subject networks can be secondary to organisation-wide priorities for 'closing the gap' and raising attainment. Even where Teaching Schools provide school-to-school support through the deployment of Specialist Leaders of Education (SLEs), these outstanding middle and senior leaders often, inevitably, focus on whole school priorities. Where geography SLEs exist their reach and impact in other schools depends on their availability and their own school's commitment to deployment: indeed, SLEs can themselves feel 'reluctant to miss their own classes' (NCTL, 2016, p. 120). In the most recent White Paper *Educational Excellence Everywhere* (DfE, 2016) the government pledged 300 more SLEs 'to reach vulnerable schools' (p. 19). It remains to be seen how many of these are geographers.

Equally, policy level decisions have had significant impact on where and how beginning teachers are increasingly being prepared. Teacher education departments in universities have been systematically undermined by governments for 20 years now, driven by the belief that teacher training is best done in school following a kind of apprentice model. This is a form of anti-intellectualism wrapped up in beguiling talk of a mature and responsible profession being able to take 'ownership' of training. Such a view disregards almost totally the need for any professional group to make and remake the knowledge that defines it. In schools, which are intensely practically oriented places, often very inward-looking and with constant, urgent busy-ness to attend to, it is very difficult indeed to do this, *especially* in the field of subject knowledge development.

In the White Paper *Educational Excellence Everywhere* (DfE, 2016) we also learn that efforts to reduce underperformance in the system are to be driven by 'great leaders' and 'great teachers'. Initial teacher training (ITT) will be through 'the best schools – those up to date with what works best in the classroom' (ibid.,

1970	Conservative Government takes office. Schools Council secondary school geography projects announced: *Geography for the Young School Leaver* ('Avery Hill') and *Geography 14–18* ('Bristol').
1974	Labour Government takes office.
1976	Prime Minister James Callaghan stimulates the 'great debate' in his Ruskin College speech. Schools Council A level Project announced *Geography 16–19 Project* (London).
1977	(DES) *Educating our Children.* (DES) *Education in Schools: Consultative Document.* (HMI), (DES) *Curriculum 11–16 Working Papers.* Geographical Association (GA) response to these documents: e.g.see *Teaching Geography*, 3, (2).
1978	(DES) *The Teaching of Ideas in Geography* (HMI 'Matters for Discussion' series).
1979	Conservative Government takes office.
1980	(DES) *A View of the Curriculum.* (DES) *A Framework for the School Curriculum.* GA Response: e.g. see *Geography*, 65, (3).
1981	(DES)*Geography in the School Curriculum 11–16*(HMI). (DES)*The School Curriculum.*
1985	(DES) *Better Schools.* (HMI) (DES) *Curriculum Matters,2:Curriculum from 5–16.*
1986	(HMI) (DES) *Curriculum Matters,7:Geography from 5–16.*
1987	(DES) *The National Curriculum 5–16: A Consultation Document.* GA response: Bailey and Binns (eds) *A Case for Geography* Sheffield: GA.
1988	Education Reform Act (geography becomes a 'foundation subject' –compulsory for 5–16-year-olds).
1989	(DES) *National Curriculum: From Policy to Practice.*
1990	(DES) *Geography National Curriculum Working Group Final Report.*
1991	(DES) *Geography in the National Curriculum (England) (1st version).* (SEAC) *Geography in the National Curriculum: Non-statutory Guidance for Teachers.*
1992	(CFAS) National Curriculum Standard Assessment Tasks (SATs). Geography pilot tests in 41 schools: students sit two 1 hour papers (tiered entry at levels 1–3; 3–5; 5–7 and 7–10).
1993	(CFAS) *Evaluation of KS3 Geography Pilot Tests.* (SEAC) *Pupils' Work Assessed Geography KS3.* (Ofsted) *Geography: Keys stages 1, 2 and 3. Report on the First Year* (1991–92). School Curriculum and Assessment Authority (SCAA) formed. (SCAA) *Final Report: The National Curriculum and its Assessment* (known as the *Dearing Report*) – recommendation for geography to become optional at KS4. (CCW) *Developing a Curriculum Cymreig, Advisory Paper,18.* (CCW) *An Enquiry Approach to Learning Geography at Key Stages 2 and 3.*
1994	KS3 Geography SATs did not proceed. Curriculum and Assessment Council for Wales (ACAC) formed.
1995	(DFE) *Geography in the National Curriculum (2nd version).* (Welsh Office) *Geography in the National Curriculum (Wales).* (Ofsted) *Geography: A Review of Inspection Findings 1993/94*
1996	(SCAA) Consistency in Teacher Assessment: Exemplification of Standards KS3. (SCAA) Key Stage 3 Optional Tests and Tasks: Geography.
1997	Labour Government takes office. (SCAA) *Geography and the Use of Language: Key Stage 3.* Qualifications and Curriculum Authority (QCA) formed.
1998	(QCA) *Geographical Enquiry at Key Stages 1–3: Discussion Paper,3.* Geography and history suspended from the primary curriculum for one year, to allow schools to focus fully on the numeracy and literacy strategies.
1999	(DfEE/QCA) *Primary Geography National Curriculum.* (DfEE/QCA) *Geography: The National Curriculum for England Key stages 1–3 (3rdversion).* The National Assembly (Wales) starts work.

Figure 0.1 Key events and official publications. The policy setting in England and Wales 1970–2018.

2000	(Ofsted) *Subject Reports 1998/99:Primary Standards in Geography* (HMI). (QCA/DfEE) *Geography: A Scheme of Work for Key Stages, 1, 2 and 3.*
2001	Department for Education and Skills (DfES) *Schools:Achieving Success.* (Ofsted) *Subject Reports 1999/2000 Primary Geography; Secondary Geography.*
2002	National Curriculum in Action website launched. (DfES) *KS3 National Strategy: Literacy in Geography.* (DfES) *KS3 National Strategy: Access and Engagement in Geography: Teaching Pupils for whom English is an Additional Language.* (Ofsted) *Subject Reports 2000/01 Geography in Primary Schools: Geography in Secondary Schools.*
2003	(DfES) *14–19: Opportunity and Excellence.* (Ofsted) *Subject Reports 2001/02: Geography in Primary Schools: Geography in Secondary Schools.*
2004	(DfES) *Five Year Strategy for Children.* (DfES) *Every Child Matters: Change for Children.* (DfES) *KS3 National Strategy Literacy and Learning in Geography.* (DfES) *KS3 National Strategy: ICT across the Curriculum: ICT in Geography.* (Ofsted) *Subject Reports 2002/03:Geography in Primary Schools* (HMI 1998) and *Geography in Secondary Schools* (HMI 1985).
2005	(DfES) *Higher Standards, Better Schools for All.* (DfES) *KS3 National Strategy Leading in Learning: Exemplification in Geography.* (Ofsted) *Annual Report 2004/05 Geography in Primary Schools* and *Geography in Secondary Schools* (Last in Series).
2006	DfES renamed the DCSF (Department for Children, Schools and Families). (GA/RGS) 'Action plan for geography' launched.
2007	(DCSF) *Children's Plan: Building Brighter Futures.* (QCA) *Geography National Curriculum (4th version –for KS3 only).*
2008	(Ofsted) *Subject Report Geography in Schools: Changing Practice.* (GA/RGS) 'Action plan for geography' funded for a further three years. (WAG) *Geography in the National Curriculum for Wales KS2–3.*
2009	(GA) *Manifesto: A Different View.* *Cambridge Primary Review.* *Independent Review of the Primary Curriculum Final Report.*
2010	Liberal Democrat-Conservative Coalition Government takes office. DCSF renamed DfE (Department for Education). *Wolf Review on Vocational Education.* (DfE) *The Importance of Teaching: Schools White Paper.* (Parliament) Academies Act makes it possible for all publicly funded schools to become academies. (Ofsted) *Subject-specific Guidance for Inspectors (for subject survey visits).*
2011	(GA/RGS) *Action Plan for Geography* ends. (GA) *Geography Curriculum Consultation Report.* (Ofsted) subject report *Geography: Learning to Make a World of Difference.* English Baccalaureate (EBacc) (Geography or History named as one of the five core academic subjects). National Strategies website closed. QCDA abolished (bringing an end to over 40 continuous years of a curriculum body (starting with the Schools Council in the 1960s). (DfE) Expert Panel Report: *Framework for the National Curriculum.*
2012	(GA) *National Curriculum Proposals* published for consultation. (GA) *Geography Education 4–18 years Annual Monitoring Report 2011 (First Report).*
2013	(GA) Response to Ofqual on GCSE Reform. DFE announce end of the official use of National Curriculum levels for assessment. (GA) Response *Feedback on Final Draft of Geography Programmes of Study.* (DfE) *National Curriculum Geography, Programmes of Study KS1, KS2 and KS3.*
2014	First teaching of latest iteration of National Curriculum Geography. (DfE) Geography GCSE subject content published. (ALCAB) *The A Level Content Advisory Board: Report of the ALCAB Panel on Geography.* Consultation responses to Ofqual on GCSE/GCE by GA and by RGS (with IBG). (DfE) Geography GCE AS and A Level subject content published. Awarding Bodies begin work on new specifications for GCSE and GCE Geography.

Figure 0.1 Continued.

2015	Conservative Government takes office. *Carter Review of Initial Teacher Training* (ITT). (GA) *Response to DfE:A standard for Teachers' Professional Development.* (GA) *Geography Initial Teacher Education and Teacher Supply in England: A National Research Report by the Geographical Association.* *Final report of the Commission on Assessment without Levels.* (DfE) Consultation on implementation of EBacc – intention that all pupils take GCSEs in EBacc subjects from 2020. Welsh Government publishes *A Curriculum for Wales: A Curriculum for Life.* <u>Draft GCSE and GCE specifications produced.</u>
2016	DfE introduce new performance measures – Attainment 8 and Progress 8. (DfE) *Educational Excellence Everywhere White Paper.* (GA) Response to DfE: Consultation on Implementing the English Baccalaureate. (GA) Response to Commons Education Committee call for evidence on *The Purpose and Quality of Education in England.* Welsh Government – Pioneer network established. (DfE) *Reducing Teachers' Workloads* reports on marking, planning and data management. (Ofqual) all GCSE & GCE specifications fully approved. First teaching of new GCSE and GCE Geography specifications from September.
2017	First examinations of new GCE AS-level Geography in Summer.
2018	First examinations of 2016 specifications for GCSE and GCE A-level Geography in Summer. Wales – New curriculum and assessment arrangements become available.

Figure 0.1 Continued.

p. 12). As if aware that this may sound a bit technocratic, we also learn that strengthened new ITT content will equip new teachers with 'sufficient subject knowledge' (ibid.) It behoves the profession to ask: 'sufficient for what?' and 'for what purpose?' For one thing, subject expertise requires teachers to have more than subject knowledge, as they require 'a good grounding in subject pedagogy' (Tapsfield, 2016, p. 107). But what does *that* mean exactly?

Although there is an acknowledged shortage of qualified geography teachers (resulting in generous training bursaries being introduced from 2016) secondary school geography appears to be in a healthy state with growing numbers opting for geography at GCSE (following the introduction of the EBacc in 2014). But how do we ensure that those students are well taught, and that school geography continues to be seen as a curriculum innovator? It has never been more important to nurture and sustain professional debate in school and we hope the chapters in this book help you do this.

Looking ahead

> You can't connect the dots looking forward; you can only connect them looking backwards. So you have to trust that the dots will somehow connect in your future. You have to trust in something – your gut, destiny, life, karma, whatever.
>
> (Jobs, 2005)

According to Steve Jobs, the future is impossible to plan out in detail. It is impossible to predict. If for historians the past is a 'foreign country', then the future is extra-terrestrial. This is possibly why future tellers are sometimes described as star gazers.

Well neither of us is a star gazer, and in 'looking ahead' we are not about to make predictions – at least not in a precise manner. On the other hand, we do see some continuities. And, like Steve Jobs, we trust that joining the dots from the past – having a sense of lineage and where we have come from – will somehow connect to the future. Without that sense of trust, we permit a Maoist approach to continuous 'cultural revolution' utterly dismissive of the past and deeply pessimistic of human potential and achievement. That said, it is astonishing how frequently in the world of education we seem to suffer pendulum-like swings: the continuous unfolding of fresh starts, new beginnings, and revolutions. To some there is even a sense of chaos in recent educational policy making[4], making 'joining the dots looking backwards' of limited use in coming to an understanding of where we are going. If there is an overarching policy direction, it appears to be to dismantle the notion of a national education service based on shared aims and aspirations in favour of competing schools accountable only to 'the market'.

The dismantling of national professional bodies has also been unsettling, such as the General Teaching Council, Qualifications and Curriculum Development Agency and the Training and Development Agency: all abolished in the Education Act of 2011. This can be illustrated, for example, by the powerful Public Accounts Committee, which concluded the following in its rather damning 2016 report on the training of new teachers:

- The Department for Education (the Department) has missed its targets to fill teacher training places for 4 years running and has no plan for how to achieve them in future.
- The Department does not understand the difficult reality that many schools face in recruiting teachers.
- The myriad routes into teaching are confusing for applicants and it is the Department's responsibility to end this confusion.
- The Department's approach means that a growing number of pupils are taught by teachers who are not subject specialists.

(Public Accounts Committee, 2016:
Conclusions and recommendations)

Issues such as these are entirely foreseeable and possible to address. It is not that the Department does not receive advice – not least from the Geographical Association (GA, 2015, 2016), which has repeatedly alerted government to the possible consequences of the final bullet point above. If we attempt to join the dots looking backwards, it is possible to see that for many years, from at least the early 1990s, successive governments have been drawn into taking teacher education and training away from the universities and placing it more in schools. As we acknowledged in the previous section, this has been an understandable development that sought to make the teaching profession more responsible for its own training and standards. Indeed, in the beginning it was welcomed: university–school partnerships have been repeatedly praised by Ofsted (e.g. see 2010, 2011). But flying in the face of such evidence universities have been undermined and sidelined, risking the making of a 'crisis' (Brighouse, 2013) now acknowledged by the Public Accounts Committee.

However, when we note that according to ministers, neither Academies nor Free Schools need to employ staff with Qualified Teacher Status we can see that this is a crisis that at least some in government do not recognise as significant – in the market system, apparently, anyone can be a teacher. As Sir Tim Brighouse dryly observed: 'This is very disturbing' (ibid.). In the world of geography education, these trends are disturbing because university-based teacher educators, that is the practically oriented academics who are in a position to research and make scholarly contributions to the knowledge base on which the profession can draw, are about to become few and far between. Increasingly, new teachers of geography are going to be trained in 'what works *here*' (in this school) rather than be encouraged to think creatively and critically about broader aims and purposes (such as those introduced by Clifford, Firth, Morgan and others in this volume). They are increasingly going to be trained in general teaching techniques (pedagogy) rather than be encouraged to truly take responsibility for curriculum enactment (what the GA and others refer to as curriculum making, discussed by Mary Biddulph in the volume). Increasingly, it appears that graduate teacher trainees are not required to possess a geography degree: for instance, the much lauded Teach First organisation does not require anything more than a good A level in the subject to be accepted for training.

All this matters if we regard being a geography teacher to be part of a high status profession with a clear professional identity. As Clare Brooks (2016) has shown, specialist teachers have complex identities. This includes specialist training which the system may dismantle only at great risk. Although comparisons are always dangerous, for illustrative purposes what is happening to the profession of geography teaching is akin to the state deciding that prospective General Practitioners, armed with an A level in Biology, get recruited to a GP practice or Health Centre and learn on the job, topped up with some university lectures and workshops. It is unlikely that this would be deemed adequate as the trainee would lack sufficient depth of knowledge and experience from which to draw.

Looking forward then, we need to 'trust in something'. Like Steve Jobs, we are not sure that merely joining the dots into the future is possible. But we can nourish a sense of *belief* in our identity and function as teachers and geography educators. In the circumstances that now exist, where government has relinquished direct responsibility for the curriculum (that is, for what is taught in schools) it may be time to re-assert our professional subject specialist identity. That means taking responsibility especially for what is taught in geography classrooms, including how this is selected and sequenced.

One of the challenges in debating the importance of subject expertise in schools, particularly for a subject like geography, taught in elementary schools since the nineteenth century in England and in secondary schools since really the inception of state-funded secondary education at the beginning of the twentieth century, is that we sometimes feel the burden of 'tradition'. Even within the subject community – amongst friends, so to speak – we sometimes bend over backwards to express our disdain for traditional approaches to geography. We reject old-fashioned regional geography; we tut-tut at the very suggestion that textbooks might be a useful teaching aid (not least for non-specialist teachers of geography); we wince knowingly if a parent (or government minister) asks why their child doesn't 'know' the rivers of England, the capital cities of Europe, or the countries of Africa. Traditional approaches are often considered inadequate to contemporary educational needs, especially if one is concerned with some of the big challenges to arise from global citizenship or education for sustainable development; the educational 'guru' Ken Robinson famously asserts that 'we are educating people out of their creative capacities'[5]. The argument runs that the traditional subject curriculum overemphasises what is taught, when we should be focused on opening up learning processes. In his contribution to this 'learning revolution', Ian Gilbert asks: 'How much of what goes on in schools is the development of children's own thinking – "education" – and how much of it is training them to think our thoughts ...?' (2010, p. 3). In responding to Gilbert's book, which proactively asks *Why Do I Need a Teacher When I've Got Google?*, Ben Major (2010) has written:

> (Whilst) a conservative sees tradition as an inheritance, ... a radical conception of tradition sees it in a very different light. Here, tradition is something produced through a critical or deconstructive engagement with that inheritance. If we adopt this radical sense of tradition as an educator, we still, like the conservative, recognise the need for an inheritance of knowledge that helps us to make sense of the world, but rather than accepting it with blind faith, this sort of tradition calls for an attitude of critical engagement, a sifting through, or a recovery of sorts. As Critchley notes, 'what this radical idea of tradition is trying to recover is something missing, forgotten or repressed in contemporary life' (Critchley, 2010: 32). The radical traditionalist understands that we have to sometimes look back in order to go forward. Engaging with tradition in this way might help us to avoid a situation in which education is reduced to a concern only with themes of contemporary relevance, and with preparing young people for 'the 21st century'.
>
> (Major, 2010)

Thus, genuine educational encounters should look to tradition, 'joining the dots' to the present and future. For thoughtful specialist teachers of geography, it is in large part engaging with the disciplinary resource[6] that enables this. For the ideas we wish our students to grasp, in order that they make better sense of the world, comes from here. Substantive ideas like 'continental drift', 'central places' or the rainforest 'biome' do not just exist. They are not just 'given'. They are created, disputed, refined and developed, sometimes over many years or even decades. More abstract concepts (sometimes referred to as the discipline's big ideas) such as space, place and scale are also socially constructed through the processes and procedures of disciplinary enquiry. They are powerful and help shape the discipline's priorities and ultimately what is taught in school. Thus today, following the work of geographers such as Doreen Massey (Painter, 2016), the discipline points us towards teaching young people to grasp the significance of a 'global sense of place' rather than 'environmental determinism', the potentially racist concept which, arguably, underpinned secondary school geography from the start of the twentieth century to the post-Second World War conceptual revolution. These big ideas are the meta-concepts that sit above the substantive material which make up the scheme of work or examination specification and, in a sense, express the worth or the 'power' of the discipline (what the GCSE criteria refers to as 'thinking like a geographer'). It almost goes without saying that a non-specialist teacher of geography would struggle to see this; and their teaching would inevitably be diminished as a result.

Conclusion

In presenting a number of 'debates' we hope to encourage a radical sense of tradition in geography education, showing a due respect to where we have come from, as well as suggesting alternatives. The overarching principle underpinning the book is the possibility of a progressive 'knowledge-led' geography curriculum, which invests in the emancipatory power of education in initiating all young people into forms of specialised knowledge and powerful thought. This borrows the core argument proposed by the GeoCapabilities project[7] which is that teachers need to think hard about what they teach. If we do not accept this professional responsibility, we risk giving up on the power and significance of geography in our teaching – and, the project argues, depriving and restricting the personal and intellectual growth of young people to become fully capable adults. This is quite a claim of course – that if you are not taught how to think geographically you are not fully educated.

The type of curriculum experience we are thinking of here does not exist in the words of curriculum documents or prescribed content of examination specifications, ready for transmission or 'delivery'. It requires a curriculum made by subject specialist teachers who appreciate the discipline's rich legacy as well as its educational potential. We hope the chapters in this fully revised second edition will stimulate continued deliberation and debate on the importance and significance of geography education.

Key readings

1   Butt, G. (ed.) (2015) *MasterClass in Geography Education: Transforming Teaching and Learning*, London: Bloomsbury. This is an edited collection of chapters aimed at postgraduate study of the field of geography education with a firm emphasis on research (explicitly supporting the achievement of Masters

level assignments and dissertations). In addition to the chapters, arranged into four parts (contextualising, construction, researching and producing research in geography education), it has commissioned leading scholars to discuss the chapters, thus creating a dynamic and lively reference book. It also contains excellent bibliographies and a way in to the extensive literatures.

2   Brooks, C. (2016) *Teacher Subject Identity in Professional Practice: Teaching with a Professional Compass,* London: Routledge. This is a book based on doctoral research and provides an interesting insight into teachers' professional practice and development – not least because it has a distinctive longitudinal element (over 14 years). However, its main value is that the professional identities which Brooks explores are of secondary geography teachers.

Notes

1 It is in Lambert's Inaugural lecture in 2009 that the possibility of subject 'capabilities' was first mooted. This has now developed into the GeoCapabilities project: www.geocapabilities.org.

2 The Action Plan for Geography was jointly and equally led by the GA and the Royal Geographical Society (with IBG). The evaluation report can be read and downloaded at http://www.geography.org.uk/projects/actionplanforgeography/. It was financed by the government, instigated by schools' minister Stephen Twigg and brought into full fruition by his successor Andrew Adonis.

3 The number of academies grew dramatically under the coalition government, from 203 in May 2010 to 2,075 by May 2016 (out of a total of 3,381 secondary schools) BBC News 7 May 2016.

4 The incoherence, for example, of reforming the national curriculum in order to restore knowledge and 'the importance of teaching' (DfE, 2010) and yet, almost in the same breath, announcing that the national curriculum does not apply to Academies and Free Schools, which make up the majority of secondary schools in England.

5 Ken Robinson's TED talk 'Do schools kill creativity? filmed February 2006 available at: https://www.ted.com/talks/ken_robinson_says_schools_kill_creativity?language=en [Accessed 10 August 2016].

6 Disciplinary resource was a phrase used by the GA in its 2009 manifesto *A Different View*. It is intended to conjure a deeper more textured idea of the subject than merely a list of contents. It's the amalgam of ideas that serve the discipline – or as Maude (2016) and others have suggested – the meta-concepts (of Place, space and environments) as well and the substantive concepts.

7 The GeoCapabilities project (www.geocapabilities.org) is an EU funded project (2013–16) on curriculum leadership in schools. (See Lambert and Morgan 2010: chapter 4; and Lambert 2011 for early discussions of the capabilities approach. See Lambert, Solem and Tani, 2015 for a fuller account.)

References

Bailey, P. and Binns, T. (1986) *A Case for Geography*, Sheffield: Geographical Association.

Ball, S. J. (2003) 'The teacher's soul and the terrors of performativity', *Journal of Education Policy*, 18 (2), 215–28.

Brighouse, T. (2013) *Government Induced Crisis in Initial Teacher Education, New Visions for Education: Statement from the Chair*, Available at: http://www.new-visionsforeducation.org.uk/2013/04/15/government-induced-crisis-in-initial-teacher-education/ [Accessed 10 September 2016].

Brooks, C. (2016) *Teacher Subject Identity in Professional Practice: Teaching with a Professional Compass*, London: Routledge.

Burgess, T. (2004) 'What are the key debates in education?' in D. Hayes (ed.) *The Routledge Guide to Key Educational Debates in Education*, London and New York: Routledge.

Butt, G. (ed.) (2011) *Geography, Education and the Future*, London: Continuum.

Critchley, S. (2010) *How to Stop Living and Start Worrying*, Cambridge: Polity Press.

Department for Education (DfE) (2010) *The Importance of Teaching: The Schools White Paper*, London: HMSO.

Department for Education (DfE) (2011) *The Framework for the National Curriculum: A Report by the Expert Panel for the National Curriculum Review*, Available at: www.education.gov.uk/publications/standard/publicationDetail/Page1/DFE-00135-2011 [Accessed 12 August 2016].

Department for Education (DfE) (2016) *Educational Excellence Everywhere*, London: HMSO.

Department for Education and Skills (DfES) (2003) *Subject Specialisms: A Consultation Document*, London: Department for Education and Skills.

Geographical Association (2015) *Geography Initial Teacher Education and Teacher Supply in England: A National Research Report by the Geographical Association*, Sheffield: Geographical Association, Available at: http://geography.org.uk/news/papersandresponses/ [Accessed 24 August 2016].

Geographical Association (2016) The Purpose and Quality of Education in England – Response from the Geographical Association to the Commons Education Committee Call for evidence 25 January 2016, Available at: http://geography.org.uk/news/papersandresponses/ [Accessed 24 August 2016].

Gilbert, I. (2010) *Why Do I Need a Teacher When I've Got Google? The Essential Guide to the Big Issues for Every 21st Century Teacher*, London: Routledge.

Hayes, D. (ed.) (2004) *The Routledge Guide to Key Educational Debates in Education*, London and New York: Routledge.

Jobs, S. (2005) Commencement address at Stanford University delivered by Steve Jobs, CEO of Apple Computer and of Pixar Animation Studios', on 12 June 2005, Available at: http://news.stanford.edu/2005/06/14/jobs-061505/ [Accessed 10 September 2016].

Lambert, D. (2009) *Geography in Education: Lost in the Post? A Professorial Inaugural Lecture*, London: Institute of Education.

Lambert, D. and Morgan, J. (2010) *Teaching Geography 11–18: A Conceptual Approach*, Maidenhead: Open University Press.

Lambert, D., Solem, M. and Tani, S. (2015) 'Achieving human potential through geography education: a capabilities approach to curriculum making in schools', *Annals of the Association of American Geographers*, 105 (4), 723–35.

Major, B. (2010) 'Subjects and tradition' blog post, Available at: http://insearcho-flostplace.blogspot.co.uk/search/label/tradition [Accessed 10 September 2016].

Marsden, W. (1997) 'On taking the geography out of geography education; some historical pointers', *Geography*, 82, (3), 241–52.

Maude, A. (2016) 'What might powerful geographical knowledge look like?' *Geography*, 101 (2), 70–6.

National College for Teaching and Leadership (NCTL) (2016) *Teaching Schools Evaluation Final Report*, Available at: https://www.gov.uk/government/uploads/system/uploads/attachment_data/file/503333/Evaluation_of_Teaching_schools_FINAL_FOR_PUB_25_feb_final_.pdf [Accessed 12 August 2016].

Ofsted (2010) *The Annual Report of Her Majesty's Chief Inspector of Education, Children's Services and Skills 2009/10*, London: HMSO.

Ofsted (2011) *The Annual Report of Her Majesty's Chief Inspector of Education, Children's Services and Skills 2010/11*, London: HMSO.

Painter, J. (2016) 'Doreen Massey (1944–2016): an appreciation', *Soundings*, Available at: https://www.lwbooks.co.uk/sites/default/files/s63_04painter.pdf [Accessed 10 September 2016].

Public Accounts Committee (2016) *Report: Training New Teachers*, Available at: https://www.parliament.uk/business/committees/committees-a-z/commons-select/public-accounts-committee/inquiries/parliament-2015/training-new-teachers-15-16/ [Accessed 10 September 2016].

Roberts, M. (2010) 'Where's the geography? Reflections on being an external examiner', *Teaching Geography*, 35 (3), 112–13.

Roberts, M. (2011) What makes a geography lesson good? Available at: http://www.geography.org.uk/projects/makinggeographyhappen/teachertips/ [Accessed 20 March 2012]

Standish, A. (2011) Comment on the GA's national curriculum consultation made at 15:49 on 03 October 2011, Available at: http://www.geography.org.uk/get-involved/geographycurriculumconsultation/feedback/ [Accessed 2 March 2012]

Tapsfield, A. (2016) 'Teacher education and the supply of geography teachers in England', *Geography*, 101 (2), 105–9.

Walford, R. (2001) *Geography in British Schools 1850–2000*, London: Woburn Press.

Wooldridge, S.W. and East, W.G. (1951) *The Spirit and Purpose of Geography*, London: Hutchinson.

Part I

Policy debates

Chapter 1

Geography in the National Curriculum for Key Stages 1, 2 and 3

John Hopkin and Fran Martin

[There is] a muddled discourse about subjects, knowledge and skills which infects the entire debate about curriculum, needlessly polarises discussion of how it might be organised, parodies knowledge and undervalues its place in education and inflates the undeniably important notion of a skill to a point where it too becomes meaningless.

(Alexander, 2010, p. 252)

Introduction

At the time of writing, it is still possible to find serving teachers in England and Wales able to look back, often with some nostalgia, to teaching geography before the advent of the National Curriculum. However, in the quarter-century since its inception in the 1988 Education Act, it is the National Curriculum which has dominated discussion about what should be taught, how and by whom in primary and the early years of secondary schools. In exploring the question 'What is geography's place in the curriculum for Key Stages 1, 2 and 3?', this chapter suggests that these discussions are part of several interlinked and wider debates about who constructs and develops the curriculum, its purpose and the nature of knowledge, the status of geography and the role of teachers.

To some extent these debates turn on the evolution of the Geography National Curriculum (GNC) in England. However, it is worth pointing out that Scotland, Wales and Northern Ireland have their own distinct national curricula, the outcome of similar debates and decisions as in England, at policy, school and classroom level. We will turn to these debates after briefly reviewing the position of geography before and during successive iterations of the English National Curriculum.

The evolution of the Geography National Curriculum

In the years between the 1944 and 1988 Education Acts, teachers in all phases had considerable autonomy in planning the curriculum, largely free of any oversight from (or a sense of accountability to) local or central government. This was particularly so in primary schools and 'lower' secondary schools, whereas at age 14 pupils embarked on public examination courses, whose syllabi, then as now, largely defined what was taught. The freedom of schools and individual teachers to select aims, content and approaches ensured that pupils' experience of geography varied considerably from one to another.

This was a period that Lawton (1980, p. 22) called 'the golden age of teacher control (or non-control) of the curriculum', when many schools in both phases did little to ensure progression and continuity or a sufficiently broad and balanced set of experiences for their pupils (Simon and Chitty, 1993, p. 108). Fran Martin, writing about teaching geography in primary schools before the National Curriculum, points out that this situation

> gave great freedom to teachers, (but) it also meant that pupils' experience of geography could be very hit and miss. If a teacher loved geography, and saw its relevance in primary pupils' education, then it was included; if they did not, it was often neglected.
>
> (Martin, 2013a, p. 17)

As HMI reports at the time showed, in primary schools geography did not always appear on the curriculum, and neither was its planning or quality of teaching consistent:

> Some work of a geographical nature was undertaken in three fifths of the 7 year old classes and nine out of ten 9 and 11 year old classes ... (however) much of the work tended to be superficial and there was often little evidence of progression ... Though good work was being done in some classes, in the majority essential skills and ideas were seldom given sufficient attention.
>
> (DES, 1978, p. 74)

By contrast in secondary schools, geography was a recognised part of the curriculum, 'a popular and well-respected subject' (Rawling, 2001, p. 9) and the focus of important debates about curriculum, pedagogy and the relationship of the subject with society. It was a period of significant school-based curriculum development in geography, with national support from the Schools Council (Hopkin, 2013a), although much of this activity focused on examination courses for older pupils.

Before the National Curriculum, this period of decentralised curriculum development brought gains such as the development of a robust model of geographical enquiry; however it also had a number of weaknesses, notably a lack of attention to place and locational knowledge, and an over-emphasis on themes in human geography at the expense of physical geography (Rawling, 2001; Hopkin, 2011). At the whole-school scale, curriculum innovation in the first years of some comprehensive schools often promoted a more cross-curricular approach. An HMI survey (DES, 1974) noted that 29 per cent of secondary schools taught geography in combination with subjects such as history and RE, leading to concerns about a loss of geographical focus and dilution of teachers' expertise.

In 1991, the first National Curriculum, by introducing direct state control over the content of the curriculum, thus represents a very significant discontinuity to this period of curricular freedom. Its overt aims were to 'raise standards' and 'develop the potential of all pupils and equip them for the responsibilities of citizenship' (DES, 1987, pp. 2–3), as well as to remedy the very heterogeneity of approaches outlined above, and to restore a model of the curriculum based on subjects and focused on knowledge. In geography, a key concern was to re-establish a more traditional view of the subject which put knowledge and understanding of places at its heart (Walford, 1992; Rawling, 1992, 2001).

Almost from the outset, the National Curriculum was subject to successive revisions. At the time of writing, the Geography National Curriculum (GNC) had gone through four different versions for Key Stages 1 and 2 (see Martin, 2013a, b), and five for Key Stage 3 (DES 1991 [for 1992], DfE 1995, DfEE/QCA1999a, b [for 2000] and DCSF/QCDA 2007[1] [for 2008] and DfE 2013 [for 2014]). (For a more detailed account see Hopkin 2013a and Lambert and Hopkin 2014).

In part, these revisions reflect the exigencies of government policy rubbing up against the realities of school life, most evidently in the very considerable changes in the curriculum and assessment arrangements in the second (1995) version, and in the further reductions in content at each subsequent revision. In part, the changes also reflect the development of wider ideas in society, and in the case of geography, to some extent developments in the discipline as well as changes in its status. In part, they also reflect the ideological priorities of different governments, played out in different views about the purposes of the curriculum and the nature of knowledge, between central control and professional autonomy in the selection of content and approach, and between different concepts of 'entitlement' and 'standards'. It is to these debates and their impact on the geography experienced by pupils that we now turn.

Debate 1: 'curriculum as specification' or 'curriculum as framework'?

Successive changes to the shape and content of the GNC suggest our first, and perhaps most fundamental debate: what are the respective roles of the state and the teaching profession in specifying and developing the curriculum?

In 1991, the first GNC focused on geographical knowledge, understanding and skills, specified and assessed in great detail, allowing little space or opportunity for curriculum development by teachers. In sheer volume, as well as intent, it became a curriculum of delivery. To some extent, over successive versions the GNC developed on the basic template of the original, with considerable continuity in its basic framework of locational and place knowledge, knowledge and understanding of geographical themes and skills. This evolution was evident in:

- an increased articulation of aims for geography;
- very significant overall reductions in prescribed content, together with reductions in the detail specified and more use of illustrative examples to frame teachers' increased choice;
- increasingly articulated geographical enquiry;
- a development of themes based on geography's links with society and environment, and some reduction in physical geography;
- a clearer model of assessment and progression.

(Hopkin, 2013a; Lambert and Hopkin, 2014)

By 2007, these evolutionary processes created a fairly sparse framework for geography at all three Key Stages which, rather than attempting comprehensive coverage, sampled from the discipline and was thus designed to secure a basic entitlement for pupils (see Tables 1.1 and 1.2). The 2007 version of the National Curriculum was designed to strengthen the whole curriculum and cross-curricular learning in secondary schools, and coincided in many primary schools with the widespread adoption of the creative curriculum, an approach which aims to be driven by the pupils' needs rather than subjects, in particular the skills they need to learn (Burgess, 2007). In some secondary schools, the 2007 National Curriculum also stimulated the development of generic skills-based courses and, for the first time since before the National Curriculum, saw an increase in the number of Key Stage 3 courses which integrated the teaching of geography, often with history and RE, and thus an increase in geography lessons taught by non-specialists.

Moreover, whereas the original National Curriculum was widely seen, not least by politicians at the time, as a curriculum of control (Bennetts, 1993; Goodson, 1994), behind this evolution a shift was also evident in the balance of influence on National Curriculum policy from the politicians, strong in the first GNC, towards professionals and the geography subject associations in later versions. So alongside a sparser framework went increased professional responsibility for teachers to develop a balanced curriculum.

The 2013 version of the National Curriculum represents a disjuncture in these broadly evolutionary processes, both in form and construction. In geography, this produced more specific and content-rich Programmes of Study, albeit expressed in considerably less detail than the 1991 original, with a notable strengthening of a distinctive place and locational knowledge at each Key Stage, together with a weakening of geographical enquiry and very little attention to progression and assessment.

In an echo of 1988, this change represents another attempt by government to restore a model of the curriculum based on 'traditional' subjects and again led by a 'core of essential knowledge' (Hirsch, 1987; 2007), in spite of at least a rhetorical commitment to free teachers up from 'prescription, bureaucracy and central control' and allow 'schools and teachers … greater control over what is taught' (DfE, 2010, p. 40). We are reminded of a basic tension hard-wired into

Table 1.1 Four versions of physical geography at Key Stage 2

GNC version	Programme of Study (exemplification omitted)
1992 (DES, 1991, p. 37)	Pupils should be taught (levels 2–4) • to identify and describe landscape features … with which they are familiar • how site conditions can influence surface temperatures and affect wind speed and direction, the effect of differences and slopes • the nature and effects of earthquakes and volcanic eruptions, and how the latter produce craters, cones and lava flows • to identify water in different forms • that rivers have sources, channels, tributaries and mouths, that they receive water from a wide area, and that most eventually flow into a lake or a sea • that rivers, waves, winds and glaciers erode, transport and deposit materials • to recognise seasonal weather patterns • about weather conditions in different parts of the world • to investigate and compare the colour, texture and organic content of different types of soil.
1995 (DfE, 1995, pp. 5–6)	Rivers. In studying rivers and their effects on the landscape, pupils should be taught: • that rivers have sources, channels, tributaries and mouths, that they receive water from a wide area and that most eventually flow into a lake or a sea • how rivers erode, transport and deposit materials producing particular landscape features Weather. In studying how weather varies between places and over time, pupils should be taught: a how site conditions can influence the weather b about seasonal weather patterns c about weather conditions in different parts of the world.
2000 (DfEE/QCA, 1999a, p. 114)	Knowledge and understanding of patterns and processes Breadth of study: themes • Water and its effects on landscapes and people, including the physical features of rivers or coasts, and the processes of erosion and deposition that affect them.
2014 (DfE, 2013, p. 3)	Pupils should be taught to … describe and understand key aspects of: • physical geography, including: climate zones, biomes and vegetation belts, rivers, mountains, volcanoes and earthquakes, and the water cycle.

Source: Hopkin 2013b.

the National Curriculum enterprise from the start, as between competing impulses for central control, ultimately founded in neo-conservatism, and freedom, choice and market forces, ultimately founded in neo-liberalism (see Rawling, 2001, pp. 30–45 for an overview of ideologies in relation to the curriculum). Since 2010

Table 1.2 Five versions of environmental issues at Key Stage 3

GNC version	Programme of Study (exemplification omitted)
1992 (DES, 1991, p. 37)	Pupils should be taught (levels 3–6) [with three further points for level 7] • how the extraction of natural resources affects environments • the differences between manufactured goods and natural resources • about fresh water sources and means of ensuring a reliable water supply; why rivers, lakes and seas are vulnerable to pollution and to investigate ways in which pollution can be prevented • the differences between renewable and non-renewable resources • the effect on the environment of the development of at least two energy resources • ways in which people look after and improve the environment; some of the ways in which damaged environments can be restored and damage prevented; and to consider whether some types of environment need special protection • how attempts to plan and manage environments can have unintended effects, using case studies • how areas of great scenic attraction can give rise to conflicting demands on them and the issues which arise as a result.
1995 (DfE, 1995, pp. 5–6)	Environmental Issues. In investigating environmental issues, pupils should be taught: a why some areas are viewed as being of great scenic attraction, and how conflicting demands on the areas can arise b how attempts are made to plan and manage such environments and how these can have unintended effects c how considerations of sustainable development, stewardship and conservation affect environmental planning and management; **and either** d about provision of a reliable supply of fresh water and the causes, effects and prevention of water pollution, **or** e about provision of a reliable supply of energy and the effect on the environment of the development of two different energy sources.
2000 (DfEE/QCA, 1999b, p. 103)	Knowledge and understanding of environmental change and sustainable development. Breadth of study: themes • environmental issues, including: i how conflicting demands on an environment arise ii how and why attempts are made to plan and mange environments iii effects of environmental planning and management on people, places and environments

(*continued*)

Table 1.2 Continued

GNC version	Programme of Study (exemplification omitted)
2008 (DCSF/QCDA 2007)	Range and content: • interactions between people and their environments, including causes and consequences of these interactions, and how to plan for and manage their future impact.
2014 (DfE 2013, p. 2)	Pupils should be taught to … • understand how human and physical processes interact to influence, and change landscapes, environments and the climate; and how human activity relies on effective functioning of natural systems

this tension played out in the enactment of a revised National Curriculum designed to restore high standards in maintained schools, simultaneously with the active promotion of Academies and Free Schools, whose professed advantages included freedom from the National Curriculum – in order to secure high standards.

In the context of an increasingly centralised education policy environment, Rawling sees the process of writing the 2013 GNC as 'strongly political, with occasional moments of direct input from Ministers over topics such as climate change, enquiry and global citizenship' (see Table 1.2) representing 'the extension of control over geography subject knowledge from the centre, with a corresponding decline in influence of the subject community' (2016, pp. 164–5). The result is that the position of subject professionals in the process of curriculum and examination change has become fragile, making the need for teachers' curriculum development skills never greater (ibid., p. 168).

It is also worth remembering that, 'the curriculum as defined by policy documents and the curriculum as it is articulated in schools are two different things' (Martin, 2013a, p. 17). Thus, the curriculum experienced by pupils in the classroom is mediated by a wide range of factors including school aims, the selections and emphases made by teams of teachers and individuals, the resources used, teachers' pedagogy and assessment arrangements as well as teachers' 'potential for innovation and creativity' in curriculum making (Lambert, 2011, p. 149).

Thus, it might be argued, as Rawling does in relation to the 2013 GNC, that 'despite the apparent high level of detail, at every key stage these documents should still be viewed as curriculum frameworks for further development … ultimately (by) teachers' (2015, p. 6). Lambert and Hopkin go further, suggesting that, particularly compared with its 1991 predecessor, by avoiding detailed lists of content 'it invites teachers to create a curriculum of engagement rather than delivery. It is an opportunity for specialist geography teachers to break away from the dead hand of 'deliverology'' (op. cit. p. 75). And as with successive previous versions of the GNC, the GA's professional journals *Primary Geography* and

Teaching Geography contain many interesting examples of curriculum planning advice (see Martin, 2013b; Kinder and Owens, 2014) and practice from teachers keen to apply the GNC and make it work for their pupils in their circumstances (see for example Aston and Renshaw, 2014; Cook, 2014; Howarth et al., 2015).

Debate 2: the purpose of the curriculum and the role of geographical knowledge

Alongside the debate about the balance of forces and interests in national curriculum change, lies another fundamental debate about the purpose of the curriculum, linked with differing views about knowledge, particularly in relation to skills. Because these debates are intrinsic to people's deeply held convictions (or ideologies) about education in society, they are of course also inherent in the above debates about the National Curriculum. However, they also have a significant impact on the way schools organise the curriculum, and the choices made by individual teachers from day to day in the classroom. Here we use three different frames used by different geographers to help illuminate the way these selections and omissions play out at all these levels.

- Mary Biddulph (2014), writing about different perspectives on the curriculum, explores the impact of different curricular aims on what and how we choose to teach and the quality of the geography curriculum. She distinguishes between three different models for the curriculum:
  - cultural transmission – aiming to transmit the culture of society (or particular versions of it) to young people through education. This model tends to tradition, and is often teacher centred with pupils positioned to steadily acquire knowledge handed down to them;
  - objectives-led – aiming to train or instruct learners and often focused on competences and the acquisition of skills, which are then broken down into small nuggets, acquired in a linear way and then frequently measured;
  - curriculum as process and praxis – active curriculum making by teachers, which prioritises the development young people's geographical thought and understanding.

Biddulph suggests the evolution of the GNC represents a move from a cultural transmission model in the 1980s and early 1990s, represented in the first GNC, through to objectives led models in the 2000s, represented by generic skills-based curricula and high levels of measurability.

- Roger Firth (2012, 2013), uses Young's (2008) and Young and Muller's (2010) analysis of different approaches to the knowledge required for young people to operate as active citizens and workers in different futures to explore the impact on geography:

- Future 1 knowledge (F1) – based on the delivery of knowledge through traditional subjects. Proponents consider knowledge to be valuable for its own sake and so 'handed down' to pupils, although in the classroom this can make it static and unresponsive to a rapidly changing world.
- Future 2 knowledge (F2) – focused on the development of learners' skills and capacity to learn. Proponents often represent knowledge as merely socially constructed and so arbitrary, and subjects as artificial and irrelevant to young people's (working) futures; in the classroom this view prioritises learning over teaching, and teachers' pedagogic skills over subject knowledge.
- Future 3 knowledge (F3) – regards knowledge as the outcome of conceptual thinking which is founded in deep disciplines (and so 'powerful'), and particularly valuable in preparing young people for future active citizenship. Proponents see disciplinary knowledge as neither immutable nor arbitrary, useful attributes for a dynamic subject like geography. In the classroom teachers' subject knowledge as well as pedagogic skills (for example in geographical enquiry) are deployed in developing young people's understanding.

For Firth, the 1991 GNC represents an F1 curriculum, with limited recognition of a dynamic discipline and focused on a traditional view of the subject, to be delivered and learned for its own sake. Partly in reaction to these shortcomings; the GNC's evolution represents a move towards aspects of an F2 curriculum by 2007. As the above discussion on teachers' role in the curriculum suggests, the 2013 GNC, although in many ways an attempt to restore a view of the curriculum and of knowledge rooted in F1, may suggest, in practice, the possibility of an F3 curriculum, not least because of the Geographical Association's work to promote its Manifesto (GA, 2009) along with the concept of 'Curriculum Making', and to promote alternative ways to frame the GNC (see Hopkin, 2013b).

- Bill Marsden (see for example 1995) bases his analysis on differing orientations of geography related to historical changes in the school subject and its purpose. He sees geography as being in a dynamic state of flux between an emphasis on the subject dimension (selecting from the discipline), the educational dimension (understanding the needs of the child) and the social dimension (the relationship with wider social concerns). For Marsden, good practice resides in a balance between subject, educational and societal purposes; in particular an over-emphasis on the educational and social dimensions is ever-present in disciplinary history and represents a risk to its integrity (Marsden, 1997; Lambert and Morgan, 2009). In these terms, the GNC evolved from an originally strong orientation to the subject in 1991 towards a greater focus on education and society by 2007, but returned towards the subject dimension in 2013.

It is worth pointing out that these analyses are not uncontested (see for example Catling and Martin [2011] and Roberts [2014] on Powerful Knowledge).

However, it will be evident that, whether considering curriculum aims, views of knowledge or orientations within school geography, there is considerable alignment between these three ways of framing fundamental debates about the purpose of the curriculum, and the value and form of knowledge, as well as understanding the development the National Curriculum between 1991 and 2013. Hopkin (2014) showed how these debates were evident in the way that particular aspects of geography are taught and the quality of pupils' learning. Looking at global learning, an important ingredient of pupils' experiences of geography in both primary and secondary, he compared:

- a 'traditional geography' approach – focused on the acquisition of objective facts and world knowledge, and sceptical about the role of enquiry and contemporary global issues;
- a 'global citizenship approach' – emphasising links with other subjects, teachers' expertise in pedagogy and learners' skills and values, with some scepticism about the value of knowledge about the world; and
- a 'knowledgeable geography' approach – emphasising the merit of geographical knowledge in understanding the world, based on core geographical ideas such as place and connection, together with a recognition of the value of enquiry and critical thinking in developing knowledge, including about contemporary global issues.

Individual teachers may not necessarily be familiar with the specific models outlined above or explicitly use their language. However, we argue that they encapsulate some fundamental ideas which have a significant and direct influence on decisions about how the geography curriculum is organised and taught in different primary and secondary schools, so influencing pupils' experience of geography and its quality.

Moreover, underlying these debates is the relative complexity of disciplinary knowledge – a mixture of content (propositional knowledge such as the location of places), concepts (organising concepts and principles such as geographical processes) and contexts (everyday and social knowledge). This complexity can represent a huge challenge for some, particularly non-specialist secondary teachers but more so for primary teachers who 'whilst highly knowledgeable about teaching and learning approaches … and pupils' experiences and interests, but [are] less so about the subject knowledge' (Martin, 2013b, p. 10); thus, they may struggle to confidently reinterpret the implicit understandings and ways of seeing the world that the discipline represents. Thus, an integrated, creative curriculum designed to develop critical and reflective thinking and transferable skills is very appealing, particularly for generalist primary teachers: it does not require them to grapple with this tricky conceptual and organisational territory. In the case of geography, there is evidence that this leads to a focus on contexts such as sustainable behaviours and skills such as enquiry, while content and concepts in the form of geographical knowledge and understanding may be underplayed or lost.

Debate 3: the status of geography in the curriculum and the role of teachers

Although the National Curriculum has ensured that geography has a statutory place in the curriculum, this has not been stable and it appears that, particularly in primary schools, it has often suffered from low status compared with other subjects. Whereas in secondary schools geography is often (but not always) led and taught by geography specialists with high levels of subject and pedagogic knowledge founded in the discipline, the reverse is true in primary schools where geography is often (but not always) led and taught by teachers with limited training or specialist expertise.

An important feature of primary schools is that, for the most part, pupils are taught the whole curriculum by their class teacher. This is significant for a number of reasons.

- Not only does geography have to find a place in the primary curriculum as a whole, but it also has to find a place in each class teacher's mind as being worthy of inclusion. Moreover, as research by Catling et al., (2007) has shown, if geography is to find a place alongside all other subjects, it has to be seen as *relevant* by primary school headteachers and senior management teams, as well as by individual teachers.
- However, the majority of primary headteachers and class teachers are not geography specialists and so their *image* of the subject may be one that is outdated and seen to lack relevance in terms of its contribution to primary pupils' education, and they also have difficulty interpreting the *nature* of geography as expressed in the National Curriculum orders.
- This makes geography's place (and the place of other foundation subjects) more vulnerable and subject to variations in the *status* accorded to it at local levels, no matter what status it is accorded nationally.

Due to the nature of primary education, and the politically driven overemphasis on the core subjects of English and Mathematics, primary geography has found itself in a 'Catch 22' situation. It is a subject that is not well understood outside the geography community (and also by some school leaders); primary student teachers come to their training with a limited and outdated view of what the subject has to offer; but there are limited opportunities within ITE courses to change these views so teachers enter the profession lacking subject knowledge and confidence; teachers therefore struggle to see the relevance of the subject, and either avoid teaching it, or teach it in such a way that does not enthuse their pupils.

As well as putting pressure on teaching time for geography, the relentless focus on raising standards in the core subjects in both primary and secondary schools also limits teachers' access to professional development; even for secondary subject specialists, Continuing Professional Development (CPD) often focuses on preparation for examination courses and improving geography results, rather than improving subject knowledge or subject-specific pedagogy in Key Stage 3. The re-emergence of integrated courses in Key Stage 3, which are based on general 'themes' taught by non-specialist teachers (often interpreted as providing continuity with a primary model of the curriculum), may also be to some extent a response to restrictions on teaching time for geography, but they also reflect a particular view of the purpose of the curriculum and of knowledge. As the Ofsted reports (2008, 2011) make clear, in both primary and secondary schools, the pressure on curriculum time and the demands on teachers' expertise can limit pupils' experience of a high quality geography curriculum and so their attainment; and put at risk the notion of a broad and balanced range of subjects.

A key aspect of this debate concerns the interaction of status, time and teacher expertise with the purpose, form and function of each Key Stage. The model of generalist class teachers teaching a non-core curriculum organised in broadly thematic or cross-curricular way is likely to continue in the majority of primary schools in the foreseeable future, although successive Ofsted reports suggest that this can lead to classrooms where 'the subject was often peripheral ... or there was too great a focus on skills, rather than on knowledge and understanding' (Ofsted, 2011, p. 19), so how can provision and achievement best be improved within this model? At what point should pupils begin to experience a greater degree of specialisation; in particular, should Key Stage 3 be regarded as an extension of primary education, with its traditional emphasis on integration, or as the platform for secondary education with its emphasis on the development subject knowledge, conceptual depth and intellectual challenge?

Martin (2013) points out that the subject associations have been particularly active in creating diverse opportunities for CPD (pp. 23–4), and argues there may be more innovative ways of developing teachers' geographic confidence and capability. She suggests the adoption of a new paradigm 'ethnography' for primary geography that draws on teachers' and pupils' everyday geographies and understanding of knowledge, and helps primary teachers to connect pupils' knowledge productively with knowledge beyond the 'everyday' and the key concepts that underpin them (Martin, 2006, 2008). Generalist teachers need subject specialists to share with them the narrative (organising conceptual framework) of subjects, so that they can use their own personal experience to make better sense of them and decide which aspects of the academic subject (outside their experience) they might then teach. This would also support pedagogical reasoning, deciding which activity was appropriate at which point and in which order; what Tim Oates (2010) refers to as curriculum coherence.

Conclusion

Referring to the three interlinked debates discussed in this chapter, we are not suggesting that these are necessarily binary choices, and to some extent the emphases between perspectives will differ according to circumstances – although we clearly have our own views about these debates. However, the decisions made in relation to them, particularly by school leaders and teachers, do have a direct impact on how pupils experience geography in the classroom (and outside it), as well as the quality of that experience. Ofsted reports covering the period from 1993 to 2011 showed steady improvements in achievement, teaching and curriculum over two decades in primary and secondary schools, as well as persistent weaknesses since the early years of the National Curriculum (Hopkin 2013a). These include some whole-school issues, such as limitations on curriculum time for geography and poorly thought-out thematic courses, weaknesses in teachers' subject knowledge leading to poor teaching of locational knowledge, places and geographical skills, together with limitations on achievement caused by limited challenge, differentiation and weak assessment.

The Geography National Curriculum established a framework for pupils' geographical education for the (previously neglected) primary and early secondary years. After a quarter of a century, it is likely that significantly more pupils at Key Stages 1 to 3 now experience a high quality geography education. However, progress has been only modestly successful in some significant aspects including issues that predate the National Curriculum, suggesting that they are deep-seated within school geography. We suggest that, in the interests of future progress, informed engagement with these debates, supported by the systematic professional development needed to foster a 'cultured profession' (HoC, 2009, para 47), is an important responsibility of professionals able to make informed judgements about the geography curriculum (rather than compliant technicians) for Key Stages 1, 2 and 3.

Key readings

1   Catling, S. and Martin, F. (2011) 'Contesting powerful knowledge: The primary geography curriculum as an articulation between academic and children's (ethno-) geographies', *Curriculum Journal,* 22 (3), 317–15. Catling and Martin discuss the idea of ethno-geographies in relation to academic geographies and, drawing on the work of Paulo Freire and Michael Young, examine the claims that each makes to be a form of powerful knowledge. The authors propose that ethno-geographies, rather than being encountered as in some way deficient and in need of replacing by academic disciplined knowledge, could 'be brought into dialogue as a democratic partner in the mutual interplay of learning' (Catling and Martin, 2011, p. 332).

2   Young, M. (2011) 'The future of education in a knowledge society: The radical case for a subject-based curriculum', *Journal of the Pacific Circle Consortium for Education,* 22 (1), 21–32. Michael Young argues that if we are to give the importance of education in a knowledge society any serious meaning, we need to make the question of knowledge our central concern and this involves developing a knowledge-led and subject-led, and not, as much current orthodoxy assumes, a learner-led approach to the curriculum. He explores what this means for the curriculum, subjects and the purpose of schooling.

Note

1 The DCSF/QCDA (2007) Geography National Curriculum applied to Key Stage 3 only, Primary schools continued to teach using the DfEE/QCA (1999) orders.

References

Alexander, R. J. (ed.) (2010) *Children, their World, their Education*, London: Routledge.

Aston, R. and Renshaw, S. (2014) 'Planning a new Key Stage 3', *Teaching Geography*, 39 (2), 64–5.

Bennetts, T. (1993) 'Reflections on the development of geography in the National Curriculum', in R. Walford, and P. Machon, (eds.) *Challenging Times: Implementing the National Curriculum in Geography*, Papers from the Charney Manor Conference 1993, Cambridge: Cambridge Publishing Services.

Biddulph, M. (2014) 'What kind of curriculum do we really want?', *Teaching Geography*, 39

Burgess, T. (2007) *Lifting the Lid on the Creative Curriculum: How Leaders Have Released Creativity in their Schools through Curriculum Ownership*. Research report for the National College for School Leadership, Available at: http://dera.ioe. ac.uk/7340/1/download%3Fid%3D17281%26filename%3Dlifting-the-lid-on-the-creative-curriculum-full-report.pdf [Accessed 2 August 2016].

Catling, S. and Martin, F. (2011) 'Contesting powerful knowledge: the primary geography curriculum as an articulation between academic and children's (ethno-) geographies', *The Curriculum Journal*, 22, 317–35.

Catling, S., Bowles, R., Halocha, J., Martin, F., and Rawlings, S. (2007) 'The state of geography in English primary schools', *Geography*, 92 (2), 118–36.

Cook, K. (2014) 'Planning a new Key Stage 3', *Teaching Geography*, 39 (1), 16–17.

DCSF/QCDA (2007) *The National Curriculum: Statutory Requirements for Key Stages 3 and 4*, London: DCSF/QCDA.

DES (1974) 'School geography inn the changing curriculum', *Education Survey* 19, London: HMSO.

DES (1978) *Primary Education in England* London: HMSO, Available at: http:// www.educationengland.org.uk/documents/hmi-primary/hmi-primary.html#05 [Accessed 6 August 2016].

DES (1991) *Geography in the National Curriculum: England*, London: HMSO.

DfE (1995) *Geography in the National Curriculum: England*, London: HMSO.

DfE (2013) National Curriculum in England: Geography Programmes of Study, Available at: https://www.gov.uk/government/publications/national-curriculum-in-england-geography-programmes-of-study [Accessed 6 May 2016].

DfEE/QCA (1999a) *The National Curriculum Handbook for Primary Teachers in England*, Key Stages 1 and 2, London: DfEE/QCA.

DfEE/QCA (1999b) *The National Curriculum Handbook for Secondary Teachers in England*, Key Stages 3 and 4, London: DfEE/QCA.

Firth, R. (2012) 'Disordering the coalition government's 'new' approach to curriculum design and knowledge: the matter of the discipline', *Geography*, 97 (2), 86–94.

Firth, R. (2013) 'What constitutes knowledge in geography?' in D. Lambert and M. Jones (eds.) *Debates in Geography Education*, London: Routledge.

Geographical Association (GA) (2009) *A Different View: A Manifesto from the Geographical Association*. Sheffield: Geographical Association.

Goodson, I. F. (1994) *Studying Curriculum: Cases and Methods*, Buckingham: Open University Press.

Hirsch, E. D. (1987) *Cultural Literacy: What Every American Needs To Know*, Boston: Houghton Mifflin.

Hirsch, E. D. (2007) *The Knowledge Deficit*, Boston: Houghton Mifflen.

HoC (1999) House of Commons Children, Schools and Families Committee, *National Curriculum: Fourth Report of Session 2008–9*. London: The Stationary Office.

Hopkin, J. (2011) 'Progress in geography', *Geography*, 96 (3), 116–23.

Hopkin, J. (2013a) 'What is Key Stage 3 for?' in D. Lambert and M. Jones (eds.) *Debates in Geography Education*, London: Routledge.

Hopkin, J. (2013b) 'Framing the Geography National Curriculum', *Geography*, 98 (2), 60–7.

Hopkin, J. (2014) A 'knowledgeable geography' approach to global learning', *Teaching Geography*, 40 (2), 50–4.

Howarth, L. et al. (2015) 'Brazil: beyond the stereotypes' *Primary Geography*, 86 (1), 8–9.

Kinder, A. and Owens, P. (2014) 'Preparing for curriculum 2014', *Primary Geography*, 83 (1), 28–9.

Lambert, D. (2011) 'Reviewing the case for geography, and the 'knowledge turn' in the English national curriculum', *The Curriculum Journal*, 22 (2), 147–57.

Lambert, D. and Hopkin, J. (2014) 'A possibilist analysis of the Geography National Curriculum in England', *International Research in Geographical and Environmental Education*, 23 (1), 64–78.

Lambert, D. and Morgan, J. (2009) 'Corrupting the curriculum? The case for geography', *London Review of Education*, 7 (2), 147–57.

Lambert, D. and Morgan, J. (2010) *Teaching Geography 11–18: A Conceptual Approach*, Maidenhead: Open University Press.

Lawton, D. (1980) *The Politics of the School Curriculum*, London, Routledge: Kegan & Paul.

Marsden, W.E. (1995) *Geography 11–16: Rekindling Good Practice*, London: David Fulton.

Marsden, W.E. (1997) 'On taking the geography out of geographical education', *Geography*, 82 (3), 241–52.

Martin, F. (2006) *Teaching Geography in Primary Schools: Learning to Live in the World*, Cambridge: Chris Kington Publishing.

Martin, F. (2008) 'Ethnogeography: towards a liberatory geography education', *Children's Geographies*, 6 (4), 437–50.

Martin, F. (2013b) 'The place of knowledge in the new curriculum, *Primary Geography*, 82 (3), 9–11.

Oates, T. (2010) *Could Do Better: Using International Comparisons to Refine the National Curriculum in England*, Cambridge: Cambridge Assessment.

Ofsted (2008) *Geography in Schools: Changing Practice*, London: Ofsted.

Ofsted (2011) *Geography: Learning to Make a World of Difference*, London: Ofsted.

Rawling, E. (1992) 'The making of a national geography curriculum', *Geography*, 77 (4), 292–309.

Rawling, E. (2001) *Changing the Subject: The Impact of National Policy on School Geography 1980–2000*, Sheffield: Geographical Association.

Rawling, E. (2015) 'Spotlight on: curriculum change and examination reform for geography 14–19', *Geography*, 100 (3), 164–8.

Rawling, E. (2016) 'The geography curriculum 5–19: what does it all mean?' *Teaching Geography*, 41 (1), 6–9.

Roberts, M. (2014) 'Powerful knowledge and geographical education', *The Curriculum Journal*, 25, 187–209.

Simon, B. and Chitty, C. (1993) *Save Our Schools*, London: Lawrence and Wishart.

Walford, R. (1992) 'Creating a national curriculum: a view from the inside', in D. Hill. (ed.) *International Perspectives on Geographical Education*, Boulder: Centre for Geographical Education, University of Colorado.

Young, M. (2008) *Bringing Knowledge Back In*, London: Routledge.

Young, M. and Muller, J. (2010) 'Three educational scenarios for the future: lessons from the sociology of knowledge', *European Journal of Education*, 45 (1), 11–27.

Chapter 2

Geography in the examination system

David Gardner

> Our changes will make these qualifications more ambitious, with greater stretch for the most able; ... and will give pupils, parents, teachers, universities and employers greater confidence in the integrity and reliability of our qualifications system.
>
> (Gove, DfE, 2014a)

Introduction

In the previous edition of this book the implications of the Schools White Paper, *The Importance of Teaching* (DfE, 2010), were still difficult to envisage, not least the kind of geography that would emerge from 14–19 reform (Gardner, 2013). The changing picture is now becoming clearer.

In 2014 the Secretary of State for Education, Michael Gove, made clear what reforms post 14 were designed to achieve, as shown above. This chapter will consider how this has impacted on the kind of geography now emerging post 14; the changes to the way fieldwork will be assessed at GCSE and A level; the overall changes to assessment in geography; and importantly, the way in which geography teachers will need to adapt to these changes.

Progression in geography 11–19

The Department for Education and Ofqual have approached both GCSEs and A levels in a more direct interventionist manner since 2010. Rawling (2015) has pointed to 'the centralised nature of the exercise and the strong element of political control exerted throughout' (Rawling, 2015, p. 166) Thus, both for national curriculum and GCSE reform there was no permanent subject expert or committee to advise government, as the Qualifications and Curriculum Authority (QCA) has been abolished. For A level the situation was different, as in 2013 the Secretary of State invited the Russell Group of universities to take a leading role in discussions over subject content. This led to the formation of the A level Content Advisory Board (ALCAB): the ALCAB Geography Panel was established in January 2014 chaired by Professor Martin Evans of the University of Manchester (Evans, 2016). This panel consisted mainly of academic geographers plus representatives of the GA and RGS-IBG. As Rawling (2015) points out, these geographers had a key role in subject discussions, with Ministers content to stand back from the process – at least at A level.

New GCSEs and A levels have been driven by 'a political desire to define subjects through content' (Digby, 2015, p. 104). The DfE (2014b) subject content documents for GCSE make clear the purpose of the prescribed content:

> The GCSE subject content sets out the knowledge, understanding and skills common to all GCSE specifications in a given subject. Together with the assessment objectives it provides the framework within which awarding organisations create the detail of their specifications, so ensuring progression from key stage 3 national curriculum requirements and the possibilities for development into A level.
>
> (p. 3)

The last part of this statement is of significance in current curriculum reform. In previous post-14 curriculum reviews, the government provided a framework of subject criteria via its 'arm's length' agency, the Qualifications and Curriculum Authority (QCA). These criteria provided broad guiding principles such the proportion of physical geography that should be included in a GCSE geography specification. This approach provided awarding bodies with the flexibility to develop specifications in different ways. However, the flipside was that across the variety of GCSE (and A level) specifications, there was arguably a lack of coordinated effort to support progression from KS3 into GCSE and onto A level. The amount of flexibility has now been significantly reduced with the new subject content frameworks at GCSE and A level: all awarding bodies have to comply with the new subject content requirements in order to gain approval from Ofqual.

Teachers are now required to teach aspects of geography they may not previously have covered in their GCSE courses: for instance, the geography of the UK, both in overview and through some in-depth study, is a significant departure from former GCSE specifications. This requires more than just providing 'case studies' from within the UK, but developing holistic knowledge of UK landscapes, environmental challenges, changing economy and society. On the other hand, it is, perhaps for the first time, possible to map 'progression' in geography from 5 to 19 years old. Eleanor Rawling (2016), in her role as lead Geography Consultant and Writer for the government (encompassing National Curriculum, GCSE and AS/A-level reviews), has had a unique opportunity to 'coordinate' the full range of what is to be covered at each level, as Figure 2.1 shows.

As she points out:

> Looking across the guidelines as a whole, it is clear that there is a focus on subject knowledge and a detailed listing of particular topics and themes to be covered. There is also a stronger emphasis than in previous versions on physical geography and it is apparent that the AS/A-level content introduce some human geography content that may be considered new to schools.
>
> (Rawling, 2016, p. 6)

National curriculum 11–14 years	GCSE 14–16 years 14–16 years	AS/A level 16–19 years 16–19 years
Knowledge-led, emphasis on locational knowledge, a regional study in Africa and one in Asia, coverage of traditional physical and human topics, including rocks, weathering, weather/climate, population, urban development, economic activity, resources. Brief aspects of progression. Not all aspects of geography present (e.g. people-environment). No mention of enquiry.	Detailed subject knowledge via headings: locational knowledge; place; human geography; people-environment; physical geography; maps, fieldwork, geographical skills (including enquiry). 'Place' includes 'Geography of UK' in overview and in some depth. Fieldwork strengthened – in two contrasting environments. Full statement about progression from key stage 3. Terminal examination only.	Subject knowledge framed within clear rationale and structure (from A level Content Advisory Board [ALCAB] report). Core (60%) content includes two human and two physical themes for A level (1 each for AS). Updated content especially in human geography – place meaning, identity, representation; and in physical geography – water/carbon cycles. Progression from GCSE stated. Independent learning and research stressed (student investigation 20%).

Figure 2.1 Geography for ages 11–19 (Rawling, 2016).

Thus, the DfE subject content documents provide an excellent starting point for planning for pupil progress across the secondary geography curriculum. In addition, the explicit *aims* for GCSE and A level in these documents can help teachers establish a clear vision for what they are trying to achieve for pupils at each key stage. The GCSE aims are particularly helpful stating that GCSE specifications in geography should enable students to:

- develop and extend their knowledge of locations, places, environments and processes, and of different scales and social, political and cultural contexts (know geographical material);
- gain understanding of the interactions between people and environments, change in places and processes over space and time, and the interrelationship between geographical phenomena at different scales and in different contexts (think like a geographer);
- develop and extend their competence in a range of skills including those used in fieldwork, in using maps and Geographical Information Systems (GIS) and in researching secondary evidence, including digital sources; and apply the cycle of collecting, presenting and analysing (geographical) data, including categorising and evaluating information and hypotheses (study like a geographer);
- apply geographical knowledge, understanding, skills and approaches appropriately and creatively to real world contexts, including fieldwork, and to contemporary situations and issues; and develop well-evidenced geographical argument drawing on their knowledge and understanding (applying geography).

(DfE, 2014b, p. 3)

The summaries in brackets for each aim – to know, think, study and understand like a geographer – are particularly useful devices to support teachers and pupils. Jo Debens, a school teacher, has created a simplified version of this for her pupils (Figure 2.2).

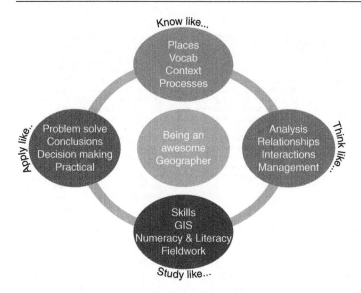

Figure 2.2 GCSE aims: a version for pupils.

Source: Jo Debens.

It is also useful to note the *approach* to geography adopted by the Awarding Bodies who have had to interpret and develop the content. As Digby (2015) has pointed out across the seven new GCSE specifications offered by the Awarding Bodies, two models have emerged:

- a thematic approach, defining content by physical/human themes;
- an issues-based approach, which defines content largely by its topicality, embedded in a people-environment approach.

Both models have a clear fieldwork and geographical skills requirement.

Evans (2016) has usefully described the debate that took place between teachers and academics in developing the DfE (2014c) subject content for A Level geography. Academics tended to favour less choice than teachers. The result is a specified 60 per cent common core of knowledge across all A level specifications. This, it is argued, will help to ensure that university entrants have a common base of thematic knowledge. Academic geographers were also keen to ensure new specifications reflected some of the developments that have taken place in the last 30 years, particularly in human geography. Examples include elements of the *Changing Place; Changing Places* unit. In addition, steps have been taken to encourage greater rigour in understanding physical systems and processes. Approaches to understanding geographical information and geo-located data, as well as some ethical dimensions to fieldwork are also new developments.

Taken together, reforms to geography 14 to 19 make progression in geography significantly clearer and provide new and stronger integrity for the subject, which is to be welcomed (see Clifford in this volume). The changes at A Level in particular represent an important step forward, in realigning and possibly reconnecting school and university geography (but also see Butt and Collins, and Firth in this volume). All changes create significant challenges for teachers. These include updating and enhancing their own geographical knowledge and pedagogies, to successfully support new generations of pupils to develop as geographers, and to succeed in these new qualifications.

The place of fieldwork

Lambert and Reiss (2016) make a strong case for fieldwork in geography (and science) qualifications across the 14–19 age range – uncontroversially, for ever since the introduction of GCSE in 1986, fieldwork has been a key component of 'coursework assessment' or more recently 'controlled assessment'. These forms of assessment were designed to encourage students to undertake fieldwork investigations, but in the most recent reforms have now been removed. Fieldwork remains a clear, unambiguous requirement (students must experience 'different approaches to fieldwork … in at least two contrasting environments') but is assessed as part of the terminal examination.

Assessing fieldwork at GCSE through terminal examination is both problematic and controversial and a significant matter for debate. It is perhaps worth quoting, at some length, from the Geographical Association's letter to Michael Gove, Secretary of State for Education at that time:

> In our view, written examinations are an inadequate tool for assessing the broad range of complex skills involved in fieldwork design, data collection and interpretation and fieldwork evaluation, as well as broader skills such as teamwork, self-management and research. Fieldwork skills and knowledge are best assessed through practical activity and the reports which can arise from this activity, rather than through examination questions which test the theory of fieldwork. Such questions tend to be formulaic, and are therefore a less valid and reliable form of assessment. We argue that setting questions that distinguish candidates who have acquired the practical skills they need for further study and employment will not be possible in practice. We also fear that, if opportunities for writing longer fieldwork-based reports are removed from GCSE geography, the curriculum for students will be narrowed and that the knowledge and skills identified above will be neglected, as schools focus on the more theoretical demands of a written examination.
>
> (Geographical Association, 2013)

Only the experience of successive GCSE examinations will determine how far the GA's concerns about fieldwork are vindicated. An opposing view, discussed briefly in Lambert and Reiss (2014) is that coursework (and its successor, controlled assessment) themselves led to formulaic fieldwork experiences. The government also expressed concern that assessments undertaken outside examination conditions can be manipulated and encourage various forms of inequalities (e.g. some students getting more 'help' than others).

Moving to A level, the ALCAB panel for geography is also very clear about the importance of fieldwork: 'Fieldwork is an essential component of geography. The ability to conduct field investigations in order to test ideas, build evidence, reflect on concepts, and create new geographical knowledge is one of the defining characteristics of a geographer' (ALCAB, 2014, p. 23). Furthermore, the panel believe that the only appropriate method of assessment for fieldwork at A Level is through a non-examination assessed independent investigation. A piece of field research and extended writing is required, for it was the panel's view that 'nothing students can write in an examination can demonstrate the synthesis of skills, knowledge and practical ability that is the hallmark of excellent fieldwork' (ibid., p. 25). As Evans (2016) points out,

> fieldwork needed to be a core part of the new content. The content requires four days of field experience for A level students. While prescription around this issue has its challenges, strong views were expressed to the panel that without this requirement the timetabling and logistical issues around fieldwork meant that field experience ran the risk of being lost from the curriculum.
>
> (Evans, 2016, p. 159)

Lambert and Reiss (2016) make the point that if the educational arguments for coursework can be accepted for A level it is unclear why they do not also apply to GCSE. They sense that this is an argument that is not yet settled. While few, if any, geography educators would deny that fieldwork should be an essential component of qualifications at 16+, the form it takes and the assessment arrangements that apply is a continuing debate. What is clear is that no matter how fieldwork is assessed, the pedagogic choices made by individual teachers regarding the provision of high quality fieldwork experiences, and how this is embedded into their strategic planning for the GCSE or A level course as a whole, are vital.

New approaches to assessment

The 2010 Schools White Paper, *The Importance of Teaching*, set out the government's intentions to restore confidence in GCSEs. The resultant reforms have aimed to increase the 'rigour' of the qualifications, with an increased focus on linear examinations with all assessments taken at the end of the course or study. The abolition of modular assessment structures would avoid repeated ('bite sized') assessment, and require students to demonstrate the full breadth of their abilities in the subject; this would allow standards to be set fairly and consistently. Schools Minister, David Laws, in a speech explained the rationale for the changes:

> During the past few years, too many students in our schools system have spent too long preparing for and taking tests in years 10, 11, 12 and 13. During the past decade, we have been in danger of creating an "exam factory" in our schools, particularly in the last four years of education, rather than creating places of deep learning where teachers and students are given the time and space to develop deep knowledge of subjects, rather than just preparing constantly for public examinations. That is one of the key reasons why the Government have made these changes.
>
> (Laws, 2013)

This sounds educationally appealing, but there is little doubt that the key driver behind the reforms from the government's point of view was to halt the perceived erosion of standards – and restore 'rigour' in the public examination system. Other significant changes at GCSE include the following:

- the abandonment of 'higher' and 'foundation' tiers of entry; GCSE geography is now a common examination paper for all students;
- an increase in the number and length of examination papers;
- the introduction of four Assessment Objectives (AOs); the 'weighting' for AO3 'Application' – probably the toughest of the four AOs – is set at 35 per cent;
- standardising the use of 'rigorous' command words; examination questions will use words such as 'analyse', 'evaluate', 'assess', or 'discuss';
- increasing the expectation for extended writing in examinations;
- the inclusion of maths and statistics worth 10 per cent of final grade;
- a new grading scale that uses the numbers 1–9 to identify levels of performance, with 9 being the top level; the standard for a 'good pass' (grade 5) is also being raised.

Changes to A Level reflect the above list. Thus, to preserve 'linearity' AS and A levels have been decoupled, so that AS levels are taken as qualifications in their own right. Any student wishing to take an A level course after doing the AS level would be reassessed on the AS level material. However, as we have seen, A level has seen the introduction of an independent investigation worth 20 per cent of the final grade; the linear examination is reduced to 80 per cent of the final grade

Although very challenging for school geography departments, the fact that the reform of examinations has been undertaken concurrently with national curriculum reform, is a significant development that has the potential to enhance the curriculum design process in schools. Table 2.1 illustrates a clear progression pathway from 11 to 19. The progression strands along the top are taken from the

Table 2.1 A progression pathway in secondary school geography from 11 to 19

Progression Strands	Know geographical material	Think like a geographer applying geography	Study like a geographer
NC aspect of pupil achievement	Contextual world knowledge of locations, places and geographical features.	Understanding of the conditions, processes and interactions that explain geographical features, distribution patterns, and changes over time and space.	Competence in geographical enquiry, and the application of skills in observing, collecting, analysing, evaluating and communicating geographical information.
GCSE Assessment Objectives	AO1 Demonstrate knowledge of locations, places, processes, environments and different scales. (15%)	AO2 Demonstrate geographical understanding of concepts and how they are used in relation to places, environments and processes, and the inter-relationships between places, environments and processes. (25%) AO3 Apply knowledge and understanding to interpret, analyse and evaluate geographical information and issues and to make judgements. (35%: 10% applied to fieldwork contexts)	AO4 Select, adapt and use a variety of skills and techniques to investigate questions and issues and communicate findings. (25%: 5% used to respond to fieldwork data and contexts)
GCE A Level Assessment Objectives	AO1 Demonstrate knowledge and understanding of places, environments, concepts, processes, interactions and change, at a variety of scales. (30–40%)	AO2 Apply knowledge and understanding in different contexts to interpret, analyse and evaluate geographical information and issues. (30–40%)	AO3 Use a variety of relevant quantitative, qualitative and fieldwork skills to: investigate geographical questions and issues interpret, analyse and evaluate data and evidence construct arguments and draw conclusions. (20–30%)

GCSE aims (see Figure 2.1 above). These are aligned to the Assessment Objectives (AOs) for GCSE and A level – and to National Curriculum (NC) 'aspects of achievement' devised by the Geographical Association (2014). Table 2.1 aims to demonstrate the interlinkage and potential for school geography department to plan for progression in geography from 11 to 19 years.

Teacher reaction and support needs

As we have seen, the reforms to geography examinations (and the National Curriculum – see Hopkin and Martin in this volume) are many and represent a significant attempt by policy makers to increase 'rigour' and demand. This presents a major challenge for both teachers and their students. Whilst there are advantages in this in terms of providing a real opportunity for teachers to stand back and consider the big picture of geography 11–19, the reality is that teachers are grappling with massive change on top of the normal, day-to-day running of their classrooms, geography departments and wider school life.

To begin with, one of the crucial initial decisions teachers need to make is to select appropriate GCSE and A level specifications. Digby (2015) provided an excellent overview of GCSEs and offered key questions to consider when deciding which was appropriate. For example:

- Do you prefer a thematic approach or an issues-based approach?
- Do you have particular favourite physical or human topics?
- For fieldwork, do you prefer:
  - a specified content approach (Edexcel);
  - a skills and concepts approach (WJEC Eduqas);
  - to choose whichever fieldwork topics you like from within the specification content (AQA and OCR)?

During this period of decision making, between February and March 2016, teachers were surveyed to ascertain their approaches to new GCSEs.[1] In all 42 teachers provided responses (at professional development events and meetings across the country). Figure 2.3 a-d charts the results of several questions.

It is interesting that almost 50 per cent of schools in the survey opted for AQA with a distinct possibility that many decided to stay with the same Awarding Body (see Figure 2.3a and b). This indicates an understandable inertia, but it also implies that many did not spend much time comparing the different specifications and considered the sorts of questions outlined by Digby. Although fieldwork assessed by examination and the inclusion of mathematics and statistics appeared to be the initial concerns of most teachers surveyed, some of the new content also appeared to be a significant issue (Figure 2.3c).

It would seem, from the responses in Figure 2.3d that many of the teachers eagerly await the publication of new GCSE textbooks, to resource and support their training needs for the new content: clearly the responsibility that falls to

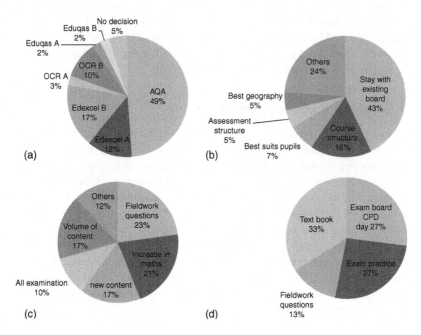

Figure 2.3a–d Results of a 2016 survey of teachers' views on the new specifications for GCSE Geography.

authors and publishers is enormous. This understandable (and in the Schools Minister Nick Gibb's view, desirable) reliance on textbooks assumes that the textbooks themselves are of high quality – raising a very important set of questions about the characteristics of good textbooks. Many teachers also see the Awarding Bodies as an important provider of continuing professional development (CPD). Awarding Bodies have been quick to provide such training, both in house and in partnership with subject associations. However, feedback from teachers showed the limits of such CPD, which clearly focuses heavily on 'delivering' the new specification and less on wider questions of quality, advancing the 'vision' of 11–19 progression as outlined in this chapter and deepening subject knowledge.

Geography teachers contributing to the Schoolszone (2014) survey on examinations reform provide evidence that seems to mirror the findings of my initial survey. For example, according to Schoolzone teachers regard input from 'exam boards' as essential: they are reassured by information direct from the source – the 'rules of the game', as it were. There is also recognition that becoming an examiner for the relevant specification provides invaluable experience and understanding (although this clearly adds to workloads).

According to Schoolzone the abolition of 'controlled assessment' might be quite popular, some teachers remarking that this might provide more teaching time (preparing for the examination). There was however some scepticism as to whether headteachers will facilitate the time to undertake two contrasting fieldwork enquiries: this is clearly an issue that need to be closely monitored.

There is absolutely no doubt that teachers will require a great deal of support in order to bring into fruition the intentions of examinations reform, this will be provided in the short term by the Awarding Bodies. In addition, both the RGS and GA have developed online guidance and support for the new content areas for A levels, together with various face-to-face opportunities, locally, regionally and nationally such as the GA's annual conference in April.

As the qualifications develop, and when several cohorts of students have worked through the examinations, many of the *initial* training needs will disappear. However, these will be replaced by new issues and concerns, as teachers come to terms with the full implications of the new qualifications, which have been designed stretch and challenge all pupils to develop them as geographers.

Conclusion

In the 2013 version of this chapter, written in the years immediately following the 2010 White Paper we observed that the

> early signs of new policy seem very encouraging for the future of geography 14–19; the question still to be debated, however, is what kind of geography this will be and how well will it be taught across a wider spectrum of the age cohort.
>
> (Gardner, 2013, p. 53)

These questions remain, although it is certainly worth recording that since geography and history were given equal status within the English Baccalaureate (EBacc) from 2014, the number of geography GCSE students has grown strongly (after years of decline). A level candidature is also growing, following the Russell Group of universities identification of geography as one of the favoured 'facilitating' subjects.

Thus, the post-14 scene is currently a good news story, not least the opportunities the reforms have created for coherent planning for genuine progression and continuity 11–19. Real challenges remain and some of these are to do with geography becoming increasingly identified as a shortage subject in so far as teacher supply is concerned. The kind of advances alluded to in this chapter are only possible with properly prepared, specialist teachers.

Key readings

1   Stobart, G. (2008) *Testing Times: The Uses and Abuses of Assessment*, London: Routledge. This book explores controversial questions about current uses of assessment and provides a framework for understanding them. It examines how assessment and qualifications, driven by accountability, have become central to schools, leading to teaching to the test strategies.

2   The A Level Content Advisory Board (ALCAB) (2014) *Report of the ALCAB Panel on Geography*, Available at: https://alcab.org.uk/reports/ [Accessed 13 August 2016]. This report of the findings and recommendations of the geography panel provides an excellent overview of the reform process at A level, and the thinking behind new A level specifications.

Note

1   This small-scale research was conducted by the author and based upon a short questionnaire.

Questions included:

2.3a   Which specification are you adopting?
2.3b   What factors contributed to your choice?
2.3c   Which aspects of the new GCSEs will be most challenging for teachers?
2.3d   What are your resource and training needs for the new GCSEs?

References

Department for Education (DfE) (2010) *The Importance of Teaching: The Schools White Paper 2010, London*: The Stationery Office, Available at: www.gov.uk/government/uploads/system/uploads/attachment_data/file/175429/CM-7980.pdf [Accessed 5 June 2015].

Department for Education (DfE) (2014a) Education Secretary Michael Gove's Statement About The Publication of Reformed GCSE and A Level Content, Available at: www.gov.uk/government/speeches/gcse-and-a-level-reform [Accessed 4 August 2016].

Department for Education (DfE) (2014b) *GCSE Subject Content for Geography*, Available at: www.gov.uk/government/ publications/gcse-geography [Accessed 24 August 2016].

Department for Education (DfE) (2014c) *GCE AS and A Level Subject Content for Geography*, Available at: www.gov.uk/government/publications/gce-as-and-a-level-geography [Accessed 24 August 2016].

Digby, B. (2015) 'Choosing a new GCSE specification', *Teaching Geography*, 40 (3), 104–8.

Evans, M. (2016) 'Reflections on the changes to A Levels', *Geography*, 101 (3), 156–63.

Gardner, D. (2013) 'What is geography's place in post-14 education?' in D. Lambert and M. Jones (eds.), *Debates in Geography Education*, London: Routledge.

Geographical Association (2013) Reform of GCSE geography, letter to Michael Gove 2 July, 2013, Available at: http://www.geography.org.uk/news/gcsereform/thegcsereformprocess/ [Accessed 4 August 2016].

Geographical Association (2014) An assessment and progression framework for geography, Available at: http://www.geography.org.uk/news/2014nationalcurriculum/assessment/ [Accessed 9 August 2016].

Gove, M. (2014) GCSE and A level reform, written statement to parliament, Available at: https://www.gov.uk/government/speeches/gcse-and-a-level-reform [Accessed 4 August 2016].

Lambert, D. and Reiss, M (2016) 'The place of fieldwork in geography qualifications', *Geography*, 101 (1), 28–34.

Laws, D. (2013) AS-levels and A-levels, speech on 16 April 2013 in Westminster Halls, Available at: http://www.publications.parliament.uk/pa/cm201213/cmhansrd/cm130416/halltext/130416h0002.htm [Accessed 12 August 2016].

Qualifications and Curriculum Authority (QCA) (2007) *GCSE Subject Criteria for Geography*, London: QCA.

Rawling, E. (2015) 'Spotlight on: curriculum change and examination reform for geography 14–19', *Geography*, 100 (3), 164–8.

Rawling, E. (2016) 'The geography curriculum 5–19: what does it all mean?', *Teaching Geography*, 41 (1), 6–9.

Royal Geographical Society (with IBG) (2014) Royal Geographical Society (with IBG) welcomes A Level reforms Media release (2014), Available at: http://www.rgs.org/PressRoom/Media+releases.htm [Accessed 9 August 2016].

Schoolzone (2014) Teachers' response to curriculum reforms: secondary, Available at: http://www.schoolzone.co.uk/schools/NCres/GCSE/Curriculum_reform_report_Secondary.pdf [Accessed 9 August 2016].

Part II

'Classroom' debates

Chapter 3

Place in geography

Change and challenge

Eleanor Rawling

> Place is one of the two or three most important terms for my subject –
> geography. If pushed, I would argue that it is the most important of them all.
> (Cresswell, 2015, p. 1)

Introduction

Geography developed formally as a discipline in the nineteenth century when the greatest stimuli to its formation and character were travel and exploration. The focus was on accurate observation, description and eventually on the recognition of regions with distinctive characteristics. It was regional geographers such as Herbertson, Fleure and Vidal de la Blache, and the American cultural geographer, Sauer, whose work dominated in geographical work in the nineteenth and early twentieth centuries. School geography, developing from the late nineteenth century, followed this lead. In 1939, Richard Hartshorne (whose book I was given to read in my sixth form geography studies in 1966) could claim that geography was all about what he called 'areal differentiation', or what I understood as regional geography, and about the attempt to recognise 'the total combination of phenomena in each place, different from those in every other place' (p. 462).

It was in the 1960s and 70s that first academic geography and then school geography began to move away from regional geography, dissatisfied with what seemed to have become a largely descriptive and unchallenging approach. Many academic geographers sought to redefine geography as a spatial science and to give greater emphasis to spatial theory and quantitative techniques in research and teaching (e.g. Chorley and Haggett 1967; Abler, Adams and Gould 1971). School geography began to reflect these changes too. For many schoolchildren, geography had become a tedious educational journey, learning facts about the regions of the world. The new ideas, seen in the A level reforms of the 1970s, the new GCSE syllabuses of the late 1980s, and even in primary and lower secondary textbooks of the 1970s and 1980s, enlivened geographical work with investigation of patterns and networks and the use of statistical techniques and games. Significantly, however, this meant more focus on the generalities of space and less interest in particular places, regions and landscapes. By the mid-1970s, when I began my teaching career, most school geography was a strange mixture of traditional regional geography and some newer thematic and spatial emphases. Locations and links[1] were in the ascendant; place as an object of study in its own right was beginning to slip into the background.

The 1980s were a time of ferment in academic geography as critical human geography questioned some impacts of the spatial revolution, particularly the narrow dehumanising effects of seeing geography purely as a spatial science. In school geography, the debate was started through the Schools Council Geography projects, during one of which I started my second career as a curriculum developer. New teacher magazines (e.g. *Contemporary Issues in Geography Education*) and numerous conferences and courses brought academic geographers and their school teacher colleagues together (e.g. DES Short Courses; Charney Manor Conferences 1970s and 80s). Unfortunately, time was running out for school innovation and there was no pause for reflection about the impact and appropriateness of new ideas. The new mood was symbolised in 1984 by the closure of the Schools Council, the body that had encouraged innovation in school subjects. After 1987, geography was engulfed in the 'Great Education Debate', which led inexorably to the National Curriculum and increasing state control of education. From this date can be traced the gradual separation of academic and school geography. Whereas academic geography became more diverse and innovative, school geography was subject to greater restriction giving fewer opportunities for innovation and change. At school level, place is one of the big ideas of geography that has suffered the most from this unhelpful divide.

Place: change and development in academia

In academic geography, one of the most influential movements in relation to place has been the humanistic, in which geographers such as Yi-Fu Tuan (1974) and Relph (1976) drew on the works of philosophers, particularly Heidegger (1962) and Merleau-Ponty (1962) to reassess the fundamental significance of place to human existence. Humanistic geography grew rapidly, exploring themes about image, identity and experience (e.g. Lynch 1960; Buttimer and Seamon 1980). The emphasis moved away from places as objects of study to focus on place as an idea. Humanistic approaches, with their emphasis on immediate experience and on different ways of seeing, have huge educational potential, but they had only a minor impact on mainstream school geography through, for example, Schools Council Projects (Geography 16–19 with its A level unit on Changing Urban Environments; Art and the Built Environment with its interest in urban landscapes and sensory walks) and ideas promoted by the Bulletin of Environmental Education. All these innovations were side-lined when the National Curriculum was established.

From the mid-1970s, a range of critical analytical approaches flourished in academic geography including, for example, welfare, radical, Marxist, feminist and post-structuralist. Through the influence of writers such as David Smith, David

Harvey, Edward Soja, Derek Gregory, Jan Monk, Doreen Massey, these were focused on uncovering the underlying social, economic and political processes affecting human lives and the spaces and places in which they lived. Again, the beginnings of school geography's engagement with some of these ideas was seen in books aimed at teachers (Hall, 1976; Huckle, 1983), themes of conferences (e.g. Charney Manor 1980s and 90s), HMI guidance (DES 1978) and even in the more thematic and process-based GCSE syllabuses of 1986 (see Rawling, 2001, p. 111).

David Harvey (1996, p. 261) claimed that place 'in whatever guise is, like space and time, a social construct ... The only interesting question that can then be asked is: by what social processes is place constructed?' His view reflected the feeling of many human geographers that the study of process was more pressing than the pursuit of an abstract idea of 'sense of place', but this was not an assertion accepted by all geographers. Sack suggested that

> privileging the social in modern geography and especially in the reductionist sense that "everything is socially constructed" does as much disservice to geographical analysis as a whole as has privileging the natural in the days of environmental determinism or concentrating only on the mental or intellectual in some areas of humanistic geography.
>
> (Sack, 1997, p. 2)

Sack thought that both kinds of analysis – critical social and humanistic were important. Similarly, at a joint geography projects conference in 1980, it had been suggested that the role of place and locational geography in a critical and process-based school geography was a burning issue that needed to be addressed (Rawling, 1980) but the changes consequent on centralised curriculum control made that impossible.

Whilst an understanding of place as an idea has stalled in school geography, in academic geography humanistic research has seen a big resurgence in recent years, partly stimulated by renewed interest from philosophers in the idea of place. Malpas (1999, 2006) is a key name here and his research, focusing on the primacy of place as the basis for human existence, has stimulated geographers to explore new approaches such as the non-representational and the performative (see e.g. Anderson and Harrison 2010), to rediscover landscape (e.g. Wylie, 2007) and to refocus on the dynamics of 'being in place' rather than merely describing, representing or critiquing place. As Hayden Lorimer (2005) writes about what he calls this 'more-than-representational' trend in geography, 'the focus falls on how life takes shape and gains expression in shared experiences, everyday routines, fleeting encounters, embodied movements, precognitive triggers ...' (p. 84).

Whilst school curriculum debates have become narrowly focused on traditional subject disciplines, geography in higher education has been opening up its borders and working with other disciplines interested in 'place' such as anthropology, archaeology, performance studies, literature, art and creative writing (e.g. Dewsbury 2000; Lorimer 2005). It is significant that a new term 'geohumanities' has been created to refer to the rapidly growing zone of interaction between geography and the humanities. The introduction to a recent publication, *GeoHumanities*, claims that 'the traditions of these various disciplines are being actively breached by a profusion of intellectually and artistically challenging scholarship and practice' (Robinson et al., 2011, p. 3). Little of this 'buzz' has yet been felt in school geography, though the opportunities do exist.

One of the most recent new directions in place study is concerned with 'assemblage', deriving from the work of French philosophers Gilles Deleuze and Felix Guattari (1987). Assemblage arises predominantly from post-structuralist analysis and is concerned with the idea of gathering and combining things together to create a whole 'whose properties emerge from the interaction between the parts' (DeLanda, 2006, p. 5). Geographers are still exploring these ideas (e.g. Anderson and MacFarlane, 2011). However, Cresswell points out that it is possible to see the early claims of regional geography to understand the totality and distinctiveness of phenomena in a place as 'early statements of a view of the world that is now referred to as assemblage theory' (2015, p. 52). According to DeLanda (2006) assemblage theory concerns itself both with the expressive (e.g. meaning, emotion) and the material (e.g. landscape features), so current thinking harks back to both humanistic and regional geography as well as bringing new insights and provocations.

Place: stagnation and centralisation in the English school curriculum

Cresswell suggests a threefold summary of approaches to the study of place (see Table 3.1). In *descriptive* regional geography, the aim is to identify and describe particular places and to draw out the salient characteristics of each distinct place. *Social constructionist* approaches, represented by a range of different critical geographies such as radical, post structural, feminist, post-colonial, are interested in particular places predominantly as instances of underlying social, economic or political processes, while *phenomenological* approaches are focused on recognising place as an essential part of being human. In summary, regional geographers are interested in *places*; social constructionists are interested in *processes*; and phenomenologists are interested in *place* as an idea and as a way of *being-in-the-world*. Ideally school geography should introduce young people to all of these different approaches, but the reality seen in national guidelines has been quite different.

In the first English National Curriculum[2] for Geography (1991), there was strong representation of locational knowledge, regional descriptive approaches to place (study of places) and an equally strong emphasis on facts in thematic human and physical geography. The formulation was lacking in opportunities for more critical or humanistic geography. Throughout successive reviews (1995, 1999, 2007) of the National Curriculum, there were attempts to reduce the prescriptive detail of the requirements and to promote ideas and processes, but no real

Table 3.1 Place in National Guidelines 2013–16 (based on Cresswell's approaches 2015)

Approaches to Studying Place (Cresswell)	How Place Is Understood	Representation in National Curriculum 2013	Representation in GCSE and AS/A Level 2014–16
Descriptive Geographers aim to identify and describe each particular and unique place and to draw out the salient characteristics. e.g. regional geographers, common sense idea of geography	Places are discrete areas of land with their own characteristics and ways of life. (understanding of **places**)	2013 NC provides strong representation of descriptive regional approaches. Emphasis on locational and place knowledge.	GCSE – importance of locational and contextual knowledge. Key emphasis on 'Geography of UK' incl. descriptive, regional and sense of place/identity. AS/A level – locational/ contextual knowledge expected and local place in 'Changing Place' theme.
Social Constructionist Geographers are interested in particular places as instances of more general underlying social processes. e.g. radical, postcolonial, feminist geographers	Places are reflections of the processes and power relations that formed them. (understanding of **process**)	Poorly represented except at KS3 where this is opportunity to examine processes in physical and human geography 'through use of place-based exemplars' and to 'examine links between places'	GCSE 'Geography of UK' gives key opportunities for process and relationships underlying UK economy, society, landscapes. AS/A strong representation in core theme of 'Changing Place' esp. via relationships and connections. Also in core theme 'Global Systems'
Phenomenological Geographers are interested in how place is an essential part of being human and how this is revealed.e.g. humanistic and phenomenological geographers	Place is a fundamental way of 'being in the world' (idea of **'place'** and **'being in the world'**)	Poorly represented, though potential to pick up 'curiosity and fascination' (KS1) first-hand experience (KS1 and interpreting variety of data sources (KS3)	Not signposted in GCSE but opportunities in 'Geography of UK' and in 'Cities and Urban Society'. AS/A – strongly emphasised in core theme 'Changing Place' esp. in 'meaning and representation'

clarity about place study (Rawling, 2001). In the 1995 and 1999 revisions, places appeared as one of three key emphases for study but still outlined undemandingly, implying that challenging issues about people, environment and society were the preserve of thematic studies. It was in 2007 that the term 'place' appeared as a key concept in the national requirements, ostensibly with the possibility of applying descriptive, critical social constructionist and more phenomenological approaches (the latter represented by the term 'geographical imagination'), but since there was little explanatory guidance for teachers, it was unclear whether the opportunities would be taken up (Rawling, 2011, pp. 69–70). The 2010 elections heralded a change of direction yet again (see Rawling, 2015a) with the Coalition Government focusing on what was described as an increase in rigour and traditional subject knowledge, so that the current 2014 version of the National Curriculum for KS1, 2 and 3 (5–14-year-olds) seems to have returned to a traditional listing of locational knowledge, places and physical and human geography themes (DfE, 2013a; 2013b).

For GCSE and A level, the changes of the 1980s gave early promise of some new developments being recognised particularly in relation to process studies. The examining bodies embraced theories, quantitative techniques and emphases on themes in geography. The linking of GCSE to National Curriculum requirements, the onset of increasing examination regulation and the establishment of SEAC (the Schools Examination and Assessment Council, 1988) all militated against further innovative curriculum thinking. By the 1990s, the 14–19 system moved from being curriculum-led to being assessment-led. New developments at this time emphasised accountability (e.g. reduction in coursework assessment, narrowing of types of examination questions) and new structural elements (modularisation, introduction of AS levels). Geographers in universities were busy with their own managerial and structural changes so there was less time for subject dialogue. In 2001, I suggested that 'after 10–15 years of regulation without curriculum development, the geography specifications at all levels have become relatively static and technical documents' (p. 113). By the time of the 2010 elections, the lack of time and opportunity for subject content appraisal was particularly acute with regard to physical geography and place. Although GCSE and AS/A level syllabuses showed a reasonable variety of thematic emphases, attention to global challenges and a strong focus on environmental issues, place was seen primarily as an adjunct to thematic work. In an article in *Geography* in 2008, Cresswell remarked that 'place' as an idea had barely penetrated even A level geography.

The processes of curriculum and assessment change for GCSE and A level in the 2010–14 period were highly centralised; what is more for GCSE, the lack of attention that had been given to place over the past twenty years meant that even talking about it proved difficult. As I explained

> misunderstandings between the Department for Education (DfE) and Ofqual (the regulatory body for school examinations) led to difficulties over

whether the term place referred only to locational knowledge (an interpretation used by default in most pre-2010 specifications) or whether it summed up a vibrant area of modern geography concerned with place processes, inter-relationships and meanings. This particular debate had to be re-run several times to allow place to appear as a heading and a big geographical idea in addition to the heading locational knowledge.

(Rawling, 2015b, p. 167)

For A/AS level, the establishment of the A Level Content Advisory Board (ALCAB), with its strong representation from academic geographers, ensured the possibility of some genuine dialogue about subject. Significantly, this resulted in challenging new ideas about place meaning and representation appearing as a core requirement in the new Criteria for AS/A level specifications.

The last two columns of Table 3.1 summarise the way in which the study of place is represented in the current national requirements from KS1 to A level (KS5). It is important to note that 'locational knowledge' as a crucial foundation for other geographical learning can be traced as a thread in national requirements from the prescribed details at KS1, 2 and 3 through a locational knowledge statement at GCSE to an expectation at AS/A level that study will extend existing locational and contextual knowledge.

Descriptive place study is the main focus at KS1–3 (though with the beginnings of explanatory process study) through exploring localities and understanding similarities and differences between specified regions in Europe, US, North and South America and Asia.

At GCSE level, the guidelines (DfE, 2014a) require a focus on the 'geography of the UK' as a means of developing a more mature understanding of processes and relationships within and between places (potentially *descriptive, social constructionist* and some aspects of *phenomenological* approaches).

At AS/A level, the requirements (DfE, 2014b) for place study are more detailed still, focusing explicitly on the idea of place, and on relationships, connections, meanings and representations of place (predominantly *social constructionist* and *phenomenological)* that shape how we see the world. To study this fully, students are required to revisit the idea of the local place (first encountered in KS1) in a way that involves 'moving out from the local place to encompass regional, national, international and global scales in order to understand the dynamics of place' (DfE, 2014b).

Place: challenge and opportunity

The current national geography requirements do allow the opportunity for place to be represented more diversely but the extent to which this potential will be realised depends on implementation.

For the KS 1–3 National Curriculum, teachers have the opportunity to plan a curriculum that enlivens the rather terse specifications and introduces places as well as themes, giving attention to people's feelings and lived experiences of places (being-in-place), perhaps through stories, performances and drawing on children's own geographical experiences. These are all aspects of good practice used by confident teachers and encouraged by resource writers (e.g. Catling and Willy, 2009) and support agencies such as the Geographical Association. However, the realities of the school context, with shortage of subject specialist teachers and difficulties of timetabling against core subjects, mean that the challenge at KS1–3 may be in keeping a sound geographical presence at all. Although the increasing numbers of academies[3] are, ironically, freed from central curriculum control, anecdotal evidence would suggest that much depends on the individual school circumstances of geography expertise and leadership, and that academies are no more likely than their maintained school counterparts to provide curriculum innovation.

At GCSE and A level, much will depend on interpretation of the national criteria. In this respect, a consideration of the newly approved GCSE specifications reveals a reluctance on behalf of awarding bodies to address the place opportunities. Despite the requirements making clear that 'students must study the UK as a country and draw across physical and human characteristics to summarise significant geographical features and issues' (DfE, 2014a), not one specification of the six that have now been approved by Ofqual (May 2016) provides the opportunity for such a place-focused approach. Some do have a section of the specification that focuses on UK themes (e.g. 'Living in the UK Today', OCR A) or on UK issues (e.g. UK Geographical Issues as a content section and examination paper, Edexcel B), but these are, by their own admission, thematic and issues based rather than place-based. In a presentation given at the Geographical Association Conference in 2016, two representatives of AQA awarding body, explained that the key consideration in dealing with the new criteria was 'continuity with previous specifications' and as a result 'the Geography of the UK is integrated into the physical and human geography themes studied' (Durman and Taylor, 2016), and there will be no examination paper on the Geography of the UK. Was there a lack of knowledge about new developments in place? Did those developing the specifications fear a return to an 'old-fashioned regional geography'? This is not a criticism of one awarding body – more a reflection that such organisations are by their nature conservative in a curriculum sense and likely to be motivated by a desire to keep schools 'on board', rather than present them with risky new challenges.

However, what happened to the role of Ofqual in ensuring that the curriculum intentions of the GCSE Criteria are met? It could be argued that the GCSE requirements demand a drawing on all approaches to studying place – descriptive, social constructionist and phenomenological – in order to draw out an understanding of the complex geography of landscapes, regions and localities and of the social, cultural and political relationships that create a place like the UK. Surely, the rubric implies a place-based focus at some point? Yet all the GCSE specifications have reverted to the idea of exemplifying themes or issue in human and physical geography with UK examples, rather than taking the opportunity to refocus on place as a dynamic concept in its own right.

Doreen Massey's advice, as far back as 1994, was that it is not necessary to see the study of place as reactionary: 'Can't we rethink our sense of place?' she asked. In this paper and in later writings (e.g. 2005) she argued that study of place can be progressive, open and outward-looking rather than self-enclosing and inward-looking. She coined the term 'global sense of place' and advocated an approach that studies connections, flows and interactions within and across all kinds of place boundaries. Massey (who can probably be described as a social constructionist in Cresswell's definition) suggested four characteristics of this more dynamic approach to place study:

1   Places are dynamic rather than static and 'can be conceptualized in terms of the social interactions which they tie together'.
2   Places 'do not have to have boundaries in the sense of divisions which frame simple enclosures' – linkage to the outside is part of what constitutes the place.
3   'Places do not have single unique 'identities'; they are full of internal conflicts'.
4   None of the above arguments deny place or the importance of the uniqueness of place. 'The specificity of place is continually reproduced'.

                                                        (Massey, 1994, pp. 155–6)

Massey's own research included her looking at Kilburn, her own locale in northwest London; at London as a capital city and living place for millions of people; and, at Skiddaw, a physical/natural place in the Lake District (Massey, 2005). Despite the range of human, social, economic and even physical processes she studied, each of these (social constructionist) explorations needed to start with and focus on a place, not on a theme. How different might some, at least, of the GCSE specifications look if this kind of approach could be followed in relation to students' own localities, cities, regions and the wider context of the UK as a dynamic outward-looking place, especially in the context of discussions about immigration, refugees, EU membership and the identities of the UK countries?

Preparation of the new AS and A level specifications have been given a direct steer towards current approaches by the detailed core criteria for the *Changing Place; Changing Places* section (DfE 2014b). The rubric makes clear that descriptive, process-based and more humanistic/phenomenological approaches to study will all be required. In the rationale for this, the A Level Content Advisory Board explained that

> the topic ('Changing Places') outlines a conceptual framework which emphasises both the social, economic and demographic character of places and also the cultural meanings and representations attached to places. The key social and demographic content of the previous specifications is therefore preserved

but will be studied in a way which is more in line with the approaches current in higher education geography.

(ALCAB, 2014)

Looking at the four new specifications for A level prepared by the Awarding Bodies (2 accredited and 2 awaiting accreditation, May 2016), each has a focus on place as a core element of the requirements; each attends to social and cultural processes and global contexts of change; and, each provides opportunity to focus on place-making, on lived experiences and identities, and on the varying representations of place. In this respect, all of Cresswell's three approaches may be developed by teachers and students. It is interesting to note, however, that place is still cast as a thematic study. No specification has taken the opportunity to give a more locality-based or regional-based flavour within its requirements. As at GCSE, there seems to be a desire to avoid anything that might smack of old-fashioned regional geography.

And yet, many human geographers have recently been exploring places in a way that features some of the characteristics of earlier regional geographies, but informed by phenomenology and assemblage theory. Cresswell draws attention to a more creative kind of place-writing which he suggests uses 'a number of creative strategies to present the place to the reader as an entanglement of diverse elements and strands using stories of people and things to recreate what Doreen Massey has called the 'thrown-togetherness of place' (2015, p. 57). He refers to Patricia Price's work *Dry Place* (2004) and Laura Ogden's *Swamplife* (2011), account of the Florida Everglades. One can note the similarities with recent popular place and nature writing (e.g. Atkins, *The Moor* 2014; McFarlane, *Landmarks* 2015; Jamie, *Sightlines* 2012) and suggest that at least some mention of these more humanistic perspectives might have a role in a twenty-first-century 'Geography of the UK' (GCSE) or a focus on 'Changing Places; Changing Place' (AS/A level). As Cresswell points out, it is in more recent place writings that we can see

all three levels of place theory in practice simultaneously. They are certainly descriptive accounts of individual places but they are also grappling with the phenomenological significance of place to its inhabitants (human and non-human) and the ways in which power and society are producing and being produced by place.

(Cresswell, 2015, p. 58)

Conclusion

I would argue that place is one of the biggest challenges for school geography. There is a pressing need for dialogue with academic geographers about interpreting and developing the subject in the school curriculum. Experience seems to confirm that central government bodies are not well-placed to undertake this kind of curriculum thinking. Teachers, resource writers and those working in the qualifications and assessment system all need time and CPD opportunities to appreciate the range of opportunities in the national requirements and the possibilities for implementation. In our interconnected world, the idea of place has more not less resonance in the challenge of understanding people's struggles with wider social, economic, and political forces. Place is a word used in public discourse, in newspaper headlines and in poetry, art, and theatre. To study place is not to retreat to an outmoded world of 1950s regional geography; to describe and imagine past, present and future places is not to take an intellectual 'soft option'. Place is one of the most important interdisciplinary concepts of the twenty-first century, and it should be at the heart of school geography.

Key readings

1   Cresswell, T. (2008) 'Place; encountering geography as philosophy', *Geography*, 93 (3), 132–9. Cresswell suggests that at school level we are too focused on the specifics of place seeing it as a simple and uncontroversial term. In fact, he claims that our views of place deeply affect how we see ourselves and understand a range of issues. We should also be encouraging young people to think about place as a fundamental idea in geography (the philosophy of place).

2   Massey, D. (2005) *For Space*, London, Sage: Publications. Massey (pp. 155–9) draws our attention to the need to look at London as a place which is a large and intense constellation of trajectories, not just social, ethnic and cultural trajectories but also those of finance and capital. City life is inescapably political. The character of London and its direct influence on the character and identity of the rest of the UK is a direct result of what Massey calls the 'thrown-togetherness' of place. An understanding of the different ways of looking at place is fundamental to any study of the geography of the UK.

Notes

1   'Locations and links' was the title of a series of school textbooks by M J Walker, 1970s/80s.
2   All references in this paper are to the National Curriculum in England.
3   On current projections, around three-quarters of secondary and a third of primary schools would convert to academy status by 2020. Nicky Morgan April 2016 address to NAHT, Available at: https://www.gov.uk/government/speeches/nicky-morgan-speech-at-the-naht-annual-conference-2016). Plans to make all state schools become academies (2016) were finally abandoned in May 2016.

References

Abler, R., Adams, J. and Gould, P. (1971) *Spatial Organization: The Geographer's View of the World*, New Jersey: Prentice Hall.

ALCAB (The A Level Content Advisory Board) (2014) *Report of the ALCAB Panel on Geography*, London: ALCAB.

Anderson, B. and Harrison, P. (2010) *Taking-Place: Non-Representational Theories and Geography*, Farnham: Ashgate Publishing.

Anderson, B. and MacFarlane, C. (2011) 'Assemblage and geography', *Area*, 43, 124–7.

Atkins, W. (2014) *The Moor; Lives, Landscape, Literature*. London: Faber and Faber.

Buttimer, A. and Seamon, D. (1980) *The Human Experience of Space and Place*, New York: St Martin's Press.

Catling, S. and Willy, T. (2009) *Teaching Primary Geography*, Exeter: Learning Matters Ltd.

Chorley, R. J. and Haggett, P. (eds.) (1967) *Models in Geography*, London: Methuen.

Cresswell, T. (2008) 'Place: encountering geography as philosophy', *Geography*, 93 (3), 132–9.

Cresswell, T. (2015) *Place: An Introduction* 2nd edn, London: Wiley Blackwell.

Department for Education, (DfE) (2013a) *Geography Programmes of Study Key Stages 1 and 2.*

Department for Education, (DfE) (2013b) *Geography Programmes of Study Key Stage 3.*

Department for Education, (DfE) (2014a) *Geography GCSE Subject Content.*

Department for Education, (DfE) (2014b) *Geography GCE AS and A Level Subject Content.*

DeLanda, M. (2006) *A New Philosophy of Society: Assemblage Theory and Social Complexity*, London: Continuum.

Deleuze, G. and Guattari, F. (1987) *A Thousand Plateaus; Capitalism and Schizophrenia*, Minneapolis: University of Minnesota Press.

Department of Education and Science, (DES) (1978) *The Teaching of Ideas in Geography: Some Suggestions for the Middle and Secondary Years of Schooling*, A Discussion Paper by HMI, London: HMSO.

Dewsbury, J. D. (2000) 'Performativity and the event: enacting a philosophy of difference', *Environment and Planning D: Society and Space* 18, 473–96.

Durman, S. and Taylor, B. (2016) *AQA; Meeting the Challenge of GCSE Geography Reform*, Presentation at GA Conference 2016, Available at: http://www.geography.org.uk/cpdevents/annualconference/#1 [Accessed 5 August 2016].

Hall, D. B. (1976) *Geography and the Geography Teacher*, London: George, Allen and Unwin.

Hartshorne, R. (1939) *The Nature of Geography: A Critical Survey of Current Thought in the Light of the Past*, Lancaster PA: The AAG.

Harvey, D. (1996) *Justice, Nature and the Geography of Difference*, Cambridge, MA. Blackwells.

Heidegger, M. (1962) *Being and Time*, Oxford: Blackwell Publishing.

Huckle, J. (ed.) (1983) *Geographical Education: Reflection and Action*, Oxford: Oxford University Press.

Jamie, K. (2012) *Sightlines*, London: Sort of Books.

Lorimer, H. (2005) 'Cultural geography; the busy-ness of being 'more-than-representational' *Progress in Human Geography*, 29 (1), 83–94.

Lynch, K. (1960) *The Image of the City*, Cambridge MA: MIT Press.

McFarlane, R. (2015) *Landmarks*, London: Hamish Hamilton (Penguin/Random House).

Malpas, J. E. (1999) *Place and Experience: A Philosophical Topography*, Cambridge: Cambridge University Press.

Malpas, J. E. (2006) *Heidegger's Topology: Being, Place, World*, Cambridge Mass: MIT Press.

Massey, D. (1994) *Space, Place and Gender,* Cambridge: Polity Press.

Massey, D. (2005) *For Space*, London: Sage Publications.

Merleau-Ponty, M. (1962) *Phenomenology of Perception,* London and Henley: Routledge and Kegan Paul.

Ogden, L. (2011) *Swamplife: People, Gators and Mangroves Entangled in the Everglades*, Minneapolis: University of Minnesota Press.

Price, P. L. (2004) *Dry Place: Landscape of Belonging and Exclusion*, Minneapolis: University of Minnesota Press.

Rawling, E. (ed.) (1980) *Geography into the 1980s*, Sheffield: The Geographical Association.

Rawling, E. (2001) *Changing the Subject: The Impact of Curriculum Policy on School Geography 1980–2000*, Sheffield: The Geographical Association.

Rawling, E. (2011) 'Reading and writing place', in G. Butt (ed.) *Geography Education and the Future,* London: Continuum.

Rawling, E. (2015a) 'The geography curriculum 5–19; what does it all mean?', *Teaching Geography*, Sheffield: The Geographical Association.

Rawling, E. (2015b) 'Spotlight on curriculum change and examination reform for geography 14–19', *Geography*, 100 (3), 164–8.

Relph, E. (1976) *Place and Placelessness*, London: Pion.

Robinson, D., Luria, S., Ketchum, J. and Dear, M. (2011) 'Introducing the GeoHumanities' in M. Dear et al., (eds.) *GeoHumanities; Art, History, Text at the Edge of Place*, London: Routledge.

Sack, R. D. (1997) *Homo Geographicus*, Baltimore: John Hopkins University Press.

Tuan, Y.-F. (1974) *Topophilia: A Study of Environmental Perception, Attitudes and Values*, Englewood Cliffs NJ: Prentice-Hall.

Wylie, J. (2007) *Landscape*, London: Routledge.

Chapter 4

The place of regional geography

Alex Standish

> What are the inter-relationships among phenomena that produce this
> particular set of features?
>
> (Slater, 1982, p. 3)

Introduction

What is the place of regional geography in the modern school subject? This is a
question of how geographical knowledge is structured, rather than a matter of
logic or proposition. In order to answer this question, I examine the evolution of
the discipline, leading to an explanation of its epistemology. Next, the chapter considers some implications for contemporary school geography curricula and pedagogy, including how teachers can construct a curriculum to introduce pupils to the
discipline. However, I begin with the idea of a region, and concepts related to this.

Concepts

A region is an area of the earth's surface displaying a degree of homogeneity
in one or more of its geographical features or characteristics that distinguish it
from surrounding areas. Region is in the same genre as place (the ideographic
tradition), both of which 'focus on particular areas of the earth's surface and
the qualities that makes these areas different and unique from the areas around
them' (Cresswell 2013, p. 58). The term region derives from the Latin *regionem*
meaning 'a district, portion of a country, territory; a direction, line; boundary
line, limit' (Online Etymology Dictionary, 2016). Preceding Roman times,
Plato used the terms *chora* and *topos* in his discussion of the process of becoming
(Cresswell, 2013). *Chora* refers to the place or setting for becoming and *topos* was
the achieved place. Cresswell reports that Aristotle, following Plato, used *chora* to
describe a country and *topos* as a particular region or place within it.

As intellectual constructs, both the concepts of place and region became fundamental disciplinary tools in what Hartshorne (1939) and others thought of
as the classical period of geography (1750–1850). Specially, place refers to a
general location while regions are bounded areas. Regions also exist in common

vernacular, as well as being used for administrative purposes. In many countries around the world people identify with a region and hence they have a lived reality (Clavel, 1998). In the discipline of geography, regions are a tool for analysing and categorising the surface of the earth, a means for simplifying that which is too complex to study as a whole. When we draw a line around an area, we are making an informed judgement about the geographical properties of the phenomena that lie within the region: we are highlighting what we see as a significant degree of homogeneity. Regions are a means of classifying the surface of the earth, the geographical equivalent of history's periods, but not an end in themselves. This is not to dismiss the obvious heterogeneity within the region (generalisations are precisely so), but rather to say that there is something that is common to the area.

The concept of a region also implies that it is a part of something larger – a region of the world or country. Hence, geographers identify world regions (also called realms), but also sub-regions, that are smaller. Scale, then, is another geographical concept related to region. While regions can be as large as continents, they can also be used to distinguish parts of a country or town. Scale matters, for at the scale of landmasses, a mountain range such as the Pyrenees may be a boundary between two regions, while at a more local scale the Pyrenees could be its own region. In general, the smaller the scale of the region, the greater the degree of heterogeneity likely to be found within it.

This brings us to another related concept: transition zone. While we draw lines to demarcate one region from another, change is usually graduated rather than abrupt. For instance, driving from Austria into Italy, one will see combined cultural influence on both sides of the borders. Of course, some borders do result in sharp differences, such as that between North and South Korea.

A region also implies a sense of wholeness, and this helps us to understand why the concept is fundamental to geography. Regions are a product of the interlacing of geographical phenomena, the inter-connectedness of human and environmental factors that together produce unique qualities, leading to the quintessential geographical question posed by Slater (1982) at the beginning of this chapter. Geographers distinguish between different types of region: *thematic* (generic), *functional* and *formal*. Thematic regions (e.g. climatic, agricultural or religious) are delineated by type rather than by location. If we divide the earth surface according to climate type, the same climatic region (e.g. humid temperate) will be found in different parts of the world. While thematic regions clearly display homogeneity with respect to at least one geographical feature, their purpose is not to explore the inter-relationships between phenomena in a given area; and, thus, it can be argued, that they are more useful for systematic geography. Formal regions, on the other hand, are contiguous and aim to synthesise different geographical features into a unique whole, for example, the northeast of England or Sub-Saharan Africa. Functional regions are a product of the functional relationships between people within a given geographical extent rather than geographical form. A metropolitan area like New York City, extending into New Jersey and southern Connecticut, connected through infrastructure is one example. A nation state can also be viewed as a functional geographical territory.

Regional method of enquiry

Cresswell suggests that two questions underpin the geographical tradition: 'what is the connection between the human and physical worlds?' And, 'how can we account for spatial difference?' (Cresswell, 2013, p. 58). The human quest to comprehend differences between areas of the earth's surface can be traced back to Ancient Greece and Rome. For one, Herodotus went beyond the description of routes to demarcate areas on a map according to their geographical ensembles and geometry (Clavel, 1998). In Roman times, the 'science of regions' or chorology was established by early geographers[1]. Strabo identified five climatic regions in the known world of his time, extending from the northern arctic through two temperate zones and an equatorial region.

Geography was much later established as a formal discipline in the classical period (1750–1850), especially through the work of German geographers. In 1650, Varenius made reference to special (regional) geography in contrast to that of systematic geography. However, it was the exhaustive work of Alexander Humboldt and Karl Ritter that established the modern method of regional study. Following the Enlightenment tradition, both took an empirical approach to their studies of Central America (Humboldt) and Central Asia (Ritter). Following in Ritter's footsteps, Alfred Hettner further developed the chorological tradition through his work on Europe and South America. In Germany, the concept of *Landshaft* (a small regional unit) became popular amongst geographers. In a period which emphasised environmental determinism, some geographers were looking for natural regions as a way of accounting for human actions and spatial differences. A similar tradition evolved in France with French *pays* identified in *Tableau de la Geographie de la France* (Vidal de La Blache 1908). In contrast to earlier environmental determinists, de la Blache identified both natural regions but also how different forms of sociability characterised different regions. His ideas influenced the cultural geography of Carl Sauer in twentieth-century America.

With the benefit of hindsight, we can be critical of some of the European regional geographies. In particular, the endeavour to discover natural regions as definitive objects on the surface of the earth was misplaced. In *The Nature of Geography* Richard Hartshorne (1939) reminded us that regions are intellectual constructs that the student applies somewhat arbitrarily, or at least by making decisions about the relative importance of different geographical features. He noted that geography does not have its own specific objects of study, beyond the surface of the earth. While most sciences aim to comprehend the nature of objects and, hence, develop concepts, principles and laws about their character and behaviour, geographers study objects in relation to each other: 'Geography does not claim any particular phenomena as distinctly its own, but rather studies all phenomena that are significantly integrated in the areas which it studies'

(Hartshorne, 1939, p. 372). This means that geography, like history, is an integrative discipline. Geographers are not interested in one particular phenomenon, but how objects are related in space.

Here, we can begin to see how the regional method captures the very essence of geography: that the character of different places is necessarily a product of the inter-relationships between phenomena. Therefore, it is the task of regional geography to comprehend the nature of the inter-relationships at a given place or within a region, a task that requires *synthesising knowledge*:

> Cultural, political and economic processes together shape and structure the specific regions under investigation and it is only through the study of their interrelationships that the regional specificity can be retraced. Such a study involves a process of synthesis, a process that takes the results of analysis, the detailed studies of particular aspects of society and draws out the web of relationships that generates and binds them to produce spatial differentiation.
>
> (Gilbert, 1988, p. 218)

Here, Gilbert explains how the regional method moves from analysis of different geographical features, and how they are related to other features, to the more demanding task of synthesising knowledge. Because places and regions are a product of a complex web of interactions, this presents the problem of selecting the geographical criteria and also the starting point. Hartshorne suggests that no phenomena should be discounted if one is aiming to depict something whole. However, not all phenomena are equally significant in shaping the character of a region. Mountainous regions, such as the Himalayas or the Andes are distinctive by the nature of the terrain, which in turn influences climate and land use, including vegetation. Other regions can be characterised by their distinctive geography including islands (Caribbean), hot deserts (Sahara), cold deserts (Antarctica), abundance of hydrocarbons (Gulf States), rainforest (Amazon), the cultural patterns of Arabic speaking states or the distinctive combinations of religion in South Asia. This is not for one minute to suggest that these are the only significant phenomena, but rather that their influence is geographically *significant*.

The student of geography must make a determination of which geographical factors and features they see as important for their particular geographical description. The selection of these is subjective, but purposeful: exploring the relationships that account for spatial differences. The student must account for their selection and how their regions are constructed. An important curricular principle arises from this approach: that the selection of geography to include in a regional study should aim for contextual coherence. Clavel notes how the regional method depends upon substantial knowledge of the region in question. Ideally, geographers will use a combination of primary and secondary data in classifying regions. This data is best presented on a reference map or Geographical Information System; such that spatial configurations can be observed.

When characterising regions geographers must be attuned to the history of the area in question. The regional method does not demand a history of the region, but rather the student or teacher should select those aspects from the past that are significant for its contemporary geography. For example, an account of the geography of the Middle East would be incomplete without acknowledging the significance of Jerusalem to the three Abrahamic religions, as well as the modern-day founding of the state of Israel. It is this history, as well as the division of Islam, that helps to account for current-day conflict in the region. Here, we need to be careful to distinguish between regional geography's use of the past to explain the present and historical geography. The latter explores geography at different points in time. Any regional map is a product of geographical interaction at a given point in time and therefore changes from one period to the next. For instance, Eastern Europe during the Cold War period was very much under the sphere of influence of the Soviet Union. In historical geography, it would be possible to construct any number of regional geographies varying by date.

With the above example, we can see that the dynamism of regions is not just a product of the interactions taking place within a region. Regions are connected to, and influenced by, what is happening outside of them. Therefore, the regional method demands the study of the relationships between regions. This can be in terms of trade, migration, politics, ideas and culture, or climate (global warming) and volcanic activity.

Regional geography was heavily criticised in the middle part of the twentieth century for being overly descriptive and lacking scientific credibility. After a period in the shadows, a 'new regional geography' was enacted in the late 1980s (Gilbert, 1988; Sayer, 1989; Clavel, 1998). This modern take on regional geography emphasised how regions were constructed through social processes.

Geography's epistemology

In this section I will show how regional geography is intimately related to systematic (or thematic) geography and that the failure to maintain the relationship between the two ultimately undermines the scientific credibility of both. To do this we need to understand a little more about these two traditions in geography.

While above I have noted that regional geography, being concerned with the particular or unique, is part of an ideographic tradition. In contrast, systematic geography is a nomothetic pursuit in that it aims to develop generalisations (concepts), models, theories and principles about how things are spatially related. Geographers do this by examining one geographical phenomenon (e.g. glaciation or population) at a time – how it varies in space and how it is influenced by other phenomena. Systematic geographical knowledge evolved as a series of sub-disciplines (geomorphology, climatology, urban geography, political geography) each of which is related to its own branch of science (geology, meteorology, planning/urban studies, political science – see Figure 4.1).

Geographers draw from these individual sciences using the concepts each has constructed for the study of its object (lithosphere, atmosphere, settlements, political ideas/organisations/institutions). However, the geographer utilises

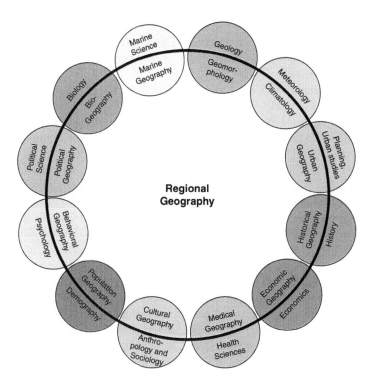

Figure 4.1 The relationship between regional and systematic geography (de Blij, H. and Muller, P. [2012] *Geography: Realms, Regions and Concepts*, New York: Wiley).

these concepts for a different purpose: to comprehend spatial relationships and patterns. Because geographers are interested in how objects are associated with other objects, they may modify generic concepts or invent new ones (e.g. sphere of influence). This is important because no concept can capture all the characteristics of an object; each discipline will view an object from its own perspective and devise concepts related to its particular intellectual quest. As Hartshorne notes, the concept is simply 'a scientific tool' whose purpose is 'to provide a single statement of a collection of common characteristics shared by objects which otherwise differ' (Hartshorne, 1939, p. 387).

The value of nomothetic science is that by abstracting from the real world we can begin to see patterns of behaviour and relationship that are not apparent at a more concrete level. With the nomothetic tradition scientists are seeking explanations of the behaviour and patterns of phenomena. Its knowledge structure is therefore hierarchical – aiming for greater precision, certainty and truth (Bernstein, 1999). Some examples of geographical theories and models include the Bradshaw Model, the Demographic Transition Model, the Gravity Model, the Burgess Land Value Model, the Core/Periphery Model, Von Thunen's Land Use Model, Weber's Industrial Location Theory, Dependency Theory, the Heartland Theory, Christaller's Central Place Theory and Butler's Model of Tourist Resort Development.

The risk in constructing *propositional (conceptual) knowledge* is that it becomes too removed from the real world and therefore is unable to explain phenomena and their behaviour. All sciences experience this tension between the need for universal laws and the facts and circumstances of particular cases. For example, a virus can be studied in a laboratory to learn about its general characteristics and behaviour, but in the blood stream of individual patients these may vary in unanticipated ways due to the individual's particular biology. For this reason, disciplines need *contextual (empirical) knowledge* – the facts, data and observations of human and physical features of the earth's surface, in geography's case. By its very nature contextual knowledge cannot be abstract and therefore does not give rise of generic concepts or theories. In contrast to propositional knowledge, it is horizontal in structure; so that studying new places and regions adds to existing knowledge – but sideways rather than hierarchically.

The two branches of geography, systematic and regional, can be illustrated in the following way (Figure 4.2). Systematic geography focuses on one geographical phenomenon or 'layer' of the earth's surface at a time and explores how it varies with respect to other geographical layers. Regional geography examines the totality of geographical phenomena or layers, and how they are related, at a given locale or region.

Let us consider now, in a little more depth, how the two branches of geography work together. We have already noted that propositional knowledge develops by abstracting from context. However, if its generalisations, models and principles are of value they must necessarily explain aspects of the real world. This can be done by testing or applying them in different contexts. This does

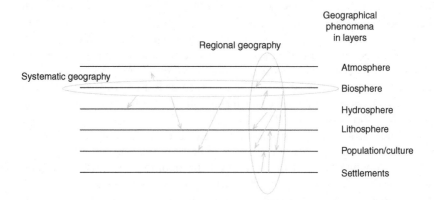

Figure 4.2 Conceptualising systematic and regional geography. (A. Standish)

not mean that models will perfectly predict patterns and behaviour on the surface of the earth. However, in order to say something meaningful about spatial arrangements we should be able to find evidence of their principles at work. In the course of applying generic models and principles, the geographer may well discover imperfections and errors, forcing them to go away and refine their ideas and models. The process of hypothesising, testing, analysis and verification of knowledge is known as *procedural knowledge*, being the third element of disciplinary knowledge.

So, while the reliability and value of generic concepts and theories may be considered dependent upon their application in different contexts, 'regional geography in itself is sterile; without the continuous fertilisation of generic concepts and principles from systematic geography it could not advance to higher degrees of accuracy and certainty in interpretation of its findings' (Hartshorne, 1939, p. 468). Without the 'continuous fertilisation' of conceptual knowledge from systematic geography, regional geography can approximate a simple cataloguing of geographical data about regions, as was too often the case in the first half of the twentieth century. Where this is the case, there is insufficient attempt to analyse relationships and to synthesis knowledge.

Regional geography in curriculum and pedagogy

The dualistic nature of geography is expressed aptly by Phil Gersmehl (2008) in his book *Teaching Geography*. Gersmehl likens systematic geography (he calls it topical geography) and regional geography to two blades of a scissors. Each is its own analytical tool with the potential to dissect the earth's surface, but the blades are much sharper when kept together. As we turn our attention to schools and classrooms, we must consider how best to organise the geography curriculum and to teach the subject to pupils. Gersmehl proposes, and I think he has a point, that it does not matter how the curriculum is organised: it can take either a systematic or regional approach. What matters more is that pupils are introduced to both approaches such that they can begin to appreciate and comprehend how the two complement one another.

'Keeping the blades together' can be achieved through a curriculum that takes a regional approach, but embeds systematic geography within it (ibid.). Or, a curriculum that is organised through systematic geography but includes extensive case studies and regional methods can be equally successful. My own view, in terms of school geography, is that a combination of approaches should be taken in each key stage of the curriculum. Having said that one can argue that synthesising across multiple knowledge-layers, as demanded by regional geography, is one of the more taxing aspects of thinking geographically – certainly an aspiration we aim for towards the later stages of a child's education. But again, that doesn't mean that pupils should not be introduced to this way of thinking earlier in their geography education. Learning the conceptual content for topics such as rivers, glaciation, population and development is arguably more straightforward, as concepts are organised hierarchically and the inferential connections (Brandom, 2000) more tenable.

A further case for embedding more systematic geography earlier on in the child's development is that in order to synthesis different areas of geographical knowledge, the pupil must have the knowledge in the first place. This suggests there is a strong case for ensuring a broad coverage of systematic knowledge in the early secondary curriculum. On the other hand, continually returning to regional geography is important from a pedagogical perspective because, 'The interplay between topical and regional perspectives is what stimulates thought' (Gersmehl, 2008, p. 23). One of the signature features of geography is that context matters a great deal. Thus, in constructing a school curriculum there are important decisions to be made about which areas of systematic and regional geography to include and when in the course of a child's education they should be introduced to most of geography's sub-disciplines (Figure 4.1), not to mention how to cover a reasonable selection of the world's regions.

Teaching children to use both blades of the scissors will only happen where the teacher plans for this. While schools will often plan units of work for both regional and systematic geography there is plenty of scope for teachers to move between the two within units and even within lessons. For instance, a unit of work on South America may include a significant focus on tectonic movement and earthquakes, or a topic on trade and development may focus on the geography of East Asia. Teachers themselves can be creative in the way they move between the two approaches. They could divide their classroom so that one wall takes a regional approach and another wall systematic geography.

Teachers need to be mindful that pupils need *to be taught* to explore relationships between geography's layers, although later this will become more habitual. The first step is to look for associations between different features (geology and soil, trade and development, migration and political system) and begin to recognise relationships. American teacher Mark C. Jones (2014) reports on a teaching method he uses to accomplish this with high school juniors and seniors. When looking at a region he takes the pupils through each of five themes: physical and environmental geography, population geography, economic and social geography, cultural geography and political geography. Towards the end of the unit he gives his pupils an 'integration exercise' in which they have to identify connections between the topics. Figure 4.3 illustrates the final outcome from an integration exercise for the region of Southwest Asia/North Africa.

Another example which perhaps takes us beyond simple regional classification is the French tradition of creating *croquis* (Uhlenwinkel, 2013). While a map is a representation of the earth's surface a *croquis* (meaning rough sketch) is 'understood as a simplified representation of space aiming to explain its organisation' (Uhlenwinkel, 2013, p. 297). Uhlenwinkel suggests that *croquis* are less factual representations and more maps that tell a story or give an answer to a geographical question. In the example of Brazil (see Figure 4.4), the student has aggregated data (economic activities and population density) and linked them

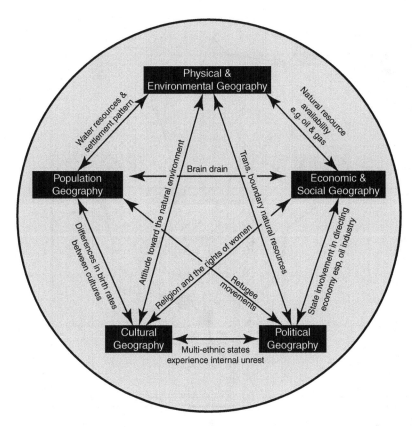

Figure 4.3 Examples of relationships using Southwest Asia and North Africa (Jones, M.C., 2014).

to a model of core and periphery. This example suggests the type of work pupils could be undertaking in order to think in regional terms: identifying associated phenomena that together give a geographical account or narrative. While such tasks can be undertaken individually there is also scope for the class working together on maps projected onto a SMart Board®.

Finally, mention must be made of the potential use of GIS for teaching regional geography. If the regional approach demands the analysis and synthesis of different layers of the earth's surface, a GIS is an ideal tool for putting geographical layers into relation with one another on a map. Its versatility to not only add and subtract layers at the discretion of the student, but also to interrogate, analyse and then display geographical data, give the user potential powers that the likes of Humboldt and Ritter could not have conceived of. As such, a GIS takes the student well beyond the scope of a reference map, although the latter are still probably a better starting point.

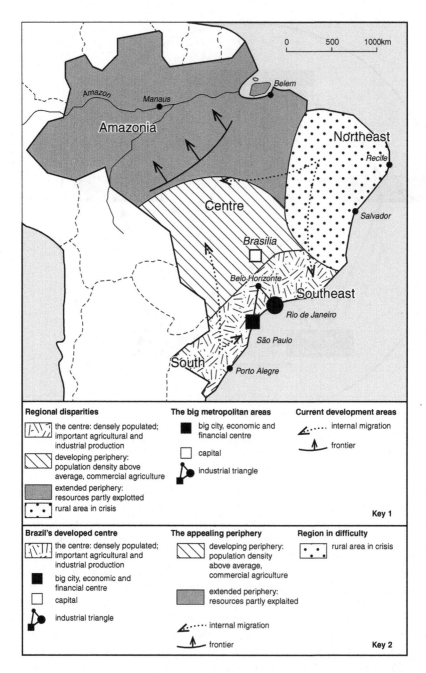

Figure 4.4 French *croquis* showing disparities in regional development (based on Jalta *et al.* 2008, cited by Uhlenwinkel 2013, p. 298).

Conclusion

In conclusion, this chapter has argued for a return to the dual nature of geography as both a nomothetic and an ideographic tradition. Attention has been drawn to the danger of potential fragmentation resulting from increasing specialisation and sub-division within university departments (Matthews and Herbert, 2008). But this is also not a new concern. Hettner also warned that to only study systematic geography 'runs the risk of leaving the ground of geography entirely' (Hartshorne, 1939, p. 458). 'He who does not understand regional geography is no true geographer' added Hettner (ibid.). While Matthews and Herbert settled upon space, place and environment as geography's core concepts, providing one solution, it can be argued that this does not account for the relationships between these concepts within the discipline. The advantage of an epistemology that encompasses systematic *and* regional geography is that the two branches are intimately related, and disciplinary concepts can sit comfortably within such a framework of knowledge.

A good geography teacher must, therefore, appreciate the complementary nature of systematic and regional geography, and introduce their pupils to both approaches early in their education (although they won't necessarily use these terms). As the child progresses through, school teachers must find ways of 'keeping the blades together' such that moving between the two approaches becomes second nature. This way, as the pupil matures and their knowledge of systematic geography and the world expands, they will be well-positioned to accomplish the synthesis demanded by the regional approach.

Key readings

1   Hartshorne, R. (1939) *The Nature of Geography*, Lancaster, PA: Association of American Geographers. Chapter 11: What Kind of Science Is Geography? This is the best explanation of the dynamic interplay between systematic and regional geography one can find.

2   Jones, M. C. (2014) 'Seeking Synthesis: An Integration Exercise for Teaching Regional Geography.' *The Geography Teacher*, 11 (1), 25–8. American author Mark C. Jones provides a modern example of how to teach through regions. Teachers will be able to adapt his ideas and approach for their own purposes and for different year groups.

Note

1   For example, Strabo's (7AD) 17 volumes of *Geographica* have been preserved and are available on the Internet.

References

Bernstein, B. (1999) 'Vertical and horizontal discourse: an essay', *British Journal of Sociology of Education*, 20 (2), 157–73.

de Blij, H. and Muller, P. (2012) *Geography: Realms, Regions and Concepts*, New York: Wiley.

de la Blache, V. (1908) *Tableau de la Geographie de la France*, Paris: Librairie Hachette.

Brandom, R. (2000) *Articulating Reasons: An Introduction to Inferentialism*, Cambridge, Massachusetts: Harvard University Press.

Clavel, P. ([1993] 1998) *An Introduction to Regional Geography* (translated by Ian Thompson), Oxford: Blackwell.

Cresswell, T. (2013) *Geographic Thought: A Critical Introduction*, Chichester, West Sussex: Wiley-Blackwell.

Gersmehl, P. (2008) *Teaching Geography* (2nd edn), New York: Guildford Press.

Gilbert, A. (1988) 'The new regional geography in English and French-speaking countries', *Progress in Human Geography*, 12 (2), 208–28.

Hartshorne, R. (1939) *The Nature of Geography*. Lancaster, PA: Association of AmericanGeographers.

Jones, M. C. (2014) 'Seeking synthesis: an integration exercise for teaching regional geography.' *The Geography Teacher* 11 (1), 25–8.

Matthews, J. and Herbert D. (2008) *Geography: A Very Short Introduction*, Oxford: Oxford University Press.

Sayer, A. (1989) 'The "new" regional geography and the problem of narrative', *Environment and Planning: Society and Space*, (7), 253–76.

Slater, F. (1982) *Learning through Geography*, London: Heinemann.

Uhlenwinkel, A. (2013) 'Spatial thinking or thinking geographically? On the importance of avoiding maps without meaning' In: T. Jekel, A. Car, J. Strobl and G. Griesebner (eds.) *GI Forum 2013 Creating the GISociety*, Berlin: Herbert Wichmann Verlag.

Vidal de La Blache, P. (1908) *Tableau de la Geographie de la France*, Paris: Librairie Hachette.

Chapter 5

Physical geography

Duncan Hawley

> One area where more content would be appreciated was Physical Geography. This was because it was felt that gaining a geographer's understanding of, say, how Hurricane Katrina affected America, requires a clear understanding not just of the social effects but how the physical surroundings contributed to those social effects. Physical Geography was also felt to develop important scientific skills, which can be underdeveloped if an A level student focuses primarily on Human Geography.
>
> (Higton et al., 2012, p. 60)

Introduction

When revisions to the curriculum and examination specifications in England were announced in 2008, a topic thread on a popular Internet forum for geography teachers asked, 'Will students know less about physical processes?' (SLN[1] Geography Forum, 2008). Similar concerns were also expressed in the consultation reviews commissioned by government leading up to the 2013–14 revisions, which highlighted issues over the content and quality of physical geography being taught (Higton et al., 2012; Ofqual, 2012). In essence, these discussions and concerns, at both teacher and policy level, centre on the place, role and impact of physical geography in a twenty-first century (geography) school education. This chapter asks, 'What is the rightful place of physical geography?'; it aims to open up debates over the position and relationship of physical geography with cognate subject disciplines and with the broader collective of ideas within geography.

It provokes questions over the construction of knowledge and methods that can influence discourse, thinking and approaches to teaching physical geography in schools.

What is physical geography and can it be defined by subject matter?

We tend to think of physical geography as being 'out there', its substance is in 'the field', it is the 'natural' dimension of geography. A brief description of physical geography might be 'dealing with all the non-human processes and features which occur on or near the Earth's surface' (Trend, 2008). This is a wide remit, which makes for reaching a comprehensive definition difficult (Tadaki et al., 2012). One effect in universities is increasing specialisation, where physical geography has become a complex blend of various sub-disciplines, shifting emphases and methodologies that in recent years has been increasingly positioned within larger units of environmental or Earth sciences (Matthews and Herbert, 2004; Pitman, 2005).

Pitman (2005) argues physical geography is synonymous with 'Earth System science'. Aimed at creating a (holistic) synthesis of disciplines, Earth System science accepts and emphasises a scientific process-oriented approach based on systems modelling that investigates how energy and mass flows and is cycled across boundaries of the Earth's four major spheres (geosphere, atmosphere, hydrosphere and biosphere). It stresses the links between physical, biological and social systems to investigate large-scale issues, including human induced change. However, a systems approach over-emphasises process, function and generalised explanation at the expense of pattern, the spatial approach and (physical) characterisation of place (Kent, 2009); concepts which, in highlighting variation and diversity across a range of scales, arguably lie at the heart of geographical study, these being rooted in 'real world' environments occurring at specific locales. With this perspective, physical geography promotes a distinctive conceptual outlook in considering the physical world when compared to more conventional sciences, and is less 'diluted' than in global modelling approaches such as Earth System science (Gregory, 2009; Inkpen and Wilson, 2013). Notwithstanding the perspective it can offer, a systems approach to physical geography overlaps with other cognate disciplines and subjects taught in schools and universities. The study of ecosystems is (naturally) part of the biological sciences; studies of earthquakes, volcanoes and tectonics form fundamental aspects of study in geology, which draws on strong connecting roots in physics and chemistry; climatology and weather are allied with physics. These rooted links prompts Gregory to ask: 'Is the position of physical geography within geography as a whole appropriate?' (Gregory, 2000, p. 22). Collectively, these are the Earth sciences and this content overlap provokes debate about the school subject in which Earth science content should be situated.

Should aspects of physical geography be part of the science curriculum?

Different nations situate the Earth sciences in different curriculum subject locations and internationally there is variable and uneven distribution of approaches to teaching Earth science in schools (King, 2013). For some nations this has meant shifting geography's 'Earth science tradition' (Pattison, 1964) to science so the school geography curriculum is dominated by human geography, often taught within a social studies or humanities context (Butt and Lambert, 2014). This raises the question of whether geography can properly exist without regard to physical geography and consideration of natural landscapes, but if physical geography (in whatever form) is essential to geographical study, how might curriculum 'overlap' be resolved?

When the National Curriculum of England was first established, 'territorial' claims and counter-claims were made for what aspects of Earth science should be part of the science curriculum and which should be taught in geography (King, 1986; Wilson, 1990; Trend, 1995; Hawley, 1997). The geography curriculum contained key aspects of physical geography whilst the science curriculum also featured the study of rock types, the rock cycle and plate tectonics, and both retained the overlap in subsequent 'slimmer' versions (DfES/QCA, 2004). Between 2011 and 2013 a major review was tasked to produce a national curriculum with a core of 'essential knowledge' in key subject disciplines and 'coherence in what is taught in schools' (DfE, 2012). Duplication of subject content was not considered acceptable, and the 'dilemma' this placed on where to position Earth science in the curriculum is clear in the generic label given to this 'discipline'. Earth is 'naturally' seen as the study domain of geography, but a claim is also made for science being the rightful place to teach this aspect (King, 2011). Using international test data, King argued that in nations where Earth science is a significant and distinct part of the science curriculum, and taught by teachers who are Earth science specialists, the students outperform students from the UK and other nations where Earth science is not so strongly demarcated. The 2011–13 review was remitted to develop a curriculum that compares favourably with other successful curricula in high performing jurisdictions, so King's argument for Earth science being a distinct 'strand' of the science curriculum could claim to have some legitimacy. The Geographical Association, however, argued for a complementary approach to understanding physical environments, claiming physical geography 'naturally' sets the study of earth processes in real world contexts that aid the capacity for interpretation and meaning, particularly in appreciating the aesthetic, moral and ethical dimensions and not least for understanding their application and usefulness. They distinguished this from a concept of 'deep Earth science', which focuses on investigation into the chemical and physical properties of the Earth (such as the composition and viscosity of magmas or the mechanics of seismic waves), and suggested such knowledge is appropriately developed in the context of science lessons. The idea of deep Earth science playing a part in understanding physical geography has become widely practiced in higher education in recent years through interdisciplinary collaborative work that seeks to find new ways of understanding environmental issues. As Urban and Rhoades state:

physical geography draws on knowledge of a wide range of ancillary disciplines including physics, chemistry and biology', so in this sense it is a composite science with a 'strong dependency on theoretical knowledge drawn from other natural sciences, many of which are viewed as foundational with respect to physical geography.

(Urban and Rhoades, 2003, pp. 212–13)

According to this line of argument, teaching about the Earth, its systems and how people respond to its environments, requires neither appropriation nor duplication but a harnessing of both perspectives (Geographical Association, 2011) (Figure 5.1). There are planning implications, but the debate about the rightful place of physical geography becomes less about 'territory' and more about its place within geography.

Should physical geography always be taught within a social/environmental issues context?

Curriculum-making engages geography teachers to become (critically) active in recontextualising the subject content of the curriculum to engage students in purposeful geography and meaningful knowledge (Morgan, J. 2006; GeoCapabilities, 2016). Questions about the curriculum-making of physical geography have existed for some time. David Pepper was, perhaps, the first to resonate with his article 'Why teach physical geography?' (Pepper, 1985), in which he railed against what he saw as the predominant mode of school physical geography at that time (driven by exam syllabus content), arguing it didn't allow students (and teachers) to set knowledge within the context of human society and problems. He thus claimed the physical environment was seen as a system entirely separated from society.

Twenty years on, Brooks (2006) evaluated the knowledge presented in a lesson which aimed 'to identify the causes and effects of acid rain' by looking at the environmental impacts (in Europe and Canada), and then suggest how they might be managed. Thus, it might be assumed that this lesson went some way towards satisfying Pepper's need for 'relevance' in placing the acid rain problem in a social context. However, Brooks comments that whilst the lesson tasks and activities allowed students to gain knowledge about the physical processes and impacts of acid rain, the teacher didn't draw attention to the borderless nature of acid rain and how this could result in different 'solutions', depending on which side of a geopolitical border you happen to live. She questioned whether the knowledge presented by the teacher as a simple sequence of cause, effect and symptoms, based on the physical process, would result in students thinking the 'solution' to acid rain is a simple issue rather than one that cannot be easily resolved. Brooks argues that knowledge and understanding of physical processes are not sufficient without being referenced in the wider geographical (social) context, even if they appear to be set within the frame of an 'environmental issue'. The 'dilemma' lies in the prevailing divide between human and physical geography in schools, even if the intention is for topic context to narrow the gap. At school level this has been dealt with simplistically, often by creating 'applied problem-solving' tasks rather than teasing out the complexities of a holistic approach that involves people's perspectives on the physical environment. David Pepper would probably still be dissatisfied.

Atherton (2009) suggests that the teaching and delivery of many physical geography topics in school tends to rely on extreme simplification of complex topics,

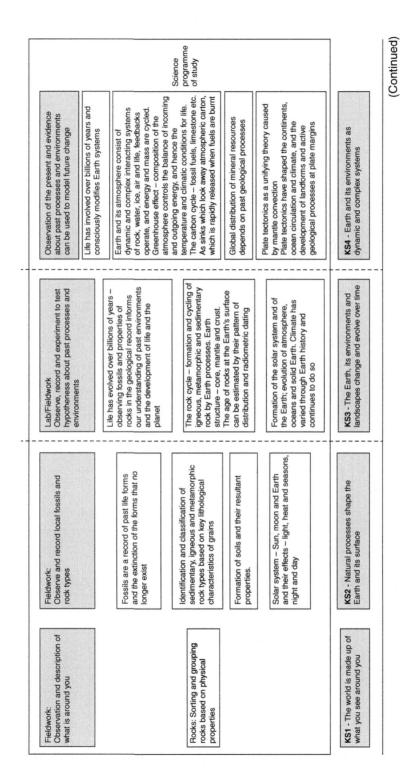

Figure 5.1 A curriculum map of earth science and physical geography in the national curriculum.[2]

(Continued)

Landscapes and Environments: Identifying key landforms, soil, vegetation, water bodies and weather

The world's major physical features – locations, patterns, characteristics and scale: continents, oceans and currents, mountain chains, river basins and hot and cold deserts

World climate zones and distribution and characteristics of major ecosystems

The water cycle: major phases and flows, atmosphere to surface and sub-surface, surface to lakes/oceans, oceans/lakes to atmosphere.

The UK: Climate and weather patterns; types of landscapes

The processes shaping the Earth's surface including the role of water, weathering and erosion and the formation of soils. Landscapes as distinctive collections of landforms, soils and Earth surface processes

Weather systems, climate zones and ocean currents; their properties, processes and patterns

People–Environment interactions
Humans depend on resources provided by the Earth and its atmosphere.
Human activity affects climate, oceans and landscapes.
Parts of the planet are more prone to natural hazards than others.
Humans are affected by natural hazards

Geography programme of study

Ecosystems as the balance and interconnections between climate, soil, water, plants and animals

Fragile landscapes and environments e.g. deserts, polar regions, mountains and reefs, are vulnerable to change, especially through human interventions and choices

Human life has rapidly modified Earth's systems and surface resulting in climate change, ocean pollution, land degradation and flood risk.

Use and sustainability of renewable and non-renewable resources.

Geohazards are managed by assessing risk perception, monitoring events and evaluating mitigation strategies.

Fieldwork:
Observation of what is around you

Fieldwork:
Observe and record local landscapes and weather

Fieldwork:
Observe, map, measure, analyse and interpret UK landscapes/surface processes

Fieldwork:
Observe, map, measure, analyse, interpret and evaluate landscapes/surface processes.

Figure 5.1 Continued.

especially in lower secondary school, due to students' level of intellectual capacity and lack of time to explore the concepts in any depth. Before students are able to make considered arguments and decisions about complex socio-scientific issues that are well supported, qualified and justified, they need to develop a content and conceptual knowledge base that is significant in terms of breadth, depth and organisation (Sadler and Fowler, 2006). Setting physical geography in an issues-based context (which may be known to students from popular information sources) is one thing, but it is quite another to teach deep understanding of the 'science' context by which informed decisions about the issue can be made (Reinfried et al., 2012).

These observations raise questions about the extent to which teaching physical geography in a 'social context' leads to superficial understanding of the way the natural world works and develops misconceptions, thereby diminishing a key aim of the social context approach of encouraging and empowering informed participation, decision making and actions over issues rooted in the physical environment.

Atherton (2009) also suggests that new ideas in physical geography only trickle through to schools and into the curriculum when it appears that they pass through a test for 'how does this apply to humans?', which aims to ensure relevancy of the content to young people. Atherton gives the example of tackling sea level rise from the point of view of its impacts rather than studying the underlying scientific processes. Here, the processes are supplementary and only introduced to further the understanding of the component of human impact. However, Gregory (2000) contests this approach, stating that

> the greater tendency at pre-university level to focus on the impact of human activity and upon management of the environment, with much less, if any, emphasis on the mechanics and principles of landscape development, is rather like putting the cart before the horse. It is very difficult later to take up the study of the horse when all the emphasis has been placed upon the cart!
>
> (p. 109)

Gray (2009) agrees, arguing that landscape is made up of physical, biological and cultural layers and, by way of its foundational relationship, the physical requires study in its own right before making sense of the other layers, and appreciating their part in creating the character of landscapes and their management and conservation.

An underlying assumption of Atherton's 'applicability test' is that relevance is recognised by students as being something worthwhile and so becomes of interest. Decisions about the context of teaching are usually made by teachers with little regard for students' views, which begs the question of whether students prefer physical geography being taught within a social (issues-based/integrated) context or as a branch of geography in its own place. Referring to Earth science in mass popular culture, Iain Stewart asserts that social contexts are interesting, but it is the awe and wonder that captivates and inspires, stating 'that modern Earth science is ripe for public consumption but ironically, this ripeness stems less from "pressing social relevance" than from an inherent sense of narrative' (Stewart, 2012).

Few studies have looked into physical geography as a focus of students' interest (Trend, 2009) but, in researching interest in geosciences he found 'Girls have a preference for phenomena perceived as aesthetically pleasing and boys have a preference for the extreme and catastrophic' (Trend, 2005, p. 271). Hopwood researched the responses of students to their experiences of physical geography and their conceptions of the people-environment theme. He discovered different understandings and not all were persuaded by the 'social context' despite being acknowledged as part of the geography. He reports that

> evidence suggests equally if not more strongly that physical phenomena *per se* interest Matt, and his desire to study them reflects a fascination with the physical world and how it works rather than an ultimately social concern.
> (Hopwood, 2006, p. 5)

Perhaps physical geography being always passed through the 'applicability test' risks negating the spiritual and intellectual stimulation (the awe and wonder) to 'discover' the natural world. As Hopwood asks, 'Are we in danger of losing sight of education about the environment?' (ibid.).

Concerns about the 'weakening' of physical geography in the school curriculum have surfaced periodically. The rise of humanistic geography and the emergence of environment as a focus of political concern led to a drift towards 'concentrating attention on human geography in the school curriculum' considered as 'potentially damaging' (Mottershead, 1987, p. 80). The people-environment framework was thought insufficiently rigorous to give proper attention to physical process (Adamczyk et al., 1994), giving academic physical geographers and policy advisors concerns over whether appropriate and up-to-date knowledge and ideas are being taught in schools (Keylock, 2006; Knight, 2007; Higton et al., 2012). The A-Level Content Advisory Board Panel on Geography report emphasised the importance of people-environment themes to geography but noted this should be balanced and not 'at the expense of understanding physical processes' (ALCAB, 2014, p. 6). So a key debate revolves around the extent to which physical geography taught in a social context, via a people–environment or issues-based approach, weakens or strengthens understanding and engagement with the physical world. We have returned to the question mentioned in the introduction: 'Will students know less about physical processes?' and are forced to consider the implications.

What counts as 'knowledge' in physical geography?

So far this discussion on the rightful place of physical geography has focused on how it is situated in terms of content and context. I now want to turn attention to the process and production of (new) knowledge in physical geography.

Morgan, J. (2006) recalls his experience of physical geography at school in the 1980s; there was a lot of teaching about hydrology involving quantification and correlation of variables, studying glaciers as a 'system' and coasts as 'process studies'. The intention, he suggests, was to give students experience of how geographers practiced the subject. The outcome, he argues, was inculcation into one particular type of knowledge that breaks the world down into discrete parts, offering a limited view of how physical geography knits into the wider landscape. What was portrayed as a neutral and objective scientific approach is built on assumptions, and is only one way of constructing meaning? Newson (1997) illustrates this with an anecdote based on a conversation with a Lake District farmer about management of a river channel: 'I wish the bloody boffins would come here in a spate and watch how this beck eats my land; they'd not waste money making it deeper then – it's deep water what drowns sheep' (p. 22). Morgan, J. (2006) suggests that if teachers are aware of types of knowledge (and how these are produced), they will be better equipped to give a considered answer as to what it is they want students to learn. It raises questions about the process of how we teach physical geography and what worldview students are likely to derive from how they are being taught.

The dominant type of knowledge experienced in school physical geography tends to be that of machine and system driven by process (Lambert and Morgan, J. 2010, p. 138), portraying the way nature works in geography as determined by a set of stable, 'fixed' processes where facts fit together in a given way according to 'laws', that is a positivist perspective. It is manifested through predetermined models presented in the classroom by descriptions, diagrams and definitions, system boxes and the classic (single) hypothesis-testing approach. At one level, this knowledge can convince of rational explanation and is intellectually seductive (Harrison, 2009). However, it can also lead to belief in an outdated machine that doesn't match with a dynamic understanding of nature, leading teachers to passively depict a machine that doesn't meet reality. It can encourage students to learn the model and slot the components in, even if they don't fit, gripped by the 'tyranny of models' (Trudgill, 2003, p. 34).

Academic understanding has shifted from this empirical, rigid world to acknowledge simplicity doesn't exist and the real world is more 'naughty', complex, approximate and our interpretations of it are socially constructed (Kennedy, 1979; Tadaki et al., 2012). There is no objective 'truth' but there are better approximations to the truth (Inkpen and Wilson, 2013) and in this sense, physical geography should be exploratory, engaging in debate about validity of data and reasoning, in addition to being explanatory.

In knowledge as text, physical geography isn't just 'out there' as information in physical object, but its meaning is constructed through heuristic or swayed by paradigm (Kennedy, 2006). Constructs (interpretative frameworks) offered by teachers help stimulate seeing the world in new ways, although teachers need to be aware of the limitations and alternatives as the 'tyranny of models' also warns caution in 'storytelling' (Trudgill, 2003; Kastens and Chayes, 2011). When a construct is oversimplified, outdated, offered as the sole explanatory model, or as though no understanding about the physical world existed previously, and without critical evaluation, it can obfuscate rather than clarify. For example, according to popular textbooks the 'recipe' to create a waterfall is simple. Take bands of 'hard' and 'soft' rock, erode the soft rock carefully for a period of time until the hard rock is undercut, the hard rock collapses, a plunge pool is created and the waterfall will retreat to form a gorge. While such happy endings make us feel comfortable, they are not always the most helpful outcome as they do not encourage examination of the range and complexity of processes that could have produced the same outcome (the concept of equifinality). In this case, glacial action to produce a hanging valley or isostatic uplift and faulting are other processes that might create a waterfall (Atherton, 2009). In focusing on the seductive detail of one story, it misses the more significant meaning beyond description; waterfalls tell us about changes in base level and the volatility of the Earth.

Accounts of the 'one size fits all' model can be temptingly found in many aspects of physical geography, especially in textbooks. However, when teachers only consider a limited number of the facts in order to fit the theory we teach (and tell the story), it results in a lesser rather than a better approximation of the 'truth'; and, usually, the lesser approximation does a disservice to students, as they make sense of the world in a less powerful way, developing diminished ability to explain novel situations (Kastens and Chayes, 2011). If the paradigms taught in school are not explored and the limits of their reasoning is not 'tested', then the knowledge produced makes it more difficult for students to make worthwhile distinctions between 'trend' (nearer the truth) and 'noise' (exceptions that don't fit) in the real world.

Atherton (2009) suggests students develop skills of acceptance rather than enquiry, whereas in reality, the world is riddled with uncertainty so that students should be taught to deal with ambiguities, and therefore a constructivist approach is more appropriate to physical geography teaching. Trend (2009) and Morgan A. (2006) advocate the use of argumentation as a pedagogic approach to empower students with a more critical understanding of the world's natural systems, and that there is a role for introducing the history of ideas into teaching, thus creating opportunities for students to argue, debate and re-create the intellectual struggles that brought about our current constructs in understanding of the physical world (Sack, 2002; Trend, 2008).

The key debate here revolves around how best to help students make sense of a complex and dynamic physical world: whether, when and how to use paradigms as constructs and simple, singular explanatory models, or whether it is more appropriate and effective to introduce a range of different (sometimes historical) interpretive tools to explore the validity of ways of explaining and understanding that helps students make worthwhile distinctions.

Conclusion

This exploration of the 'rightful place' has clearly identified that school geography could not exist without physical geography; the interdependence between the physical world and cultural and social worlds, in a range of direct and indirect ways, is too strong to be dismissed. However, the physical world is wide-ranging, complex and dynamic. The content matter of physical geography lies within a collective of scientific disciplines called Earth sciences, but our current understanding shows that there is value in a geographical dimension brought to a 'hard science'-driven systems approach. The debate for teachers is over what to emphasise in choosing to teach and how to develop students' thinking to enable a fresh, distinctive perspective to be gained in understanding the physical world. The idea of physical geography as emphasising the surface, spatial and social, as opposed to 'deep' Earth science, is attractively simple, but this throws up debates over balance of studying processes, for it is in the conceptual understanding of processes that the power of applicability lies. Applicability seems to be a current filter for much physical geography taught in school that gives a social justification to the place of physical geography. The dilemma of 'cart before horse' can lead to insufficient knowledge and understanding in how the physical world works, and so the application becomes detached from reality. Applicability could also limit the development of a 'richer', more spiritual, appreciation of the physical world. The challenge for teachers is in deciding appropriate starting points and routes for study. Shifts in constructing our understanding of the physical world have moved from a fixed positivist view as a stable, 'lawful' place to exploring multiple knowledges, which interpret contingent contexts and aim to reveal evermore 'approximate truths'. Here the challenge for geography teachers is to critically examine their own biographical knowledge of physical geography so as to evaluate decisions over how to help students envisage and develop understanding of the 'naughty world'. The rightful place of physical geography cannot be thought of as a fixed location in the minds of geography teachers or their students, but it should be debated to understand the context in which we find ourselves making sense of the world.

Key readings

1   Trudgill, S. and Roy, A. (eds.) (2003) *Contemporary Meanings in Physical Geography: From What to Why?* London: Arnold. This book offers a collection of refreshing, stimulating, reflective, cultural interpretations of physical geography which challenge how meanings derived from physical geography are framed.

2   Atherton, R. (2009) 'Living with natural processes – physical geography and the human impact on the environment', Chapter 6, in Mitchell, D. (ed.) *Living Geography: Exciting futures for teachers and students*, London: Chris Kington Publishing. This chapter discusses linking natural processes and human activity in an applied context to engage young people's interest in physical geography.

3   Gregory, K. J. (2000) *The Changing Nature of Physical Geography*, London: Arnold. The focus of Ken Gregory's book is self-explanatory and whilst there have been some further changes in the last decade or so it provides an enduring overview of ideas that have influenced our conceptions of physical geography as taught in schools.

Notes

1 SLN is the Staffordshire Learning Net, its geography pages although no longer updated are available at: http://www.sln.org.uk/geography/.
2 A curriculum map of earth science and physical geography in the National Curriculum based a document produced jointly by The Geographical Association, The Geological Society, The Earth Science Teachers' Association, The Royal Geographical Society and The Royal Meteorological Society and submitted to assist with the review of the National Curriculum for England (December 2011).

References

Adamczyk, P., Binns, T., Brown, A., Cross, S. and Magson, Y. (1994) 'The geography-science interface: a focus for collaboration', *Teaching Geography*, 19 (1), 11–14.

ALCAB (The A Level Content Advisory Board) (2014) *Report of the ALCAB Panel on Geography*. July 2014, Available at: https://alevelcontent.files.wordpress.com/2014/07/alcab-report-of-panel-on-geography-july-2014.pdf [Accessed 13 August 2016].

Atherton, R. (2009) 'Living with natural processes – physical geography and the human impact on the environment', in D. Mitchell (ed.), *Living Geography*, Cambridge: Chris Kington Publishing.

Brooks, C. (2006) 'Geography teachers and making the school geography curriculum', *Geography*, 91 (1), 75–83.

Butt, G. and Lambert, D. (2014) 'International perspectives on the future of geography education: an analysis of national curricula and standards', *International Research in Geographical and Environmental Education*, 23 (1), 1–12.

Department for Education and Skills/Qualification and Curriculum Authority (DfES/QCA) (2004) *The National Curriculum: A Handbook for Secondary Teachers*, London: HMSO, Available at: www.education.gov.uk/publications/eOrderingDownload/QCA-04-1374.pdf [Accessed 29 July 2016].

Department for Education (DfE) (2012) *Remit for Review of the National Curriculum in England*, Available at: http://webarchive.nationalarchives.gov.uk/20130123124929/ http://www.education.gov.uk/schools/teachingandlearning/curriculum/nationalcurriculum/b0073043/remit-for-review-of-the-national-curriculum-in-england/ [Accessed 29 July 2016].

GeoCapabilities (2016) *Curriculum Making and GeoCapabilities*, Available at: http://www.geocapabilities.org/training-materials/module-2-curriculum-making-by-teachers/theory/ [Accessed 29 July 2016].

Geographical Association (2011) What are the key concepts in Earth science to which all students should be introduced at school?, Available at: http://www.geography.org.uk/download/GA_AUEarthScienceNCResponse.pdf [Accessed 29 July 2016].

Gray, M. (2009) 'Landscape: the physical layer', in N.J. Clifford, S.L. Holloway, S.P. Rice and G. Valentine (eds.), *Key Concepts in Geography*, 2nd edn, London: Sage.

Gregory, K. J. (2000) *The Changing Nature of Physical Geography*, London: Arnold.

Gregory, K. (2009) 'Place: The Management of Sustainable Environments', in N.J. Clifford, S.L. Holloway, S.P. Rice and G. Valentine (eds.), *Key Concepts in Geography*, 2nd edn, London: Sage publications.

Harrison, S. (2009) 'Environmental systems: philosophy and applications in physical geography', in N.J. Clifford, S.L. Holloway, S.P. Rice and G. Valentine (eds.), *Key Concepts in Geography*, 2nd edn, London: Sage.

Hawley, D. (1997) 'Cross-curricular concerns in geography Earth science and physical geography', in D. Tilbury and M. Williams (eds.), *Teaching and Learning Geography*, London: Routledge.

Higton, J., Noble, J., Pope, S., Boal, S., Ginnis, S., Donaldson, R. and Greevy, H. (2012) *Fit For Purpose? The View of The Higher Education Sector, Teachers and Employers on the Suitability of A Levels.* Ipsos MORI Social Research Institute, Available at: http://webarchive.nationalarchives.gov.uk/20141031163546/http://www2.ofqual.gov.uk/downloads/category/95-qualification-standards-reports?download=1371%3Afit-for-purpose-the-view-of-the-higher-education-sector-teachers-and-employers-on-the-suitability-of-a-levels [Accessed 28 July 2016].

Hopwood, N. (2006) Pupils' perspectives on environmental education in geography: 'I'm not looking at it from a tree's point of view', Paper presented at the University of Bath Centre for Research in Education and the Environment, 16 February 2006, Available at: http://www.bath.ac.uk/cree/resources/hopwood.pdf [Accessed 29 July 2016].

Inkpen, R. and Wilson, G. (2013) *Science, Philosophy and Physical Geography*, 2nd edn, London: Routledge.

Kastens, K. and Chayes, D. (2011) Telling lies to children, *Earth and Mind: the Blog Reflections on Thinking and Learning about the Earth*, Available at: http://serc.carleton.edu/earthandmind/posts/lies_children.html [Accessed 29 July 2016].

Kennedy, B. A. (1979) 'A naughty world', *Transactions of the Institute of British Geographers*, 4 (4), 550–8.

Kennedy, B. A. (2006) *Inventing the Earth: Ideas on Landscape Development Since 1740*, Malden, MA: Blackwell Publishing.

Kent, M. (2009) 'Space: making room for space in physical geography', in N.J. Clifford, S.L. Holloway, S.P. Rice and G. Valentine (eds.), *Key Concepts in Geography*, 2nd edn, London: Sage.

Keylock, C.J. (2006) 'Reforming AS/A2 physical geography to enhance geographic scholarship', *Geography*, 91 (3), 272–9.

King, C. (1986) 'Will physical geography join the sciences?', *Teaching Geography*, 12 (1), 32.

King, C. (2011) 'Where should Earth science be situated in the curriculum?', *Teaching Earth Sciences*, 36 (2), 56–60.

King, C. (2013) 'Geoscience education across the globe – results of the IUGS-COGE/IGEOsurvey', *Episodes*, 36 (1), 19–30, Available at: http://www.episodes.org/index.php/epi/article / view/57426 [Accessed 29 July 2016].

Knight, P. (2007) 'Physical geography: learning and teaching in a discipline so dynamic that textbooks can't keep up', *Geography*, 92 (1), 57–61.

Lambert, D. and Morgan, J. (2010) *Teaching Geography 11–18: A Conceptual Approach*, Maidenhead: Open University Press.

Matthews, J.A. and Herbert, D.T. (2004) 'Unity in geography: prospects for the discipline', in J.A. Matthews and D.T. Herbert (eds.), *Unifying Geography: Common Heritage, Shared Future*, London: Routledge.

Morgan, A. (2006) 'Argumentation, geography education and ICT', *Geography*, 91 (2), 126–40.

Morgan, J. (2006) 'Geography – a dynamic subject', in D. Balderstone (ed.), *Secondary Geography Handbook*, Sheffield: Geographical Association.

Mottershead, D. (1987) 'Physical geography', *Teaching Geography*, 12 (2), 80–81.

Newson, M. (1997) *Land, Water and Development: Sustainable Management of River Basin Systems*, 2nd edn, London: Routledge.

Ofqual (2012) *Review of Standards in GCE A level Geography 2001 and 2010,* Available at: http://webarchive.nationalarchives.gov.uk/+/http:/www.ofqual.gov.uk/ files/20120427 review-of-standards-in-gce-a-level-geography.pdf [29 July 2016].

Pattison, W.D. (1964) 'The four traditions of geography', *Journal of Geography,* 63 (3), 211–16.

Pepper, D. (1985) 'Why teach physical geography?', *Contemporary Issues in Geography and Education,* 2 (1), 62–71.

Pitman, A.J. (2005) 'On the role geography in earth system science', *Geoforum,* 36, 137–48.

Reinfried, S., Aeschbacher, U. and Rottermann, B. (2012) 'Improving students' conceptual understanding of the greenhouse effect using theory-based learning materials that promote deep learning', *International Research in Geographical and Environmental Education,* 21 (2), 155–78.

Sack, D. (2002) 'The educational value of the history of geomorphology', *Geomorphology* 47, 313–23.

Sadler, T. D. and Fowler, S. R. (2006) 'A threshold model of content knowledge transfer for socioscientific argumentation', *Science Education,* 90 (6), 986–1004.

Staffordshire Learning Net (SLN) Geography Forum (2008) *Will pupils know less about physical processes?,* Available at: http://www.learningnet.co.uk/ubb/ Forum5/HTML/ o16909.html [Accessed 2 August 2011].

Stewart, I. (2012) Tell me a story, Available at: https://www.geolsoc.org.uk/ Geoscientist/Archive/March-2012/Of-maps-means--ends/Tell-me-a-story [Accessed 29 July 2016].

Tadaki, M., Salmond, J., Le Heron, R. and Brierley, G. (2012) 'Nature, culture, and the work of physical geography', *Transactions of the Institute of British Geographers,* 37 (12), 1–16.

Trend, R. (1995) *Geography and Science: Forging Links at Key Stage 3,* Sheffield: Geographical Association.

Trend, R. (2005) 'Individual, situational and topic interest in geoscience among 11 and 12 year old children', *Research Papers in Education,* 20 (3), 271–302.

Trend, R. (2008) *Think Piece, Physical Geography (secondary),* Available at: http://geography.org.uk/download/GA_TP_S_physicalgeog.pdf [Accessed 29 July 2016].

Trend, R. (2009) 'Commentary: fostering students' argumentation skills in geoscience education', *Journal of Geoscience Education,* 57 (4), 224–32.

Trudgill, S. (2003) 'Meaning, knowledge, constructs and fieldwork in physical geography', in S. Trudgill and A. Roy (eds.), *Contemporary Meanings in Physical Geography: From What to Why?* London: Arnold.

Trudgill, S. and Roy, A. (eds.) (2003) *Contemporary Meanings in Physical Geography: From What to Why?* London: Arnold.

Urban, M. and Rhoads, B. (2003) 'Conceptions of nature', in S. Trudgill, and A. Roy (eds.), *Contemporary Meanings in Physical Geography: From What to Why?* London: Arnold.

Wilson, R.C.L. (1990) National Curriculum Geography Working Group: comments on the interim report of the National Curriculum Geography Working Group, submission from the Association for Science Education, *Teaching Earth Sciences,* 15 (1), 18–22.

Chapter 6

Making progress in learning geography

Liz Taylor

> If we did not hope that students should progress, we would have no foundation on which to construct a curriculum or embark on the act of teaching.
> (Daugherty, 1996, p. 195)

Introduction

A teacher's main task is to create opportunities for their students to progress, but what exactly is progress in learning geography? This is not an easy question to answer and is the subject of considerable intellectual effort internationally (Muniz Solari et al., 2017). Learning involves change in someone's knowledge, understanding, skills or attitudes (and the meaning of those terms and the relationship between them is complex and contested), but a neutral idea of 'change' is not enough. The change must be seen as valuable, as moving in a positive direction, as progress. This moves the issue into more contentious, political territory, for who decides what is positive or valuable? Is this determination to be made by the teacher, the school, the government, or the learner him/herself? Further, in such a broad field of study as geography, a skill or area of content which is valuable to one person may be unimportant to another. Indeed, the subject itself is continually under construction, or in 'progress', so those elements that are valued and promoted change over time.

Not only are different aspects of the subject popular or marginalised at any one time and place, but different levels of emphasis are given within education to knowledge, understanding, skills and values/attitudes. Also, the discourse of 'education' is not unitary: is education concerned with the acquisition of substantive knowledge, gaining skills, or the understanding of key concepts? Of course, most outworkings of these different dimensions are complementary rather than in opposition, and each element is likely to be present in a curriculum even if not explicitly signposted. Even with a broad agreement on the relative importance of these dimensions of learning, there would still be significant discussion over exactly *what* knowledge is valuable (see Roger Firth's chapter in this volume; Lambert, 2011a), or *which* concepts are most powerful for the geographer to deploy in selecting and organising the potential mass of content (see Clare

Brooks' chapter in this volume; Taylor, 2008). In recent years, debates around the role of knowledge in geography education have led to attention being focused on *what* students are expected to make progress in rather than the characteristic *ways* in which that progress happens. Both are important.

It is useful to have theoretically clear and empirically-informed work on how children and young people make progress in geography. Research can inform medium- and long-term planning by sharing understanding of the common patterns of progression and problems students encounter in their subject learning. Such understanding might be particularly valuable around break-points between key stages, as maintaining progression across these can be notoriously problematic (Jefferis and Chapman, 2005; Marriott, 2007). Research can also inform meaningful assessment practice, whether this is day-to-day formative practices, or construction of the overarching descriptors or benchmarks designed for summative assessment at the end of a key stage (Daugherty, 1996; Lambert, 2011b).

What should students be 'getting better at' in geography?

Various 'strands' or 'dimensions' in progression in learning geography have been proposed over time. Recent whole-scale reform of curricula and qualifications in England has given opportunity for thinking about progression in geographical learning from one stage of education to the next (Rawling, 2015, 2016; Biddulph and Lambert, 2017). Both GCSE and A-Level subject content documents (these give compulsory foundations for all geography examination specifications in England) include statements about progression (DfE 2014a, 2014b). For example, the A-Level document specifies 'that there is a clear progression in the breadth and depth of content from GCSE'. Awarding organisations must aim to:

- build on knowledge of contexts, locations, places and environments;
- ensure emphasis on deep understanding of both physical and human processes;
- require study that builds on and reinforces the conceptual understanding;
- ensure that specifications demand engagement with models, theories and generalisations (that) require a mature understanding;
- promote understanding of the rationale for, and applications of, skills and approaches used;
- ensure that (in fieldwork) study demands a high degree of responsibility from students for selecting research questions, applying relevant techniques and skills, and identifying appropriate ways of analysing and communicating findings.

(abridged from DfE, 2014a, pp. 4–5).

This reform has also provided opportunity for subject organisations to guide teachers' thinking on progress. The Geographical Association's 'Assessment and progression framework for geography' (2014), gives guidance on 'dimensions of progress' to age 16. This has been followed by discussions of how to operation-alise elements of progression in practice (e.g. Monk, 2016 on fieldwork or Knox and Simmonds 2016 on assessment).

Setting out strands or dimensions in progression is not a new phenome-non, for example, the School Curriculum and Assessment Authority (SCAA, 1994, p. 7) proposed that through Key Stage 3 (KS3), pupils in England would increasingly:

- broaden and deepen their knowledge and understanding of places and themes;
- make use of a wide and precise geographical vocabulary;
- analyse, rather than describe, geographical patterns, processes and change;
- appreciate the interactions within and between physical and human processes that operate in any environment;
- appreciate the interdependence of places;
- become proficient at conducting and comparing studies at a widening range of scales and in contrasting places and environments;
- apply their geographical knowledge and understanding to unfamiliar contexts;
- select and make effective use of skills and techniques to support their geo-graphical investigations; and
- appreciate the limitations of geographical evidence and the tentative and incomplete nature of some explanations.

Over time, various authors on geographical education theory and practice have also proposed dimensions of progression (for example, Marsden, 1995). Bennetts (2005a) drew together his thinking on the topic of geographical progression and understanding (Bennetts 1995, 2005a, 2005b), to suggest the following as 'the most significant dimensions of progression in geographical understanding' (2005a, pp. 123–4):

- distance from experience in the sense of the gap between what is required to be understood and what students have experienced or have knowledge of;
- complexity – whether of experience, information, ideas or cognitive tasks;
- abstraction – particularly of ideas about processes, relationships and values, but also forms of presentation;
- precision – in the sense of being more exact and knowing when that is appro-priate and useful;
- making connections and developing structures – ranging from applying sim-ple ideas to experience and making simple links between ideas, to the use of sophisticated conceptual models and theories;
- the breadth of context in which explanations are placed, especially spatial contexts, but also temporal and other contexts;

- the association of understanding with cognitive abilities and skills; and
- the association of understanding with affective elements, such as attitudes and values, and the value-laden nature of particular ideas.

These various interpretations of progression show significant commonality. Each mentions some form of increasing *breadth*. Breadth is often juxtaposed with *depth*, which presumably refers to greater amounts of detail or complexity for each topic or place studied. There is also a clear association of the move from the *concrete to the abstract* with progress, a move which is often seen as culminating in the understanding or use of models and theories. In addition, the influence of familiar thinking on cognitive stretch, such as that detailed in Bloom's taxonomy (Bloom, 1956; Krathwohl, 2002), can be identified in terms of progress from describing to applying, explaining or analysing. Skills are also mentioned, with the intention that students should be able to use a *wider range of techniques*, increasingly to discern which are appropriate in a given situation, and to be able to work with greater independence over time.

It is significant to note that many of the strands suggested in the above paragraph could apply equally well to education in general, or to other curricular subjects: few are inherently geographical. However, Lee and Shemilt, who have undertaken considerable research in this area of history education, suggest that a useful distinction can be made between the more general ideas of progress and 'progression'. They see progression being the more specialised term, referring to 'the way in which pupils' ideas – about history and the past – develop' (2003, p. 13). Lee and Shemilt also counterpose progression and 'aggregation', the latter defined as 'an increase in the amount of information pupils could recall' (2003, p. 13), which perhaps parallels mentions of 'breadth' above. This reflects Lee and Shemilt's desire to see their subject as *more* than accumulation of that substantive knowledge. Their research focuses on analysis of large sets of students' writing, as well as some classroom-based investigation, to illuminate key ways of thinking associated with the underlying operational structures of history (Lee and Ashby, 2000). They have created progression models in students' understanding of evidence, historical accounts and interpretations, historical explanation and causal reasoning (Lee and Shemilt, 2003, 2004, 2009). This is based on empirical evidence – in contrast to the geography lists quoted above. As the statements can be seen as aspirational rather than directly descriptive of current patterns, this is not particularly problematic. However, is there any empirical evidence regarding children and young people's progression in geography? *In what ways* do children characteristically progress?

What do we know about children and young people's progression in geography?

Although it can take some detective skills to locate it, there is a fair volume of empirically based research on children and young people's understandings of topics which come into the purview of geography education. However, not all of this research is 'badged' as geography education. To take one example, there is substantial research on children's understandings of place(s), both local and distant to them. To access this, it is necessary to draw on work originating at the interface with psychology and sociology, as well as geography and geography education. So, one key strand of this work arose from an interest within *environmental psychology*, for example the 'Clark group' in the late 1960s (see special issue of the *Journal of Environmental Psychology*, 7 (4)). The work of Blaut, Stea and Hart also explored the interface between geography and psychology, often with a focus on children's thinking and behaviours, and usually with regard to their local environment (see Blaut, 1987; Hart, 1987). Other environmental cognition research located within, or overlapping with, the discipline of psychology focused on children's mapping of the world (see Matthews, 1992, for a useful summary). For example, Gould and White's classic book *Mental Maps* (1974) explored young people's place knowledge and preferences, using cross-sectional techniques to show how the extent of knowledge was related to age. Young people's knowledge about, and attitudes towards, other countries has also formed a focus to research over time, from Piaget and Weil's influential study (1951) to more recent work carried out in the context of European integration (Axia et al., 1998; Barrett and Short, 1992; Barrett and Farroni, 1996; Rutland, 1998). These studies tend to be large-scale surveys, highlighting knowledge of location and spatial configuration, or attitudes towards nationalities, rather than in-depth explorations of a broader range of understandings about places.

Another key strand of research is in the field of children's geographies, a branch of geography which tends to be informed by *sociology*. Examples of literature on children's understandings of place from this perspective include Holloway and Valentine's (2000) study, which traced young people's imaginative geographies over sets of emails exchanged in a UK–New Zealand school-linking project, and Vanderbeck and Dunkley's (2003) research which explored young people's understandings of rural–urban difference.

Moving to research on understandings of place generated within a *geography education* context, there is considerable focus on children's world place-knowledge and map drawing (Wiegand, 1991; 1998; Harwood and Rawlings, 2001; Schmeinck, 2006). There is also research on children's understandings of their local area (for example Barratt and Barratt-Hacking, 2000), and distant places. In the 1980s, the latter often tied in with concerns about racism (for example Graham and Lynn, 1989), whilst, more recently, school-linking has been a motivator (Halocha, 1998; Disney, 2005; Pickering, 2008).

Whilst various disciplines have contributed to a substantial literature on children's understandings of place, in other areas of geography, the volume of research evidence varies considerably from topic to topic. Those physical geography topics that border or overlap with science education tend to have attracted more research. These include ecosystems (Strommen, 1995; Dove, 2000), landscape features (Eyres and Garner, 1998; Cin and Yaziki, 2002; Mackintosh, 2004) and weather and climate (Dove, 1998; Alkis,, 2007). Issues of the environment and sustainability have also received attention (for example Cabral and Kaivola, 2005; Walshe, 2008). Human geography has generally received less attention, though there is research on children and young people's understanding of rural and urban environments (e.g. Walker, 2004; Béneker et al., 2007) and globalisation (Picton, 2010). Of course, these published studies are probably the tip of the iceberg – much small-scale research about children's understandings by teachers and trainee teachers is unpublished and therefore not available to the geography education community as a whole. Recently, work in the USA has generated momentum around the ideas of 'learning progressions', with a particular emphasis so far on map interpretation, spatial reasoning processes and geospatial technologies (Huynh, Solem and Bednarz, 2015; Solem, Huynh and Boehm, 2014). This positions geography education research alongside initiatives in mathematics and science education. It provides some interesting models for research studies in learning progression, including an element of cumulation of smaller studies, but it is not yet clear how easily the idea will transfer to children's learning in less 'scientific' areas of the subject.

Insofar as research methods are concerned, most of the studies of children's understandings detailed above describe the oral, written or pictorial representations of young people on a particular geographical topic at *one point in time*. These can be useful to show us the range of different understandings with a group, and if the group is large enough, then these data might be a starting point for identifying and evaluating characteristic ways of thinking about a particular topic. This would be one way in to understanding paths in progression. *Cross-sectional research* (a snapshot of the responses of different age groups at one point in time) is commonly used as a proxy for how children's understandings change over longer periods of time (usually a number of years) and can also be used to inform progression models. However, when trying to understand the processes by which children and young people make progress, *longitudinal research* (following the same children over time) is necessary. Some work on children's understandings of distant place compares their representations at the start and end of a unit of work (Stillwell and Spencer, 1974; Harrington, 1998; Picton, 2008). This is useful in describing changes at a detailed level, but processes of change may not be evident. In my own research on young people's understanding of distant place, a detailed lesson-by-lesson system of data collection enabled a fine-grained tracking of changes as well as reflections from the students on their experiences of learning. The empirical component of this research consisted of an interpretive case study of one Year 9 class (ages 13–14), who were studying Japan in their geography lessons. Materials resulting from a wide range of methods, including in-depth interviews, visual methods, classroom observation and audio diaries, were used to explore students' representations of Japan and the ways in which these developed over time. The students' initial representations of Japan were found to be diverse and individual in nature, though it was possible to identify common themes (Taylor, 2009). Over the unit of study, some representations of Japan were found to persist, some were modified and new ones emerged. There was evidence for three processes of change taking place: prediction from knowledge of other distant places and personal experience; elicitation of new knowledge; and classification of new knowledge into both familiar and new categories (Taylor, 2011). Different learning activities provided students with distinctive opportunities for understanding and framing diversity, both within Japan and between Japan and other countries. Whilst the work does not involve the explicitly evaluative component needed for constructing a progression model, it does point to some of the learning experiences which seem to have encouraged changes in students' representations.

This leads us to research on conceptual change. This type of detailed, longitudinal work is more common within research in science and mathematics education than in geography, and the processes by which children form and change concepts over time have long been investigated by psychologists. Research on geographical topics that border on science education has given particular prominence to the identification of common 'preconceptions', 'misconceptions' or 'alternative conceptions' (Dove, 1999). These may act as barriers to further learning. Such research can be useful to warn teachers of likely misunderstandings or prior conceptions regarding a particular topic, such as the confusion between global warming and the hole in the ozone layer. However, misconceptions are not necessarily most profitably seen as enemies to be confronted and replaced. Instead, whilst their flaws and limitations of application are acknowledged, it may still be possible for them to be refined and reused in later, more sophisticated reasoning (Smith et al., 1993). Work on conceptual change has sometimes taken a purely cognitive focus, but more recently, affective factors such as motivation and attitudes to learning have interested researchers, the so-called 'warming' trend in conceptual change research (Pintrich et al., 1993). Debate also focuses around whether conceptual change is gradual and cumulative (evolutionary) or more sudden and transformative (revolutionary) (Keiny, 2008). Work in neuroscience suggests that learning is incremental and networks cannot suddenly be restructured (Goswami, 2008). However, 'certain experiences may result in previously distinct parts of the network becoming connected, or inefficient connections that were impeding understanding being pruned away' (Goswami, 2008, p. 388), suggesting an enticing yet beguiling possibility of research identifying a physical anchor to explain conceptual change.

The work of Meyer and Land (2003) on 'threshold concepts' in economics has sparked interest from some geographers (GEES, 2006; Slinger, 2011). A threshold concept refers to a core learning outcome that involves 'seeing things in a new way' (Meyer and Land, 2003, p. 1). They suggest that a threshold concept is transformative, probably irreversible, integrative, possibly bounded and potentially troublesome, with opportunity cost suggested as an example from economics. This 'troublesome knowledge' is 'conceptually difficult, counterintuitive or "alien"' (Meyer and Land, 2003, p. 1). A range of possible threshold concepts has been suggested in a geography and earth sciences context, including quantification, time, sustainability and geographical enquiry (GEES, 2006; Slinger, 2011). If we could identify and then research children's understandings of threshold concepts in geography, this would clearly be profitable for informing planning for progression. However, how would such concepts be identified?

Much of the current empirical work in geography education outlined above concerns children and young people's understandings of substantive concepts (rivers, rainforests, cities etc.) or their knowledge about particular places. There are a great many substantive concepts used in geography, from the concrete (farm) to the abstract (inequality), and complete agreement on which are the most important for a young person's progression in their learning of geography is unlikely. Lee and Shemilt commented of the equivalent work in history education that:

> It is too simple to say that research on substantive concepts failed to find patterns or change in students' ideas, but it ran into problems about whether the concepts were in any clear sense 'historical', why some should be taught rather than others, and how they related to one another.
>
> (2003, p. 14)

Instead, Lee and Shemilt focused their research on looking for characteristic pathways of development in students' understanding of second-order concepts in history, such as evidence or interpretations (Lee, 2005). This follows the interest in the history subject community on identifying Schwab's 'syntactic structures' (Schwab, 1978) within the discipline. Whilst the exact composition of history's set of second-order concepts is still debated, the general move of research focus from substantive to second-order seems to have been profitable:

> Work on pupils' second-order ideas began to provide evidence that it was possible to treat history as progressive in a somewhat analogous way to physics: pupils did not simply add to their information about the past, but acquired understandings that changed in patterned ways as they learnt about history. The concepts of progression began to mean something more specific than progress. It meant that history was not just about aggregation.
>
> (Lee and Shemilt, 2003, p. 14)

The outcome has been a series of progression models showing sets of less to more powerful ideas, which students can mobilise when learning about historical topics. Lee and Shemilt are well aware of the potential pitfalls of the ways in which such models can be understood, and their work is well sprinkled with caveats:

> The 'levels' in a progression model are not a sequence of ladder-like rungs that every student must step on as he or she climbs. Indeed, a model of the development of students' ideas does not set out a learning path for individuals

at all. Assuming it is well founded, it is valid for groups, not for individuals. That is, it sets out the ideas likely to be found in any reasonably large group of children, the likely distribution of those ideas among students of different ages, and the pattern of developing ideas we might expect.

(2003, p. 16)

Sometimes Lee and Shemilt themselves suggest teaching activities which might help students move on from an understandable, but ultimately unhelpful, idea brought from everyday life into their learning of history. At other times practising history teachers have supplied and disseminated such ideas (Lee and Shemilt, 2009). In either case, the combination of rigorous research and innovative practice is persuasive and shares some aims with the Geoprogressions project in the USA (Solem, Huynh and Boehm, 2014).

Conclusion

Where does this leave this overview of progress in geography education? We have a number of *a priori* descriptors of progress, including the four examples given earlier in this chapter. We also have a fairly large, though somewhat unsystematic, volume of research on students' understandings of substantive concepts used in geography and somewhat less on their representations of particular places. Some of this research, based on analysis of larger data sets, or on longitudinal work, suggests possible progression pathways for young people's understanding of certain substantive concepts (including some potentially troublesome ones such as 'sustainability') or in deploying geographical skills (such as graphicacy). The GeoProgressions project suggests some ways forward on collecting and consolidating research in this area, though the context and content of geography education in England are sufficiently different to that of the USA, to make a straight transfer of findings into the English planning and assessment landscape unlikely. However, the Geographical Association is offering some useful approaches to practical application in the English context, and there is clearly potential for cumulation of existing research as well as new projects here. A consideration of progression in young people's understandings of important concepts in geography, and the link between content knowledge and overarching disciplinary ways of organising, is likely to be a fruitful area of focus.

Key readings

1   Bennetts, T. (2005a) 'Progression in geographical understanding', *International Research in Geographical and Environmental Education, 14*(2), 112–32. A good overview of Bennetts' thinking in the area of progression.
2   Daugherty, R. (1996) 'Defining and measuring progression in geographical education', in E. Rawling and R. Daugherty (eds.), *Geography into the Twenty-First Century* (pp. 195–215), Chichester, West Sussex: John Wiley

and Sons Ltd. A useful overview of thinking on progression in the context of the development of the National Curriculum, including a review of available empirical research at that time; it poses some useful and still unresolved questions.

References

Alkiş, S. (2007) 'An investigation of grade 5 students' understanding of humidity concept', *Elementary Education Online*, 6 (3), 333–43.

Axia, G., Bremner, J., Deluca, P. and Andreasen, G. (1998) 'Children drawing Europe: the effects of nationality, age and teaching', *British Journal of Developmental Psychology*, 16, 423–37.

Barratt, M. and Barratt-Hacking, E. (2000) 'Changing my locality: conceptions of the future', *Teaching Geography*, 25 (1), 17–21.

Barrett, M. and Farroni, T. (1996) 'English and Italian children's knowledge of European geography', *British Journal of Developmental Psychology*, 14, 257–73.

Barrett, M. and Short, J. (1992) 'Images of European people in a group of 5–10-year-old English schoolchildren', *British Journal of Developmental Psychology*, 10, 339–63.

Béneker, T., Sanders, R., Tani, S., Taylor, L. and Van der Vaart, R. (2007) 'Teaching the geographies of urban areas: views and visions', *International Research in Geographical and Environmental Education*, 16 (3), 250–67.

Bennetts, T. (1995) 'Continuity and progression', *Teaching Geography*, 20 (2), 75–9.

Bennetts, T. (2005a) 'Progression in geographical understanding', *International Research in Geographical and Environmental Education*, 14 (2), 112–32.

Bennetts, T. (2005b) 'The links between understanding, progression and assessment in the secondary geography curriculum', *Geography*, 90 (2), 152–70.

Biddulph, M. and Lambert, D. (2017) Making progress in school geography: issues, challenges and enduring questions, in O. Muniz Solari, M. Solem and R. Boehem (eds.) (2017) *Learning Progressions in Geography Education: International Perspectives*, Cham, Switzerland: Springer International.

Blaut, J. (1987) 'Place perception in perspective', *Journal of Environmental Psychology*, 7 (4), 297–305.

Bloom, B. (ed.) (1956) *Taxonomy of Educational Objectives: The Classification of Educational Goals. Handbook 1: Cognitive Domain*, New York: David McKay.

Cabral, S. and Kaivola, T. (2005) 'Imagine the world', *Teaching Geography*, 30 (2), 86–90.

Cin, M. and Yazici, H. (2002) 'The influence of direct experience on children's ideas about the formation of the natural scenery', *International Research in Geographical and Environmental Education*, 11 (1), 5–14.

Daugherty, R. (1996) 'Defining and measuring progression in geographical education', in E. Rawling and R. Daugherty (eds.), *Geography into the Twenty-First Century*, Chichester, West Sussex: John Wiley and Sons Ltd.

Department for Education (2014a) Geography GCE AS and A level subject content, Available at: https://www.gov.uk/government/uploads/system/uploads/attachment_data/file/388857/GCE_AS_and_A_level_subject_content_for_geography.pdf [Accessed 28 May 2016].

Department for Education (2014b) Geography GCSE subject content, Available at: https://www.gov.uk/government/uploads/system/uploads/attachment_data/file/301253/GCSE_geography.pdf [Accessed 28 May 2016].

Disney, A. (2005) 'Children's images of a distant locality', *International Research in Geographical and Environmental Education*, 14 (4), 330–5.

Dove, J. (1998) 'Alternative conceptions about the weather', *School Science Review*, 79 (289), 65–9.

Dove, J. (1999) *Immaculate Misconceptions*, Sheffield: Geographical Association.

Dove, J. (2000) 'Conceptions of rainforests', *Teaching Geography*, 25 (1), 32–4.

Eyres, M. and Garner, W. (1998) 'Children's ideas about landscapes', in S. Scoffham (ed.), *Primary Sources*, Sheffield: Geographical Association.

Geographical Association (2014) An assessment and progression framework for geography, Available at: http://www.geography.org.uk/news/2014nationalcurriculum/assessment/ [Accessed 28 May 2016].

Geography Earth and Environmental Sciences (GEES) (2006) 'Special issue on threshold concepts and troublesome knowledge', *Planet*, 17. Available at: http://www.gees.ac.uk/pubs/planet/index.htm#P17 [Accessed 12 September 2011].

Goswami, U. (2008) 'Principles of learning, implications for teaching: A cognitive neuroscience perspective', *Journal of Philosophy of Education*, 42 (3–4), 381–99.

Gould, P. and White, R. (1974) *Mental Maps*, Harmondsworth: Penguin Books Ltd.

Graham, J. and Lynn, S. (1989) 'Mud huts and flints: children's images of the Third World', *Education 3–13*, 17 (2), 29–32.

Halocha, J. (1998) 'The European dimension', in S. Scoffham (ed.), *Primary Sources: Research Findings in Primary Geography*, Sheffield: Geographical Association.

Harrington, V. (1998) 'Teaching about distant places', in S. Scoffham (ed.), *Primary Sources: Research Findings in Primary Geography*, Sheffield: Geographical Association.

Hart, R. (1987) 'Environmental psychology or behavioural geography? Either way it was a good start', *Journal of Environmental Psychology*, 7 (4), 321–9.

Harwood, D. and Rawlings, K. (2001) 'Assessing young children's freehand sketch maps of the world', *International Research in Geographical and Environmental Education*, 10 (1), 20–45.

Holloway, S. and Valentine, G. (2000) 'Corked hats and Coronation Street: British and New Zealand children's imaginative geographies of the other', *Childhood*, 7 (3), 335–57.

Huynh, N. T., Solem, M. and Bednarz, S. W. (2015) 'A road map for learning progressions research in geography', *Journal of Geography*, 114 (2), 69–79.

Jefferis, T. and Chapman, S. (2005) 'Using ICT as a bridging unit', *Teaching Geography*, 30 (2), 108–12.

Keiny, S. (2008) "Conceptual change' as both revolutionary and evolutionary process', *Teachers and Teaching: Theory and Practice*, 14 (1), 61–72.

Knox, H. and Simmonds, M. (2016). Assessment without levels – a new start. *Teaching Geography*, 41(2), 56–9.

Krathwohl, D. (2002) 'A revision of Bloom's taxonomy: An overview', *Theory into Practice*, 41 (4), 212–18.

Lambert, D. (2011a) 'Reviewing the case for geography, and the 'knowledge turn' in the English National Curriculum', *Curriculum Journal*, 22 (2), 243–64.

Lambert, D. (2011b) 'The lie of the land (revisited)', *Teaching Geography*, 36 (1), 24–5.

Lee, P. (2005) 'Putting principles into practice: understanding history', in M. Donovan and J. Bransford (eds.), *How Students Learn: History in the Classroom*, Washington, DC: The National Academies Press.

Lee, P. and Ashby, R. (2000) 'Progression in historical understanding among students ages 7–14', in P. Stearns, P. Seixas and S. Wineburg (eds.), *Knowing Teaching and Learning History: National and International Perspectives*, New York: New York University Press.

Lee, P. and Shemilt, D. (2003) 'A scaffold, not a cage: progression and progression models in history', *Teaching History*, 113, 13–23.

Lee, P. and Shemilt, D. (2004) '"I just wish we could go back in the past and find out what really happened": progression in understanding about historical accounts', *Teaching History*, 117, 25–31.

Lee, P. and Shemilt, D. (2009) 'Is any explanation better than none? Over-determined narratives, senseless agencies and one-way streets in students' learning about cause and consequence in history', *Teaching History*, 137, 42–9.

Mackintosh, M. (2004) 'Children's understanding of rivers: is there need for more constructivist research in primary geography?', in S. Catling and F. Martin (eds.), *Researching Primary Geography (Register of Researching Primary Geography Special Publication No. 1)*, London: Register of Research in Primary Geography.

Marriott, A. (2007) 'The transition from A level to degree geography', *Teaching Geography*, 31 (2), 49–50.

Marsden, W. (1995) *Geography 11–16: Rekindling Good Practice*, London: David Fulton.

Matthews, M. (1992) *Making Sense of Place: Children's Understanding of Large Scale Environments*, Hemel Hempstead, UK: Harvester Wheatsheaf.

Meyer, J. and Land, R. (2003) *Threshold concepts and troublesome knowledge: linkages to ways of thinking and practising within the disciplines, Enhancing Teaching-Learning Environments in Undergraduate Courses Project, Occasional Report 4*, Edinburgh: University of Edinburgh, Available at: http://www.etl.tla.ed.ac.uk/docs/ETLreport4.pdf [Accessed 28 May 2016].

Monk, P. (2016) 'Progression in fieldwork', *Teaching Geography*, 41 (1), 20–1.

Muniz Solari, O., Solem, M. and Boehem, R. (eds.) (2017) *Learning Progressions in Geography Education: International Perspectives*, Cham, Switzerland: Springer International.

Piaget, J. and Weil, A. (1951) 'The development in children of the idea of the homeland and of relations with other countries', *International Social Science Bulletin, UNESCO*, 3, 561–78.

Pickering, S. (2008) 'What do children really learn? A discussion to investigate the effect that school partnerships have on children's understanding, sense of values and perceptions of a distant place', *GeogEd*, 2 (1), Article 3, Available at: http://www.geography.org.uk/gtip/geogede-journal/vol2issue1/article3/ [Accessed 28 May 2016].

Picton, O. (2008) 'Teaching and learning about distant places: conceptualising diversity', *International Research in Geographical and Environmental Education*, 17 (3), 227–49.

Picton, O. (2010) 'Shrinking world? Globalisation at key stage 3', *Teaching Geography*, 35 (1), 10–17.

Pintrich, P., Marx, R. and Boyle, R. (1993) 'Beyond cold conceptual change: the role of motivational beliefs and classroom contextual factors in the process of conceptual change', *Review of Educational Research*, 63 (2), 167–99.

Rawling, E. (2015). Curriculum change and examination reform for geography 14–19. *Geography*, 100 (3), 164–8.

Rawling, E. (2016). The geography curriculum 5–19: what does it all mean? *Teaching Geography*, 41 (1), 6–9.

Rutland, A. (1998) 'English children's geo-political knowledge of Europe', *British Journal of Developmental Psychology*, 16, 439–45.

SCAA (1994) *Geography in the National Curriculum, Draft Proposals*, London: SCAA/HMSO.

Schmeinck, D. (2006) 'Images of the world or do travel experiences and the presence of media influence children's perception of the world?', in D. Schmeinck (ed.), *Research on Learning and Teaching in Primary Geography*, Karlsruhe, Germany: Pädagogische Hochschule Karlsruhe.

Schwab, J. (1978) *Science, Curriculum and Liberal Education*, Chicago: University of Chicago Press.

Slinger, J. (2011) *Threshold concepts in secondary geography education*, Paper presented at the Geographical Association Annual Conference, Guildford, University of Surrey April 2011, Available at: www.geography.org.uk/download/GA_Confl1Slinger.pdf [Accessed 28 May 2016].

Smith, J., diSessa, A. and Roschelle, J. (1993) 'Misconceptions reconceived: a constructivist analysis of knowledge in transition', *Journal of the Learning Sciences*, 3 (2), 115–63.

Solem, M., Huynh, N. T., and Boehm, R. (eds.) (2014). *Learning Progressions for Maps, Geospatial Technology, and Spatial Thinking: A Research Handbook*. Washington DC: the Association of American Geographers, Available at: http://www.ncrge.org/wp-content/uploads/2014/02/GeoProgressions-Handbook_FINAL.pdf [Accessed 28 May 2016].

Stillwell, R. and Spencer, C. (1974) 'Children's early preferences for other nations and their subsequent acquisition of knowledge about those nations', *European Journal of Social Psychology*, 3 (3), 345–9.

Strommen, E. (1995) 'Lions and tigers and bears, oh my! Children's conceptions of forests and their inhabitants', *Journal of Research in Science Teaching*, 32 (7), 683–98.

Taylor, L. (2008) 'Key concepts and medium term planning', *Teaching Geography*, 33 (2), 50–54.

Taylor, L. (2009) 'Children constructing Japan: material practices and relational learning', *Children's Geographies*, 7 (2), 173–89.

Taylor, L. (2011) 'Investigating change in young people's understandings of Japan: a study of learning about a distant place', *British Educational Research Journal*, 37 (6), 1033–54.

Vanderbeck, R. and Dunkley, C. (2003) 'Young people's narratives of rural-urban difference', *Children's Geographies*, 1 (2), 241–59.

Walker, G. (2004) 'Urban children's perceptions of rural villages in England', in S. Catling and F. Martin (eds.), *Researching Primary Geography*, London: Register of Research in Primary Geography.

Walshe, N. (2008) 'Understanding students' conceptions of sustainability', *Environmental Education Research*, 14 (5), 537–58.

Wiegand, P. (1991) 'The "known world" of primary school children', *Geography*, 76 (2), 143–9.

Wiegand, P. (1998) 'Children's free recall sketch maps of the world on a spherical surface', *International Research in Geographical and Environmental Education*, 7 (1), 67–83.

Chapter 7

Understanding conceptual development in school geography

Clare Brooks

> Place, space and scale are arguably the three really big ideas that underpin school geography. Opening up these ideas a little ... shows their scope and potential. We can see the relevance of being able to 'think geographically' to anyone living in the world and wanting to understand and respond to the challenges facing them during the 21st century.
>
> (Lambert, 2009, p. 4)

Introduction

Concepts are at the centre of geography education. However, even in the fairly recent past, concepts and in particular their role in the geography curriculum, have been somewhat contested. The 2007 Geography National Curriculum (GNC) expressed the Programme of Study through Key Concepts and Key Processes. However, this approach was critiqued due to its lack of specific reference to geographical knowledge, and the seemingly knowledge-weak school curriculum it produced (see DfE, 2010). In its place, the 2014 Geography National Curriculum and the Department for Education's public examination guidance makes little explicit reference to concepts. And yet, geographical concepts and conceptual understanding are fundamental to structuring and supporting how people learn geography. The lack of explicit reference to concepts in official curriculum documents has shifted the focus onto teachers to consider how to use geographical concepts to support geographical thinking. It is the aim of this chapter to offer some ways that geography educators can think about geography concepts.

As the opening quotation to this chapter suggests, how we understand concepts determines how we use them, and can affect our understanding of geographical phenomena. This chapter will explore how concepts have been used and understood in geography education, and how they relate to concepts in academic geography.

Concepts in the curriculum

An examination of the Department for Education's guidance for Geography reveals an interesting shift in the role that concepts play in the educational vernacular. The word 'concept' itself is missing from both the National Curriculum Programmes of Study for Key Stages 1 and 2, and that for Key Stage 3 (see DfE, 2013a, b). Whilst, there are no direct references to concepts themselves, place knowledge does appear in Key Stage 1 and 2, and frequent references are made to the intention that pupils will be able to 'understand' and 'interpret'. At Key Stage 3, one reference is made to concepts, but this is in relation to models and theories, and no explicit mention is made of any particular geographical concept.

The Department for Education guidance for GCSE (DfE, 2014a) and GCE AS and A Level subject content (DfE, 2014b) also tend to focus on content rather than concepts but concepts are more evident. Within the GCSE Progression statement, reference is made to 'the subjects' conceptual frameworks' (2014a, p. 4), although these are not defined, and pupils are encouraged to develop their ability to make generalisations, abstractions and synthesis. Some reference is also made to conceptual understanding around Place (ibid., p. 5).

It is at advanced level that concepts make an explicit appearance. In the DfE (2014b) guidance on GCE AS and A Level subject content, four concepts are listed (p. 3): place, space, scale and environment. Furthermore, a claim is made that these concepts underpin the previous National Curriculum Programmes of Study and GCSE guidance. Despite this claim that geographical concepts underpin the curriculum, they are not an explicit part of it until GCSE and GCE level. If we understand concepts as being a vital part of how one develops geographical understanding, then it is essential that they feature in teachers' plans to follow the above programmes of study. But to do that, teachers need to be clear on what geographical concepts are and how they can be useful.

What is a concept?

Before exploring the meaning of the term 'concept', and how it has been used in geography education, it is useful to consider why they are important. 'Concept' is a fairly general term that is used in a variety of contexts to mean different things. Concepts can be concrete and fairly unambiguous (like 'rain') or more abstract and difficult to define (like 'culture'). Within geography education, concepts have been used to describe and categorise geographical knowledge and understanding. However, there has not been a consensus as to which concepts are 'key' or how they should be used by teachers. To help us to understand these differences, I suggest that concepts are used from three different perspectives each relating to a different approach to teaching and learning. Key to this categorisation is an understanding that there are three dimensions to education: the curriculum, pedagogy and the learner, as represented in GA's curriculum making diagram (see Lambert and Morgan 2010, p. 50). Each of the categorisations below foreground one of these dimensions:

- *hierarchical* – concepts as a content container, with the focus on the subject;
- *organisational* – concepts helping the linking of ideas, experiences and processes, with the focus on pedagogy;

- *developmental* – concepts reflecting the process of deepening understanding, with the focus on the learner.

I suggest that these categorisations are useful to distinguish which particular perspective is being emphasised. However, these categorisations are not inherent to the concepts themselves but illustrate how they can be used in curriculum making. In this respect they are a useful tool for examining curriculum documents critically. In the next section, I take each dimension in turn.

Hierarchical concepts

One of the most common uses of 'concepts' is to group the contents of the subject: as a container for geographical ideas or content. In this respect, the word is used to represent ideas, generalisations or theories. When concepts are used in this way, they are represented as hierarchical: so some concepts are described as 'key', or 'foundational' or 'main'. Taylor (2008) refers to concepts of this type as 'classifiers', as they classify the geographical knowledge to be taught.

In his review of concepts in geography (at the time of the introduction of the 'concept-free' Original Orders of the Geography National Curriculum), Marsden (1995) suggested that concepts have two dimensions: abstract–concrete, and technical–vernacular (everyday). In my adaption of Marsden's classification (see Figure 7.1), we can see how these dimensions result in different types of concepts.

It is worth noting that some readers may disagree with my categorisation in Figure 7.1. Indeed, it is debatable whether 'beach' is indeed a concrete concept. Geomorphologists and surfers may have some disagreement about what constitutes a 'beach'. The precise meanings of concepts are often debated, for example a concept such as 'place' will mean different things to different specialists: one person's concrete concept, can be highly abstract for another. In addition, there will be some discussion as to whether some concepts are geographical: time is a key part of geographical analysis, but is not always considered a geographical concept.

The examples used in Figure 7.1 were chosen from a list of 'Main Concepts' taken from the Physical Geography section of a Singaporean Geography 'O' level (equivalent to GCSE) examination syllabus. My reason for doing this is twofold: first, to demonstrate how concepts can be used in different contexts (i.e. a 'main

		Dimension 2	
		Technical	Vernacular
Dimension 1	Abstract	Abstract-technical e.g. Adaption	Abstract-vernacular e.g. Erosion
	Concrete	Concrete-technical e.g. Abrasion	Concrete-vernacular e.g. Beach

Figure 7.1 Dimensions of hierarchical concepts (adapted from Marsden, 1995).

concept' in Singapore is not necessarily the same as a 'key concept' in the English Geography National Curriculum). Second, concepts can demonstrate both these dimensions of being abstract-concrete and technical-vernacular. The two dimensions are useful because they show that some concepts are more commonplace (vernacular) and more concrete than others. Concepts that are abstract–technical are more 'difficult' to understand than those that are concrete-vernacular. For curriculum makers this differentiates substantive geographical content, and enables them to structure content from the concrete-vernacular towards abstract-technical concepts: in this sense these concepts are hierarchical. This kind of classification is often used in examination specifications and other curriculum documents.

The key concepts in the 2007 Geography National Curriculum (e.g. Place and Space) can be viewed as hierarchical concepts. They are used to represent geographical ideas that are both technical and abstract. In Rawling's book *Planning your Key Stage 3 Geography Curriculum*, she refers to these concepts as 'fundamental ideas in geography' (2007, p. 17). Written specifically to support geography teachers implementing the 2007 Geography National Curriculum, Rawling's book breaks down each of the GNC key concepts, illustrating how the concept is understood within geography, and how students can experience them. This breakdown illustrates the hierarchical nature of these concepts, and Rawling shows how the curriculum can be designed to scaffold students' learning towards understanding the abstract-technical concepts. In particular, Rawling draws attention to the hierarchical nature of the key concepts, describing Space and Place as the most generalised and abstract of these ideas which are 'standing at the top of a hierarchy of ideas in geography' (pp. 23–4). Rawling's approach to the handling of these concepts is very clear. As content containers and abstract ideas, she argues that they should not be used as a starting point for curriculum planning, but more of a skeleton 'on which to hang the more detailed curriculum flesh' (p. 17). When concepts are used as content containers, it is possible to distinguish between the abstract-concrete, and technical-vernacular nature of content knowledge (and hence are often referred to in the academic literature as substantive concepts). In this respect they are helpful in determining the 'ends' or outcomes of the curriculum, but not necessarily the process or 'means' of how to achieve that end.

This way of thinking about concepts is particularly valuable when they are so absent in the Department for Education's Programme of Study. A programme of study articulated without concepts, runs the risk of focusing entirely on knowledge or skill acquisition, and not on how to develop the building blocks of geographical understanding. Not only will this affect progression in geographical learning, but it will also affect how we distinguish what is distinctively different about learning geography from other school subject areas.

Organisational concepts

Another approach to the use of concepts in geography education is to view them as organisational. Whilst the hierarchical nature of concepts described above has a degree of organisation embedded within it, the focus is not on how the concept is used, but in how it relates to geographical knowledge. Both Leat's (1998) 'big concepts' and Taylor's (2008) 'organisational concepts' use concepts as a way of linking everyday experience with higher-level geographical ideas. The distinction here is that the concepts are seen as a tool in developing geographical learning.

Leat used the term 'big concepts' in his *Thinking through Geography* publication (1998). This, and subsequent publications, became very influential in geography education, as the geographical interpretation of the Thinking Skills movement (and in line with other cognitive acceleration strategies). Thinking Skills were adopted as part of the New Labour Key Stage 3 Strategies and influenced geography education pedagogy in the first decade of the twenty-first century. *Thinking through Geography* featured a series of thinking skills activities relevant to geography education. The focus of the publication (and the strategies contained within) was to promote children's thinking, and so the concepts emphasised were those that would promote 'thinking'. Rather than seeing these concepts as goals of learning in geography education, Leat suggests they function as a way of developing understanding in geography:

> We believe that it is helpful to conceive of geography in terms of a number of central underpinning concepts, through which much subject matter is understood.
>
> (Leat, 1998, p. 161)

He acknowledges that the list of Big Concepts is not a definitive one and is likely to change, but includes:

- cause and effect;
- classification;
- decision making;
- development;
- inequality;
- location; and
- planning and systems.

Taylor (2008) describes these concepts as generic cognitive processes, and whilst they each have a role in geography education, they are not uniquely or distinctly geographical in nature. Indeed, a similar list would not look out of place in history or science education. Leat (1998) acknowledges this by arguing that 'the main concern of this book is students' learning, not the sanctity of the subject' (p. 167), and that these concepts are useful to help students to make sense of the thinking scenarios that they are faced with, in the sense that they are used organisationally to develop the learning.

Taylor (2008) differentiates Leat's list of concepts from her own 'organisational' concepts. Taylor outlines that her four organisational concepts were developed from engagement with the work of Massey (see 2005) and so they have a distinctively (but not exclusively) geographical function:

- diversity;
- change;
- interaction; and
- perception and representation.

The organisational nature of these concepts stems from how Taylor suggests they are used, particularly in how they create a bridge between the hierarchical substantive concepts of place, space and time and the geographical enquiry questions which relate to the topic being studied. This is illustrated in Figure 7.2 below, adapted from Taylor's original article (2008).

These concepts are organisational because they provide a link between the abstract concepts of place, time and space, and the enquiry questions that relate to the topic being studied. Taylor does not suggest that these concepts should necessarily be shared with students, but that these organisational concepts are useful in curriculum planning.

Taylor acknowledges that her work on organisational concepts has been influenced by 'second order concepts' as they appear within school history. (Indeed, it is also interesting to note that Taylor includes time as a geographical concept, when other categorisations explored in this chapter prefer to emphasise Place and Space as stronger geographical concepts.) In history education, second order concepts (cause, consequence, significance, change) are used to shape enquiry that will lead to deeper understanding of substantive concepts (such as democracy, revolution and empire). Within history education, there is a clear demarcation between these second order concepts, which are organisational and enquiry-based, from the more substantive (content-based) historical concepts (see Counsell, 2011).

PLACE		SPACE	TIME
DIVERSITY	INTERACTION	CHANGE	PERCEPTION AND REPRESENTATION
- How and why does it vary over space? (Differences in form, function, patterns of distribution etc.) - How does this affect different groups and how is it managed?	- How are different elements linked? (Inc. physical-human; human-human; physical-physical) - How does change in one element knock on to others? How might this affect different groups? - What are the 'power-geometries' of the links? -What can we learn about it by 'zooming in and out' of scales?	- How and why has it been different in the past? - What has the nature, rate and extent of the change been like? - How might it be different in the future?(Prediction) - Which of the different future paths are more/less desirable? - How can the more desirable outcomes be achieved?	- How do different people experience it? (Directly or indirectly) - How do they communicate this experience? How does this affect their own and other people's views and actions?

Figure 7.2 Questions afforded by each organising concept (adapted from Taylor, 2008, p. 52).

Organisational concepts are different to hierarchical concepts, as they are not the goal of learning geography but a facilitating tool to get to those goals, and hence they emphasise linking processes and ideas rather than outcomes.

Developmental concepts

The third approach to discussing concepts is the least common in geography education. The definition of key concepts in the 2007 Geography National Curriculum helped to define hierarchical concepts as the dominant approach in geography education. Prior to that, concepts were often referred to in relation to the child and their own learning, rather than on concepts as a way of structuring or organising knowledge.

In Hopwood's research, he explored students' own conceptualisation of school geography, which he argues is an important influence on their learning (2004, 2011). Hopwood demonstrates how students use their conceptualisation of the subject as a way of filtering and processing their geography lessons: as a way of making meaning. In this respect, concepts are ideas, internally held, that are adapted or modified in the light of new information.

I have included this distinction because I think it is a particularly useful one for teachers. Research into concepts in education generally illustrates that views of knowledge in the curriculum can be divided into two schools of thought: exogenic and endogenic (Gergen, 2001). In the exogenic approach, knowledge is seen as external to the student, and the process of teaching is one in which 'outside' concepts are brought to the student. In this sense concepts are determined by the teacher (as the subject's conduit) and could be hierarchical and/or organisational. In the endogenic approach, knowledge is developed from within. In this respect, concepts are developmental, and are used by the student to make sense of a lesson's content.

With this alternative way of understanding concepts, Hopwood's research is particularly important because he illustrates that students' conceptual understanding of geography is often different to the hierarchical or organisational way of presenting concepts, and also that students' concepts are unique to the individuals. The implication of this finding is that whilst teachers may organise their curriculums around hierarchical or organisational concepts, the way that students make sense of their lessons may be determined by their own conceptual frameworks.

Using concepts to build understanding

The absence of any explicit mention of concepts in the 2014 Geography National Curriculum Programme of Study, requires geography teachers to take their own stance on how they introduce, use and develop geographical concepts in their teaching. Whether concepts are seen as hierarchical, organisational or developmental, teachers need to consider how they can support learners in developing

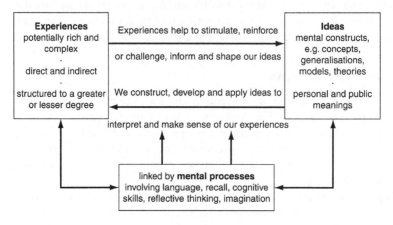

Figure 7.3 The roots of understanding (Bennetts, 2005).

geographical understanding, and how they can be used in planning meaningful geographical learning experiences.

Bennetts (2005) represents the process of developing understanding in geography education with the diagram in Figure 7.3.

In this diagram, concepts are grouped together with generalisations, models and theories as the ideas and mental constructs that enable learners to make sense of their experiences. To use the language analogy made popular by the Geographical Association's manifesto *A Different View* (2009), concepts can then be viewed as the 'grammar' of geography that we use to make sense of the world (or the vocabulary) and how we experience it. Bennett's diagram places concepts with both personal and public meanings, illustrating that they can come from the subject as well as from the student.

Geographical concepts

The idea of threshold concepts has become influential in geography education. However, it is important to distinguish threshold concepts from academic geography, and, how they both relate to the typology already used in this chapter. Firstly, it is important to outline what threshold concepts are.

The idea of threshold concepts was developed by Meyer and Land (2005) in relation to economics in higher education. They define a threshold concept as:

A threshold concept can be considered as akin to a portal, opening up a new and previously inaccessible way of thinking about something. It represents a transformed way of understanding, or interpreting, or viewing something without which the learner cannot progress. As a consequence of comprehending a threshold concept there may thus be a transformed internal view of subject matter, subject landscape, or even world view.

(p. 174)

They identify that threshold concepts have particular characteristics that distinguish them from other (lesser) concepts. For a concept to be 'threshold', it is likely to have the following features: it is:

- *transformative* – in that once it has been understood, it changes the way one views the phenomena;
- *troublesome* – in that it can seem counter-intuitive, alien or incoherent;
- *irreversible* – so that once understood, one cannot go back to how they thought before;
- *integrative* – in that it brings together aspects of the subject that did not appear to be related;
- *bounded* – and so delineates a particular conceptual space;
- *discursive* – and therefore incorporates an enhanced and extended use of language.

Jonathan Slinger's research for the MA in Geography Education, sought to identify a framework for looking at threshold concepts in school geography (2010). Slinger describes threshold concepts as 'existing in relational web-like patterns' which includes the following:

- using the discipline as a resource;
- viewing students as active, enquiring learners who bring their own experience to the learning processes; and
- teachers as working with the subject and the students to construct knowledge collaboratively.

Whilst Slinger doesn't go so far as to list what these concepts might be, he does acknowledge that they can operate at different levels (which he describes as basic, disciplinary and procedural) and that they can adopt a relational and situated view of knowledge, acknowledging the contested and plural nature of approaches within the discipline. In this respect, threshold concepts can be viewed from a variety of perspectives: the subject, the pedagogy and the learner, and so can be seen to cross the categorisations offered in this chapter.

Slinger's analysis highlights the geographical potential of threshold concepts, but he also concludes that defining threshold concepts in geography is not straightforward. It has been argued by proponents of the idea of threshold concepts that they are what constitute the nature of disciplinary thinking: they are in effect what distinguishes 'thinking like a geographer' from other ways of thinking.

The literature does suggest then that there may be a strong link between disciplinary concepts and threshold concepts, but that they are not necessarily the same. Once a threshold has been crossed, it changes the way you think, and much of the literature on threshold concepts suggests that it then becomes tacit and difficult to explain to others. The example used by Meyer and Land (2005) is that of price in economics. One cannot understand many of the ideas in economics without a precise understanding of 'price', and yet once understood, price becomes difficult to articulate clearly.

In geography, the concepts of place or space, are also still an area of widespread theoretical debate. Academic concepts like these are an important link between the school subject and the academic discipline, which Maude (2016) explains is because they have analytical power. However, their analytical power does not necessarily make them easy for learners to grasp.

Within academia, concepts help structure and define the future development of the discipline. For example, Jackson (2006) has argued that the geographical concepts of space and place, scale and connection, proximity and distance emphasise relational thinking, which he argues is a distinctive geographical contribution to knowledge. However, views on the significance of certain concepts can change. For instance, Castree (2005) presents a strong case for Nature as a powerful concept within geography. His book on nature is part of a series entitled Key Ideas in Geography that includes titles on *The City, Migration, Landscape, Citizenship, Rural, Mobility, Home, Scale.* Each of these titles can be seen as geographical concepts, and their focus as titles within this popular series illustrates a shifting dynamic in academic geography. This is symptomatic of the changing nature of disciplines, and is representative of our growing understanding of the world, and the ideas that shape it.

It is to be expected then that important concepts within the academic discipline will change over time. This will in turn influence school geography. Lambert and Morgan (2010) focus on the concepts of Place, Space, Scale and Interdependence, which they take care not to define in a hierarchical way (i.e. they don't refer to them as core or key), but as 'significant ideas' within geography. They argue that geography uses these 'ideas' to make sense of the world, whilst acknowledging the historical development of the concepts themselves. In the detail of their analysis, they explore the development and interpretation of these concepts, and illustrate that the concepts are sites of contestation with the academic discipline, with multiple meanings. With each of the concepts they consider the implications this has for school geography.

Lambert and Morgan (2010) hold a position that a conceptual approach shows the promise of geography education. They see concepts as a powerful mechanism to support and develop geographical understanding.

Conclusion

In this chapter, I have suggested a categorisation of concepts in geography education. Concepts can be seen as hierarchical, organisational and developmental. In each of these categorisations, concepts are used by geography educators to support the learning process, by emphasising the subject, pedagogy or the students' experiences (respectively). In this respect, concepts can be understood as powerful tools for the geography curriculum maker. The GA (Lambert, 2011) has suggested that it is useful to distinguish between:

- core knowledge (the extensive world knowledge or vocabulary of geography);
- content knowledge (the key concepts and ideas, or grammar of geography); and
- procedural knowledge (thinking geographically, and the distinctly geographical approaches to learning such as enquiry).

Should geography teachers seek to adopt or develop this approach as a way of thinking about geographical content in the curriculum, then they will need to clarify which geography concepts they wish to focus on (hierarchical), and how they will support students to develop their understanding of those concepts (organisational) and the extent to which they will support students to develop their own conceptual frameworks (developmental). Further work on threshold concepts in geography could help to achieve this.

Key readings

1   Lambert, D. and Morgan, J. (2010) *Teaching Geography 11–18: A Conceptual Approach*, Maidenhead: Open University Press. Anyone interested in exploring geography's key concepts more should start with this book. In the opening chapters David Lambert and John Morgan outline their approach to teaching with concepts, and subsequent chapters take key concepts in turn and explore how they have changed over time and their relevance for school geography.

2   Taylor, L. (2008) 'Key concepts and medium term planning' in *Teaching Geography*, 33 (2), 50–4. This article is a good introduction to organisational concepts. In this article, Liz Taylor outlines her interpretation of them, how they relate to more substantive concepts and how they can be used to identify enquiry questions.

References

Bennetts, T. (2005) 'Progression in geographical understanding', *International Research in Geographical and Environmental Education*, 14 (2), 112–32.

Castree, N. (2005) *Nature*, London: Routledge.

Counsell, C. (2011) 'What do we want students to do with historical change and continuity?', in I. Davies (ed.), *Debates in History Education*, London: Routledge.

Department for Education (DfE) (2010) *The Importance of Teaching: the Schools White Paper*, London: HMSO.

Department for Education (DfE) (2013a) *Geography Programmes of Study: Key Stages 1 and 2; National Curriculum in England*. DfE Reference: DFE-00186-2013.

Department for Education (DfE) (2013b) *Geography Programmes of Study: Key Stage 3; National Curriculum in England*. DfE Reference: DFE-00186-2013.

Department for Education (DfE) (2014a) *Geography; GCSE Subject Content*. DfE Reference: DFE-00345-2014.

Department for Education (DfE) (2014b) *Geography; GCE AS and A Level Subject Content*. DfE Reference: DFE-00693-2014.

Geographical Association (2009) *A Different View: A Manifesto from the Geographical Association*, Sheffield: Geographical Association.

Gergen, K. (2001) 'Social construction and pedagogical practice', in K. Gergen (ed.), *Social Construction in Context*, London: Sage.

Hopwood, N. (2004) 'Pupils' conceptions of geography: towards an improved understanding international research', in *Geographical and Environmental Education*, 13 (4), 348–61.

Hopwood, N. (2011) 'Young people's conceptions of geography and education', in G. Butt (ed.), *Geography, Education and the Future*, London: Continuum.

Jackson, P. (2006) 'Thinking geographically', *Geography*, 91 (3), 199–204.

Lambert, D. (2009) 'Introduction – part 1: What is living geography?', in D. Mitchell (ed.), *Living Geography*, Cambridge: Chris Kington Publishing.

Lambert, D. (2011) *The Geography National Curriculum: GA Curriculum Proposals and Rational*, Sheffield, Geographical Association.

Lambert, D. and Morgan, J. (2010) *Teaching Geography 11–18: A Conceptual Approach*, Maidenhead: Open University Press.

Leat, D. (1998) *Thinking Through Geography*, Cambridge: Chris Kington Publishing.

Marsden, W. (1995) *Geography 11–16: Rekindling Good Practice*, London: David Fulton Publishers.

Massey, D. (2005) *For Space*, London: Sage Publications.

Maude, A. (2016) 'What might powerful geographical knowledge look like?' *Geography*, 101 (2), 70–6.

Meyer, J.H.F. and Land, R. (2005) 'Threshold concepts and troublesome knowledge (2) Epistemological considerations and a conceptual framework for teaching and learning', *Higher Education*, 49, 373–88.

Rawling, E. (2007) *Planning your Key Stage 3 Geography Curriculum*, Sheffield: Geographical Association.

Slinger, J. (2010) 'Threshold concepts in secondary geography education', Unpublished dissertation, Institute of Education: University of London.

Taylor, L. (2008) 'Key concepts and medium term planning', *Teaching Geography*, 33 (2), 50–4.

Chapter 8

The enquiry approach in geography

Jane Ferretti

> The GA believes that teachers should be accountable, but also that they
> are autonomous professionals driven by educational goals and purposes.
> (Geographical Association, 2009, p. 27)

Introduction

In geography 'enquiry learning' has long been advocated as an important approach
for teachers; however, evidence (Ofsted, 2008, 2011) suggests that, although
excellent in some schools, its use in both Key Stage 3 (KS3) and Key Stage 4
(KS4) is limited. Although no longer explicit in the geography programmes of
study (DfE, 2013), enquiry is specified in the GCSE subject content (DfE, 2014),
which states that all GCSE specifications should enable students to 'develop their
competence in applying sound enquiry and investigative approaches to questions
and hypotheses (study like a geographer)' (p. 3). Whether explicit or not in curriculum documentation and specifications, enquiry learning remains an important approach to teaching geography. This chapter considers ideas surrounding
geographical enquiry, starting by linking enquiry to established-learning theories, particularly constructivism, and the importance of students being actively
involved in their own learning, and the key role that teachers play in facilitating
this. Although there may be a lack of consensus about what teachers understand
by the term 'geographical enquiry', the key debate must be about why only limited use of an enquiry approach is used in schools, whether or not this is an
inevitable result of the current demands being made on teachers and schools,
and whether the educational goals and purposes advocated by the Geographical
Association (GA) in the opening quotation are being lost as a result of the pressures of the performativity agenda.

Theory into practice

Before discussing what enquiry learning is, we need to remind ourselves that
teachers have for many years been swamped by changing policies and frequently

repeated dogma, so it is understandable that for some there is a tendency to comply with rather than question the demands made of them. This has included advice about 'pedagogy', or put rather simply 'how to teach' but pedagogy is more complex than this (for a more detailed discussion see Ferretti, 2013). It is perhaps unsurprising that many teachers rarely challenge what they are asked to do, although, as Adams (2008) points out, many feel 'frustrated and constrained' (p. 379) by the expectation that they should teach in a particular way. The danger is that teachers will increasingly focus on their daily routine, rarely drawing on their wider professional knowledge and beliefs unless specifically encouraged to consider evidence, look at research and discuss and reflect on their pedagogic practice.

One way in which teachers might build up their pedagogical expertise is through developing a better theoretical understanding of what goes on in the classroom. Freeman (2010) suggests that 'for many teachers the notion of engaging with theory may seem like an additional burden on their time; a distraction from the real world of teaching and learning' (p. 139); however, key questions such as 'how do young people learn?' and 'how can teachers encourage and support their learning?' require us to engage with and develop an understanding of learning theories (see Moore, 2000 for a useful summary of learning theories).

Constructivists including Piaget, Vygotsky and Bruner believe that learners need to build on ideas they already have in order to understand and internalise new information. Central to 'constructivism' is that learning occurs 'by making sense of what happens to us in the course of actively constructing a world for ourselves' (Barnes, 2008, p. 3). The role of teachers is vital by creating situations which will challenge young people and enable them to improve their understanding; providing information which has no connection with a learner's current view, will soon be forgotten. The constructivist view of learning stresses that learners need to be *actively* involved in their own learning, which Barnes (2008) suggests 'does not imply moving about the room or manipulating objects (though either of these might be involved), but rather attempting to interrelate, to reinterpret, to understand new experiences and ideas' (p. 2). The link between this and enquiry learning is clear and indeed is developed by Roberts (2003) who relates geographical enquiry to constructivism and especially the work of Vygotsky. The essence of enquiry learning is that students are 'enquiring actively into questions, issues or problems' (Naish et al., 1987, p. 45), and in order to do this they are using some form of 'data' to explore and develop their knowledge and understanding.

What is geographical enquiry?

The term geographical enquiry was used within the Schools' Council geography projects developed in the 1970s and 1980s and in the Geography 16–19 project. Enquiry has been included within the geography programmes of study for Key Stages 1, 2 and 3 since the inception of the Geography National Curriculum

(GNC) in 1991, although it is not explicit in the 2014 GNC. Margaret Roberts' research (1998, 2003) examined what secondary geography teachers understood by the term geographical enquiry and how they incorporated it into schemes of work for Key Stage 3. She found an impressive variety of enquiry work going on in schools, both inside and outside the classroom, with students working individually and in groups. However, perhaps her most striking finding was the considerable range of different understandings of geographical enquiry held by the teachers she interviewed, and the differences in the extent to which enquiry-based work was incorporated into lessons, not only between schools but also within departments. She found some schools making extensive use of enquiry-based learning but others only incorporating enquiry into fieldwork investigations and rarely using it in the classroom.

Roberts developed her ideas about geographical enquiry in her book *Learning through Enquiry* (2003) and a decade later in *Geography through Enquiry* (2013). She emphasises the need for students to be actively involved in their own learning and identifies four essential characteristics of enquiry: starting by creating a need to know, then using data, making sense of the data, and, finally, reflecting on learning. She recognises that geographical enquiry may take different forms and that it is not always appropriate for classes to have an open-ended project, based on independent research lasting several weeks, and suggests that 'by narrowing the scope of enquiry work, it is possible to carry out a complete enquiry from initial stimulus to the reaching of conclusions and debriefing within one or two lessons' (Roberts, 2003, p. 46).

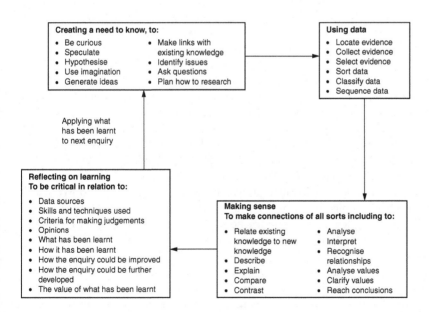

Figure 8.1 A framework for learning through enquiry (Roberts, 2003, p. 44).

The framework which Roberts suggested is not intended to show a prescribed route that all geographical enquiries should follow, although that is what some teachers may think. An investigation which is structured by the teacher but worked on independently by students is at one end of a spectrum of enquiry approaches, which also includes much more tightly structured activities, where teachers provide a stimulus that generates students' questions and helps them to find answers. Any activity which opens up problems and issues, encourages questions and begins to find solutions can be described as enquiry, and the key to this is the teacher who provides the structure to allow this to occur (Rawling, 2001). Most important of all, in my view, is the way in which teachers inspire curiosity and 'a need to know'; failing to do this, will inevitably lead to lessons that simply cover prescribed content, which may not interest or have any relevance to students and is thus likely to limit their learning.

The 2007 programme of study (POS) for KS3 geography (QCA, 2007) put considerable emphasis on geographical enquiry, which it highlighted as one of four key processes, itself a change from the previous three POS where it was listed as a skill. The 2007 POS stated that 'pupils should carry out a range of enquiries, from structured to more open ended and active' (p. 4). It provided a list of seven aspects of geographical enquiry which pupils should be able to do, the first of which is to 'ask geographical questions, thinking critically, constructively and creatively' (p. 4). Beyond the list little guidance is provided, meaning teachers had to make their own decisions about how, and how often to include geographical enquiry in schemes of work, nor did it clarify that it is not necessary for all these steps to be followed at the same time. The 2013 geography programmes of study (DfE, 2013) consists largely of a list of knowledge and skills which pupils should be taught, leaving decisions about how it should be taught to teachers themselves.

Sadly, evidence from Ofsted's 2011 report into geography teaching *Learning to Make a World of Difference* suggested that in many schools very little enquiry learning takes place at all, reporting that 'in too many of the lessons seen, there were not enough opportunities for enquiry through research, discussion, collaboration and allowing pupils to use their initiative' (p. 26); they also observed that starter activities often had little relevance to the main part of the lesson and plenaries were weak and unlikely to stimulate reflection (Ofsted, 2011). Furthermore, the Ofsted (2015) report *Key Stage 3: The Wasted Years?* while not mentioning enquiry specifically, identified geography, along with history and MFL, as a subject where 'pupils were not challenged or engaged sufficiently' (p. 6). This highlights the reluctance of some teachers to engage with geographical enquiry, which may reflect a lack of understanding of generally accepted ideas about how people learn.

Perhaps there is another related issue here too in terms of how teachers see their role: is it simply the transmission of information or should teachers be enabling students to investigate something geographical? Some of the most familiar Key Stage 3 textbooks, such as Waugh and Bushell's Key Geography series, tend to present information without encouraging students to question or challenge and indeed the increasing use of PowerPoint® presentations can tempt teachers simply to provide information as fact rather than inspire their students to ask questions and investigate for themselves. As Margaret Roberts has pointed out, enquiry as a teaching method implies a state of mind which is not about the transmission of information but about engaging students with data and in making meaning (Roberts, 2011).

The lack of consensus about the meaning of geographical enquiry, which Roberts identified in her research during the 1990s, is almost certainly the same for today's teachers, who will also have different understandings of the term geographical enquiry. Rawling (2007) suggests that 'some people think of enquiry as meaning open ended activities in which students are independently discovering things for themselves; others see it, certainly at key stage 3, as a tightly controlled set of training activities' (p. 42). But Rawling also points out that neither of these views is entirely correct because geographical enquiry can include both, and a range of other 'more-or-less structured approaches in between' (p. 42). Differences in interpretation and the issue of whether geographers need consensus are worth considering and discussing but are probably not a 'key debate'. What matters is that teachers are able to stimulate curiosity, help their students learn by investigating issues and considering evidence, and can encourage them to adopt a critical and questioning approach, which in turn helps them to widen their geographical knowledge and understanding. Of course, there are schools with strong geography departments, where students are involved in geographical enquiry, and where geography is seen as relevant and important, but perhaps too few of them. The debate must therefore be about what is threatening the place of geographical enquiry and why it is not used more frequently in geography classrooms. Young people need to be engaged in challenging enquiries to help them to develop their ability to 'think geographically', perhaps best defined as 'a unique way of seeing the world, of understanding complex problems and thinking about inter-connections at a variety of scales' (Jackson, 2006, p. 199).

Why is there a lack of geographical enquiry in schools?

In this section I consider three concerns which may be responsible for a lack of geographical enquiry in schools. These are lesson structure, assessment and issues related to skills, competencies and core knowledge.

Lesson structure

Over the last decade or more, teachers have been given extensive advice, particularly through the National Strategy (1997–2010), about teaching and learning strategies, learning styles, assessment, behaviour management and lesson structure. The publications produced by the National Strategy were advisory rather than statutory, however, schools often felt pressured to adopt advice given by Local Authorities through their Strategy consultants and also by Ofsted, whose inspectors expected to see evidence of these preferred practices. One of the results has been that teachers feel, and sometimes are, obliged to structure learning by planning three-part lessons, including a starter, development activities and a plenary, and to share lesson objectives and learning outcomes with the class at the start of each lesson. There is much which could be debated about the three-part lesson, but one particular aspect to consider is the impact it can have on enquiry learning. Roberts' (2003) four essential characteristics of the enquiry process can certainly be incorporated into the three-part model, for example, by creating 'a need to know' as a starter and using the plenary as an opportunity to 'reflect on learning', but it seems this rarely happens. One reason for this, as Davidson (2006) points out, is the impact which sharing learning objectives at the start of lessons can have on the way students engage with lessons. Davidson stresses the importance of starting lessons in ways which stimulate and engage students, providing them with a purpose for learning and encouraging them to ask questions and to make sense of information for themselves. Davidson also points out that sharing lesson objectives at the start of lessons can have a demotivating effect and curtail the process of enquiry. Furthermore, opportunities for linking with students' own lives and experiences are lost, and there is a tendency for information to be presented as fact rather than debatable issues worth investigating (Davidson, 2006). This is supported by comments from Ofsted (2011), which reports seeing geography lessons where lesson objectives were simply copied off the board, starters had little relevance to the rest of the lesson and plenaries were no more than a summary, often foreshortened by lack of time.

Unfortunately, some teachers have focused on lesson structure at the expense of adopting teaching strategies, such as geographical enquiry, which might not fit easily into the three-part formula. Starters may be chosen to grab the class's attention rather than to encourage curiosity or speculation about a geographical issue, and plenaries may simply summarise rather than encourage reflection. School leaders often implement changes hoping to impress Ofsted and certainly the three-part lesson is now almost ubiquitous, thus it is somewhat ironic that Ofsted's 2011 report into geography found that

> lessons which consistently used a rigid three-part structure did not allow sufficiently for spontaneity and creativity in students' learning. Such lessons also did not always allow them opportunities, the most academically able pupils in particular, to develop the skills of planning and organisation, take responsibility for their own learning or work independently.
>
> (p. 26)

In other words, the three-part lesson, especially when rigidly adhered to, can stifle geographical enquiry.

Assessment

Another concern is to do with assessment. Since 1997, the UK government has increasingly 'sought to inform teachers not only what to teach ... but also how to teach' (Adams, 2008, p. 377). Adams points out that government guidance, such as that issued through the National Strategies, clearly suggests that adopting particular teaching methods 'will directly lead to high quality teaching that will result in increases in pupil attainment' (p. 377). Going hand in hand with this is an assumption that test results are the only way to demonstrate student attainment, with little acknowledgement that learning can take place in different ways and with different outcomes. A consequence of this results-driven approach is the unrelenting pressure on teachers to show that pupils are making progress week by week, term by term, and year by year, resulting in frequent 'levelled' assessments with increasing use of sublevels to show the all-important 'progression'. The demise of national curriculum levels seems to have done little to abate this practice with schools now using a variety of ways to mark pupils' work with numbers and grades and record 'progress'. Teachers are accused of 'teaching to the test' especially at GCSE and A Level but who can blame them? This quotation from Barker (2010) will resonate with many:

> [T]he dominance of the performance regime has masked ... the extent to which official curriculum requirements, and the selected measures of success (e.g. the five A* to C GCSE grades threshold), have distorted and changed the nature of education. Schools teach to the test ... reduce the time devoted to non-examinable activities and concentrate attention on borderline candidates.
>
> (pp. 113–14)

It may also explain why some teachers are rarely using geographical enquiry, as evidenced by Ofsted (2011), which refers to narrow prescriptive approaches and a focus on covering the content suggesting that 'teaching programmes met the examination requirements but lacked imagination and stimulus for the students' (p. 33). Teachers naturally worry about examination results, but this concern can lead them to focus on 'delivering' content and they perhaps feel that using an enquiry approach will impact on their results. On the other hand, some examination specifications explicitly advocate enquiry learning; for example, the Edexcel GCSE Geography specification B 'is framed by geographical enquiry questions that encourage an investigative approach' (Edexcel 2016), and the Eduqas GCSE Geography A specification states that it

> develops an enquiry approach allows enquiry-based learning to the study of geographical information, issues and concepts. It is based on the principle that geographical education should enable learners to become critical and reflective thinkers by engaging them actively in the enquiry process.
>
> (Eduqas, 2016, p. 3)

Teachers often remain unconvinced by this rhetoric, anxious to focus on the content and examination skills they feel are needed for success. Despite expecting students to undertake two days of enquiry *through* fieldwork, its assessment through examination at GCSE may potentially curtail these experiences of the enquiry process.

Skills, competencies and core knowledge

A further concern relates to the different emphasis placed on skills, competencies and 'core' knowledge in the curriculum. The 2007 KS3 Curriculum review resulted in the publication of a curriculum overview called the Big Picture (QCDA); this emphasised the importance of skills, particularly personal, learning and thinking skills (PLTS), and led some schools to redesign their KS3 curriculum with a focus on competencies and skills-based curricula, often through the integration of geography with other humanities subjects. Lambert (2008) points out the dangers of this asking: 'Don't we care *what* young people are taught? Aren't we interested in *what* they are learning?' (p. 209). Reorganising the curriculum to focus on skills instead of subjects threatens geography in a number of ways, including threatening investigative geography and geographical enquiry. It usually leads to less time being allocated to the subject and a reduced focus on subject knowledge; and, in addition, these changes may also involve non-specialists teaching geography and geographers themselves teaching other subjects. Although we should be pleased that geography is a subject which can contribute to developing skills, there is a risk that this approach devalues it as a subject in its own right; it should be emphasised that genuine geographical enquiry is not a means of learning transferrable skills but an approach to learning *geography* and developing a better understanding of geographical issues.

On the face of it, the White Paper, *The Importance of Teaching* (DfE, 2010) might have been seen to address this issue. It indicated that teachers should be given more responsibility for what they teach, claiming that 'at present, the National Curriculum includes too much that is not essential knowledge, and there is too much prescription about how to teach' (p. 10) and that this is 'weighing teachers down and squeezing out room for innovation, creativity, deep learning and intellectual exploration' (p. 40). It promised a revised National Curriculum with a greater focus on subject content which would 'outline core knowledge in the traditional subject disciplines' (p. 42). In the event, the geography programmes of study for 2014 were presented as lists of content divided into sections: locational knowledge, place knowledge, human and physical geography and geographical skills and fieldwork. Far from relieving teachers, it became much more prescriptive, creating a long list of topics that had to be taught, which was far more extensive than in the previous programmes of study. It presents considerable problems for teachers in both primary and secondary state-funded schools, which have a statutory obligation to teach the national curriculum, and it is hard to see how everything can be covered especially where geography is taught infrequently (as in many primary schools), or where schools have moved to a 2-year Key Stage 3. Further questions will be raised as increasing numbers of schools become academies, where teaching the national curriculum is not a requirement.

The 2010 White Paper also announced the introduction of the English Baccalaureate (E.Bacc) awarded to students who secure A* to C passes at GCSE in English, mathematics, a science, a language and a humanity, which must be either history or geography. This has provided opportunities for geography; the status of the subject has improved and uptake at GCSE has increased substantially rising from 187,022 entries in 2012 to 228,078 (Geographical Association, 2015), remaining the eighth most popular subject at GCSE; this is probably as a result of schools striving to improve the percentage of students achieving the E.Bacc. Encouraging young people to ask questions about real issues, to search for answers using a wide range of skills and information, and to think critically about issues is an essential ingredient in helping them to 'think geographically', and I see it as important that an enquiry approach is not thrown out in a rush to rationalise and create space in the curriculum.

Conclusion

Teachers need to have time to read and reflect on their pedagogy, not only independently but with other teachers and teacher educators. Their reflection should go beyond simply deciding what particular teaching strategy or approach to use and most teachers certainly realise that improving their practice depends on more than adopting particular approaches advocated by government agencies, and that these alone are not the key to transforming their own performance or that of the young people they teach. Indeed, it could be argued that some of these approaches, including the three-part lesson, have had a negative impact on geography lessons and may be partly responsible for the fact that geographical enquiry is not a strong feature of practice in many schools. Both Davidson (2006, 2009) and Roberts (2010) have raised concerns about the way in which starters and plenaries are used as part of a routine, and that lessons can lack any focus on geography's big ideas or how students' *geographical* understanding can be developed. Ofsted continues to see schools where geography teachers are reluctant to change teaching approaches in order to make geography more relevant and challenging, relying instead on textbooks and work that occupies rather than engages students (see Ofsted, 2011, 2015).

An enquiry approach to geography starts with an engaging and worthwhile question about a real issue, something which intrigues learners and inspires them to find out more. It leads them to use different kinds of information and skills to find answers and construct their own knowledge. It helps them to evaluate information and to empathise and respect the views of others. It is a very powerful way in which young people can understand contentious issues and develop their geographical knowledge and understanding. So is this incompatible with the demands of teaching today? In my view the very opposite is true. Young people learn when they are interested and engaged and when they have questions for which they want answers; they are less likely to learn if they are told the answers or if information is simply provided for them by the teacher, from a PowerPoint® slide or a textbook. Many geography teachers responded to the changes brought by the new KS3 POS in 2007, which had less prescription and more opportunities to innovate, by redesigning their schemes of work and incorporating current and relevant topics which appeal to young people. The more recent changes in 2014 have also led to teachers redesigning schemes of work and further updating of case studies and examples. The efforts of the GA and RGSIBG to encourage teachers to make changes through the Action Plan for Geography (2006–11) helped many to have the confidence to become curriculum makers. As the GA points out, teachers should be accountable, but they are also professionals with educational goals. Perhaps all they need is the confidence to be autonomous in their classrooms, to focus on inspiring young people and encouraging them to ask questions and to engage with the geography around them, something which is at the heart of the enquiry approach.

Key readings

1   Roberts, M. (2013) *Geography through Enquiry,* Sheffield: Geographical Association. This book draws on the author's own research and her experiences as a PGCE Tutor. It outlines the key characteristics of geographical enquiry and provides suggestions for how teachers might incorporate enquiry into their teaching.
2   Barker, B. (2010) *The Pendulum Swings. Transforming School Reform,* Stoke on Trent: Trentham Books. This book is a fascinating discussion of education reform since 1988 and particularly of New Labour's education policies. The author argues that teaching and learning will not improve through regulation, inspection and measurement, and that the time is right for completely new thinking from policy makers. Published in 2010, it is particularly interesting to read in the context of both the Coalition government (2010–15) and the Conservative government's education policies.

References

Adams, P. (2008) 'Considering "best practice": the social construction of teacher activity and pupil learning as performance', *Cambridge Journal of Education*, 38 (3), 375–92.
Barker, B. (2010) *The Pendulum Swings: Transforming School Reform*, Stoke on Trent: Trentham Books.
Barnes, D. (2008) 'Exploratory talk for learning', in N. Mercer and S. Hodgkinson (eds.), *Exploring Talk in School*, London: Sage.
Davidson, G. (2006) 'Start at the beginning', *Teaching Geography*, 31 (3), 105–8.

Davidson, G. (2009) GTIP *Think Piece: Geographical Enquiry*, Available at: http://geography.org.uk/gtip/thinkpieces/geographicalenquiry [Accessed 8 September 2011].

Department for Education (DfE) (2010) *The Importance of Teaching: Schools White Paper*, Available at: https://www.education.gov.uk/publications/standard/publicationdetail/ page1/CM%207980 [Accessed 22 August 2011].

Department for Education (DfE) (2013) *National Curriculum in England: Geography Programmes of Study*, Available at: https://www.gov.uk/government/publications/ national-curriculum-in-england-geographyprogrammes-of-study [Accessed 1 August 2016].

Department for Education (DfE) (2014) *Geography GCSE Subject Content*, Available at: https://www.gov.uk/government/uploads/system/uploads/attachment_data/ file/301253/GCSE_geography.pdf [Accessed 1 August 2016].

Edexcel (2016) *Specification Edexcel GCSE (9–1) Geography B*, Available at: http:// qualifications.pearson.com/en/qualifications/edexcel-gcses/geography-b-2016. html [Accessed 1 August 2016].

Eduqas (2016) *Specification GCSE in Geography A*, Available at: http://www.eduqas. co.uk/qualifications/geography/gcse-a/ [Accessed 1 August 2016].

Ferretti, J. (2013) 'Whatever happened to the enquiry approach?' in D. Lambert and M. Jones (eds.) *Debates in Geography Education* 1st edn, London: Routledge.

Freeman, D. (2010) 'Engaging with theory', in C. Brooks (ed.), *Studying PGCE Geography at M Level*, London: Routledge.

Geographical Association (2009) *A Different View: A Manifesto from the Geographical Association*, Sheffield: Geographical Association.

Geographical Association (2015) *Geography GCSE Entries and Results 2015*, Available at: http://www.geography.org.uk/news/2015gcseresults/#top [Accessed 1 August 2016].

Jackson, P. (2006) 'Thinking geographically', *Geography*, 91 (3), 199–204.

Lambert, D. (2008) 'Why are school subjects important?', *Forum*, 50 (2), 207–13.

Moore, A. (2000) *Teaching and Learning: Pedagogy, Curriculum and Culture*, London: Routledge Falmer.

Naish, M., Rawling, E. and Hart, C. (1987) *Geography 16–19: The Contribution of a Curriculum Project to 16–19 Education*, London: Longman.

Ofsted (2008) *Geography in Schools: Changing Practice*, London: Ofsted, Available at: http://www.ofsted.gov.uk/resources/geography-schools-changing-practice [Accessed 10 August 2016].

Ofsted (2011) *Geography: Learning to Make a World of Difference*, London: Ofsted, Available at: http://www.ofsted.gov.uk/resources/geography-learning-make-world-of-difference [Accessed 10 August 2016].

Ofsted (2015) *Key Stage 3: The Wasted Years?*, Available at: https://www.gov.uk/ government/uploads/system/uploads/attachment_data/file/459830/Key_ Stage_3_the_wasted_years.pdf [Accessed 1 August 2016].

QCA (2007) Geography National Curriculum, Available at: http://curriculum. qcda.gov.uk/key-stages-3-and-4/subjects/key-stage-3/geography/index.aspx [Accessed 12 September 2011].

Rawling, E. (2001) *Changing the Subject: The Impact of National Policy on School Geography 1980–2000*, Sheffield: Geographical Association.

Rawling, E. (2007) *Planning your Key Stage 3 Geography Curriculum*, Sheffield: Geographical Association.

Roberts, M. (1998) 'The nature of geographical enquiry at Key Stage 3', *Teaching Geography*, 23 (4), 164–7.

Roberts, M. (2003) *Learning through Enquiry*, Sheffield: Geographical Association.

Roberts, M. (2010) 'Where's the geography? Reflections on being an external examiner', *Teaching Geography*, 35 (3), 112–13.

Roberts, M. (2011) *What Makes a Geography Lesson Good?*, Available at: http://www.geography.org.uk/download/GA_PRMGHWhatMakesAGeographyLessonGood.pdf [Accessed 12 August 2016].

Roberts, M. (2013) *Geography through Enquiry*, Sheffield: Geographical Association.

Chapter 9

Personalising learning in geography

Mark Jones

> Interpretations of policy are situated and contextualised; interpretations are
> 'meaning-making' processes – a 'what does this mean for us' and 'do we
> have to do this' and 'does this fit with what we do already' conversation.
>
> (Maguire et al., 2013, pp. 328–9)

Introduction

Geography teachers aim to make the curriculum exciting and engaging for students by translating government policy, new curricula and examination specifications into 'meaningful educational encounters' (Lambert and Morgan, 2010, p. 52). However, for teachers this meaning-making process is situated both within the policies, practices and *politics* of the school and in the broader context of what can appear constantly changing national priorities. In discussing this process, this chapter initially focuses on 'personalised learning', part of the Labour government's (1997–2010) wider 'personalisation' agenda. Under the Liberal-Conservative Coalition (2010–15) personalisation was quickly curtailed; the Schools White Paper, *The Importance of Teaching* (DfE, 2010) heralded instead a renewed emphasis on 'core knowledge' and 'teaching' and more rigorous examinations. In this new policy environment (e.g. The English Baccalaureate (EBacc), Progress 8 and Attainment 8), we might ask 'whatever happened to personalised learning?' (Maguire et al., 2013). In attempting to answer this question, this chapter briefly traces the concept's emergence as policy before discussing in practice its association with the differentiation of teaching and learning and Assessment for Learning (AfL).

We also examine the original conception of personalisation where Labour's polices for public services were influenced in part by the think tank *Demos* (see Leadbeater, 2004a, 2006). For Charles Leadbeater a clear distinction exists between shallower forms of practice and deeper forms of personalisation which prioritise increased choice and voice; and which potentially invite a more radical and disruptive agenda in schools.

> Personalised learning would provide children with a greater repertoire of
> scripts for how their education could unfold. At the core would still be a

common script – the basic curriculum – but that script could branch out in many different ways, to have many different styles and endings.

(Leadbeater, 2004a, p. 68)

Personalised learning's potential to increase *choice* in what students learn, how they approach learning and where and when learning occurs was to be accompanied by opportunities for students to operate as 'co-author[s] of the script' (ibid., 2004b, p. 16). With more authentic student *voice* in their experience of school and schooling, this 'radical collegiality' (Fielding, 2004) challenges the traditional roles of students and teachers. In the second part of this chapter, we discuss the transformative potential of personalising learning in geography, through teachers and students co-constructing learning and 'curriculum making'.

Personalisation and personalised learning

As part of Labour's priorities, the policies of personalisation promised to give more choice and voice to people in transforming public services (DfES, 2004). Personalised learning was not to be imposed from above but developed by schools 'around the needs, interest and aptitudes of individual pupils' (Miliband, 2004, p. 3). However, personalised learning was a contested concept from the outset. Johnson (2004) suggested it was simply 'a development of the standards agenda' (p. 4), supporting the government's pursuit of maximising students' attainment by paying attention to individuals. Maguire et al. (2013) suggest it is representative of 'a polyphonic, multiple policy agenda' (p. 324); a policy that in practice requires significant 'interpretation and translation' (p. 323). Numerous government publications (e.g. DfES, 2004; DfES, 2007; DCSF, 2008) and pamphlets (e.g. Leadbeater 2004a; Hargreaves, 2004a-b, 2006) provided alternative interpretations which meant that a wide range of existing practices within schools became labelled as 'personalised learning' (Sebba et al., 2007; Maguire et al., 2013).

The publication, *A National Conversation on Personalised Learning* (DfES, 2004a) listed five key components: assessment for learning; effective teaching and learning strategies; curriculum entitlement and choice; a student-centred approach to school organisation; and strong partnership beyond the school. Even so, despite its beguiling common-sense appeal, personalised learning lacked theoretical underpinning. (Johnson, 2004; Campbell et al., 2007). In terms of policy consistency, Pollard and James (2004) warned of the potential to lose sight of the focus on learners and learning by more restricted interpretations based on 'teaching provision and associated systems' (p. 5) emanating from New Labour's National Strategies. In his paper, *Personalised Learning – An Emperor's Outfit?* Johnson (2004) suggested it really provided little more than a 'box' for all the good practice already in existence in many schools.

Personalised learning: attempting meaning making

In order to gain clarity about personalised learning, David Hargreaves adopted a distributed approach working with headteachers to produce six pamphlets claiming to give the concept substance through nine themes or 'gateways' (see Table 9.1). Assessment for Learning (AfL) was identified by many as the most developed aspect in their schools (Hargreaves, 2006a) and it quickly became a key feature of personalised learning (NCSL, 2008). For Hargreaves the gateways represented a more transformative twenty-first-century vision of education summarised into four 'Deeps' (Hargreaves, 2006b). At the same time an independent review of teaching and learning presented a vision of how personalised learning could become a reality in every classroom by 2020 (Gilbert et al., 2006). The review concluded personalised learning was strongly connected with developing a shared understanding of pedagogy, although the recommended model was so wide-ranging it could be 'interpreted as almost anything and everything in the school system' (Campbell et al., 2007, pp. 144–5). Thus, lack of clarity among school leaders, teachers and learners has remained widespread (Sebba et al, 2007; Courcier, 2007; Underwood and Banyard, 2008). Furthermore, the promise of personalised learning becoming a deep culture shift has often been reduced to a standardised checklist for schools to audit themselves against, stripping away its 'radical democratic potential' (Williamson and Morgan, 2009, p. 290). In government policy and exemplification documents there was little emphasis on Leadbeater's (2004a) deep personalisation in which user voice was central and the learner seen as the 'co-author of the script'. This is not uncommon in education

Table 9.1 Conceptions of personalised learning (2004–2008)

Five Key Components (DfES, 2004a)	Nine gateways (Hargreaves, 2004a) Four Deeps (Hargreaves, 2006b)	Nine features of pedagogy of personalisation (DCSF, 2008)
1. Assessment for learning.	1. Assessment for learning (DL)	1. High quality teaching and learning.
2. Effective teaching and learning strategies.	2. Student voice (DL)	2. Target setting and tracking.
3. Curriculum entitlement and choice.	3. Learning to learn (DL)	3. Focused assessment
4. A student centred approach to school organisation.	4. Curriculum (DE)	4. Intervention.
5. Strong Partnership Beyond the School.	5. New Technologies (DE)	5. Pupil grouping.
	6. Mentoring and coaching (DS)	6. The learning environment.
	7. Advice and guidance (DS)	7. Curriculum organisation.
	8. Design and organisation (DLe)	8. The extended curriculum.
	9. Workforce reform (DLe)	9. Supporting children's wider needs.
	DL Deep Learning DE Deep Experience DS Deep Support DLe Deep Leadership	

policy and public service reform where student voice often resides 'at the very margins of policy' (Ball, 2008, p. 132).

Before exploring personalised learning in a geography-specific context, it is worth examining Table 9.1 in more detail to consider the extent to which these different representations of personalised learning are still a focus in schools today.

Conceptions of personalised learning in geography: differentiation and AfL

In the classroom, teachers naturally try to make sense of ideological or policy shifts in the context of their tried and tested practices, and for some geography teachers personalised learning has become synonymous, or at least associated, with 'differentiation'. Government publications under Labour reinforced the differentiation of teaching and learning as fundamental to the success of personalised learning (DCSF, 2008) and Burton (2007) has argued that personalised learning's 'pedagogical and political roots' are located in the concept of differentiation (p. 14). However, Courcier (2007) has reported confusion among teachers concerning the differences between 'differentiation' and 'personalised learning'.

If we associate differentiation with personalising learning, then a persistent question that arises, specifically because of differentiation's concern for the individual is: *who to differentiate for?* Is it all students or just those with *identified* learning needs? The orthodoxy seems to be that any interventions should 'make a difference for all pupils' (Lambert and Balderstone, 2010, p. 205) and, as Battersby (2002) reminds us, differentiation should occur at the planning stage in all classrooms and for all pupils. This is a fine aspiration but difficult to achieve with integrity. Ofsted (2008) has reported that differentiation in geography lessons still needs to improve as 'too often, teaching is directed at pupils of average ability' (para 42); teaching to the majority of students with little deviation from a single script. However, where teachers do meet the needs of particular groups of students, Sebba et al., (2007) have equally identified concerns over teachers' lack of engagement with *invisible* middle-ability students.

In broad terms, there are two approaches to differentiation: through adapting classroom practice or by outcome (providing the single script). The former may mean adapting resources, providing alternative tasks, organising pupils in different groupings, using different levels of support or asking questions with differing levels of challenge. If differentiating by outcome, there are usually little or no changes to a 'planned' lesson based on students' individual needs – the variation in outcome is due to students' performance on the day. Whichever approach is utilised, if differentiation simply means engaging students and then monitoring their progress, it inevitably results in accepting different levels of performance or attainment.

One practice in schools labelled as 'differentiation' is the use of differentiated learning objectives, where objectives with tripartite stems such as *All, Most, Some* or *Must, Should, Could* are used at the start and at different points in the lesson. While well intentioned as tools to support students in seeing the 'big picture', and, arguably, provide reference points to identify *measurable* learning gains or signal 'progress' in lessons, their use can place artificial ceilings on students' attainment; for if students are encouraged to focus on one objective at the expense of others, this can narrow a student's lines of enquiry and engagement. Differentiated objectives may in any case be misdirected, bound up with what Lambert (2010) has called the 'AfL paraphernalia' – that is, bureaucratic systems to demonstrate compliance with AfL policies but which, literally, get in the way of planning and teaching motivating worthwhile geography. In addition, Burton (2007) reminds us that whilst theory and ideas concerning learning develop, educators should 'resist reductionist attempts to produce neat, digestible, commercialised chunks of pedagogy' (p. 16).

If differentiation dominated educational discourse in the 1990s, then personalised learning, particularly through the visible form of AfL, dominated the first two decades of the 2000s. Original work on formative assessment produced evidence of subsequent improvement by two GCSE grades (Black and Wiliam, 1998) and improved attainment in the core subjects at KS3 (Black et al., 2003). However, this effectiveness, and, indeed, the very purpose and principals, of AfL can be lost when superficial *representation* of AfL occur in classrooms. Lambert (2010) has warned that the principles of formative assessment can be 'lost in translation' (p. 1) in to practical, visible actions. In addition, Ofsted (2011) has reported that in geography lessons:

> AfL has had a limited impact on improving teaching and learning … what schools needed to focus on was how best to ensure that the students actually made progress.
>
> (para. 58)

Pollard and James (2004) have argued that to be effective teachers' use of AfL requires 'deeper changes in practices and relationships' (p. 6). This presents considerable challenges for those teachers operating within restrictive school policies where standardised-operating procedures may result in formulaic lesson structures (see Roberts, 2010). Sharing differentiated objectives at the start of a lesson, checking students' 'progress' at regular intervals in lessons or focusing on feedback through 'triple impact marking' may merely represent what Hartley (2006) calls 'personalised standardisation'. Where such approaches, labelled as 'AfL', become accepted routine classroom practice it can be difficult to change, particularly if perceived as supporting whole school improvement or what Ofsted require for inspections outcomes of 'good' or 'outstanding'.

Making significant changes to routinised classroom practice is challenging, especially those that demand teachers can demonstrate the 'progress' of their students. For example, the use of 'progress checks' within lessons, perhaps every 20 minutes, recently became a feature of lessons in many schools preparing for inspection. This is despite Ofsted (2012) asserting that it is only zealous senior leaders in schools that demand this, and not the Inspection body itself (Ofsted has had to dispel a number of myths about inspection: see Ofsted, 2015b; GA, 2016, p. 5). The AfL acoustics around 'progress' may have resulted in an over technical, bureaucratised form of teaching where the formative potential of assessment is not realised (see Weeden and Simmons in this volume). The constant review of learning may actually interrupt and intrude on students' learning. Indeed, Ofsted (2012) reported that

> significant periods of time were spent by teachers on getting pupils to articulate their learning, even where this limited their time to complete activities and thereby interrupted their learning. Pupils need time to complete something before they can valuably discuss and evaluate it.
>
> (p. 3)

Personalising learning in geography

In this section examples of personalising learning, where students have increased choice and voice in the curriculum, are discussed. It is important to stress the finding from the Young People's Geographies Project that although, pedagogically, more voice and choice are productive, students do not see themselves as responsible for the curriculum. It is for teachers to make selections of what is important to teach, not students (see Biddulph, 2011a). Two projects funded by the Action Plan for Geography, which are particularly valuable here, are: 'Young People's Geographies' (YPG)[1] and 'Making Geography Happen' (MGH)[2] .

The YPG brought together young people, geography teachers and academics for a geography 'curriculum-making' project (see Firth and Biddulph, 2009; Biddulph, 2011a). The MGH project involved five schools exploring what makes good quality, innovative curriculum-making; two schools involved their pupils in co-construction of the curriculum. In the YPG the use of inclusive pedagogies and 'respectful conversations', enabled students to co-construct a range of geographical experiences for their school curriculum, from exploring feelings about different local places to scenarios such as 'What if gas was cut off tomorrow?' Through using dialogic pedagogies, outcomes included increased student enthusiasm and motivation. However, the YPG also showed up dilemmas relating to curriculum, and in particular the teachers' and students' roles in its formation (see Biddulph, 2011b, pp. 395–6).

Personalising learning in geography at Key Stage 3

For many geography teachers who are not involved in funded projects or research, opportunities for increased student participation in decision making, relating to what students learn, how they learn, and how they are assessed, may appear somewhat limited, not least due to accountability. Underwood and Banyard (2008) found secondary pupils perceived that personalisation declines over time in school; however, Key Stage 3 provides ample opportunity for increased student choice and voice in learning geography. That said, Ofsted in their 2015 publication *Key Stage 3 – The Wasted Years?* report this key stage is not a priority for school leaders; concluding that in improving teaching and assessment school leaders 'must not allow Key Stage 3 (KS3) to become a lost opportunity' (Ofsted, 2015a, p. 27). For geography teachers wanting and able to create a dialogic KS3 environment, there is the potential to offer students choice in topic (curriculum), approach (pedagogy), and outcome (assessment); although in practice there may be significant variation in what represents 'choice' (see Figure 9.1).

At KS3, opportunities exist for student choice within project-based learning and through enquiry, although the latter may vary from tightly controlled teacher-led to more flexible and dynamic student-led enquiry (Roberts, 2003). *Restricted* choice is where a teacher decides the overall theme and students have options within, for example, giving students' choice over which country to study in a project on 'development'. Within an established 'geography of sport' unit, Berry (2011) acknowledges that while allowing students choice over groups and outcomes, all students carried out the same enquiry on 'child labour', thus

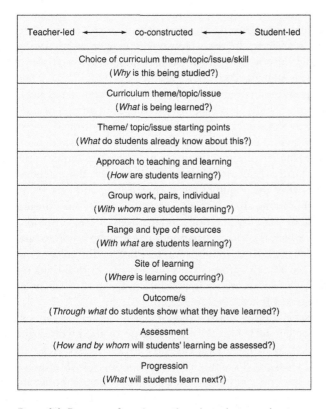

Figure 9.1 Degrees of teacher and student choice and voice.

restricting choice and allowing the teacher to maintain control. In the MGH project, one school provided Year 7 students with a choice of four different assessment approaches including making an artefact to show their understanding of a unit on Australia. Approaching the concept of deep personalisation through more *open* choice, Morgan (2010) permitted Year 8 students the freedom for planning lessons to be taught by teachers. The Year 8 students created lessons covering super-volcanoes, endangered species and environmental impacts of music festivals. Students clearly valued the experience and wanted more *negotiated* choice of topic and activities (Morgan, 2010), but they respected the teacher's vital role in the curriculum-making process (Hopwood, 2007; Morgan, 2011). This echoes Biddulph's (2011a) point that curriculum making is primarily teachers' work and is further supported by Campbell et al. (2007), who identified important features of effective personalised pedagogy including teachers' high level of subject expertise; and their control of the overall structure of lessons including 'pace, direction and transition' (p. 150).

Personalising learning in geography at GCSE and GCE

Any *real* choice for students can disappear altogether after KS3 as the focus becomes examination orientated where teachers prioritise content coverage and may even feel pressures to 'teach to the test'. However, it may be worth noting that in examination specifications where fieldwork is mandatory, there may yet be real opportunities to provide some student choice and control.

From 2016, GCSE specifications require students to have completed fieldwork experiences in two contrasting locations; this presents both an opportunity and a challenge for teachers and students. With the ending of controlled assessment, students' participation and understanding of their fieldwork 'experiences' will be assessed through terminal examination questions. Despite a requirement for schools to evidence that the fieldwork element has been met, the extent to which students fully experience the enquiry process (pre, during and post visits) could vary significantly. For some students, independence may be encouraged through making choices about enquiry questions and methods of data collection, presentation and analysis, which is good preparation for those who go on to take the subject at GCE. For other students, the situation may not be dissimilar to the days of GCSE coursework where the process skills of creativity, critical thinking and independent learning were 'of secondary importance to the goal of achieving a good GCSE grade' (Reid and Jones, 2002, p.125).

At GCE, the 2016 specifications introduced 'independent investigations' requiring a significant element of fieldwork; one outcome of the involvement of academic geographers on the A Level Content Advisory Board (see ALCAB, 2014, pp. 23–9). The ALCAB panel's view (ironic considering GCSE requirements) was 'that nothing students can write in an examination can demonstrate the synthesis of skills, knowledge and practical ability that is the hallmark of excellent fieldwork' (ibid., p. 25). The independent investigation has the potential for authentic student voice and choice, but it brings challenges, not least in teachers providing genuine opportunities for students to define and develop a question or issue to address, whilst also acknowledging the logistics of planning for group fieldwork in specific locations. The reality may be that despite well intentioned for supporting progression to higher education, the independent investigation may still 'become predictable, 'safe' and formulaic'' (Lambert and Reiss, 2014, p. 11). Opportunities for more student voice and choice in what is essentially 'coursework' post-16 may be influenced by similar factors to its GCSE predecessor where Martin et al.'s (2002) research indicated that for the different stakeholders involved independent learning was secondary to

> getting marks in the bank (students), constraints from assessment criteria (teachers) and pressure from accountability e.g. league tables (parents and teachers), [which] all promote the importance of maximising students' grades.
>
> (p. 39)

Conclusion

Geography teachers are key players in how government priorities such as personalised learning and changes to curriculum and assessment policies are enacted in practice. This chapter has discussed how teachers often try to make sense of policy in relation to what currently happens in their schools (e.g. personalised learning and its relationship to differentiation and AfL). Under current policy directives where core knowledge is more prescribed', deeper forms of personalising learning, through co-construction and creative conversations between geography teachers and their students, is a challenge but still possible. It is only where geography teachers take account of their students' motivations, preferences and interests that policy potentially translates into educational encounters which have shared meaning, significance and relevance. Returning to the opening quotation by Maguire et al. (2013), if we want students to be part of the meaning-making process then 'conversations' firstly need to involve them, but then where this occurs it also needs to be an authentic experience rather than students' views 'merely treated as minor footnotes in an unaltered adult text' (Fielding and Prieto, 2002, p. 20). Perhaps, in the end we should resist the trends to technicise issues like personalisation (e.g. to meet supposed Ofsted 'requirements') and simply trust our professional instincts that getting to know our students in a crucial part of effective teaching and learning.

Key readings

1   Biddulph, M. (2011) 'Young people's geographies: implications for secondary school geography', in G. Butt (ed.), *Geography, Education and the Future*. Using the metaphor of *conversations*, Mary Biddulph's chapter

provides a valuable insight for teachers wanting to collaborate with students in the curriculum-making process.

2   Firth, R. and Biddulph, M. (2009) 'Whose life is it anyway? Young people's geographies', in D. Mitchell (ed.), *Living Geography,* London: Chris Kington Publishing, a useful highlighting of academic geography's engagement with young people's lives and explanation of the YPG approach.

Notes

1   YPG (2006–11) has been promoted to the wider geography community through the YPG website (launched 2008); the Summer 2010 edition of *Teaching Geography,* which focused entirely on young people's geographies and the projects page of the GA website.
2   MGH (2009–11), see the projects page of the GA website and Paul Weeden's chapter in this volume.

References

A Level Content Advisory Board (ALCAB) (2014) *Report of the ALCAB Panel on Geography,* Available at: https://alevelcontent.files.wordpress.com/2014/07/alcab-report-of-panel-on-geography-july-2014.pdf [Accessed 12 August 2016].

Ball, S. (2008) *The Education Debate,* Bristol: The Policy Press.

Battersby, J. (2002) 'Differentiation in teaching and learning geography', in M. Smith (ed.), *Teaching Geography in Secondary School,* London: RoutledgeFalmer.

Berry, S. (2011) 'What are the barriers to achievement for Year 9 boys within geography and how can the classroom teacher begin to narrow the gap?' Unpublished dissertation, University of the West of England, Bristol.

Biddulph, M. (2011a) 'Young people's geographies: implications for secondary school geography', in G. Butt (ed.), *Geography. Education and the Future,* London: Continuum.

Biddulph, M. (2011b) 'Articulating student voice and facilitating curriculum agency', *The Curriculum Journal,* 22 (3), 381–99.

Black, P. and Wiliam, D. (1998) *Inside the Black Box: Raising Standards through Classroom Assessment,* London: King's College.

Black, P., Harrison, C., Lee, C., Marshall, B. and Wiliam, D. (2003) Assessment for Learning: Putting it into Practice Maidenhead: Open University Press.

Burton, D. (2007) 'Psycho-pedagogy and personalised learning', *Journal of Education for Teaching,* 33 (1), 5–17.

Campbell, R., Robinson, W., Neelands, J., Hewston, R. and Mazzoli, L. (2007) 'Personalised Learning: Ambiguities in theory and practice', *British Journal of Educational Studies,* 55 (2), 135–54.

Courcier, I. (2007) 'Teachers' perceptions of personalised learning'. *Evaluation and Research in Teacher Education,* 20 (2), 59–80.

Department for Children, Schools and Families (DCSF) (2008) *Personalised Learning: A Practical Guide,* Nottingham: DCSF publications.

Department for Education (DfE) (2010) *The Importance of Teaching: The Schools White Paper,* London: The Stationery Office.

Department for Education and Skills (DfES) (2001) *Schools Achieving Success*, Norwich: The Stationery Office.

Department for Education and Skills (DfES) (2004) *A National Conversation about Personalised Learning*, Nottingham: DfES publications.

Department for Education and Skills (DfES) (2007) *Pedagogy and Personalisation*, Nottingham: DfES publications.

Fielding, M. (2004) 'Transformative approaches to student voice: theoretical underpinnings, recalcitrant realities', *British Educational Research Journal*, 30, 295–311.

Fielding, M. and Prieto, M. (2002) 'The central place of student voice in democratic renewal: a Chilean case study', in M. Schweisfurth, L. Davies and C. Harber (eds) *Learning Democracy and Citizenship: International Experiences*. Oxford: Symposium Books.

Firth, R. and Biddulph, M. (2009) 'Whose life is it anyway? Young people's geographies', in D. Mitchell (ed.), *Living Geography: Exciting Futures for Teachers and Students*, Cambridge: Chris Kington Publishing.

Geographical Association (2016) The purpose and quality of education in England – response from the Geographical Association to the Commons Education Committee call for evidence 25 January 2016.

Gilbert, C., August, K., Brooks, R., Hancock, D., Hargreaves, D. and Pearce, N. (2006) *2020 Vision: Report of the Teaching and Learning by 2020 Review Group*, Nottingham: DfES publications.

Hargreaves, D. (2004a) *Personalising Learning 1: Next Steps in Working Laterally*, London: Specialist Schools Trust.

Hargreaves, D. (2004b) *Personalising Learning 2: Student Voice and Assessment for Learning*, London: Specialist Schools Trust.

Hargreaves, D. (2006a) *Personalising Learning 6: the final gateway school design and organisation*, London: Specialist Schools Trust.

Hargreaves, D. (2006b) *A New Shape for Schooling*, London: Specialist Schools and Academies Trust.

Hargreaves, D. (2008) *Leading System Redesign-1*, London: Specialist Schools and Academies Trust.

Hartley, D. (2006) 'Excellence and enjoyment: the logic of a 'contradiction', *British Journal of Educational Studies*, 54 (1), 3–14.

Hopwood, N. (2007) Young People's Geography Evaluation Report, Available at: http://www.youngpeoplesgeographies.co.uk/about-ypg/evaluation-reports/ [Accessed 12 July 2011].

Johnson, M. (2004) *Personalised Learning: An Emperor's Outfit?* London: Institute for Public Policy Research.

Lambert, D. (2010) Issues in Geography Education, *8, Progression,* Available at: http://www.geography.org.uk/download/GA_PRMGHProgressionThinkPiece.pdf [Accessed 12 September 2011].

Lambert, D. and Balderstone, D. (2010) *Learning to Teach Geography in the Secondary School*, 2nd edn, London: Routledge.

Lambert, D. and Morgan, J. (2010) *Teaching Geography 11–18: A Conceptual Approach*, Maidenhead: Open University Press.

Lambert, D. and Reiss. M.J. (2014) The Place of Fieldwork in Geography and Science Qualifications, London: IoE, University of London.

Leadbeater, C. (2004a) *Personalisation through Participation: A New Script for Public Services*, London: DEMOS.

Leadbeater, C. (2004b) *Learning about Personalisation: How Can We Put the Learner at the Heart of the Education System*, London: DfES/NCSL.

Maguire, M., Ball, S.J. and Braun, A. (2013) What ever happened to ...? 'Personalised learning' as a case of policy dissipation, *Journal of Education Policy*, 28 (3), 322–338.

Martin, S., Reid, A., Bullock, K. and Bishop, K. (2002) *Voices and Choices in Coursework*, Sheffield: Geographical Association.

Miliband, D. (2004) *Personalised Learning: Building a New Relationship with Schools*, North of England Education Conference, Belfast, 8 January, 2004.

Morgan, L. (2010) 'Young people's voice in geography today: to what extent can they be heard in curriculum development?' Unpublished dissertation. University of the West of England, Bristol.

Morgan, L. (2011) Research paper: 'How far can young people's voices be heard in geography today?', Geographical Association Annual Conference University of Surrey, 14–17 April, 2011.

National College for School Leadership (NCSL) (2008) Leading Personalising Learning National Survey, Available at: www.nationalcollege.org.uk/index/leadershiplibrary/leadingschools/personalisedlearning/leading-personalised-learning-survey [Accessed 10 August 2011].

Ofsted (2008) *Geography in Schools: Changing Practice*, London: Ofsted, Available at: http://www.ofsted.gov.uk/resources/geography-schools-changing-practice [Accessed 12 August 2011].

Ofsted (2010) *The National Strategies: A Review of Impact*, London: Ofsted, Available at: http://www.ofsted.gov.uk/node/2416 [Accessed 18 August 2011].

Ofsted (2011) Geography: Learning to make a world of difference, London: Ofsted, Available at: http://www.ofsted.gov.uk/resources/geography-learning-make-world-of-difference [Accessed 15 August 2011].

Ofsted (2012) *Moving English Forward: Action to Raise Standards in English*

Ofsted (2015a) Key Stage 3: The Wasted Years, London: *Ofsted*, Available at: https://www.gov.uk/government/uploads/system/uploads/attachment_data/file/459830/Key_Stage_3_the_wasted_years.pdf [Accessed 12 August 2016].

Ofsted (2015b) Ofsted Inspections: Clarification for Schools, Available at: https://www.gov.uk/government/uploads/system/uploads/attachment_data/file/463242/Ofsted_inspections_clarification_for_schools.pdf [Accessed 12 August 2016].

Pollard, A. and James, M. (eds.) (2004) *Personalised Learning: A Commentary by the Teaching and Learning Research Programme*, London: Economic and Social Research Council/TLRP.

Reid, A. and Jones, M. (2002) 'Learning from GCSE coursework', *Teaching Geography*, 27 (3), 120–5.

Roberts, M. (2003) *Learning Through Enquiry*, Sheffield: Geographical Association.

Roberts, M. (2010) 'Where's the geography? Reflections on being an external examiner', *Teaching Geography*, 35 (3), 112–13.

Sebba, J., Brown, N., Steward, S., Galton, M. and James, M. (2007) *An Investigation of Personalised Learning Approaches Used by Schools*, Nottingham: DfES Publications.

Underwood, J. and Banyard, T.S. (2008) 'Managers', teachers' and learners' perceptions of personalised learning: Evidence from Impact 2007', *Technology, Pedagogy and Education*, 17 (3), 233–46.

Williamson, B. and Morgan, J. (2009) 'Educational reform, enquiry based learning and the re-professionalisation of teachers', *Curriculum Journal*, 20 (3), 287–304.

Chapter 10

Formative assessment

Paul Weeden and Michael Simmons

> Assessment for learning (AFL) or formative assessment is any assessment for which the main purpose is promoting students' learning. It thus differs from (summative) assessment designed primarily to serve the purposes of accountability, ranking, or certifying competence.
>
> (Weeden and Lambert, 2006, p. 25)

Introduction

Formative assessment is more effective when both teachers and students know 'Where are we now?', 'Where are we trying to get to?' and 'How can we make progress?'.

> 'What do you have to do to make progress Luke?'
> 'Get a Level 5a'.
>
> (Hesslewood, 2016, p. 28)

Using the shorthand of levels has imposed a straitjacket on teaching for many years with a tendency for students, teachers, schools and parents to define attainment and progress by numbers rather than fostering a more productive conversation about geographical knowledge, understanding and skills. The removal of levels from the English National Curriculum in 2015 provided opportunities and challenges for teachers as they seek to promote learning without the framework of progression they have used for the last twenty years.

Effective AfL involves purposeful dialogue between student and teacher about geography; it provides an opportunity to create an assessment system that is 'fit for purpose' rather than driven by the data collection needs of schools (Hesslewood, 2016). Teachers can use assessment to develop a dialogue with students through strategies such as more effective questioning, feedback and self/peer assessment (Weeden, 2005; Weeden and Lambert, 2006; Rooney, 2006, 2007; Hodgen and Webb, 2008; Swaffield, 2008; Wood, 2009).

The welcome increase in the use of AfL within schools during the last decade is the result of activity promoted by research evidence (Black and Wiliam, 1998a, b;

Black et al., 2003). This research suggested the use of formative assessment with its focus on deep learning boosts performance because learning is more effective. However, despite research-based principles for classroom practice (ARG, 2002a), as with any mass implementation there is a danger that formative assessment has been watered down to a series of strategies that are used without full understanding of the underpinning principles (Marshall and Drummond, 2006). One issue is whether assessment is used to provide effective feedback about current attainment and feed-forward about next steps or whether it is merely a bureaucratic data collecting exercise for accountability purposes. There may be a conflict between teacher values which support AfL and the requirements of a school system that is judged by performance outcomes (James and Pedder, 2006; Lambert, 2010).

Assessment therefore has two different, often conflicting, but both important purposes:

1 Formative purposes that promote day-to-day learning in the classroom.
2 Summative purposes that summarise students' attainment at a particular point in time that have increasingly been used to judge school performance.

AfL principles

One approach to formative assessment and working without levels in the classroom is illustrated by the Making Geography Happen Project (Geographical Association, 2010). The teacher was attempting to establish what the students knew at the beginning of the module, and using this information to plan the teaching and learning activities that would get them to the intended outcome of a more complex, precise and critical understanding of 'uneven development' and the linkages between places and people.

At the start of a module on uneven development, Year 9 students completed the phrase 'Uneven Development is ...'. The teacher used student responses to identify their understanding at the start of the unit:

> Pupils are aware that it is about difference and there are multiple reasons for it. Some are aware that it is about change though very few refer to scale or place except to refer to the familiar terms 'rich and poor countries'. Many related the term to their own lives in a rich country. Many referred to the selfishness of rich countries.
>
> (Cooper, 2010)

The teacher in designing the module made decisions about three assessment issues which will be considered here: assessing progress; integrating assessment with teaching and learning; and fitness for purpose. The 'golden thread' of progression was the concept of uneven development (QCA, 2008). This was explored in different places and scales so students considered the complexity of their place in the world, as well as developing their criticality and precision in handling geographical ideas. Choices were made about content, teaching and assessment methods. The assessment was varied and practical arising out of day-to-day work. It was not 'polished and neat' and 'oral evidence was particularly valued and recorded' (Cooper, 2010). Assessment purposes were mostly formative (Gardner, 2006; Gardner et al., 2010):

> Lesson planning became very interesting as I tried to plan the appropriate 'next step' for students rather than simply teach the next thing on a scheme of work. I found that we were not labouring points but rather moving on with our thinking and the ongoing dialogue with students provided evidence of progression in understanding and also helped me tailor lessons to their needs.
>
> (Cooper, 2010)

By the end of the unit, the teacher was able to identify the progress made by both individuals and the group. By incorporating the assessment into day-to-day work, she used her knowledge of the strengths and weaknesses of different assessment instruments and the evidence they provided. This allowed her to both evaluate whether the assessment was 'fit for purpose' and to build up a profile of evidence that was not just based on one assessment. She was focused on the evidence of progress in geographical understanding not merely on collecting the grades or marks that so often are the outcome of end of unit assessments. Her purpose here was to help 'all' the students develop their understanding of ideas associated with uneven development, not to grade them for management and tracking purposes. This could allow her to report progress in a descriptive manner to parents and students against the intended outcomes rather than as a level; although she might have used terms such as not secure/secure/exceeding expectations.

The process outlined above has been developed further by the Geographical Association (2014) in their guidance for assessing the 2014 National Curriculum (see Figure 10.1). The key elements are that assessment is built into the planning process and that teachers have a vision of what they are hoping students will achieve. As formative assessment is a daily occurrence, every interaction between teacher and student has the potential to be an assessment and learning opportunity that may not be formally recorded but is part of the ongoing process of helping students become better geographers.

Life without levels and beyond: assessing progress in geography

A major challenge is conceptualising progress in geography in a way that is helpful for student learning, teacher planning and tracking within the school. A frequent approach has been to draw on the practice and understanding of teachers, but a second approach has been to analyse students' responses and to link them to theoretical models (Davies, 2002, p. 185).

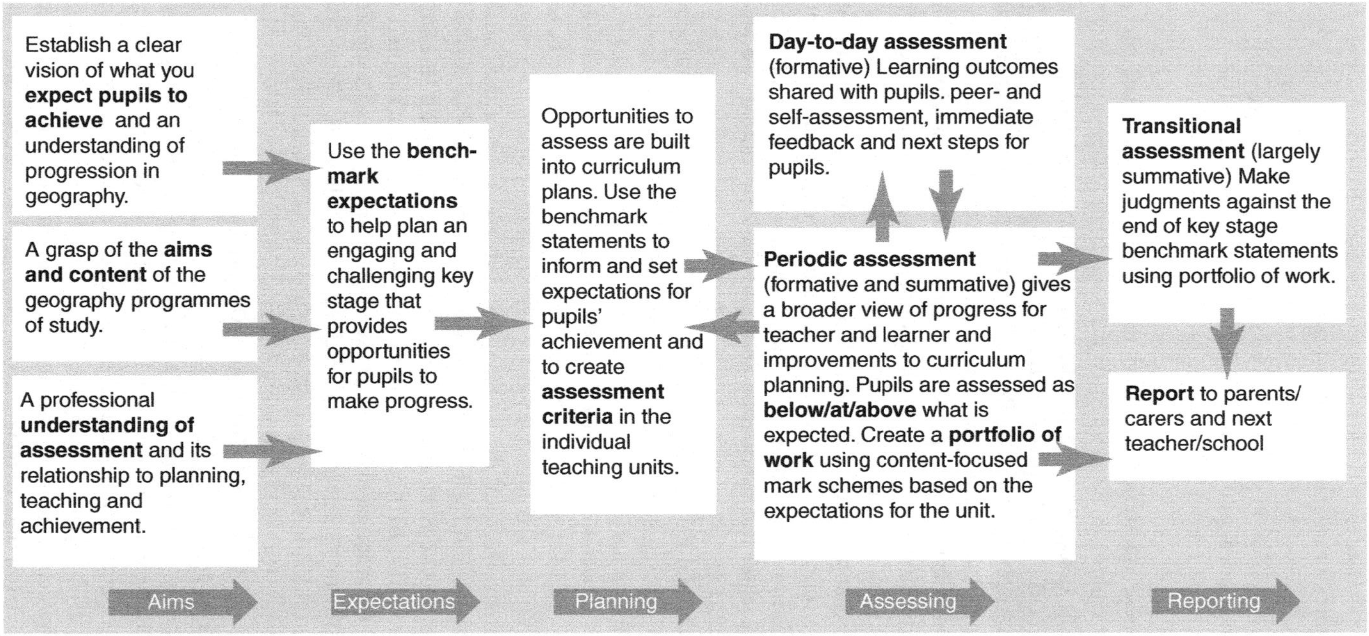

Aims

Establish a clear vision of what you **expect pupils to achieve** and an understanding of progression in geography.

A grasp of the **aims and content of** the geography programmes of study.

A professional **understanding of assessment** and its relationship to planning, teaching and achievement.

Expectations

Use the **bench-mark expectations** to help plan an engaging and challenging key stage that provides opportunities for pupils to make progress.

Planning

Opportunities to assess are built into curriculum plans. Use the benchmark statements to inform and set expectations for pupils' achievement and to create **assessment criteria** in the individual teaching units.

Assessing

Day-to-day assessment (formative) Learning outcomes shared with pupils. peer- and self-assessment, immediate feedback and next steps for pupils.

Periodic assessment (formative and summative) gives a broader view of progress for teacher and learner and improvements to curriculum planning. Pupils are assessed as **below/at/above** what is expected. Create a **portfolio of work** using content-focused mark schemes based on the expectations for the unit.

Reporting

Transitional assessment (largely summative) Make judgments against the end of key stage benchmark statements using portfolio of work.

Report to parents/carers and next teacher/school

Figure 10.1 Using the benchmark expectations in the assessment process (GA, 2014).

The freedom and flexibility provided by the 2014 National Curriculum for schools to create measures of progress that are personal to their students at Key Stages 1–3, requires a revisit of the following questions:

- How has progression in geography been defined and established over time?
- Is there a theoretical underpinning for progression in geography?
- How might expectations of students' progress change over time?

In answering these questions, we need to remind ourselves that the original national curriculum in England attempted to define progression largely by content and skills through 'huge numbers of atomistic and trivial statements of attainment' (DfE, 2011, p. 43) which was problematic (Rawling, 2001, pp. 52–64; Davies, 2002). For example, if the content is 'rivers' what knowledge, understanding and skills might be expected of a 7-year-old (Y2) or a 16-year-old (Y11) and how might they be expressed? Meanders could be taught to students of any age, but decisions have to be made about the level of detail to be included and assessed. In terms of teaching, what happens to progression when the next topic is climate change or urbanisation? How can these topics be taught and assessed at an appropriate level of performance? Subsequent rewriting of national curriculum levels into broad brush criteria statements of progression remained problematic as teachers had to interpret and apply these to content (see Hopkin, 2006; Weeden, 2013).

The 2014 National Curriculum removed levels and instead set out expectations for the end of each key stage. Schools now had the freedom to devise their 'own' assessment systems to 'check what pupils have learned and whether they are on track to meet expectations at the end of the key stage, and to report regularly to parents' (DfE, 2014a). While this freedom brought challenges, one benefit of putting ownership and accountability onto schools is the potential to match an assessment system to the local demographics and ability range of their students. The freedom to plan and create their own assessment measures has also led to a wide range of approaches with many schools at the time waiting for 'the answer'. According to the DfE (2014b, p. 6) 'the removal of levels has prompted a collaborative response amongst schools', as exemplified in the research report into alternative assessment practices by 34 teaching school alliances. These include systems that are underpinned by pedagogical theories of Structure of Observed Learning Outcomes (SOLO) taxonomy (Davies, 2002; Biggs, 2011), Bloom's Revised Taxonomy (Krathwohl, 2002) and Mastery Grids in the form of 'I can do' style statements and objectives.

At the geography department level, there is a responsibility to create geography specific assessments. In many departments this is seen as an opportunity but some departments may be struggling to cope with the required changes. The Geographical Association recognised the need for sharing good practice within geography departments with different approaches presented in Teaching Geography (see Aston and Renshaw 2014; May, 2014; Weeden and Hopkin,

2014; Rogers, 2015; Hesslewood, 2016; Rawling, 2016); National CPD sessions; workshops at annual conference and a range of supporting statements and diagrams. A useful starting point for departments is to revisit the broad dimensions of progress identified by the GA as:

- demonstrating greater fluency with world knowledge by drawing on increasing breadth and depth of content and contexts;
- extending from the familiar and concrete to the unfamiliar and abstract;
- making greater sense of the world by organising and connecting information and ideas about people, places, processes and environments;
- working with more complex information about the world, including the relevance of people's attitudes, values and beliefs;
- Increasing the range and accuracy of investigative skills, and advancing their ability to select and apply these with increasing independence to geographical enquiry.

(GA, 2015)

Figure 10.2 is an overview of how expectations of students might change over time and provides a starting point for more detailed analysis of individual modules that meet the needs of students in the individual school context.

This provides a potential framework for progression but does not provide an 'off the peg' model that can be used on a day-to-day basis. This has been one of the major challenges for geography teachers over the last twenty years where there has been an increasing emphasis on having clearly defined criteria that exemplify performance. Are there some aspects of progress that can be more easily identified? It has been suggested that there are some skills such as map reading that can be defined relatively easily (Lambert, 2010). Other examples include factual recall of place names and explanations of landforms although it is difficult to see how progress can be made other than knowing more places or more obscure places. It has also been argued that 'knowing how' rather than 'knowing what' is more important nowadays because of the growth of the internet. This leads to another current debate in education – what is the core and essential knowledge that is required for the subject (Lambert and Morgan, 2010; Hopkin, 2011; Kinder and Lambert, 2011) and how will it be assessed?

For teachers to use any of these frameworks, they need to develop their knowledge and understanding of progression in geography so that they feel confident in making judgements or helping students make next steps without being constrained by formal assessment structures. It is hoped that assessment changes in the 2014 National Curriculum mean students will 'become better geographers because their progress is engendered by the curriculum itself, not by targets and levels' (Hesslewood, 2016, p. 29)

One framework for developing individual units has been developed by the Assessment and Examinations Special Interest Group of the GA (2015). The exemplar in Figure 10.3 shows part of a tectonics unit illustrating how there is a

The framework

Contextual world knowledge of locations, places and geographical features

- demonstrating greater fluency with knowledge by drawing on increasing breadth and depth of content and contexts.

Expectations

by age 7	by age 9	by age 11	by age 14	by age 16
Have simple locational knowledge about individual places and environments, especially in the local area, but also in the UK and wider world.	Have begun to develop a framework of world locational knowledge, including knowledge of places in the local area, UK and wider world, and some globally significant physical and human features.	Have a more detailed and extensive framework of knowledge of the world, including globally significant physical and human features and places in the news.	Have extensive knowledge relating to a wide range of places, environments and features at a variety of appropriate spatial scales, extending from local to global.	Have a broader and deeper understanding of locational contexts, including greater awareness of the importance of scale and the concept of global.

Figure 10.2 Overview of how expectations of students might change over time (GA, 2014).

vision of what might be achieved within the unit but the freedom to develop it in different ways dependent on the teaching context. These units are not intended to be formulaic and rigid but rather starting points for development by teachers to suit their individual context.

One final issue related to assessing progress in a formative manner is that it is important to find out what the students know already. Students entering secondary schools have a wide variance of geography knowledge based on primary

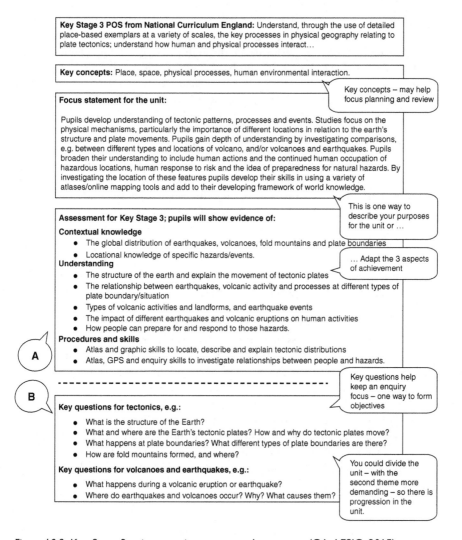

Key Stage 3 POS from National Curriculum England: Understand, through the use of detailed place-based exemplars at a variety of scales, the key processes in physical geography relating to plate tectonics; understand how human and physical processes interact…

Key concepts: Place, space, physical processes, human environmental interaction.

Key concepts – may help focus planning and review

Focus statement for the unit:

Pupils develop understanding of tectonic patterns, processes and events. Studies focus on the physical mechanisms, particularly the importance of different locations in relation to the earth's structure and plate movements. Pupils gain depth of understanding by investigating comparisons, e.g. between different types and locations of volcano, and/or volcanoes and earthquakes. Pupils broaden their understanding to include human actions and the continued human occupation of hazardous locations, human response to risk and the idea of preparedness for natural hazards. By investigating the location of these features pupils develop their skills in using a variety of atlases/online mapping tools and add to their developing framework of world knowledge.

This is one way to describe your purposes for the unit or …

Assessment for Key Stage 3; pupils will show evidence of:

Contextual knowledge
- The global distribution of earthquakes, volcanoes, fold mountains and plate boundaries
- Locational knowledge of specific hazards/events.

Understanding
- The structure of the earth and explain the movement of tectonic plates
- The relationship between earthquakes, volcanic activity and processes at different types of plate boundary/situation
- Types of volcanic activities and landforms, and earthquake events
- The impact of different earthquakes and volcanic eruptions on human activities
- How people can prepare for and respond to those hazards.

Procedures and skills
- Atlas and graphic skills to locate, describe and explain tectonic distributions
- Atlas, GPS and enquiry skills to investigate relationships between people and hazards.

… Adapt the 3 aspects of achievement

A

B

Key questions help keep an enquiry focus – one way to form objectives

Key questions for tectonics, e.g.:
- What is the structure of the Earth?
- What and where are the Earth's tectonic plates? How and why do tectonic plates move?
- What happens at plate boundaries? What different types of plate boundaries are there?
- How are fold mountains formed, and where?

Key questions for volcanoes and earthquakes, e.g.:
- What happens during a volcanic eruption or earthquake?
- Where do earthquakes and volcanoes occur? Why? What causes them?

You could divide the unit – with the second theme more demanding – so there is progression in the unit.

Figure 10.3 Key Stage 3 unit: tectonic patterns and processes (GA AESIG, 2015).

school coverage and personal experiences. Geography as a discipline involves a wide range of skills and 'core knowledge' that incorporates quality of written understanding and expression, numerical statistical analysis and interpretation and cartographic proficiency. To plan appropriately, geography teachers should assess students early in their secondary school career to establish their strengths and areas for development.

Summative purposes

Alongside the increase in AfL, there has also been a huge expansion in tracking student performance and progress because teachers and schools in England are increasingly judged by performance through the league tables (James, 1998; Black et al., 2003; Harlen, 2007; Stobart, 2008). This may result in 'teaching to the test' to maximise performance rather than learning. The question here is whether student' learning is deep (resulting in understanding) or surface (knowledge sufficient to pass the assessment). The implications of tracking progress are discussed later.

Implicit or explicit beliefs about learning and the model of progression adopted can have implications for assessment. If the assumption is that learners 'capacity to learn, and achieve, is determined by innate endowment of fixed intelligence (ability)' (DfE, 2011, p. 45 para 8.6), then this can limit expectations of children and have a negative impact on performance. Expectations of 'intelligence' can be further complicated by socio-economic factors such as class, gender, race, ethnicity and income.

Overall, performance in England, as measured by test and examination outcomes, has improved significantly over the last thirty years but the gap in the performance of different sub-groups has widened. For example, about 75 per cent of candidates of Chinese origin get at least 5 A*-C grades at GCSE compared to about 35 per cent of Black African or Caribbean candidates (Torrance, 2009, p. 223). White working-class boys have the lowest performance at GCSE (Cassen and Kingdon, 2007; EHRC, 2015). Data from the 2011 school performance tables have been used to highlight these issues with schools and teachers held accountable:

> Children only have one chance at education. These tables show which schools are letting children down. We will not hesitate to tackle underperformance in any school, including academies. Heads should be striving to make improvements year on year, and we will not let schools coast with mediocre performance
>
> (DfE, 2012)

The issue here is the role of 'assessment' outcomes in quantifying complex social issues and influencing practice in schools through the threat of punitive measures (Ball, 2008, pp. 152–93). Does accountability raise 'standards' overall or merely focus teaching and learning too much on 'passing the test' which can limit the curriculum (Torrance, 2009)? Effective formative assessment provides crucial inputs in improving performance although it is debatable whether education can be the panacea for all society's social and economic problems.

Finally, it is important to recognise that learning is related to interest and motivation (Trend, 2005) with topics engaging and motivating students in different ways (Hopwood, 2004; Biddulph and Adey, 2004). Assessment can also motivate or discourage. One view is that testing raises levels of achievement, but an alternative view is that it is only motivating for those who anticipate success. This has the effect of widening the gap between high and low achieving students (ARG, 2002b, p. 1). 'A strong emphasis on testing produces students with a strong extrinsic orientation towards grades and social status, i.e. a motivation towards performance rather than learning goals' (Harlen and Deakin-Crick, 2002).

Can assessment be used for different purposes?

This leads to another debate in the literature about whether different purposes of assessment can easily sit together (Black et al, 2003; Taras, 2005). Can one assessment serve a number of different purposes? This has implications for classroom practice because if summative and formative purposes can be more closely linked then assessment for learning will not be an additional burden on teachers (Harlen, 2007; Weeden, 2008).

Can day-to-day formative assessment sit alongside ostensibly AfL data collection procedures, such as detailed mark schemes, self-assessment charts, peer-assessment criteria that are used on a regular basis to collect detailed numerical or grade information about performance? These tools are used to set ongoing targets and to track progress but do they help learning?

Any assessment can be formative or summative. What is important is the way the information collected is used. Formative assessment involves the student in actively engaging with the feedback provided and using it to aid their learning. This can range from classroom questioning that helps students understand a topic better to the detailed analysis of answers to mock exam questions that helps them improve their performance. Summative assessment just provides them with a grade or mark that is a record of attainment at that point in time. The grade only tells the student their performance in relation to their peers or their last piece of work. Only if the reasons underpinning the award of that grade are explored can there be potential for improved learning.

Figure 10.4 shows how a variety of types of assessment should be used over time (GA, 2014). Short-term assessments will be largely formative, may not be formally recorded, but may be stored for future reference as the teacher and student gather more evidence about strengths and areas for development. Longer term assessments may have a more summative purpose and be formally recorded for example in summarising progress at the end of a year or key stage. However,

Scale/focus	Practice, for example:	Progress and standards
Short term Day-to-day	Assessment for learning classroom practice, e.g. questioning, formative feedback/response, etc.	Evident in teaching and learning, in pupils' ongoing work, response to feedback, etc.
Frequent basic knowledge/skills	Short test, identified piece of homework More in-depth marking	Progress check (confidence vs concern?) can give you a number
Half/Termly conceptual, procedural knowledge	Short research task, problem-solving exercise, etc. Access to work at particular standards, e.g. display Peer/self assessment	Criterion marking and feedback Linked to pitch/age-related expectations
Long term (Year/Key stage) substantial, conceptual development	A major piece of work, e.g. enquiry, decision-making exercise, extended writing End of year: perhaps synoptic, drawing learning together	As above, plus an opportunity to develop portfolio of geography work exemplifying and sharing standards and illustrating progress

Figure 10.4 Monitoring progress at different scales (GA, 2014).

if there is dialogue about the outcomes of this summative assessment then this has formative potential as the student may engage with learning how to improve their responses and not just focus on the assigned grade.

The 2014 National Curriculum performance is to be reported as descriptive profiles while GCSEs will use a numerical system of 1 (lowest grade) to 9 (highest grade). Levels or grades imply that learning is a series of sequential steps but geography with its varied topics result in variable progress by students. Some students will find weather more interesting and motivating while others will engage better with development issues.

Separating the ever increasing need to collect data for performance purposes (The English Baccalaureate, Attainment 8 and Progress 8 Measures) from day-to-day formative assessment in the classroom is a challenge. Pressure to publish school attainment on institution websites in a standard format (DfE, 2014a) has resulted in schools monitoring and tracking student data throughout their time at school to ensure that the student progress is strong and reflected in the school headline figures. To track students' progress schools are increasingly using sophisticated data analysis (Midyis, Yellis, Allis; FFT; Raiseonline[1]: Go4Schools: Value Added) to 'predict' student progress or to evaluate the comparative performance of departments (Howes, 2009; FFT, 2007, 2011; CEM, 2017).

Removal of the national curriculum levels has taken away a system that provided a national framework. Schools are now required to have an agreed system within their own school without the support of national benchmarking criteria (levels). This has caused uncertainty but provides teachers with the opportunity to promote better learning in the classroom because they no longer need be constrained by levels. If the assessment system is coherent and progress can be shown through students demonstrating their understanding of geography, then the need to collect large quantities of evidence for accountability purposes is reduced:

> Without levels, schools can use their own assessment systems to support more informative and productive conversations with pupils and parents. They can ensure their approaches to assessment enable pupils to take more responsibility for their achievements by encouraging pupils to reflect on their own progress, understand what their strengths are and identify what they need to do to improve. Focusing assessment on the content of the school's curriculum will allow for communications with parents and carers to provide a clearer sense of how to support their children to build and consolidate learning.
>
> (McIntosh, 2015, p. 14)

At the time of writing, one major issue facing schools during the transition to 'life without levels' is how to replace numerical targets with a more descriptive system. Some schools may find it easier to retain the common currency, or an adapted version, of the 'old national curriculum' levels and 'old GCSE grades' when monitoring student progress. The shorthand of grades or levels, while giving the opportunity to produce graphs showing progress over a series of modules, do not guarantee effective learning or even a 'good' GCSE pass. In fact, they could become the focus of the exercise and can get in the way of dialogue with students. If a grade is attached to a piece of work the student will tend to focus on the grade rather than the comments the teacher has made (Black and Wiliam, 1998a, b; Weeden and Lambert, 2006, p. 13). It can be difficult to get students, parents and school managers to accept that if the purpose is to improve dialogue and engage students with analysing their own work, grades get in the way but the outcomes have been shown to be beneficial (Black et al., 2003, pp. 43–9). Hesslewood (2016) gives an interesting example of a formative assessment system that promotes geographical understanding using feedback, dialogue, metacognition and self/peer assessment rather than targets and grades.

Conclusion

> An assessment activity can help learning if it provides information that teachers and their students can use as feedback in assessing themselves and one another and in modifying the teaching and learning activities in which they are engaged. Such assessment becomes "formative assessment" when the evidence is actually used to adapt the teaching work to meet learning needs.
>
> (Black et al., 2004, p. 10)

Assessment for learning starts with teachers obtaining information about what students know, understand and can do. This information provides the baseline from which a route to the intended geographical learning outcomes can be planned. It has been suggested that progression in geography is encapsulated by students' ability to demonstrate learning through their increasingly complex use of scale, breadth, depth, context, interaction, diversity, generalisation, precision and communication.

The removal of levels within the English National Curriculum has provided an opportunity for teachers to develop assessment systems tailored to the needs of their students. However, the dominance of school assessment systems that largely track students' progress for accountability purposes may have impacted on teachers' confidence in their ability to judge progress. Assessing progress post-levels provides a unique opportunity to enhance the geography taught in schools by encouraging teachers and students to consider for themselves what makes deeper geographical understanding. As in the past, during times of curriculum change and challenge, geography teachers are willing to grasp this opportunity, as illustrated by the articles in geography journals and on teacher websites. By using formative assessment processes that create opportunities for a dialogue about learning geographically, teachers can help students become more autonomous learners and better geographers.

Key readings

1   Weeden, P. and Lambert, D. (2006) *Geography Inside the Black Box*, London: nferNelson/GA. One of a series of booklets about AfL offering advice to teachers on how to interact more effectively with students, on a day-to-day basis, promoting their learning.

2   Gardner, D., Weeden, P. and Butt, G. (2015) *Assessing Progress in your Key 3 Geography Curriculum*, Sheffield: Geographical Association. This revised digital version of the 2007 title has been updated for the 2014 National Curriculum and includes new chapters with advice and guidance on assessing without levels.

Notes

1   Raiseonline, Available at: https://www.raiseonline.org/login.aspx?ReturnUrl=%2f [Accessed 12 August 2015].

2   GO 4 Schools (2017) *Pupil tracking with GO 4 Schools*, Available at: https://www.go4schools.com/PupilTracking.aspx [Accessed 21 June 2017].

References

Assessment Reform Group (ARG) (2002a) *Assessment for Learning: 10 Principles*, Cambridge: University of Cambridge, Faculty of Education.

Assessment Reform Group (ARG) (2002b) *Testing, Learning and Motivation*, Cambridge: University of Cambridge, Faculty of Education.

Aston, R and Renshaw, S. (2014) 'Planning a new Key Stage 3', *Teaching Geography*, 39 (2), 64–5.

Ball, S. (2008) *The Education Debate*, Bristol: The Policy Press.

Biddulph, M. and Adey, K. (2004) 'Pupil perceptions of effective teaching and subject relevance in history and geography at key stage 3', *Research in Education*, 71, 1–8.

Biggs, J. (2011) *The SOLO Taxonomy*, Available at: http://www.johnbiggs.com.au/solo_taxonomy.html [Accessed 15 August 2015].

Black, P. and Wiliam D. (1998a) 'Assessment and classroom learning', *Assessment in Education*, 5, 7–74.

Black, P. and Wiliam, D. (1998b) *Inside the Black Box*, Slough: nferNelson.

Black, P., Harrison, C., Lee, C., Marshall, B. and Wiliam, D. (2003) *Assessment for Learning: Putting it into Practice*, Maidenhead: Open University Press.

Cassen, R. and Kingdon, G. (2007) *Tackling Low Educational Achievement*, York: Joseph Rowntree Foundation.

Centre for Educational Management (CEM) (2017) *Assessment Monitoring Systems* Available at: http://www.cem.org/assessment-monitoring-systems [Accessed 21 June 2017].

Cooper, P. (2010) *Making Geography Happen: Uneven Development*, Available at: http://www.geography.org.uk/projects/makinggeographyhappen/unevendevelopment/ [Accessed 12 August 2015].

Davies, P. (2002) 'Levels of attainment in geography, *Assessment in Education: Principles, Policy and Practice*, 9 (2), 185–204.

Department for Education (DfE), (2011). *The Framework for the National Curriculum. A Report by the Expert Panel for the National Curriculum review*, London: Department for Education.

Department for Education (DfE), (2012) New data reveals the truth about school performance: Press release, Available at: http://www.education.gov.uk/a00202531/secperftables12 [Accessed 28 January 2012].

Department for Education (DfE) (2014a) *National Curriculum and Assessment from September 2014: Information for Schools*, London, Department for Education.

Department for Education (DfE) (2014b) *Beyond Levels: Alternative Assessment Approaches Developed by Teaching Schools*, London, Department for Education.

Equality and Human Rights Commission (EHRD) (2015) *Is Britain Fairer? The State of Equality and Human Rights 2015*, London: HMSO.

Fischer Family Trust (FFT), (2011) *Data Analysis Project for Schools and Las*, Available at: http://www.fischertrust.org/dap_overview.aspx [Accessed 12 November 2011].

Fischer Family Trust (FFT), (2007) *Making Best Use of FFT Estimates*, Available at: http://www.fischertrust.org/downloads/dap/Training/Making_best_use_of_FFT_estimates.pdf [Accessed 12 November 2011].

Gardner, J. (ed.) (2006) *Assessment and Learning*, London: Sage.

Gardner, J., Harlen, W., Hayward, L. and Stobart, G. with Montgomery, M. (2010) *Developing Teacher Assessment*, Maidenhead: Open University Press.

Geographical Association (2010) *Making Geography Happen*, Available at: http://www.geography.org.uk/projects/makinggeographyhappen/ [Accessed 25 January 2012].

Geographical Association (2014) *An Assessment and Progression Framework for Geography*, Sheffield: Geographical Association, Available at: www.geography.org.uk/news/2014 curriculum/assessment [Accessed 13 April 2016].

Geographical Association AESIG (2015) Assessing without Levels – practical steps to support progression and attainment in geography, Available at: http://www.geography.org.uk/cpdevents/curriculum/assessmentwithoutlevels/#top [Accessed 13 April 2016].

Harlen, W. (2007) *Assessment of Learning*, London: Sage.

Harlen, W. and Deakin-Crick, R. (2002) 'A systematic review of the impact of summative assessment and tests on students' motivation for learning', *Research Evidence in Education Library*, London: EPPI-Centre, Social Science Research Unit, Institute of Education, University of London, Available at: http://eppi.ioe.ac.uk/cms/Default.aspx?tabid=108 [Accessed 12 November 2011].

Hesslewood. A. (2016) 'Talking about assessment', *Teaching Geography*, 41 (1), 28–30.

Hodgen, J. and Webb, M. (2008) 'Questioning and dialogue', in S. Swaffield (ed.), *Unlocking Assessment: Understanding for reflection and Application*, London: Routledge.

Hopkin, J. (2006) *Level Descriptions and Assessment in Geography: A GA Discussion Paper*, Available at: http://www.geography.org.uk/download/GA_AULevelAssessments InGeography.pdf [Accessed 12 November 2011].

Hopkin, J. (2011) 'Progress in geography', *Geography*, 96, (3), 116–23.

Hopwood, N. (2004) 'Pupils' conceptions of geography: towards an improved understanding', *International Research in Geographical and Environmental Education*, 13 (4), 348–61.

Howes, N. (2009) 'How can working assessment data help students make progress in geography?' in P. Weeden and G. Butt (eds.), *Assessing Progress in your Key Stage 3 Geography Curriculum*, Sheffield: Geographical Association.

James, M. (1998) *Using Assessment for School Improvement*, Oxford: Heinemann.

James, M. and Pedder, D. (2006) 'Beyond method: assessment and learning practices and values', *Curriculum Journal*, 17 (2), 109–38.

Kinder, A. and Lambert, D. (2011) 'The national curriculum review: what geography should we teach? *Teaching Geography*, 36 (3), 93–5.

Krathwohl, D. R, (2002) 'A revision of Bloom's Taxonomy: an overview', *Theory into Practice*, 41 (4), 212–18.

Lambert, D. (2010) Think Piece: Progression, Available at: http://www.geography.org.uk/download/GA_PRMGHProgressionThinkPiece.pdf [Accessed 12 November 2011].

Lambert, D. (2011) *The Geography National Curriculum: GA Curriculum Proposals and Rationale*, Sheffield: Geographical Association, Available at: http://www.geography.org.uk/download/GA_GIGCCCurriculumProposals.pdf [Accessed 25 January 2012].

Lambert, D. and Morgan, J. (2010) *Teaching Geography 11–18: A Conceptual Approach*, Maidenhead: Open University Press.

McIntosh, J. (2015) *Final Report of the Commission on Assessment without Levels*, Available at: https://www.gov.uk/government/uploads/system/uploads/attachment_data/file/483058/Commission_on_Assessment_Without_Levels_-_report.pdf [Accessed 9 February 2016].

Marshall, B. and Drummond, M. (2006) 'How teachers engage with Assessment for Learning: Lessons from the classroom', *Research Papers in Education*, 21 (2), 133–49.

May, C. (2014) 'Planning a new key stage 3', *Teaching Geography*, 39 (3), 99–101.

QCA (2008) *Inter-subject comparability studies Study 1a: GCSE, AS and A level geography and history London*, Available at: http://www.ofqual.gov.uk/downloads/category/105-comparability [Accessed 12 November 2011].

Rawling, E. (2001) *Changing the Subject: The Impact of National Policy on School Geography 1980–2000*, Sheffield: Geographical Association.

Rawling, E. (2016) 'The geography curriculum 5–19: what does it all mean?', *Teaching Geography*, 41 (1), 6–9.

Rogers, D. (2015) 'Planning your Key Stage 3', *Teaching Geography*, 40 (2), 67–8.

Rooney, R. (2006) 'Effective feedback as a focus for CPD with a developing geography department, *Teaching Geography*, 31 (2), 84–6.

Rooney, R. (2007) 'Using success criteria', *Teaching Geography*, 32 (1), 51–5.

Stobart, G. (2008) *Testing Times: The Uses and Abuses of Assessment*, London: Routledge.

Swaffield, S. (ed.) (2008) *Unlocking Assessment: Understanding for reflection and application*, London: Routledge.

Taras, M. (2005) 'Assessment – summative and formative – some theoretical reflections', *British Journal of Educational Studies*, 53 (4), 466–78.

Torrance, H. (2009) 'Using assessment in education reform', in H. Daniels, H. Lauder and J. Porter (eds.), *Knowledge, Values and Educational Policy: A Critical Perspective*, London: Routledge.

Trend, R. (2005) 'Individual, situational and topic interest in geoscience among 11– and 12– year-old children, *Research Papers in Education*, 20 (3), 271–302.

Weeden, P. (2005) 'Feedback in the geography classroom', *Teaching Geography*, 30 (3), 161–3.

Weeden, P. (2008) Think Piece: Assessment for Learning, Available at: http://www.geography.org.uk/gtip/thinkpieces/assessmentforlearning/#6878 [Accessed 12 November 2011].

Weeden, P. (2013) 'How do we link assessment to making progress in geography?' in D. Lambert and M. Jones (eds.) *Debates in Geography Education*, 1st edn, London: Routledge.

Weeden, P. and Hopkin, J. (2014) 'Assessing without levels', *Teaching Geography*, 39 (2), 60–3.

Weeden, P. and Lambert, D. (2006) *Geography inside the Black Box*, London: Nelson.

Wood, P. (2009) 'What helps to improve assessment for learning in the geography classroom?', in P. Weeden, and G. Butt (eds.), *Assessing Progress in your Key Stage 3 Geography Curriculum*, Sheffield: Geographical Association.

Chapter 11

Curriculum enactment

Mary Biddulph

> What counts as an educated 19 year old in this day and age?
>
> (Pring et al., 2009, p. 3)

Introduction

This chapter is not about the technicalities of prescribing a geography curriculum nor to advocate particular planning frameworks: planning grids and structures or curriculum maps, and so forth. The aim of this chapter is to examine the question 'Where is the curriculum created?' and, in so doing, to consider the range of social, political, and cultural factors that impact on the curriculum making process. This examination is necessary because whilst the idea of a 'curriculum' may seem, on first encounter, relatively straightforward (a curriculum is what we teach in school isn't it?), when we try to define curriculum a little more precisely we soon find that this straightforward idea is less clear-cut than we think; closer inspection reveals that 'curriculum' is in fact a highly contested concept, not least because what we think we should teach correlates in very precise ways with what we, as a society, think is the purpose of education in the first place. As Lambert asks:

> Is education primarily to serve the needs of society and economy (providing skilful and employable people for the world of work in the global market place), or is it mainly to provide worthwhile experiences and knowledge to help individuals 'live sanely in the world' ... Or has education to serve both these purposes and more besides?
>
> (Lambert, 2003, p. 159)

This chapter attempts to raise some important questions about the nature of the school curriculum, with a particular focus on school geography. It takes curriculum as a highly significant idea and discusses some of the key influences on how this idea has emerged and developed. It concludes with an exploration of some of the consequences of curriculum thinking for teachers and students studying geography.

The making of the geography curriculum: an historical context

It is difficult to find a curriculum theorist who argues that the school curriculum is a neutral entity. Lambert and Morgan contend that the school curriculum is 'a human creation' serving a range of needs and purposes, reflecting and responding to changes in wider society' (Morgan and Lambert, 2005, p. 25). A view echoed elsewhere and in various guises by others such as Oates (2011); Young (2008); Young and Lambert (2014); Rawling (2016). Collectively, these authors agree that the school curriculum, including the geography curriculum, is subject to a range of social, political and cultural influences that shape both institutional and individual decisions about what is taught in schools and classrooms (Deng, 2016).

This non-neutrality in the curriculum is illustrated in the history of curriculum theory. At a societal level, from the late nineteenth to the early twentieth century saw marked changes in working practices driven by rationalistic management ideals. The impact of these ideals on education was marked by the development of a technical-rational approach to curriculum planning advocated by North American curriculum theorists such as Franklin Bobbit, and later Ralph Tyler. This objectives-led model, described by Graves (1979) as a linear model of curriculum planning, presented education and perhaps, more appropriately schooling, as the means by which to change behaviours. For Bobbit and others:

> The first task of the scientific curriculum maker is the discovery of those social deficiencies that result from a lack of historical, literary and geographical experiences. Each deficiency found is a call for direct training; it points to an objective that is to be set up for the conscious training.
>
> (Bobbit, quoted in Flinders and Thornton, 2004, p. 16)

The development of this rationalistic approach to curriculum planning is well documented in historical accounts of curriculum change in UK schools. In the context of school geography, the ground-breaking work of Norman Graves in *Curriculum Planning in Geography* (1979) plus the work of others (Marsden, 1997, 2003; Naish, 1997; Rawling, 2001, 2008, 2016) all provide comprehensive accounts of geography curriculum changes in the twentieth century. Defined by Smith (2000) as 'curriculum as product', which Deng (2016) argues neglects the moral and aesthetic dimensions of schools and classrooms, the rationalistic discourse *per se* provides us with a sense of the hierarchical nature of the curriculum decision-making process, positioning teachers-as-decision-makers close to the bottom of the hierarchy. This is a model that resonates with more recent approaches to curriculum change at a national level, which will be considered later in this chapter.

Pursuing questions about curriculum change in school geography necessitates some consideration of the *content* of the school geography curriculum. Geography was in fact a school subject before it was a university subject. However, once established as a university subject, the 'geography' in the school geography curriculum was heavily influenced by subject developments at university-level. The prevailing geographical paradigm of the late nineteenth and early twentieth centuries was regionalism, and as Heffernan (2003) argues, for university geography 'the otherwise vague and underdeveloped idea of the region emerged as the single most important intellectual contribution of interwar geography' (p. 17). School geography drew heavily on this paradigm, as can be seen in school textbooks with titles such as *The World-Wide Geographies* by Jasper H. Stembridge (published, 1930), which presents pupils with a regional description of places around the world, all of which are located on a map overlain with the British Empire. It is worth noting here that despite there being no national curriculum at the time, pupils across the country were learning more or less the same geographical content (Rawling, 2001), and they were learning it 'by rote' (Naish, 1997, p. 49).

A turning point for education generally, and school geography specifically, was the establishment of the Schools Council in 1964. Universal education, the raising of the school-leaving age plus concurrent technological and social shifts in wider society necessitated a shift in the purpose of education, and in response to these shifts the curriculum also changed (see Lambert and Morgan's 2010 account of this – chapters 1 and 2). The Schools Council was responsible for curriculum and assessment developments, including supporting teachers in their newly emerging role as curriculum makers.

Curriculum planning and development in the 1970s and 1980s was characterised by notions of collaboration and cooperation – between teachers, schools, educational infrastructures (examination boards, professional development initiatives, etc.) and the academy.

Eleanor Rawling (2008) provides clear and helpful distinctions between planning and development. Curriculum planning, she argues, comprises the 'organising and sorting of material' and curriculum development has more of a creative dimension to it, 'taking things beyond what is stated or provided'. Whilst such terms are often used interchangeably, it can be said that curriculum development involves planning but not all planning involves wider curriculum development. Margaret Roberts (1997) develops these ideas when she states that both curriculum planning and development 'encompass the thinking and documentation that occurs before, during and after teaching and learning takes place' (p. 35). What she implies here is that the making of the curriculum is both an intellectual process and a practical product, and that the curriculum is in a constant state of review and change because of this. She argues, despite the curricula shifts and turns at a political and policy level, what goes into the curriculum is 'ultimately a matter of professional judgement' (ibid.). Perhaps this is so, but to balance concerns about the possibilities of a somewhat permissive approach to curriculum development, it was the varying levels of cooperation and collaboration between interested parties that ensured that school geography was not underpinned by an 'anything goes' philosophy; the Schools Council provided frameworks that supported teachers' selection of both content to be taught and processes for learning. Before the 1988 Education Reform Act and the advent of the national curriculum in England and Wales, it was professional judgement in the absence of any statutory guidelines which produced a very localised process of planning and development; a state of affairs seen as problematic by the central government of the day.

The publication in 1991 of the first national curriculum for geography provided a radical shift in where the geography curriculum was made. The curricula freedoms, enjoyed under the guidance of the Schools Council projects, were lost and according to Rawling's authoritative account, this marked the end of a golden age of curriculum *development* (Rawling, 2008). The curriculum became statutory and its implementation was shored up via a new school inspection regime, the Education (Schools) Act 1992.

Whilst the initial premise of the new curriculum was to prescribe content to be taught, freeing teachers to decide on learning processes, in actuality the geography curriculum was so content heavy that teachers' roles changed considerably. For many the pressure was to 'deliver' the content knowledge and the '*curriculum as product model*', discussed by Smith (2000) and conceptualised by Bobbit and others, resurfaced (Rawling, 1996). For others, more confident in their capacities to reinterpret and make sense of the GNC, the new rules represented an opportunity to structure the requirements of the national curriculum in educationally more valuable ways (see Roberts, 1997). Generally, however, teachers' professional judgement was no longer trusted and curriculum development, the intellectual process advocated by Roberts above, was, at least in relation to the curriculum, much more difficult to exercise. One consequence, arguably, was that the curriculum links between school and university geography were severed: at a time when university geography was taking a new turn to the left with developments in cultural geography (Jackson, 1989), school geography was being forced to turn to the right, driven by the ideologies of the New Right and a 'capes and bays' perception of the subject; the school geography curriculum became 'fossilised' in an outdated view of the discipline (Lambert, 2004).

Since 1991, the national curriculum has undergone several further revisions (DfE, 1995; DfEE/QCA, 1999; QCA, 2007). However, these revisions have been accused of 'keeping interest groups happy rather than developing well-theorised content' (Oates, 2010, p. 2) and for school geography this meant merely a *reduction* in content rather than comprising any new interpretations of what actually constituted geography as a school subject. The 2007 revision was more radical, framing the curriculum around seven 'key concepts' and leaving teachers with a great deal of professional autonomy to interpret these concepts in ways they deemed appropriate; teachers were once again in a position to 'make' the curriculum for themselves, taking into account their students' views and experiences and their own geographical enthusiasms. In addition, the curriculum also comprised a series of cross-cutting themes such as 'cultural understanding and diversity', the claim being that these themes would enable greater curriculum flexibility and ensure students experienced some degree of curriculum coherence

(Nightingale, 2007). After many years, during which 'curriculum thinking' had been severely eroded in the professional preparation of teachers, this shift proved to be a complex policy setting in which teachers had to operate. The Action Plan for Geography (GA and RGS-IBG, 2011) explicitly emphasised curriculum making, precisely because of the need to rediscover and encourage curriculum thinking in schools.

The election of a new Liberal-Democrat/Conservative coalition government in 2010 marked a U-turn in education policy, which was reflected in yet another revision of the national curriculum. It has been argued that the 2014 geography national curriculum marked a return to a traditional view of the subject, reflecting an absolutist view of knowledge and a transmission view of teaching and learning (See Firth, 2013; Biddulph et al., 2015; Rawling, 2016). At the same time, GCSE and A level specifications were also undergoing a complete review. The curriculum landscape was under full-scale assault, deemed necessary by a political discourse claiming that standards needed to be raised and the system needed greater rigour if England was to become more competitive within the global economy; education, as reflected in the curriculum, would the vehicle which, in part, would ensure the nations increased competitiveness (Gove, 2012; Morgan, N., 2016).

The dash for change took place in a broader policy context. The academisation project meant that schools that chose (or were forced) to become academies did not have to teach the national curriculum at all, and new accountability measures for schools, known as 'Progress 8' repositioned school geography as one of the 'humanities', subjects that would be part of the new success indicators for schools. Whilst the question 'where is the curriculum made?' is an enduring one, it is against this recent backdrop of system-wide change that it takes on a new significance. It could seem that the ever-changing curriculum landscape is the responsibility of everyone but teachers and education professionals; however, in the next section, I will argue that it is precisely because of the policy context that teachers are central to the curriculum-making process.

Curriculum making: the current context

As we saw earlier, the term curriculum making has a historical context which is important to understand – we are where we are because of where we have been. However, at the end of the first decade of the twenty-first century, the idea of making the curriculum in school geography has acquired new significance. This is partly through the activities of the Action Plan for Geography (2006–11) and its attempts to encourage principled, localised curriculum thinking. Thus Brooks (2006) writes:

> "curriculum-making" therefore reflects "the curriculum which is experienced by students and made by teachers in school" (ibid). Although the localised curriculum is influenced by the macro-level curriculum design, the responsibility for ensuring that it is responsive to the local needs of the school and the

individual classes remains in the hands of the individual teacher. The concept of curriculum-making firmly places the ownership of the "local" curriculum in the hands of each geography teacher.

(p. 77)

The Geographical Association's (GA) 2009 *Manifesto* for school geography also presents curriculum making as an important professional activity. Here it is said, metaphorically, to draw from three separate sources of 'energy':

- The teachers' own practical skills and expertise: the craft of teaching and pedagogic choice.
- The interests and needs of students: getting to know students, what motivates them and how they learn.
- The dynamic, changing subject discipline has to offer: drawing from the concepts and ideas in the discipline that help us understand aspects of the world.

(Geographical Association, 2009, p. 27)

Lambert and Morgan (2010) present this idea in the form of a diagram (see below) where the three 'sources of energy' are presented as interacting with, and mutually dependent on, each other. The following discussion explores the role of each, as a means of unravelling the complexity of relationships between teachers, students and the discipline, in the curriculum-making process.

a Teachers

The interaction between the teacher and the learner is dependent not only on subject knowledge and skills but it is also an expression of personal values and beliefs about teaching.

(Burgess, 2000, p. 416)

In order to plan, develop, and make a curriculum that meets the educational aims of a democratic society, the selection, ordering, and interpretation of what young people learn is a tall order and carries with it enormous responsibility. Nonetheless, once a national curriculum has been constructed (with or without consultation with education professionals including teachers), it is still the case that any prescription still has to be interpreted and implemented by teachers and subsequently taught to students. Kelly (2009) describes the 'make or break role that teachers have in all curricular activities, even in relation to those which originate outside the school' (p. 13), a view supported by Pring (2011), who calls into question the much used 'delivery' metaphor when talking about teachers' work; teachers do not 'deliver' anything, and such an idea is, he argues, a significant distraction from what it really means to be a teacher.

In the context of school geography, Lambert and Morgan (2010) develop this further when they suggest that 'the curriculum *as experienced* by children and

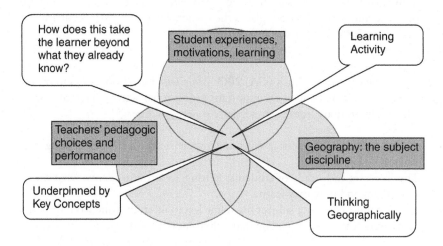

Figure 11.1 Curriculum making (GA undated; see also Lambert and Morgan 2010, p. 50).

young people is, at least in part, one that has been made by teachers. Teachers are the curriculum makers' (p. 49). Their argument runs that, in spite of prevailing political ideologies resulting in curriculum prescription, and in spite of the influences of accountability systems such as Ofsted, ultimately the curriculum comes *into being* in the day-to-day interactions between teachers, their students and the subject discipline, and it is impossible to have a living geography curriculum without this dynamic interaction. To a certain extent, it is *because* of the centralisation and institutionalisation of curriculum decisions that teachers have a moral responsibility to re-present or 're-make' (Deng, 2016: p. 90) the *curriculum as given* in ways that bring meaning and critical insight to *their* students in *their* context; without this re-presentation, young people will be learning inert, irrelevant content:

> Designing a curriculum is not just a technical matter, specifying objectives and a course of study to meet them. It is a moral concern and should reflect what we think we should be teaching.
>
> (Geographical Association, 2009, p. 27)

Such a notion of curriculum making is a radical and somewhat liberating departure from the objective-led planning approaches espoused by Bobbit, Tyler and others all those years ago. This is not to deny the significance of systematic curriculum planning, and curriculum development (after all, decisions and choices about what and how to teach still have to be made), what this alternative take on curriculum making does is force us to see the curriculum as a *process* rather than a product (Smith, 2000) and for this process to succeed, it requires creative contributions from teachers, students and geography. What this means for geography teachers is that they themselves have to 'think geographically' (Jackson and Massey, 2005; Jackson, 2006), as opposed to generically, in order to make intelligent decisions about *what* as well as how to teach. In many respects, teachers are the drivers here and, as Smith (2000) points out, 'The approach is dependent upon the cultivation of wisdom and meaning making in the classroom. If the teacher is not up to this, then there will be severe limitations on what can be achieved educationally' (p. 10). Teachers are not the only limitation to the process model, there are others; the pursuit of curriculum uniformity and accountability mechanisms, such as examination results, do little to encourage the professional individualism that characterises this process model.

b Geography

In 2010, Margaret Roberts raised concerns that new teachers were too frequently judged as 'competent' based on the proficient instrumental generic aspect of lessons rather than on the geographical understanding being developed:

> I am not arguing that teachers don't need generic skills: it is clearly necessary for classes to be well managed if students are going to learn anything. In my opinion, however, the over-riding purpose of geography lessons is to develop geographical understanding, to give students access to geographical ways of thinking, to help them make sense of their worlds. The use of starters or plenaries is not intrinsically good; it depends on whether they enhance learning or are mere routines.
>
> (Roberts, 2010, p. 113)

A great deal of attention and a significant amount of public money has been spent in recent years on attending to issues of pedagogy. National Strategies in literacy and numeracy, initiatives such as SEAL (Social and Emotional Aspect of Learning), the proliferation of learning styles inventories, and the notion of generic thinking skills have dominated education policy and school-based curriculum development for some years now. When mired in all of this 'professional paraphernalia' (see Lambert, 2011) – the three-part lesson, target setting, explicit learning objectives, etc. – we could be forgiven for thinking that 'what' we teach is almost irrelevant; the subject seems to have been forgotten.

However, the curriculum-making diagram above makes a clear case for refocusing on the subject because without this the dynamic equilibrium necessary for successful curriculum making is lost. Curriculum making at any level – national, school or classroom cannot proceed without an intellectual engagement with the kind of geographies we believe appropriate for young people growing up in the twenty-first century.

The 2011 Ofsted report for geography entitled *Learning to Make a World of Difference* is bold, not just in its attention to how students learn, but also because it articulates the significance of what they learn if geography is to contribute to pupils' broader education. The report more than suggests that school geography needs to reconnect with its disciplinary roots. This is not to say that university geography has an automatic right to shape the school curriculum, but it does suggest that while school geography has in many respects been 'prevented from a sustained engagement with developments in the discipline' (Morgan and Lambert, 2005, p. 3), the process of making a *geography* curriculum actually requires engagement with geography at a disciplinary rather than at a 'popular culture' level. This engagement with disciplinary thinking is crucial precisely because it provides ways of 'understanding the world and interpreting facts about the world' (Gardner, cited in Brooks, 2011, p. 173).

This returns us to the question: 'What kind of geography is appropriate "*in this day and age*"?' The government's 2010 White Paper (DfE, 2010) advocates a 'core knowledge' curriculum (see Roger Firth's chapter in this volume) and the 2014 National Curriculum, is framed around broad definitions of content to be taught rather than ideas to be examined and questioned. In the 'Purpose Statement' (as opposed to the 'Importance Statement' of the 2007 curriculum), geography is defined by a form of knowledge gathering whereby pupils are 'equipped with knowledge' and they 'grow knowledge' through geographical study. This 'essentials' curriculum risks failing to make a contribution to young people's understanding of the issues of the day: climate change, mass movement of people across space, global consumerism, the global economic crisis, water security, power security, contested borders, and more. I am not suggesting the need for a 'here today/gone tomorrow' curriculum built around media events and popular 'everyday' culture, but a curriculum that enables a sustained and thoughtful engagement with the space/place dimension of significant matters of our time – or, to use John Morgan's phrase, to teach geography 'as if the planet matters' (Morgan, 2011). Morgan (2008, 2011) contends that insights from social and cultural geography could make a significant contribution here, and others (Stannard, 2002; Brown, 2002; Huckle, 2002) make a clear case for a school/university interface in order to sustain the relevance of the subject in schools.

c Students

John Dewey, a contemporary of Franklin Bobbit, argued that an effective education needed a curriculum that started with the capabilities and interests of children, and that learning was essentially a social and interactive process. He was an advocate of a curriculum that enabled children to relate new learning to prior experiences and that comprised significant and relevant content: *'It is not a question of how to teach the child geography, but first of all the question what geography is for the child* (Dewey, 1972 [1897], cited in Brooks, 2009, p. 203).

Starting with the interests and capabilities of students is a challenge in the face of curriculum prescription. However, Paechter (2009), Hall and Thompson (2008), Biddulph (2011) and others suggest that failure to do so has significant consequences for many young people. They argue that many who struggle to engage with school do so because they do not acquire from *outside* school (in their homes and in their communities), the kind of elitist knowledges validated *inside* the school system:

> An exclusive and excluding curriculum that only values certain kinds of knowledges and experiences signals to many young people how we, as a society, value them now – as individuals, as members of diverse communities and as contributors to wider society. It could be deemed educationally careless to ignore the social and cultural capital of young people whose spatial lives are shaped by powerful global forces: ignoring these geographies runs the risk of alienating significant proportions of young people and runs the risk of leaving school geography out of kilter with their needs and interests.
>
> (Biddulph, 2011, p. 56)

Students do bring into their geography lessons pre-existing 'geographical behaviours, perceptions and skills' (Lambert and Morgan, 2010, p. 50; Brooks, 2011); the lives that they lead, the places and spaces that they occupy, the real and virtual connections they make, and the concerns that they have are part and parcel of young peoples' individual and collective identities, all of which contribute, either consciously or subconsciously, to their geographical imaginations. But how can, or even should school geography utilise these pre-existing geographies and in so doing 'include and validate within school more non-school student centered knowledge ...?' (Paechter, 2009, p. 165).

In answering 'should' school geography utilise these pre-existing geographies, Yi-Fu Tuan (2008), the Chinese-American geographer, suggests that:

> Blindness to experience is in fact a common human condition. We rarely attend to what we know. We attend to what we know about ... we know far more than we can tell [yet] .... Experiences are slighted or ignored because the means to articulate them or point them out are lacking.
>
> (p. 201)

If there is any validity in Dewey's notion of learning, then it may just be the case that in 'attending' to what young people already know, that is, their pre-existing geographies, rather than just what we want them to know about, school geography may be the means by which teachers can unlock and value this knowledge, and, in doing so, create a more inclusive curriculum experience for all students.

What we are exploring here is something akin to a 'curriculum as praxis' model (Smith, 2000, p. 11), namely an approach to the curriculum that is both committed to sense-making, but, in addition, has at its core an explicit commitment to emancipation. The implications of such a model are not insignificant for school geography? How can we ensure that the everyday experiences of young people are visible, valued *and* valuable to geographical understanding, and in doing so take young people beyond what they already know? Curriculum development projects such as 'Living Geography' and the 'Young People's Geographies Project'[1] have sought to better centralise the knowledge that young people bring to school with them. The outcomes of these curriculum-making opportunities demonstrate the means by which the discipline, teachers and students can collaborate in order to construct the school geography curriculum.

Conclusion

To bring this curriculum 'story' to some sort of conclusion, it seems appropriate to return to our question at the beginning of this chapter:

> *What counts as an educated 19 year old in this day and age?*
> (Pring et al., 2009, p. 3, emphasis added)

I argue that it would be difficult to claim that the education system has done its job well if our '19-year-old' left school without a critically informed understanding of the social, environmental and cultural challenges confronting us in the twenty-first century. The question is what kind of school geography would be required in order to achieve this critically informed understanding? Without a doubt, geography as a discipline has a distinct contribution to make here. However, the success of this endeavour is dependent on a number of variables, not least of which is how we construct the geography *within* the curriculum.

As this chapter has argued, and as the curriculum-making diagram suggests, the curriculum will be what teachers and their students choose to make of it. It is in a constant state of becoming and so risks being pulled in all manner of directions – and possibly badly distorted if any one interest or influence becomes too dominant. Teachers have to accept quite a lot of responsibility for holding things in balance.

And so decisions have to be made regarding what to teach (subject discipline), when to teach it (progression) and how to teach (pedagogy), and to enact all three (what, when and how) we must return to the distinction between curriculum planning, curriculum development, and curriculum making, and the interlocking levels at which these activities are played out. And so, regardless of curriculum prescription what we can be sure of is that any authorised curriculum will need interpreting and developing by teachers,, and at the classroom level it will need bringing to life through the curriculum-making process. As Tim Oates (2011) states:

> A national curriculum should include that which is essential for participation in a modern, democratic society ... It is for teachers and schools to construct programmes of learning which will be motivating for their learners – it is teachers who understand the specific keys to unlocking the

motivation of their learners (Black et al., 2003) in respect of essential bodies of knowledge.

(p. 129)

What Oates is reminding us of here is of both the relationship between the curriculum and the broader purposes of education for a democratic society (for more see Kelly, 2009) and also that it is teachers who carry the real responsibility for the curriculum as experienced by pupils. It is almost certainly the case that excitement and motivation can be encouraged best when the students are involved, but also when the teacher is oriented by a clear sense of purpose and convinced about the significance of what she or he is doing. External political and social influences play their role, but ultimately it is up to teachers and students to take what the discipline has to offer, work it into something tangible and realise the opportunities it offers.

As a challenge to the current curriculum dilemma, Hamilton (1999) argues that at present the curriculum

has been reduced to questions about instructional content and classroom delivery. The sense that a curriculum is a vision of the future and that, in turn, curriculum questions relate to human formation has been marginalised. The short-termism of 'What should they know?' has replaced the strategic curriculum question 'What should they become?

(p. 136)

To support our vision of the future I want to give the final word in this 'story' to students who, when given the opportunity, can provide us with some wise words to reflect upon. The following quote is from a student participant in the YPG project, and it captures, for me, the essence of what a geography curriculum is all about. For this 15-year–old, school geography clearly isn't just a question of 'what should he know'. What he expresses here is a more sophisticated take on the discipline, capturing his own position within it and a sense that geography connects him to others and elsewhere. School geography is not just inert content but is both present and influential in the everyday; it is up to the curriculum and those who enact it to bring this into being.

Geography is all around us. Geography effects [sic] us all. *Me, I'm geography.* This building is part of geography; everything is geography. Geography isn't just about Jamaica's there, Africa's there, Britain's there, it's about us as a community.

(Anton, age 15 years)

The skilful curriculum maker not only recognises and values this, but also discovers how to induct Anton into ways of understanding the world, using ideas that may be new, challenging and sometimes requiring painstaking effort.

Key readings

1　Firth, R. and Biddulph, M. (2009) 'Whose life is it anyway? Young people's geographies', in D. Mitchell (ed.), *Living Geography: Exciting Futures for Teachers and Students,* Cambridge: Chris Kington Publishing, pp. 13–27. This chapter discusses how the academic discipline has engaged with young people's lives and the opportunities this presents for the geography curriculum in schools.

2　Smith, M.K. (1996, 2000) 'Curriculum theory and practice', *The Encyclopaedia of Informal Education*, Available at: www.infed.org/biblio/b-curric. htm. This article is generic and provides interesting models of curriculum with sensible criticism.

Note

1　Living Geography and The Young People's Geographies Project, both funded by The Action Plan for Geography (DfES), are curriculum development projects where expertise across a range of institutions (universities, schools, the GA, and other non-education specific organisations such as town planning departments) collaborate to develop school geography. For more go to: http://www.geography.org. uk/projects/livinggeography and http://www.youngpeoplesgeographies.co.uk/.

References

Biddulph, M. (2011) 'Young People's geographies: implications for school geography', in G. Butt (ed.), *Geography, Education and the Future*, London: Continuum.

Biddulph, M., Lambert, D. and Balderstone, D. (2015) *Learning to Teach Geography in the Secondary School*, 3rd edn, London: Routledge.

Black, P., Harrison, C., Lee, C., Marshall, B. and Wiliam, D. (2003) *Assessment for Learning: Putting it into Practice*, Maidenhead: Open University Press.

Brooks, C. (2006) 'Geography teachers and making the school geography curriculum', *Geography*, 91 (1), 79–83.

Brooks, C. (2009) 'Teaching living geography – making a geography curriculum', in D. Mitchell (ed.), *Living Geography: Exciting Futures for Teachers and Students*, Cambridge: Chris Kington Publishing.

Brooks, C. (2011) 'Geographical knowledge and professional development', in G. Butt (ed.), *Geography Education and the Future*, London: Continuum.

Brown, P. (2002) 'The erosion of geography', *Geography*, 87 (1), 84–5.

Burgess, H. (2000) 'ITT: New curriculum, new directions', *Curriculum Journal*, 11 (3), 405–17.

Deng, Z. (2016) Bringing curriculum theory and didactics together: a Deweyan perspective, *Pedagogy, Culture & Society*, 24 (1), 75–99.

Department for Education, (2010) *The Importance of Teaching: The Schools White Paper*, London: DfE.

Department for Education and Employment/ Qualifications and Curriculum Authority (DfEE/QCA) (1999) *The National Curriculum Handbook for Secondary Teachers in England*, Key Stages 3 and 4, London: DfEE/QCA.

Firth, R. (2013) 'What constitutes knowledge in geography?' in D. Lambert and M. Jones (eds.) *Debates in Geography Education*, London: Routledge.

Flinders, D. J. and Thornton, S.J. (2004) *The Curriculum Studies Reader*, New York and London: RoutledgeFalmer.

Geographical Association (2009) *A Different View; A Manifesto from the Geographical Association*, Sheffield: Geographical Association.

Geographical Association/Royal Geographical Society (2011) *The Action Plan for Geography 2006–11*, Available at: http://www.geography.org.uk/projects/actionplanforgeography/ [Accessed 12 April 2016].

Gove, M (2012) Speech given to the Education World Forum, Queen Elizabeth's Conference Centre, London, Available at: https://www.gov.uk/government/speeches/michael-gove-to-the-education-world-forum [Accessed 17 April 2016].

Graves, N. J. (1979) *Curriculum Planning in Geography*, London: Heineman Educational Books.

Hall, C. and Thompson, P. (2008) 'Opportunities missed and/or thwarted? "Funds of knowledge" meet the English national curriculum', *Curriculum Journal*, 19 (2), 87–103.

Hamilton, D. (1999) The pedagogic paradox (or why no didactics in England?), *Pedagogy, Culture & Society*, 7 (1), 135–52.

Heffernan, M. (2003) 'Histories of geography', in N.J. Clifford, S. Holloway, S. Rice and G. Valentine (eds.), *Key Concepts in Geography*, London: Sage.

Huckle, J. (2002) 'Reconstructing nature', *Geography*, 87 (1), 64–72.

Jackson, P. (1989) *Maps of Meaning: An Introduction to Cultural Geography*, London: Unwin Hyman.

Jackson, P. (2006) 'Thinking geographically', *Geography*, 91 (3), 199–204.

Jackson, P. and Massey, D. (2005) *Thinking Geographically*, Geographical Association, Available at: www.geography.org.uk/download/NPOGThinking.doc [Accessed 6 October 2011].

Kelly, A. V. (2009) *The Curriculum: Theory and Practice*, 6th edn, London: Sage.

Lambert, D. (2003) 'Effective approaches to curriculum development', in R. Gerber (ed.), *International Handbook on Geographical Education*, Netherlands: Kluwer Academic Publishers.

Lambert, D. (2004) 'Geography', in J. White (ed.), *Rethinking the School Curriculum: Values, Aims and Purposes*, London: Routledge.

Lambert, D. (2011) 'Reviewing the case for geography and the "knowledge turn" in the English National Curriculum', *Curriculum Journal*, 22 (2), 243–64.

Lambert, D. and Morgan, J. (2010) *Teaching Geography 11–18: A Conceptual Approach*, Maidenhead: McGraw-Hill.

Marsden, W. (1997) 'The place of geography in the curriculum: an historical overview 1886–1976', in D. Tillbury and M. Williams (eds.), *Teaching and Learning Geography*, London: Routledge.

Marsden, W. (2003) 'Geography curriculum planning in evolution: some historical and international perspectives', in R. Gerber (ed.), *International Handbook on Geographical Education*, Netherlands: Kluwer Academic Publishers.

Morgan, J. (2008) 'Curriculum development in new times', *Geography*, 3 (1), 17–24.

Morgan, J. (2011) *Teaching Secondary Geography as if the Planet Matters*, London: Routledge.

Morgan, J. and Lambert, D. (2005) *Geography: Teaching School Subjects*, London: Routledge.

Morgan, N. (2016) *A World-Class Education System for Every Child*, Speech delivered on 23 February, 2016, to the City of London Corporation, Guildhall, London.

Available at: https://www.gov.uk/government/speeches/a-world-class-education-system-for-every-child [Accessed 17 April, 2016].

Naish, M. (1997) 'The scope of school geography: a medium for education', in D. Tillbury and M. Williams (eds.), *Teaching and Learning Geography*, London: Routledge.

Nightingale, P. (2007) 'A level English literature: learning and assessment', *Changing English: Studies in Culture and Education*, 14 (2), 135–44.

Oates, T. (2010) *Missing the Point: Identifying a Well-grounded Common Core: Comment on Trends in the Development of the National Curriculum*, Cambridge Assessment, Available at: http://www.cambridgeassessment.org.uk/ca/digitalAssets/185415_Missing_the_point. pdf [Accessed 30 September 2011].

Oates, T. (2011) 'Could do better: using international comparisons to refine the National Curriculum in England', *Curriculum Journal*, 22 (2), 121–50.

Ofsted (2011) *Learning to Make a World of Difference*, Available at: http://ofsted.gov.uk/publication/090224 [Accessed 6 October 2011].

Paechter, P. (2009) 'Schooling and the ownership of knowledge', *Pedagogy, Culture and Society*, 6 (2), 161–76.

Pring, R. (2011) Talk given to the post-graduate students' summer conference, University of Nottingham, School of Education.

Pring, R., Hayward, G., Hodgson, A., Johnson, J., Keep, E., Oancea, A., Rees, G., Spours, K. and Wilde, S. (2009) *Education for All: The Future of Education and Training for 14–19 Year Olds*, London: Routledge.

QCA (2007) Geography National Curriculum, Programme of study for Key Stage 3 and attainment target, Available at: www.rgs.org/NR/rdonlyres/2FFCE97B-5753-4A98-9291-6E652E3185AD/0/FW_GeographyNC.pdf [Accessed 15 June 2017].

Rawling, E. (1996) 'The Impact of the national curriculum on school-based curriculum development', in A. Kent, D. Lambert, M. Naish, and F. Slater (eds.), *Geography in Education: Viewpoints on Teaching*, Cambridge: Cambridge University Press.

Rawling, E. (2001) *Changing the Subject: The Impact of National Policy on School Geography 1980–2000*, Sheffield, Geographical Association.

Rawling, E. (2008) *Planning your Key Stage 3 Curriculum*, Sheffield: Geographical Association.

Rawling, E. (2016) 'The geography curriculum 5–19: What does it all mean?' *Teaching Geography*, 41 (1), 6–9.

Roberts, M. (1997) 'Curriculum planning and course development: a matter of professional judgement', in D. Tillbury and M. Williams (eds.), *Teaching and Learning Geography*, Routledge: London.

Roberts, M. (2010) 'Where's the geography? Reflections on being an external examiner', *Teaching Geography*, 35 (3), 112–13.

Smith, M. K. (2000) 'Curriculum theory and practice', *The Encyclopaedia of Informal Education*, Available at: www.infed.org/biblio/b-curric.htm [Accessed 6 October 2011].

Stannard, K. (2002) 'Waving not drowning', *Geography*, 87 (1), 73–83.

Tuan, Yi-Fu (2008) *Space and Place: The Perspective of Experience* 6th edn, Minneapolis, MN: University of Minnesota Press.

Young, M. (2008) *Bringing Knowledge Back In: From social constructivism to social realism in the sociology of education*, London: Routledge.

Young, M. and Lambert, D. (with Roberts, C. and Roberts, M.) (2014) *Knowledge and the Future School: Curriculum and Social Justice*, London: Bloomsbury Academic.

Chapter 12

The place of fieldwork in geography education

Lauren Hammond

My ideal school would be an entire planet. Cara, 14, Winchester.

(Burke and Grovesnor, 2003)

Introduction

Cara's comment resonates; she wants her school to be an entire planet. One imagines she wants to see its natural and human wonders, to explore and investigate how they have been imagined, formed, constructed and portrayed. As Tuan (1993) articulates, our diverse home and planet, Earth, provides the focus for the study of the discipline geography. Whoever Cara is, she will come to school with a wealth of experiences, and imaginations, of the world. Upon entering the geography classroom, she will begin to study the discipline in a formal way, taking her beyond her everyday knowledge and experiences of the world (Lambert and Biddulph, 2014), and learning how 'powerful knowledge' (see Young and Muller, 2010; Young et al., 2014) is created and tested in geography. She will learn to think geographically, and this chapter explores how fieldwork can contribute to a student's development as a geographer. It discusses the benefits and challenges of fieldwork, reflects on its place in the curriculum, and considers the role of geography teachers in ensuring high quality fieldwork, and how, and why, different types of fieldwork can be utilised in geography education. Through these discussions, this chapter aims to reflect on the role of fieldwork as a fundamental pillar of geography education. It considers how the geography teacher can utilise fieldwork when making the geography curriculum, and empower them to do so (even when challenges have to be overcome). Finally, we also explore the benefits of fieldwork to students in developing as geographers, both in regards to subject knowledge and skills, and also in their identity as geographers.

What is fieldwork and why take students out of the classroom?

Geography wants to take children outside the school and into the streets and fields.

(Bonnett, 2008, p. 80)

Fieldwork can be defined simply as the medium that enables formal education outside of the classroom, and provides students with first-hand experiences of creating and testing (geographical) knowledge (Holmes and Walker, 2006; Fuller et al., 2010; Lambert and Reiss, 2014). When we think back to our personal experiences of studying geography at school and university, and/or reflect on our teaching of the subject, many of us will recall (often fondly) time spent in the field (Caton, 2006a). The chapter begins by critically examining the arguments that exist for fieldwork playing an essential role in geography education, and the reasons why many of us often have such strong memories of it.

As the opening quotation from Bonnett (2008) suggests, fieldwork is for many, 'a defining feature' and an important 'mode of learning' in geography (Hope, 2009). It has been seen as part of geography's disciplinary identity, with Lambert (2011) arguing that, as it embodies exploration and enquiry (and the relationship between them), fieldwork is a key element of geography's heritage, and an expression of 'its contemporary educational power' (p. 129). The Geographical Association, in its 2009 manifesto, represents geography as a 'discovery subject', with fieldwork being an 'essential component' (p. 23) and fundamental pillar of the discipline. Indeed, Kent et al., 1979 (cited in Fuller et al., 2010) state that it is 'as intrinsic to geography as clinical practice is to medicine'. The significance of this lies within both educational and social gains for students when conducting fieldwork, but also as a method of developing and maintaining student and teacher identities as geographers (Lambert and Reiss, 2014).

Fieldwork can both stimulate students' awe and wonder about place(s) and people(s); and even when fieldwork is conducted in a familiar place; it can provide the opportunity to take students beyond their everyday knowledge of that place (Lambert and Reiss, 2014). For example, students may know the coastal town (which they call home) is prone to flooding (e.g. from stories from family and friends, the media, and even witnessing floods themselves), but geography education can enable learners to explore the physical processes that cause the flooding, the impacts the flooding has, and how people have tried to manage the flooding. Fieldwork, as part of this study, can provide students with a sensory experience of the places at risk, allow them to see first-hand the erosive power of the ocean, and the impacts flooding has on people and the environment. Lambert and Reiss (2014) express these (and many other) benefits of taking learners out of the classroom in their 'compelling case' for fieldwork as shown in Figure 12.1.

Lambert and Reiss (2014) do, however, note that none of the potential benefits of fieldwork are guaranteed, but express that fieldwork can often provide the 'unique circumstance that make the above much more attainable' (p. 9). The 'unique circumstances' of fieldwork often mean that students are given the opportunities to work together on activities and research that occurs over several hours/ days, which contrasts with students often highly compartmentalised school days (when they may have 50 minutes of geography sandwiched between English and physical education). They can also enable learners to engage in enquires and explorations (which may include developing research questions, collecting and analysing

The use of (and investigation of) 'real world' settings[10]

- Understanding the uniqueness of place context

- The motivation of working in unfamilar settings (includes 'awe and wonder')

- Experiencing the 'unfamiliar' in the familiar/local context, and stimulating curiosity

- Understanding through direct experience and/or observation of the world, linking theory and practice

Application and evaluation of knowledge, understanding and skills in 'messy contexts'

- Deepening awareness of variability, data handling and statistical modelling

- Encouraging caution in explanation, drawing conclusions and decision making

- Exploring 'ways of seeing' (surface appearances can deceive)

- Using (potentially) all the senses to explore landscapes/phenomena

Developing 'real world learning'[11]

- 'Habits of mind': Investigating; Experimenting; Reasoning Imagining

- 'Frames of mind': Curiosity; Determination; Resourcefulness; Sociability; Reflection

- Enabling critical thinking in the 'naughty world' that does not behave as systems and models predict

Social dimensions

- Extended social interaction in meaning making

- Iterative processes (e.g. discussion, redrafting) and 'independent' learning

- Extended cooperation in problem solving and decision making

- Deepen teachers' knowledge of students and their capacities

- Awareness of ethical questions, e.g. with regard to other living things

Figure 12.1 A 'compelling case' for fieldwork in geography education (Lambert and Reiss, 2014, p. 9).[1]

primary geographical data, and using it to draw conclusions and inform further study) from start to finish and in a 'hands on' manner (see Biddulph et al., 2015).

Conducting fieldwork can provide students with the opportunity to explore and test powerful (and potentially abstract) geographical knowledge and theory in real world settings. The opportunity to collect and test primary data, is an implicit benefit of fieldwork, with Roberts (2013) identifying the benefits as:

- Data is collected to address *specific questions in the particular contexts* the students are investigating
- Students know what the data refer to in the *real world*
- Students are aware of the preparations and decisions made *prior to* data collection
- They are aware of the *limits of data*, and can comment on its reliability
- Students develop awareness of how data need interpretation.

(p. 53)

Whilst Roberts also identifies some disadvantages (e.g. relatively small sets of data are often collected over small periods of time), the opportunity to collect and analyse primary data can empower students through initiating them into the ways in which the landscapes and settings can be investigated and interpreted geographically.

In other words, fieldwork provides unique opportunities for students to 'think geographically'. Biddulph et al., (2015) maintain that fieldwork's contribution to thinking geographically comes from students being provided with real world opportunities to

> experiment with their geographical imagination, to explore their geographical understanding and to demonstrate their geographical knowledge, in ways that are simply impossible to do in the classroom alone.
>
> (p. 218)

For example, in considering this in relation to one of the core concepts of geography, place, we can (following Job, 1999) suggest a variety of experiential ways to support students in making connections with place and thus deepen their understanding of place as an concept. One illustration is Job's use of Haiku poetry (ibid. p. 26), where he encourages students to sit quietly in a place and 'allow stimuli from your surroundings come to your mind (visual, sounds, smells)' before writing a poem. He explains that this can also help to develop learners' emotional connections with place. If we, for example, imagine this activity is done in an ex-mining community, which is facing social and economic challenges, then enabling students to explore their geographical imagination of the place, alongside the study of 'objective facts' about the place, can help to develop their understanding of historical geographies associated with the place, the role of the geographical imagination in the construction of place, and also (potentially) create emotional investment in the subject and locality.

On the challenges of taking students out 'in to the streets and fields'

Teachers face several challenges when planning, conducting, and assessing, fieldwork. Whilst this chapter mainly discusses the benefits of fieldwork, and consciously downplays the issues and problems associated with fieldwork, it would be wrong to ignore these altogether (see Ofsted, 2011; Kinder, 2013), also assessment considerations at Key Stages 4 and 5 (see DfE, 2014a; DfE, 2014b). Lambert and Reiss (2016) identify a variety of challenges to teachers organising fieldwork:

> The fact is that geography can be done without venturing into the field: indeed it is often simpler, and (organisationally) more straightforward (and cheaper) to avoid the messy and unpredictable real world. Fieldwork can therefore be perceived by some as expendable: desirable, but not a core requirement. Fieldwork is sometimes seen by school management as expensive – not only in monetary cost, but also of curriculum time ... Some also argue that the opportunity costs are too high in terms of risk management and 'safety'... and there are a number of more technical challenges associated with fieldwork in the context of formal qualifications structures such as the GCSE and A-level examinations.
>
> (Lambert and Reiss, 2016, p. 29)

Teachers need to be aware of the challenges, and then overcome them. To teach geography without fieldwork would be like teaching science with no practical laboratory work: possible, efficient, cheaper, but less engaging, unidimensional and ultimately inadequate. The rest of this chapter endeavours to inform, and thus empower teachers in this task, after reflecting on the place of fieldwork in the curriculum, and the opportunities and challenges associated with this.

The place of fieldwork in the curriculum

Whilst fieldwork is entrenched in both the history and identity of geography (particularly as a school subject), its position in the curriculum (both at national level, and in the enacted school curriculum) has experienced much change over the years (see Fuller et al., 2010; Lambert and Reiss, 2016). Policy makers of all perspectives have also extoled the benefits of fieldwork, so that for 14-year-old Cara, who we met at the beginning of this chapter, fieldwork is today a compulsory part of her Key Stage 3 education. The Department for Education (DfE, 2013b) and Ofsted (2011) have recognised and strongly endorsed, the contribution of fieldwork to students' geographical learning. However, Ofsted (2011) also note, with caution, that fieldwork was underdeveloped in the majority of secondary schools that they visited (90 between 2007 and 2010), with only one-fifth of schools having a fieldwork programme which 'developed fieldwork skills progressively' (p. 45). Around half of the schools had no significant fieldwork in Key Stage 3, and fieldwork in Key Stage 4 was designed mainly to meet the examination criteria.

Ofsted's observations were made before education in England and Wales embarked on a period of radical change; in 2014 new Programmes of study were introduced at Key Stage 1, 2, and 3 (DfE, 2013a, 2013b), 2016 marked the introduction of new GCSE and A level specifications. Despite fieldwork being written into the new DfE guidance for all Key Stages (see figure 12.2), the potential for all schools to become academies by 2020 (DfE, 2016) means that no school will *be required* to follow the National Curriculum at Key Stages 1, 2, and 3 after this date. Although this is a confusing national policy position, it at least demonstrates that the state has declared its support (in principle) for fieldwork. However, it is down to the schools, and geography teachers, to enact this principle, or not.

Thus, geography teachers need to reflect on the purpose of fieldwork, take professional ownership of it and then advocate fieldwork within their local contexts and settings. They need to win resources for it (not least, time) and consider how best they can utilise the library of resources (see note at the end of the chapter) and approaches to ensure that their students are able to meet both assessment requirements, and develop their geographical knowledge and skills.

Enacting fieldwork in the curriculum

Effective learning cannot be expected just because we take students into the field.

(Lonergan and Anderson, 1988 in Fuller et al., 2010)

Key Stage	DfE requirements
1	Use simple fieldwork and observational skills to study the geography of their school and its grounds and the key human and physical features of its surrounding environment (DfE, 2013a, p. 3).
2	Use fieldwork to observe, measure, record and present the human and physical features in the local area using a range of methods, including sketch maps, plans and graphs, and digital technologies (DfE, 2013a p. 4).
3	Use fieldwork in contrasting locations to collect, analyse and draw conclusions from geographical data, using multiple sources of increasingly complex information (DfE, 2013b, p. 3).
4	Different approaches to fieldwork undertaken in at least two contrasting environments. Fieldwork overall should include exploration of physical and human processes and the interactions between them and should involve the collection of primary physical and human data (but these requirements need not all be addressed in each piece of fieldwork) (DfE, 2014a, p. 5).
5	AS and A level specifications must require students to undertake fieldwork which meets the minimum requirements of 2 days of fieldwork at AS, and 4 days of fieldwork for A level. Awarding Organisations must require evidence of this fieldwork in the form of a written statement from Centres (DfE, 2014b).

Figure 12.2 DfE requirements for fieldwork across Key Stages 1 to 5.

As Lonergan and Anderson state, taking students out of the classroom to conduct fieldwork, isn't a guarantee of enabling geographical learning. How teachers plan and prepare, teach, conduct and assess fieldwork is of vital importance, and influenced by many factors (e.g. teachers' own values and experiences of fieldwork; teachers own subject identity and geographical interests; the specific needs/experiences of their students; curriculum requirements and school management in their specific context: see Job, 2002). Organising fieldwork is a specialist aspect of engaging in curriculum making – designed to help students deepen their geographical knowledge and develop the capacity to think geographically.

The familiar curriculum making model (see Geographical Association undated, Lambert and Morgan, 2010) was developed to encourage 'the specialist geography teacher relate to the school subject and wider disciplines, but also be conscious of pedagogies appropriate to the induction of young people to the disciplinary domain' (Lambert and Biddulph, 2014, p. 216). The authors argue for a 'Future 3' curriculum (see Young and Muller, 2010; Young et al., 2014). This is a knowledge-based curriculum, which:

> recognizes that specialist theoretical knowledge has been created in the subject disciplines, which are not entirely arbitrary. This knowledge exists outside of the direct experience of the student and is powerful, because it is derived in part by the specialist communities and the disciplined procedures that produce and verify it.
>
> (Lambert and Biddulph, 2014, p. 216)

If we apply this philosophy to curriculum making with fieldwork, then specific considerations need to be made by the teacher, which include:

- How can the choice of learning activity in the field enable students to be inducted into the methods of creating and testing knowledge in geography? For example, in developing their research and enquiry skills in support of the knowledge they are generating and assessing.
- How does the 'real world' setting provide students with unique experiences and imaginations of the place(s), people(s), ideas, and knowledge being studied, and how can this be linked to powerful geographical knowledge and thinking geographically?
- How can fieldwork develop students' identity as geographers, by drawing on its rich history in the discipline?

Thus, fieldwork, as part of the enacted curriculum, needs to be firmly embedded into the whole programme of learning. The GeoCapabilities project (see www. geocapabilities.org) expresses this as a curriculum *leadership* issue, requiring deep professional thinking. Figure 12.3, adapted from the project, provides a visual representation of the considerations that teachers need to make as they begin to plan fieldwork into their school curriculum.

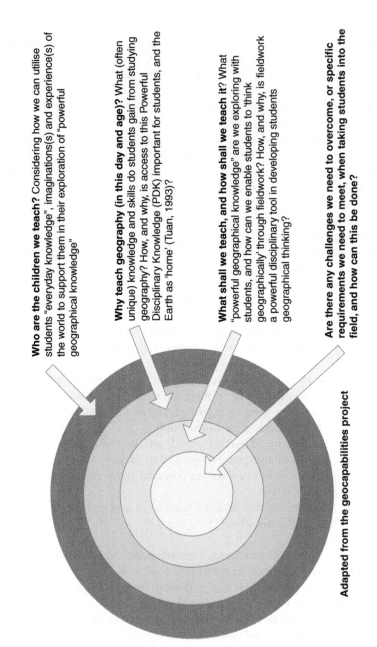

Who are the children we teach? Considering how we can utilise students "everyday knowledge", imaginations(s) and experience(s) of the world to support them in their exploration of "powerful geographical knowledge"

Why teach geography (in this day and age)? What (often unique) knowledge and skills do students gain from studying geography? How, and why, is access to this Powerful Disciplinary Knowledge (PDK) important for students, and the Earth as 'home' (Tuan, 1993)?

What shall we teach, and how shall we teach it? What "powerful geographical knowledge" are we exploring with students, and how can we enable students to 'think geographically' through fieldwork? How, and why, is fieldwork a powerful disciplinary tool in developing students geographical thinking?

Are there any challenges we need to overcome, or specific requirements we need to meet, when taking students into the field, and how can this be done?

Adapted from the geocapabilities project

Figure 12.3 Considerations for planning fieldwork (start with the questions in the outer circle and move inwards).

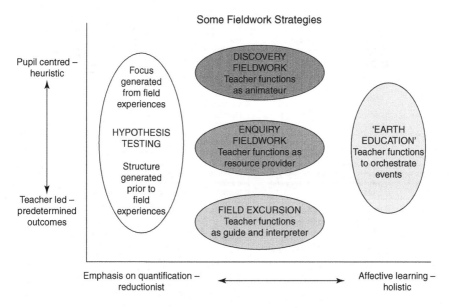

Figure 12.4 Classification of fieldwork activities (after Job, 2006).

Teachers also need to be aware of the variety of techniques and strategies that are available to them (e.g. Caton, 2006a, b; Job, 1999; Job, 2002; Holmes and Walker, 2006; Kinder, 2013), to support them planning, conducting and assessing fieldwork. Figures 12.4 and 12.5 provide an overview of the 'families' (Kinder, 2013) of fieldwork strategies available to teachers, and identify some of their advantages and limitations.

Figures 12.4 and 12.5 aim to encourage teachers to consider their role in fieldwork, what strategies would best suit their specific group of students, in their context, and how they can support their students in developing as geographers. The wealth of fieldwork strategies and resources available, and the considerable decisions that teachers have to make when planning, teaching, and assessing, fieldwork with relatively limited DfE guidance (especially in Key Stages 1–3) necessitate specialist teachers and departments, who need to work with the discipline (Lambert, 2014) to make the curriculum to ensure that fieldwork is effective. Kinder (2013) reminds us that for fieldwork to be 'effective' it needs to be 'properly conceived, carefully planned, taught to a high standard and carefully followed up' (p. 190). However, he recognises that 'engaging with the purpose(s) and associated methods of fieldwork – rather than setting out to meet statutory of examination requirements' is a challenge for geography teachers due to time, risk management, and accountability pressures on teachers.

Type of fieldwork	Purpose	Characteristic activities, some potential advantages and limitations
Field excursion	*Developing skills in geographical recording and interventions *Showing relationships between human and physical landscape features *Developing an appreciation of landscape and nurturing a sense of place	Students guided through a landscape with a teacher with local knowledge, often following a route on a map. Sites are grid referenced and sketch maps to explore the geology, the topological features, and human activity. Students listen, record, and ask questions concerning possible interpretations of the landscape *Teacher/expert-led who imparts knowledge and understanding (potentially leading to a high level of dependency on the teacher) *Teacher needs a high level of knowledge on the site/area of geographical focus
Hypothesis testing	*Applying geographical theory or generalised models to real world situations *Generating and applying hypotheses based on theory to be tested through collections of appropriate field data *Developing skills in analysing data using statistical methods in order to test field situations against geographical theory	A deductive approach which involves initial consideration of geographical theory, leading to the formulation of hypotheses which are then tested against field situations through the collection of data *Students develop their own geographical questions *Students become familiar with different techniques used to test data *Characterised by the collection of (predominantly) quantitative data *Limitations of 'applying' theories or models to different settings
Enquiry	*Students generate geographical questions to research *Students search for, collect, and classify geographical data to answer the questions *Students analyse the data and think geographically about what they have discovered *Students reflect on their learning (e.g. the information collected, the skills used and next steps) Please also refer to Roberts (2013)	A geographical question, issues or problem is identified. Ideally from student's own experience in the field. Students then gather appropriate data to answer their key questions. Findings are then evaluated, and students reflect on their learning *The posing of questions (e.g. what is this place like? What distinguishes it from other places I know?) draw on powerful geographical thinking, and spark students curiosity *Students become familiar with different techniques used to test data *It enables students to reflect on their own development as geographers and consider their next steps
Discovery	*Allowing students to discover their own interests in landscape *Students develop their own focus of study and methods of evaluation *Encourages self-motivation and self-learning	Teacher assumes the role of animateur, allowing the group to follow its own route through the landscape. When students ask questions these are countered with further questions to encourage deeper thinking. A discussion and recording session then identifies themes for further investigation in small groups. There are some strategies available to support with structure (e.g. scavenger hunts) *Driven by students own curiosity (with teachers taking a 'calculated risk') *Students develop their own research questions and data collection methods

Figure 12.5 Fieldwork strategies and purposes (adapted from Job et al., 1999; Caton, 2006a; Kinder, 2013).

Conclusion

The purpose of this chapter has been to reflect on how, and why, fieldwork is a fundamental pillar of geography education, and consider how it can be used to support students in developing their capacity to think geographically. As has been evidenced, fieldwork can provide students with opportunities for real world learning which can develop them as geographical knowledge workers (learning to create and test knowledge), help them to understand the role of theory in interpreting and representing the 'real' world, develop numerous skills (e.g. enquiry), and provides social benefits. However, the changing and challenging educational landscape means that geography teachers need to draw upon their discipline, subject identity, and subject community, to ensure that fieldwork is maintained within the enacted school curriculum.

Note

1   In figure 12.1 notes 10 and 11 in original article are:

   10 We acknowledge the potential weakness of this phrase; we do not imply, for example, that laboratories or classrooms are fake or 'unreal'. But, as one participant wrote, the 'real world' contains social, political, environmental and cultural 'complexities' that young people can be exposed to – in order to weigh up 'scientific evidence' in relation to 'public opinion' – for example, in relation to flood management or coastal retreat.
   11 This term is from Claxton, G., Lucas, B. & Webster, R. (2010) Bodies of knowledge: How the learning sciences could transform practical and vocational education, London: Edge Foundation. http://www.edge.co.uk/media/16982/' (p.19).

Key readings

1   Caton, D. (2006b) 'Real World Learning through Geographical Fieldwork' in D. Balderstone (ed.) *Secondary Geography Handbook*, Geographical Association: Sheffield. This is a clear overview of the options available to teachers in the context of the handbook which contains several other sources of tried and tested practical advice
2   Lambert, D. and Reiss, M. J. (2016) 'The place of fieldwork in geography Qualifications', *Geography* 101 (1), 28–34. This is a concise and clear overview of the place of fieldwork in geography and science, with a strong research basis. A good starting point for those wishing to get deeper into the research evidence on fieldwork.

References

Biddulph, M., Lambert, D. and Balderstone, D. (2015) *Learning to Teach Geography in the Secondary School*, 3rd edn, London: Routledge.
Bonnett, A. (2008) *What is Geography?* London: Sage Publications Ltd.

Burke, C. and Grovesnor, I. (2003) *The School I'd Like: Children and Young People's Reflections on an Education* London: RoutledgeFalmer.

Caton, D. (2006a) *New Approaches to Fieldwork*, Sheffield: Geographical Association.

Caton, D. (2006b) 'Real world learning through geographical fieldwork' in D. Baldersone (ed.) *Secondary Geography Handbook*, Sheffield: Geographical Association.

DfE (2013a) *Geography Programme of Study: Key Stages 1 and 2 National Curriculum England*, Available at: https://www.gov.uk/government/uploads/system/uploads/attachment_data/file/239044/PRIMARY_national_curriculum_-_Geography.pdf [Accessed 14 February 2016].

DfE (2013b) *Geography Programme of Study: Key Stage 3 National Curriculum in England*, Available at: https://www.gov.uk/government/uploads/system/uploads/attachment_ data/file/239087/SECONDARY_national_curriculum_-_Geography.pdf [Accessed 14 February 2016].

DfE (2014a) Geography GCSE Subject Content, Available at: https://www.gov.uk/government/uploads/system/uploads/attachment_data/file/301253/GCSE_geography.pdf [Accessed 14 February 2016].

DfE (2014b) Geography GCE AS and A level Subject Content, Available at: https://www.gov.uk/government/uploads/system/uploads/attachment_ data/file/388857/GCE_ AS_and_A_level_subject_content_for_geography.pdf [Accessed 14 February 2016].

DfE (2016) Educational Excellence Everywhere, Available at: : HYPERLINK "https://www.gov.uk/government/uploads/system/uploads/attachment_data/file/508447/Educational_Excellence_Everywhere.pdf" https://www.gov.uk/government/uploads/system/uploads/attachment_data/file/508447/Educational_Excellence_Everywhere.pdf [Accessed 14 February 2016].

Fuller, I., Edmonson, S., France, D., Higgitt, D. and Ratinen, I. (2010) 'International Perspectives on the Effectiveness of Geography Fieldwork for Leaning' in M. Healey, E. Pawson, M. Solem, (eds.) *Active Learning and Student Engagement: International Perspectives and Practices in Geography in Higher Education*, London: Routledge.

Geographical Association (undated) Curriculum Making Explained, Available at: http://www.geography.org.uk/cpdevents/curriculum/curriculummaking/ [Accessed 22 July 2016].

Geographical Association (2009) A Different View: A Manifesto from the Geographical Association, Available at: HYPERLINK "http://www.geography.org.uk/resources/adifferentview" http://www.geography.org.uk/resources/adifferentview [Accessed on 25 March 2016].

Holmes, D. and Walker, M. (2006) 'Planning geographical fieldwork' in D. Balderstone (ed.) *Secondary Geography Handbook*, Sheffield: Geographical Association.

Hope, M. (2009) 'The Importance of direct experience: a philosophical defence of fieldwork in human geography', *Journal of Geography in Higher Education* 33 (2), 169–82.

Job, D. (1996) 'Geography and Environmental Education: An exploration of Perspectives and Strategies' in M. Kent, D. Lambert, M. Naish and F. Slater (eds.) *Geography in Education: Viewpoints on Teaching and Learning*, Cambridge: Cambridge University Press.

Job, D. (1999) *New Directions in Geographical Fieldwork*, Cambridge: Cambridge University Press.

Job, D. (2002) 'Towards deeper fieldwork' in M. Smith (ed.) *Aspects of Teaching Secondary Geography: Perspectives on Practice,* London: RoutledgeFalmer.

Kinder, A. (2013) 'What is the contribution of fieldwork to school geography' in D. Lambert and M. Jones (eds.) *Debates in Geography Education,* London: Routledge.

Lambert, D. (2011) 'Reframing school geography: a capability approach' in G. Butt (ed.) *Geography, Education and the Future,* London: Bloomsbury Academic.

Lambert, D. (2014) 'Subject Teachers in Knowledge-Led Schools' in M. Young, D. Lambert, C. Roberts, and M. Roberts (eds.) *Knowledge and the Future School,* London: Bloomsbury Academic.

Lambert, D. and Morgan, J. (2010) *Teaching Geography 11–18: A Conceptual Approach,* Maidenhead: Open University Press.

Lambert, D. and Biddulph, M. (2014) 'The dialogic space offered by curriculum-making in the process of learning to teach, and the creation of a progressive knowledge-led curriculum', *Asia-Pacific Journal of Education* 43 (3), 210–24.

Lambert, D. and Reiss, M. J. (2014) 'The place of fieldwork in geography and science qualifications', Available at: http://www.field-studies-council.org/media/1252064/ lambert-reiss-2014-fieldwork-report.pdf [Accessed 14 February 2016].

Lambert, D. and Reiss, M. J. (2016) 'The place of fieldwork in geography qualifications', *Geography,* 101 (1), 28–34.

Lonergan, N. and Anderson, L.W. (1988) 'Field-based education: some theoretical considerations', *Higher Education Research and Development,* 7, 63–77.

Ofsted (2011) *Geography: Learning to Make a World of Difference,* Available at: https://www.gov.uk/government/publications/geography-learning-to-make-a-world-of-difference [Accessed 25 March 2016].

Roberts, M. (2013) *Geography through Enquiry: Approaches to Teaching and Learning in the Secondary School,* Sheffield: Geographical Association.

Tuan, Y. F. (1993) 'Foreword' in A. Buttimer. *Geography and the Human Spirit,* Baltimore: The John Hopkins Press.

Young, M. and Muller, J. (2010) 'Three educational scenarios for the future: lessons from the sociology of knowledge', *European Journal of Education* 45 (1), 11–27.

Young, M., Lambert, D., Roberts, C. and Roberts, M. (2014) *Knowledge and the Future School Curriculum and Social Justice,* London: Bloomsbury Academic.

Chapter 13

The impact of technology on geography and geography teachers

Alan Parkinson

> I think the greatest potential of the Internet lies in providing us with amazing tools and resources that enable a personalisation of learning to take place, which also needs to be reflected in a personalisation of teaching.
> (Donert, 2015, p. 9)

Introduction

Today, the majority of geography classrooms are connected with the world through the internet via the teacher's laptop, desktop or tablet. Some teachers working in these classrooms however may not necessarily have changed their practices or assumptions about what it means to teach, or appreciate the possibilities these connections offer (Leat, 1999). Where online material regularly enters classroom space perhaps more concerning is where teachers and students are uncritical of its origin, authenticity and reliability (Bartlett and Miller, 2011). These scenarios remind us that the balance between the consumption of geographical information, the critical use of new tools, and the extent to which students are involved in constructing their own learning are matters of uncertainty and flux. This chapter aims to pick a course through such matters and asks questions such as:

- What technology is used in geography classrooms and by geography teachers, and to what effect?
- What opportunities are emerging for using the latest technologies for geographical learning?
- How is the changing nature of online spaces, and the rapid rise in social media changing the relationship that learners – and teachers – have with each other and the subject?

Technology makes its way into the geography classroom

By the 1980s, the few computers that had found their way into schools were often used for programming and monitoring scientific equipment. The impact of this early use of technology or 'Computer Assisted Learning' (CAL) grew slowly (Kent, 1983). For teachers interested in using CAL in geography, the Geographical Association's journal *Teaching Geography* published articles such as Hall et al., (1985) who reported research on the use of CAL in schools. In 1986 the journal introduced the 'TG Computer Page', which offered software reviews, rather than advice on pedagogy. Despite the arrival of classroom computers pedagogic practices remained firmly rooted with the teacher as demonstrator and expert. Over the next decade, computers and software became more powerful and adaptable but it was the arrival of the internet which had the most significant impact on schooling and geography classrooms. The subsequent development of the social web or 'Web 2.0' as it became known, not only changed the nature of web content. (Murphy and Lebans, 2008) but allowed learners and teachers to have instant access to the world beyond the classroom.

The use of digital technologies in geography

One valuable use of technology is to draw out the potential that students have to explore the world beyond the classroom, often virtually. There are some landscapes students are unlikely to ever experience in person, but technology can 'take them there'. In May 1994, an article in *Geographical* magazine described a student eager to get home to start their homework, who

> puts on goggles and control gloves. Thus equipped, he flies across the world to compare average temperatures in Death Valley and the Dead Sea, making notes on his virtual palmtop to use later in an essay.
>
> (Ostler, 1994, p. 12)

With 'virtual reality' (VR) came the potential for 'virtual' fieldwork, which was temporarily sanctioned by awarding bodies when the Foot and Mouth outbreak of 2001, which closed off swathes of countryside in the UK, prevented 'actual' fieldwork taking place in many locations.

Into the twenty-first century, with more sophisticated technologies available teachers and students can utilise new types of geo-media,[1] including digital mapping and imagery, visualisation tools and geographical information systems (GIS). Students can connect remotely with distant places via webcams, engaging with real people via email, blogs, video conferencing and Voice over Internet Protocol (VOIP) services such as Skype (Taylor, 2014). Launched in 2016, Oculus Rift and similar VR headsets promise immersive experiences which for some may verge on 'edutainment'. Google Expeditions, launched in 2016, offers guided 'trips' to students wearing special goggles. The cost of this equipment is coming down, but may still be a barrier to adoption (Argles et al., 2015). Lisichenko (2015) describes a range of uses for this technology including the visualisation of geomorphology. A growing library of drone footage is also changing the way that students view their surroundings or 'experience' physical events such as floods or volcanic eruptions.

Advantages of these and other new technologies is that students can pose questions which are answered immediately and lead to deeper questions. Students can visualise large, near real-time, data sets using Cameron Beccario's Earth NullSchool atmosphere viewer. The late Hans Rosling's work with Gapminder (Rosling, 2010) and Sheffield University's Worldmapper project (Barford and Dorling, 2006) using Benjamin Hennig's compelling cartograms have found enthusiastic advocates in the classroom. Early adopters communicate the benefits through journal articles (e.g. Lang, 2011), conference presentations (e.g. Parkinson et al., 2012) and through social media such as Facebook, Ning and Twitter.

Maps have always had an important place in the geography classroom. Organisations such as the Ordnance Survey have long been supportive of education, distributing free maps to schools, and sharing teaching materials. ESRI released the collaborative StoryMap™ tool in 2014, which enabled new cartographic possibilities. New mapping tools have sharing built in. The ability to create collaborative online maps means students can take ownership of them, and add their own data. Digimap for Schools is one online mapping service, launched in 2011 and now used in over 2,700 UK schools. It offers scope for exploring maps at different scales and provides tools for creating map annotations and printing personalised maps. Maps are a surface on which stories can be told, helping students to 'write the earth'. There can however be a tension between the 'real' world and the 'virtual' one. One tool that illustrates this is Google Earth, which offers the potential for personal investigation of familiar and unfamiliar places, and has exceeded 500 million downloads. As one of several 'virtual earths' used in classrooms its community of users has shared hundreds of thousands of resources linked to specific places. For teachers and students alike it can 'capture the magic of experiencing their environment' (Buchanan-Dunlop, 2008, p. 14) although students may not always realise that what they are looking at is not the 'real world' and neither is it a particular moment in time, but a mosaic of many images and layers.

Teachers have also turned to the internet for resources, just as students rely on it for homework support. In a 'Ctrl-C, Ctrl-V' Culture, students cutting and pasting work has become common. A parallel impact for teachers is the tempting ready access to 'lessons', with over 4.5 million downloads from TES Connect every week. Although websites such as this clearly satisfy a demand, it is debatable whether they contribute to the de-skilling of teachers as curriculum makers, or encourage any personalisation of teaching and learning. Advice in a recent teacher workload paper reinforced this, with John Hattie being quoted as saying that

> there are a million resources available on the internet and creating more seems among the successful wastes of time in which teachers love to engage.
> (Hattie, 2012, p. 64)

Tools such as Apple's iBook Author, launched in 2012, challenge traditional models of publishing and the format of commercial resources is also changing with new textbooks available on subscription in addition to traditional print copies.

With a wealth of resources available at the touch of a button, or increasingly the touch of a screen, 'critical media literacy' is an important concept and one that is still developing in this era of 'fake news'. A Demos report in September 2011, *Truth, Lies and the Internet*, examined British young people's ability to critically evaluate what they consumed online; it discussed the need for students to be taught this digital literacy (Bartlett and Miller, 2011). Students must be critical of the information that they are presented with. They need to acquire the skills necessary to 'engage with misrepresentation and underrepresentation' (Kellner and Share, 2005, p. 382).

A growing number of geography teachers are using social media and digital technologies in innovative ways, including using Facebook as a context for literacy development[2] or Skype to talk to someone living a few miles from the Eyjafjallajokull volcano during the 2010 eruption.[3] Such innovative and interactive geographical activities also provide opportunities for teachers and students discussing together aspects of critical media literacy.

Challenges of using digital technologies in geography

'The teacher's traditional ally is a piece of chalk, and the closer any modern aid approaches this still indispensable material in some respects the more likely he is to use it' (Page and Kitching, 1981, p. 60). Chalk dust is no longer found in most schools, but the metaphor endures: thus, while ICT has become common in geography classrooms, its physical presence does not guarantee that it will be used effectively. Media technology can facilitate communication, but can potentially also form a barrier (Shirky, 2008).

Has the huge investment in technology in schools, approaching £2 billion between 1998 and 2008 (Ofsted, 2009), made a measurable difference to teaching and learning? Becta, the former agency for promoting educational communications technology, carried out research in a number of areas including Interactive whiteboards (Becta, 2003); the full extent of their interactive use was found to be wanting (Smith et al., 2005; Becta, 2009). This is increasingly relevant when tablet devices like Apple's iPad have been introduced into schools in large volumes. The full potential of such technologies rests in their capacity to 'give permission' to students to get involved in managing a changing relationship with information and the teacher. Some progress has been made with the development of 'sandbox' apps such as Earth Primer, which allow students to investigate a range of physical processes. Students are also producers of data as well as consumers, and many apps collect location and other information from users. The interest in 'augmented reality' (AR) games such as Pokémon GO in the summer of 2016 showed the potential for educators to harness this interest of young people for classroom use.

Teachers have a broad and expanding pedagogic toolkit with which to shape curriculum documents, and turn them into meaningful experiences for all students. An important element of a teacher's professional role is the act of 'curriculum-making' which can be enhanced by technology; for example, a downloaded enquiry-led lesson could deviate from the original, with learners following a personalised route. The Geographical Association's 'curriculum-making' model emphasises that teachers and students should both have agency and use the subject discipline as a resource; rather than seeing curriculum as inert content to be delivered (Donert, 2015). There is an alchemy that occurs in the classroom which can be improved by the addition of new elements. Technology is one of those elements. Where teachers act as 'gatekeepers' to the technology, this can inhibit progress, but gatekeepers can open as well as close the gate.

Teachers' use of technology for professional development and networking

The Geographical Association's inaugural journal, called *The Geographical Teacher* was first published in 1901. In the introduction to the very first issue, indeed on the very first page, Douglas Freshfield said:

> In Britain, teachers are for the most part too scattered and too busy to come together frequently for discussion. They require a medium through which they may readily communicate with one another, exchange experiences and learn the progress that is being made in method or in appliances in our own country and abroad.
>
> (p. 1)

Freshfield's solution was to establish the journal for which he was writing the introduction, but the challenge he describes still remains. One response by geography teachers has been to realise the benefits of new technologies for communicating, creating and collaborating online (Richardson, 2008).

Websites were an early visible and accessible form of teachers accessing information and resources. In 1999, Chris Durbin and colleagues at the advisory service for Staffordshire established a forum for geography teachers to chat and exchange ideas, using a 'bulletin board' structure: the Staffordshire Learning Network (SLN). This continues to operate as a place for geography teachers to express themselves, seek advice and share ideas.

Blogging is another form of non-face-to-face communication used within the geography community. As a free way of creating webpages, with little technical knowledge required teachers began to see the benefit of blogging over a decade ago (Parkinson, 2004; Warlick, 2005); although there are still colleagues 'discovering' blogs today. Teachers use blogs in a number of ways including reflecting on practice, sharing resources and classroom practice, or collaborating on a study or revision guide co-produced by staff and students. Wood (2009) described the emergence of a blogging community, and the value that was placed on the opportunity for global feedback. Students are also appreciative of the global audience that this potentially gives them for their work; no longer is it the 'secret exchange' between teacher and student. However, with a more 'public exchange', geography teachers need to be alert that while a digital footprint takes time to build up we should remind ourselves what is placed online has a 'permanence' which can be surprising. The Wayback machine can unearth previous iterations of websites from over 300 billion webpages archived from 1996 onwards, so teachers and students must understand the power of the medium.

Technology has enabled new opportunities for teachers to network and share each other's practice: an important element of professional development. This has come at a time when traditional models and the 'one size fits all' approach to Continuing Professional Development (CPD) are being replaced by more informal teacher-led ones (Allison, 2014). The benefits of discussing professional development are obvious. Even as little as seventy-five minutes a month discussing professional practice with colleagues through 'teacher learning communities' can be transformational for one's professional practice. Dylan Wiliam, who has researched the benefit of such professional discourse, suggests that such a regular period of focused conversation with colleagues can improve practice (Stewart, 2008). Where face-to-face opportunities are restricted, the medium that is being increasingly turned to is 'social media'. Over the last decade a range of opportunities for teachers to engage in professional dialogue with colleagues has emerged, with Facebook groups, Ning networks and more business-oriented communities like LinkedIn, providing what Leadbeater (2009) refers to as 'endless, lateral connections' (p. 5). This exposure to the experimentation of other colleagues worldwide can provide inspiration and help avoid the pitfalls experienced by others. There is also a longer-term benefit of engaging in online communities and networks. Professional reputations can extend beyond the school. Ewan McIntosh of NoTosh consultants, who developed the TeachMeet model,[4] describes the added value when 'small passionate communities' form and connect together. The internet enables educators from all over the world to meet virtually and share ideas through short presentations. Such events often have a 'back-channel' which allows teachers who can't make it physically to follow the conversations and view the presenters. Important to facilitating this in the geography community are people who have 'hubness'; a capacity to network and gather people around them. The use of hashtags allows for the collation of information and for people to follow online conversations in what would otherwise be an impossibly vast assemblage of data, which grows by the minute (Intel, 2013).

Online networks have also been adopted by the formal geography community. The Geographical Association and Royal Geographical Society moved into these online spaces, as part of the Action Plan for Geography (2006–11). The GA's Facebook page appeared in 2009, following the introduction of Ning networks, including the Geography Champions network for primary colleagues in 2008. The pace of adoption of technologies such as Twitter, founded in 2006, has been remarkable. Used by both organisations and individual teachers, there are immediate benefits of using this micro-blogging site such as the regular Thursday

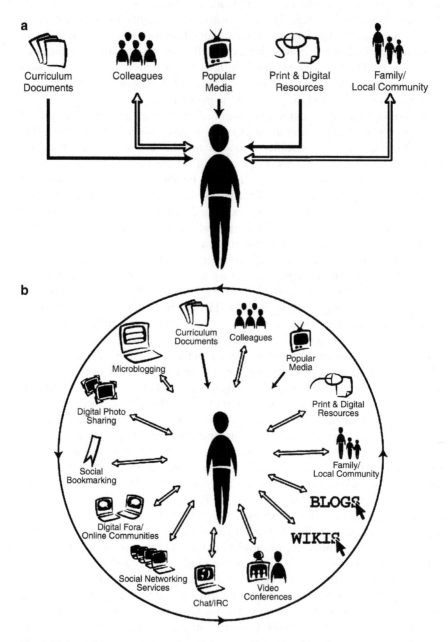

Figure 13.1 (a) Typical teacher network. (b) The networked teacher.

night meeting of educators, who debate a theme using the hashtag #UKEdChat. It is early days in terms of research into the impact of tools like Twitter but it is already attracting interest (see Watts, 2012; Willson, 2012.) The power of the tool for reporting events such as natural hazards as they happen has already been recognized (Olteanu et al., 2015).

The significant changes to a teacher's professional network, approaches to networking and the wider opportunities for professional dialogue and collaboration are usefully summarised by two diagrams created by Alec Couros of the University of Regina, Canada (see Figure 13.1a and Figure 13.1b). While continuing to recognise the importance of colleagues and family/local community in a teacher's network, 'The Networked Teacher' (Figure 13.1b) emphasises the increased possibilities for online collaboration and co-creation through a wide range of digital technologies.

How will teachers' use of digital technologies develop in the future?

In the previous section I outlined how social networking platforms and other online tools are increasingly used for CPD and networking. In this section, I raise some important questions on the challenges social media and digital technologies in general can present for schools, teachers and learners.

Does the movement of teachers into another online space mean there are now 'too many rooms'? Are we overpowered by choice and the diversity of what's on offer? How should we prioritise and select particular tools? In the past, teachers gave their attention to one room at a time, the majority of their time spent in the classroom. Should geography teachers focus their energies and professional development on this manageable, physical space? Do we spend too much time connecting and collaborating and passing on materials, with only superficial engagement of the messages and challenges that such material presents? Do we put pressure on ourselves when we see what other teachers (say they) do and feel inadequate, or have a 'fear of missing out'? There is a need for mediation by the teacher during this process, plus an element of content-curation and responsible sourcing where resources are concerned. Should such skills be written into a teacher's job description, or is this a function performed by a wider community of practice such as the GA? In a Best Practice Research Scholarship[5] focusing on the use of the internet by geography teachers, it was discovered that one early 'bad experience' of being let down would reduce the chances of using technology frequently enough for it to become embedded in practice (Parkinson, 2001). Martin (2006) reminds us that not every teacher needs 'to be an ICT pioneer' (p. 158), however, there may already be a new digital divide opening between those geographers who use social media as part of their professional as well as personal lives and those who for various reasons make limited or no use. The 24/7 nature of technology puts increasing 'pressures' on teachers to be contactable and 'online' outside school hours, and perhaps never 'clocking off'.

The first decade of the twenty-first century has seen the rise of the smart-phone, which along with the games console are becoming the device of choice of young people. Use of these digital devices outside school and the formal curriculum means the majority of young people's use of digital technologies 'is unmediated by official pedagogy' (Moore, 2012, p. 155). For many young people starting out in primary schools, the touch-screen device is what they are most familiar with, and there can be a frustration with the hardware that they find in the classroom. This echoes David Buckingham's (2003) argument that there is a growing gap between the worlds of young people outside school and their educational experiences in schools:

> While the social and cultural experiences of children have dramatically transformed over the past 50 years, schools have singularly failed to keep pace with the change. The classrooms of today would easily be recognisable to [students from] ... the mid nineteenth century: the way in which teaching and learning are organised, the kind of skills and knowledge that are valued in assessment, and a good deal of curriculum content, have changed only superficially since that time.
>
> (p. 32)

Very often early adopters of new and 'next' technologies are risk-takers, and at a time of economic uncertainty schools and teachers may well want to 'play it safe'. Will the time required to implement recent curriculum and assessment changes also limit the further adoption of new ideas? One area to work on may be the nature of progression of skills with new tools such as 'geographical information' (GI). Projects such as GI-Learner (Donert, 2015, 2016) are developing learning lines to support teachers in this area. Whatever hardware schools have now and in the future, it is how teachers and learners utilise it that will remain important. For as Mason and Rennie (2010) have concluded in relation to Web 2.0, it 'is no longer about transmission and consumption; it is about co-creating, sharing, repurposing, and above all, interacting (p. 294).

Conclusion

This chapter has provided a practitioner's perspective on the present and potential uses of technology by geography teachers. In considering different aspects of geography: teaching, learning and professional development, we should continually ask the question: 'is technology always the best tool to use?' With the speed of technological change faster than schools' responses to the potential that they offer, is the role of the teacher destined to change? Ian Gilbert (2009) argues this question in his provocatively titled book: *Why Do I Need a Teacher When I've Got Google?* Although more freedom has been given to the learner, there is still a need for the skilled subject practitioner. Whether learning online or face-to-face, it is teachers who will continue to have the crucial role of helping young people to engage critically with geography and make sense of the different forms of geographical knowledge they are presented with, whatever media this is presented through.

Key readings

1   De Bruyckere, P., Kirschner, P.A and Hulshof, C. D. (2016) 'Technology in Education – What teachers should know', *American Educator*, Spring 2016, 12–18, Available at: http://www.aft.org/sites/default/files/ ae_spring2016debruyckere-kirschner-and-hulshof.pdf [Accessed 6 August 2016]. In this short article, which is drawn from their book *Urban Myths about Learning and Education*, the authors consider five of the myths surrounding the use of technology in education. They provide a commentary, supported by research findings, on the 'truth' of ideas such as 'digital natives' requiring a new style of education and whether the internet is having a negative effect on our intellectual capabilities.

2   Mason. R. and Rennie, F. (2010) 'Social Networking as an Educational Tool', in J. Arthur and I. Davies (eds.), *The Routledge Education Studies Reader,* London: Routledge. The authors provide a very useful overview of students and teachers' engagement with digital learning. Research issues concerning the use of Web 2.0, social networking and course design provide the reader with valuable literature when debating how teachers and schools may respond to the use of digital media.

Notes

1   The term geo-media formed part of an EU-wide project to engage teachers with technology – read more at http://www.digital-earth.eu.
2   T. Cassidy; see the presentation 'What if they had Facebook' at http://www.slideshare.net/funkygeography/facebook-and-twitter-profiles.
3   V. Vannet on Twitter at https://twitter.com/# !/ValVannet.
4   The Teachmeet started amongst Scottish educators in 2005. It has evolved over time, and events based on the original model are held regularly, often with specific foci.
5   Between 2000 and 2004, the DfES funded the Best Practice Research Scholarship programme (BPRS) to promote teachers' engagement in small-scale classroom-based research.

References

Allison, S. (2014) *Perfect Teacher Led CPD*, Carmarthen, Wales: Crown House Publishing.

Argles, T., Minocha, S. and Burden, D. (2015). 'Exploring the affordances of virtual fieldwork in a multi-user, 3-D digital environment', *Higher Education Network (HEN) Annual Meeting of the Geological Society of London*, 21–22 January 2015, Plymouth University, Plymouth.

Barford, A. and Dorling, D. (2006) 'Worldmapper: the world as you've never seen it before', *Teaching Geography*, 31 (2), 68–75.

Bartlett, J. and Miller, C. (2011) *Truth, Lies and the Internet: A Report into Young People's Digital Fluency*, Available at: http://www.demos.co.uk/publications/truth-lies-and-the-internet [Accessed 21 March 2012].

British Educational Communications and Technology Agency (Becta) (2003) *What the Research says about Interactive Whiteboards*, Coventry: Becta.

British Educational Communications and Technology Agency (Becta) (2009) *Evidence on the Impact of Technology on Learning and Educational Outcomes*, Available at: http://cnp.naace.co.uk/system/files/impact_of_technology_on_outcomes_jul09.pdf [Accessed 2 February 2012].

Buchanan-Dunlop, J. (2008) 'Virtual fieldwork', in D. Mitchell (ed.), *ICT in Secondary Geography: A Short Guide for Teachers*, Sheffield: Geographical Association.

Buckingham, D. (2003) *Media Education: Literacy, Learning, and Contemporary Culture*, Cambridge and Oxford: Polity Press in association with Blackwell Publishing Ltd.

Donert, K. (2015) Innovative pedagogies series: GeoCapabilities empowering teachers as subject leaders, York: Higher Education Academy, Available at: https://www.heacademy.ac.uk/sites/default/files/karl_donert_final.pdf [Accessed 6 August 2016].

Donert, K. et al. (2016) GI-Learner: a project to develop geospatial thinking, learning lines in secondary schools – Paper at GI-Forum, Salzburg, July 2016, Available at: http://www.gilearner.ugent.be/wp-content/uploads/2016/03/GI-Forum-article.pdf [Accessed 6 August 2016].

Freshfield, D. (1901) *The Geographical Teacher*, 1 (1), 1.

Gilbert, I. (2010) *Why Do I Need a Teacher When I've Got Google*, London: Routledge.

Hall, D., Kent, A. and Wiegand, P. (1985) 'Computer assisted learning in geography: the state of the art', *Teaching Geography*, 10 (2), 73–6.

Hattie, J. (2012) *Visible Learning for Teachers, Maximising Impact on Learning*, Routledge: New York.

Intel (2013) Website infographic: What happens in an internet minute?, Available at: http://i.i.cbsi.com/cnwk.1d/i/tim/2013/03/20/internetminute.jpg [Accessed 6 August 2016].

Kellner, D. and Share, G. (2005) 'Towards critical media literacy: core concepts, debates, organizations and policy', *Discourse: Studies in the cultural politics of education*, 26 (3), 369–86.

Kent, A. (ed.) (1983) *Geography Teaching and the Micro*, York: Longman.

Lang, B. (2011) 'Gapminder: Bringing statistics to life', *Teaching Geography*, 36 (1), 17–19.

Leadbeater, C. (2009) The Art of With, Available at: http://www.cornerhouse.org/wpcontent/uploads/old_site/media/Learn/The%20Art%20of%20With.pdf [Accessed 25 March 2012].

Leat, D. (1999) 'Rolling the stone uphill: teacher development and the implementation of Thinking Skills programmes', *Oxford Review of Education*, 25 (3), 387–403.

Lisichenko, R. (2015) 'Issues surrounding the use of virtual reality in geographic education', *The Geography Teacher*, 12 (4), 159–66.

Martin, F. (2006) *E-geography: Using ICT in Quality Geography*, Sheffield: Geographical Association.

Mason, R. and Rennie, F. (2010) 'Social networking as an educational tool', in J. Arthur and I. Davies (eds.), *The Routledge Education Studies Reader*, London: Routledge.

Moore, A. (2012) *Teaching And Learning: Pedagogy, Curriculum And Culture*, 2nd edn, London: Routledge.

Murphy, J. and Lebans, R. (2008) 'Unexpected outcomes: Web 2.0 in the secondary school classroom', *International Journal of Technology in Teaching and Learning*, 4 (2), 134–47.

Ofsted (2009) *The Importance of ICT: Information and Communication Technology in Primary and Secondary Schools, 2005–2008*, Available at: http://www.ofsted.gov.uk/resources/importance-of-ict-information-and-communication-technology-primary-and-secondaryschools-20052008 [Accessed 9 August 2015].

Ostler, T. (1994) 'Revolution in reality: virtual reality applications in geography', *Geographical Magazine*, 66 (5), 12–13.

Olteanu, A., Vieweg, S. and Castillo, C. (2015) *What to Expect When the Unexpected Happens: Social Media Communications Across Crises*. Published in the proceedings of the 18th ACM Conference on Computer Supported Cooperative Work and Social Computing, New York: ACM.

Page, C. F. and Kitching, J. (1981) *Technical Aids to Teaching in Higher Education*, Guildford: Society for Research into Higher Education.

Parkinson, A. (2001) 'Best practice scholarship' unpublished.

Parkinson, A. (2004) 'Have you met GeoBlogs', *Teaching Geography*, 29 (3), 161–3.

Parkinson, A., Lyon, J. and Solem, M. (2012) Geomedia in Secondary Education, Lecture at the Geographical Association Annual Conference, University of Manchester, 12–14 April 2012.

Richardson, W. (2008) *Blogs, Wikis, Podcasts, and Other Powerful Web Tools for Classrooms*, California: Corwin Press Inc.

Rosling, H. (2010) 'How not to be ignorant about the world', TEDSalon, Berlin, Germany, June 2014, Available at: https://www.ted.com/talks/hans_and_ola_rosling_how_not_to_be_ignorant_about_the_world [Accessed 15 April 2016].

Shirky, C. (2008) *Here Comes Everybody. The Power of Organizing without Organizations*, New York: The Penguin Press.

Smith, H.J., Higgins, S., Wall, K. and Miller, J. (2005) 'Interactive whiteboards: boon or bandwagon', *Journal of Computer Assisted Learning*, 21 (2), 91–101.

Stewart, W. (2008) '75 minutes to up your game', *Times Educational Supplement*, 28 November 2008, Available at: http://www.tes.co.uk/article.aspx?storycode=6005714 [Accessed 21 March 2012].

Taylor, L. (2014) 'Diversity between and within: approaches to teaching about distant place in the secondary school curriculum', *Journal of Curriculum Studies*, 46, (2), 276–99.

Warlick, D. (2005) *Classroom Blogging: A Teacher's Guide to the Blogosphere*, 2nd edn, Raleigh: Lulu.com.

Watts, J. (2012) 'The uses of Twitter for geography teachers/students', Reporting Research session at The Geographical Association Annual Conference, University of Manchester, 12–14 April 2012, Available at: http://eternalexploration.

wordpress.com/2012/04/13/twitter-for-geography-teachers-and-students-ga-conference/ [Accessed March 2016].

Willson, A. (2012) 'Establishing a Personal Learning Network (PLN) through social media', Lulu, London.

Wood, P. (2009) 'Advances in E-learning – the case of blogging in UK school geography', *Research in Geographic Education*, 11 (2), 28–46.

Chapter 14

Using Geographic Information (GI)

Mary Fargher

Imagine for example, a young child going to a Digital Earth exhibit at a local museum. After donning a head-mounted display, she sees Earth as it appears from space. Using a data glove, she zooms in, using higher and higher levels of resolution, to see continents, then regions, countries, cities, and finally individual houses, trees, and other natural and h(u)man-made objects. Having found an area of the planet she is interested in exploring, she takes the equivalent of a 'magic carpet ride' through a 3-D visualization of the terrain.

(Gore, 1998)

Introduction

In his speech 'Digital Earth: Understanding our planet in the 21st Century', Gore encouraged us to imagine what a geographical education with GIS[1] in the twenty-first century might involve. According to Gore, Digital Earth[2] would allow us to 'capture' vast amounts of digital information about our planet. Although his speech did not quite herald the new era of geographical knowledge that its rhetoric suggested, it partially predicted the significance of geographic information (GI) and its potential influence on our geographical imaginations. In the time since he made his speech, we have become increasingly familiar with 'Digital Earth' through virtual globes such as Google Earth.[3] Some may also be familiar with more conventional GIS software and applications such as ESRI ArcGIS Online,[4] QGIS[5] and AEGIS 3 GIS[6] through university degrees or through its use in schools. GIS is a term that can be interpreted in a range of different ways. For some it is the hardware and software that makes up a computerised geographic information system capable of digitally displaying mainly mapped information about on- or near-surface geographical phenomena (Schuurman, 2004). This chapter interprets the acronym more broadly, considering GIS to include the hardware, the software and the user as part of the geographical system, as Elwood (2008) contends when she defines GIS as:

digital systems for storing and representing spatial information; they are complex arrays of social and political practices; *and* they are ways of knowing and making knowledge.

(Elwood, 2008, p. 257)

In schools, the 2013 Geography National Curriculum highlights the use of GIS use more prominently than ever before. The Key Stage 3 curriculum identifies that GIS as a key technology that pupils can use to think spatially and use maps and other geographical images to collect, present and analyse data (DfE, 2013a, p. 198). At GCSE students are now required to demonstrate how to use GIS in geographical investigations (DfE, 2013b). At A Level, students are expected to identify and synthesise geographical data from a number of different sources via GIS (DfE, 2014, p. 13).

This chapter introduces and critically examines a range of key debates about the use of GIS in geography education in terms of the nature of GI, its educational value and the role of teacher knowledge in teaching with GIS.

Conventional GIS

Despite the recent mushrooming of web-based GIS GI, it is worth remembering that GI has been around for a long time. The earliest digital geographic data appeared on the screens of computerised mainframe GIS in land use analysis and census mapping in the 1960s. Since then, GI has gradually become the cornerstone of what is now widely known as the geospatial industries, providing digitally referenced geographic information in a vast array of human contexts including industry, government and higher education. This is conventional GIS that uses a specific set of spatial tools to identify, locate and map geographical phenomena.

At the same time, evidence reflecting the educational benefits of using conventional GIS to develop student spatial skills is growing, particularly in American secondary school education (Kerski, 2008; Bednarz and Bednarz, 2008). A number of research studies have considered how GI can be used successfully in enquiry learning (Fargher, 2006; Scheepers, 2009). The cross-curricular benefits of the use of GI, particularly between geography and science, have also been explored (Sinton and Lund, 2007). Supporting teachers in developing their teaching with GIS has also been researched in the United Kingdom (see The GA's Spatially Speaking project, GA, 2006).

It is important to remember, however, that a very particular type of spatial thinking lies at the core of conventional GIS. GIS protagonists view it as a rigorous, scientific technical application, one which can be used to solve geographical problems, follow scientific enquiries, predict events such as environmental hazards and locate economic resources (Schuurman, 2004; Bednarz, 2004; National Research Council, 2006).

It is worth considering here the emphasis placed on related spatial thinking in the US education system where GI is used to teach geographical topics mainly within the science curriculum, Sinton and Bednarz (2007) summarise this approach:

> Students in pursuit of a well-rounded education must learn to think spatially [National Research Council, 2006]. Spatial thinking enables us to comprehend and address issues of spatial relationships. As students explore geographical space, they gain the facility and confidence to grasp and imagine abstract spaces, to solve multi-faceted problems, and to think critically and participate actively in our complex, multidimensional world.
>
> (Sinton and Bednarz, 2007, in Sinton and Lund, 2007, p. 19)

In their study of the Hurricane Katrina disaster, Sinton and Bednarz (2007) discuss how 'spatial data' helped people understand the event, its causes and its aftermath, and how framing this knowledge through GIS helped to build a 'cognitive geographical context'. This is an important point, that framing geographical learning is a key part of using GI. Conventional GIS does indeed provide a framework for fixing GI to specific coordinates and displaying it within a map or satellite image. Because it is digitised, the user viewing a GIS can manipulate the information displayed on the screen, transform it, analyse it. Advocates of GI use provide plenty of examples of its powerful analytical capabilities. For example, Openshaw, a GI scientist' makes this bold statement about its potentiality:

> GIS can be used to analyse river networks on Mars on Monday, study cancer in Bristol on Tuesday, map the underclass of London on Wednesday, analyse the groundwater flow in the Amazon basin on Thursday, and end the week by modelling retail shoppers in Los Angeles on Friday.
>
> (Openshaw, 1991, p. 624)

This is a GI Science view of spatial thinking; one that is subject to quite heated debate amongst the broader geography and geography education communities, particularly those involved in human geography.

Critical GIS

Since the 1990s, academic human geographers have been critical of the positivist philosophical underpinnings of GIS; the debatable ethics of military applications of GIS; the arguably non-participatory nature of a technology that only the privileged few can afford (O'Sullivan, 2006) and its potential (in their eyes) to stunt ways of thinking geographically (Schuurman, 2000). In his seminal text: *Ground Truth: The Social Implications of Geographic Information Systems*, Pickles (1995) spelt out a number of burning Critical GIS[7] issues for many in using a technology (GIS) that appeared to be able to quantify but not qualify. *Ground Truth* makes a strong case for the under- or misrepresentation of social phenomena through geographic information systems. One result of critiques of GIS has been the emergence of a more socially aware form of GIS: Critical GIS (cGIS) which aims to represent a broader range of GI than the narrowly scientific ones most often associated with conventional forms (Pavlovskaya, 2006; Dunn, 2007; Schuurman, 2009). One of the most championed movements to emerge within critical GIS has been public participatory GIS (PPGIS). Though still not short of critical review by some sceptics, public participatory GIS is considered by some to be 'GIS for the people'. PPGIS embraces an approach where local community issues drive the use of technology and where there is a stronger emphasis on community involvement with GIS. Some of the projects that adopt a PPGIS approach have included urban regeneration and sustainable development, for example the Rwandan 'Grounds for Change'[8] project that promotes fair trade coffee. In particular, PPGIS such as these differ from more traditional GIS in that they include more complex geographic information, often including indigenous geographical information. This in itself is an interesting aspect of PPGIS because it attaches importance to deep local knowledge being of value in society. There is an argument to be made that PPGIS could be used to further develop geographical understanding of local issues in schools (Fargher, 2011).

Web-based GIS

Most recently, the proliferation of device platforms (PC, laptop, network, mobile) on which GI can now be accessed has made digital geographic information more readily available (Elwood, 2008). These include geobrowsers such as Google Earth, Bing Maps and Worldwind and mobile computer apps[9] such as ESRI Collector for GIS and OpenStreetMap all which support 'annotating the planet' inside and outside the classroom.

Though research evidence of the influence of easier access to less technical GIS is not yet substantial, there are indications that geography teachers are beginning to make more use of earth viewers[10] (Kerski, 2008; Fargher, 2011). At the same time, young people are becoming increasingly more familiar with engaging with GI in informal settings; it is important that their involvement in using GI in school contribute positively to this wider geographical experience. In particular, internet users have become familiar with interacting with digital maps, scrolling satellite imagery and accessing other georeferenced GI data.[11] Some advocates of GIS[12] actually consider this kind of 'geovisualisation' to be the 'fourth R' in twenty-first-century education – as important as reading, writing and arithmetic (Goodchild, 2006).

Another aspect of using applications such as Google Earth is the ability to upload 'geographical information' (as KML files) into the virtual globe itself. Some may even argue that this is a new, quite different type of geographical knowledge which has not yet been categorised, a kind of 'neogeography' (Turner, 2006). This type of participatory GIS (for some have defined it thus) requires careful critical consideration by educators. If we are to let students loose on virtual worlds we need to be aware of the origin, validity and value of the various 'wikis',[13] podcasts,[14] vidcasts[15] and other 'geotags'[16] 'that we may be justifying and validating by facilitating their access to them. This more emancipatory, 'bottom-up' approach to using GIS and virtual globes may open up a world of opportunities for geography education particularly through the use of computer mobile apps in fieldwork. However, caution about the quality of 'geographical information' we may wittingly or unwittingly sanction seems prudent. Whichever way the use of GIS, virtual globes and GI-based mobile applications are considered, for many it is in a sense a new way of looking at the world, one in which it is important for us to consider the technology behind it and the reasons for the production of the geographic information that is visible or not visible within it (Fargher, 2009). Whatever their origin or format, it is clear that more complex GI continues to evolve at pace. Goodchild (2008) summarises this heterogeneity:

> People are indeed finding uses for the geobrowsers that are very different from typical GIS applications. They have none of the analytic modelling, and inferential power of GIS, and while oriented to visualisation are nevertheless very limited in what can be visualized .... In other ways, however, the uses of geobrowsers go well beyond those of GIS, reaching into a broad and rich domain of spatial concepts that may be very powerful aids to geographical understanding and insight.
>
> (Goodchild, 2008, p. 40)

It could be argued that more significant use of GIS in schools also requires more critical teacher understanding of how GIS frames knowledge (Fargher, 2011). By engaging more meaningfully in the type of critical debate about GIS already well-established in universities, teachers might be better placed to decide on a more productive use of GI in school geography. There are a number of related important questions for geography education here. If teachers choose to adopt conventional GI in geography, what are the implications of constructing geographical knowledge through an often quantitative technology? Which elements of geography can/cannot be measured? How can newly-evolving qualitative GIS technologies help to support the construction of a broader range of geographical knowledge? If teachers opt to use VGI in their lessons, where has that information come from? How trustworthy or reliable is geographic information uploaded on to the web? How has the move to the web released teachers from the physical restraints of GIS software and how can their access to new online data sets enhance pupils' experiences of geography? (Fargher, 2016). Several educators argue that these types of technologies will become much more important in education in the future (Kerski, 2008; Fargher, 2011). Although the technologies are emergent, the philosophy behind them ties in with earlier ideas about developing 'spatial intelligence'[17] with GI.

Hybrid GIS

The other emerging GI-related technology that should be considered in this discussion is multi-source hybrid GIS that combines elements of conventional GIS.

This idea is not new in either industry or higher education. In her GIS assessment of flood vulnerability of a core tourist area in New Orleans (*three years before the Hurricane Katrina event of 2005*), Koravec (2002) explains such an approach where conventional GIS is supplemented with a wider range of other information which reflects historical, socio-economic and political aspects of the geography of New Orleans. Several of the leading companies in GIS industries (including the market leader – ESRI) are now working on the hybrid approach to using GI. In a sense this involves using the rigour and structure of the geometry of a GIS but complementing it with the richness of web-based GIS, this could allow for some elements of space within a GIS to be quantifiable but also to bring to it the richness of more qualitative elements such as Koravec has highlighted. The geographical thinking that might lie behind such an holistic, multi-source GIS may present geographic information in ways which seem relevant and accessible to users other than conventional GIS specialists. The possibilities of geotagging (labelling/annotating digital earth representations); geoblogging (writing about places through the web); embedding photographs, video and other media alongside more traditional GIS use is an area of growing debate amongst geographers and geography educators (Goodchild, 2011). However, the need for critical use of volunteered geographic information remains paramount with regards to verifying its authenticity and source on the Internet.

Challenges to using GI

Despite the growing body of research indicating the value of using GI in geography, only a small number of UK schools are using it effectively to support geography teaching and learning (Ofsted, 2011). The small uptake continues to be connected with the fact that many teachers associate GI technologies with a steep initial learning curve, costly training and a scarcity of advice on constructing pedagogy with GIS (Fargher and Rayner, 2011). Research evidence also suggests that all ICT-related curriculum development requires teachers to develop their pedagogic strategies in considerably more complex ways than they may have done before. They need to be familiar with a range of areas of knowledge: their own subject content knowledge, knowledge about how students think and learn and increasingly in the twenty-first-century classroom, knowledge about how to use technology. Collectively this a complex set of challenges for teachers (Mishra and Koehler, 2006).

Mishra and Koehler's *TPACK framework* is useful to consider here (Figure 14.1). What kind of knowledge does a geography teacher need to bring into play to use GI in their classroom? *Technological Content Knowledge (TCK)* could involve a teacher developing their understanding of how geographic information (GI) is stored in vector or raster GIS (each of these are different ways of displaying information digitally. *Technological Pedagogical Knowledge (TPK)* could involve their being familiar with the pedagogical benefits of using Google Earth (the web-based earth viewer) for manipulating global images when teaching scale.

Technological Pedagogical Content Knowledge (*TPACK*) is the amalgam of all of these elements. TPACK requires technological competency, pedagogical skills and firm foundations in subject knowledge:

> TPACK is a form of knowledge that expert teachers bring to play anytime they teach.
>
> (Mishra and Koehler, 2006, p. 15)

It could be argued that effective GI-supported teaching and learning in geography education are more likely to occur through careful consideration of a framework such as Mishra and Koehler's TPACK. However, if we are to develop support for teachers using GIS further, consideration of a theoretical framework is likely to be only the beginning of the process. Even when teachers are trained to use particular software packages, familiarise themselves with the intricacies of new or adapted hardware or painstakingly learn associated terminologies, their training can be difficult to arrange, costly and become swiftly out of date (Mishra and Koehler, 2006). Added to this, several software packages and online GIS currently in use in schools were not designed with education in mind (ArcGIS, Google Earth). This is particularly true of conventional GIS packages (Bednarz and van der Schee, 2006).

There are also significant external and internal factors which may affect teachers' decisions to become involved with GI (Bednarz and van der Schee, 2006). Authority, manageability and consistency are important external influences. For example, seminal texts may sway teachers' attitudes towards and not away from GI; as in the case of the Mapping Our World series of texts produced by the GIS software company dominates the use of GIS in schools in the USA.[18] Decisions can be directly linked to authority too – compulsory inclusion of GIS in schools

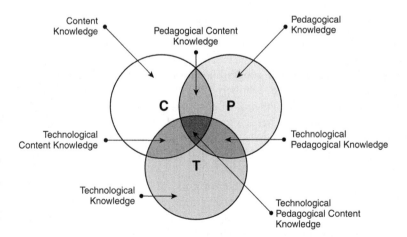

Figure 14.1 Mishra and Koehler's *TPACK framework.*

for use at GCSE level is beginning to have an effect on the uptake of GI use in schools. Manageability is seen by many as a vital factor, with teachers less likely to adopt GI practices that are difficult to master. Consistency is cited as an attractive feature of manageability too – if a GI technology 'fits in' with current practice and systems easily it becomes a more attractive proposition.

GI and the new geography curriculum

The government White Papers, *Educational Excellence Everywhere* (DfE, 2016) and *The Importance of Teaching* (DfE, 2010), offer us the lenses with which we can look at the role of GI in geography education. Emphasis on a national curriculum for the twenty-first century that is forward-looking and designed to embed strong core subject knowledge and a world-leading computing curriculum, makes the use of GI more prominent in constructing factual declarative knowledge in geography seem much more justified. Let's explore the idea that GI may be used to develop core or essential knowledge a little further. In their 2011 report on geography in UK secondary schools Ofsted states:

> Core knowledge for the majority of the students surveyed, but especially for those in the weaker schools, was poor. All but the best students interviewed were spatially naïve. The mental images they held of the world were often confused and they were not able to locate countries, key mountain ranges or other features with any degree of confidence .... Their study of geography was isolated and not set within a context that they could identify with.
>
> (Ofsted, 2011, p. 22)

According to Ofsted, core geography knowledge comprises basic factual geographic knowledge, vocabulary about and the ability to locate geographical features accurately. The argument presented in this quotation suggests that core knowledge is only one part of the complex subject of geography and its fundamental role in contributing to young people making sense of the multi-faceted world around them.

The role of GI in promoting geography's position in UK schools could be of considerable relevance, here. Lambert (2011) makes a strong case for the importance of the mutual dependence of core and powerful subject knowledge in geography education. GIS has a significant role to play in enhancing the subject's kudos and creating a curriculum that is contemporary and relevant to young people (Fargher, 2011) in the ways that the 2013 National Curriculum advocates.

Geography educators argue that the critical use of GI in constructing a synthesis of core and powerful geography subject knowledge is of considerable social significance in developing young people's awareness of major contemporary issues of our time (Annoni et al., 2011; Fargher, 2011). It is arguable that school geography could look to views on this from colleagues in the higher education sector. Cosgrove (2008), for example, offers words of warning about trying to pin geography down to distinct categories:

> We need to be vigilant in the face of a constant temptation to leap from inscribing order and pattern into (geo) graphic images to inferring something more universal. Such inference can lead – indeed too often – has led inexorably to the temptations of applied geography: imposing a single vision across the wonderful variety and individuality of geographical actuality and human freedom.
>
> (Cosgrove, 2008, p. 33)

Cosgrove is advocating multi-perspectives and not a narrowed view. Some, like Cosgrove, argue that more critical use of such technologies has much to offer in promoting geographical understanding. There is another element of this argument that perhaps needs reinforcing here. A case can be made for developing strong core geography knowledge through the use of GI but only if that constitutes part of a richer and broader geographical picture which enhances access to more powerful geographical knowledge (Fargher, 2011). For example, on a global level, at a time when climate change is at the top of many agendas some advocates of GIS and virtual globes are beginning to actively promote 'climate literacy through GI for the twenty-first century' (Herring and Leopold, 2007).

Conclusion

In its *Geography Manifesto: A Different View* (GA, 2009), the Geographical Association encourages us to take a fresh look at how we approach geography education in a way that is relevant to this discussion. By re-engaging with 'discovery' in our subject and by travelling 'with a different view', the GA's manifesto encourages teachers to invest their knowledge, expertise and energy in stimulating student interests and needs. The type of young people's geography illustrated in the manifesto is dynamic and challenging, inspiring a living geography for change in a changing world. In a broader but significantly related context, many young people are already very adept at using geo-technologies. It is important that their experiences of using GIS and virtual globes in school contribute to this wider understanding of the world. In particular, the burgeoning development of 'neogeography' and volunteered geographic information (VGI) over the last five years has changed the landscape of web-based geo-technologies, and are becoming a part of the metaphor of the 'geographical conversation' that the GA's manifesto encourages. For example, in the flatter digital world that young people experience, geography educators are best placed to explore the implications of this for the central concepts of scale and connection, and proximity and distance. Massey and Clark imply the level of responsibility that this kind of thinking shifts onto the shoulders of geography educators in the twenty-first century when they argue that:

> We are often led to believe that the 'big' global changes in the world are inevitable, that there is nothing we can do. Clearly, some things may be impossible – or extremely difficult to change. Yet there is perhaps a need to bring some of these 'big' things down to earth, to see how they are made.
>
> (Massey and Clark, 2008, p. 28)

As Massey and Clark (2008) suggest, whether we wish it or not, we are all implicated in the way worlds are 'made' and as geography educators we need to critically consider these deeper epistemological questions when choosing how to approach teaching with GIS. It could be argued that the recent exponential explosion of GI onto the Web makes our need to be conscious and critical of the language and meanings *behind* the signs and symbols present in Web 2.0 as much as when critical GIS first emerged in the 1990s. As with any semiotic medium, it is important to be aware of the different discourses which are being represented within it. GIS the commercial product comes straight from realist and pragmatic origins, and is often constructed or used to predict events and to problem solve. Web 2.0 is also commercially driven; appropriate for some types of student enquiry some might argue, but surely worthy of more careful consideration if education is to include ways of thinking about and representing ideas beyond the 'googlisation'[19] and geotagging of geography (Fargher, 2011).

The perspectives examined in this short chapter by no means exhaust the debates that could be had about the ways in which GI could or should be used in geography education. My intention has been to introduce and critically analyse a number of key issues about the nature of GI, its educational value, the role of teacher knowledge in teaching with its various conventional, Web 2.0 and hybrid guises. This chapter has argued that teachers using GI thoughtfully, critically and skilfully in education can support young people to further develop their geographical perspectives of our changing world. As Elwood states:

> GI(S) is tremendously important because it is such a powerful mediator of spatial knowledge, social and political power, and intellectual practice in geography. In short, the answer is the same as it was ten years ago: Because the stakes are high.
>
> (Elwood, 2006, p. 693)

Key readings

1   Kerski, J. Milson, A. and Demirci, A. (eds.) *International Perspectives on Teaching and Learning with GIS in Secondary Schools*, London: Springer. Very useful for following up these debates from different international perspectives, the UK chapter is Fargher, M. and Rayner, D. (2011) 'United Kingdom: realising the potential of GIS in the school geography curriculum'.

2   O'Sullivan, D. (2006). 'Geographical Information Science: critical GIS', *Progress in Human Geography*, 30 (6), 783–91. David O'Sullivan's article offers an interesting and alternative view on the contribution of more critically informed use of GIS which involves an engagement with the technology rather than just criticism of it from the outside.

Notes

1 Geographic Information System.
2 Digital Earth is an umbrella term to describe the range of digitally displayed representations of the earth (Gore, 1998).
3 Google Earth was the first widely available 'free' earth viewer – released in 2005.
4 ESRI ArcGIS Online is a web-based GIS used widely in industry, universities and increasingly in schools.
5 QGIS is a free, open source GIS.
6 AEGIS 3 GIS is a GIS specifically designed for schools.
7 Earth viewers are digital globes such as Google Earth.
8 Georeferenced GI data is digitally linked to a specific set of geographical coordinates.
9 A mobile app is a computer program designed to run on mobile devices such as smartphones and tablet computers.
10 Geographic information systems.
11 Wikis are web-based encyclopaedias.
12 Podcasts are downloadable audio recordings.
13 Vidcasts are downloadable video recordings.
14 Geotags are a form of coordinate-referenced post-it notes.
15 Spatial intelligence refers here to spatial thinking with conventional GIS.
16 *Mapping Our World – GIS Lessons for Educators* (Malone, 2005).
17 Spatial intelligence refers here to spatial thinking with conventional GIS.
18 Mapping our World – GIS lessons for Education (ESRI, 2005).
19 Googlisation is a phrase by Vaidhyanathan (2010) which casts a critical eye over the world's compulsion to 'Google'.

References

Annoni, A., Craglia, M., Ehlers, M., Georgiadou, Y., Giacomelli, A., Konecny, M., Ostlaender, M., Remetey-Füllöp, G., Rhind, D., Smits, P. and Schade, S. (2011) 'A European perspective on digital earth', *International Journal of Digital Earth*, 4 (4), 271–84.

Bednarz, S.W. (2004) 'Geographic information systems: a tool to support geography and environmental education?', *GeoJournal*, 60 (2), 191–9.

Bednarz, S.W. and van der Schee, J. (2006) 'Europe and the United States: the implementation of geographical information systems in secondary education in two contexts', *Technology, Pedagogy and Education*, 15 (2), 191–206.

Bednarz, S.W. and Bednarz, R.S. (2008) 'Spatial thinking: the key to success in using geospatial technologies in the social studies classroom', in A.J. Milson and M. Alibrandi (eds.), *Digital Geography: Geo-Spatial Technologies in the Social Studies Classroom*, New York: Information Age Publishing.

Cosgrove, D.E. (2008) *Geography and Vision: Seeing, Imagining and Representing the World*, London: Palgrave Macmillan.

Department for Education (DfE) (2013a) *National Curriculum in England: Geography Programmes of Study*. London: DfE, Available at: www.gov.uk/government/publications/national-curriculum-in-england-geography-programmes-of-study [Accessed 12 April 2016].

Department for Education (DfE) (2013b) *Geography: GCSE Subject Content and Assessment Objectives*, London: DfE, Available at: www.gov.uk/government/uploads/system/uploads/attachment_data/file/206145/GCSE_Geography.pdf [Accessed 12 April 2016].

Department for Education (DfE) (2014) *Geography: GCE AS and A Level Subject Content, July 2014*, London: DfE, Available at: www.gov.uk/government/uploads/system/uploads/attachment_data/file/330343/Geography_GCE_-_subject_content_-_final.pdf [Accessed 2 April 2016].

Department for Education (DfE) (2016) *Educational Excellence Everywhere*, Available at: www.gov.uk/government/publications/educational-excellence-everywhere [Accessed 12 April 2016].

Dunn, C.E. (2007) 'Participatory GIS—a people's GIS?', *Progress in Human Geography*, 31 (5), 616–37.

Elwood, S. (2006) 'Critical Issues in participatory GIS: deconstructions, reconstructions and new research directions', *Transactions in GIS*, 10 (5), 693–708.

Elwood, S. (2008) 'Geographic Information Science: new geovisualization technologies – emerging questions and linkages with GIScience research', *Progress in Human Geography*, 33 (2), 256–63.

Fargher, M. (2006) 'Linking lessons learnt from the classroom with research findings on pedagogies with GIS', *ESRI European Conference Proceedings, Stockholm* (2006). Available at: http://gis.esri.com/library/userconf/educ06/papers/educ_1461.pdf. [Accessed 12 April 2016].

Fargher, M. (2009) 'Putting place at the centre of digital earth', Paper presented at the Symposium for Digital Earth, Beijing.

Fargher, M. (2011) 'Geography with a different view through GIS' ESRI conference proceedings, Madrid (2011).

Fargher, M. and Rayner, D. (2011) 'United Kingdom: realising the potential of GIS in the school geography curriculum', in J. Kerski, A. Milson and A. Demirci (eds.), *International Perspectives on Teaching and Learning with GIS in* Secondary Schools, London: Springer.

Geographical Association (2009) *A Different View: A Manifesto from the Geographical Association*, Sheffield: Geographical Association.

Geographical Association (2006) Spatially Speaking, Available at: http://www.geography. org.uk/projects/spatiallyspeaking/ [Accessed 4 February 2012].

Geographical Association (2011a) 'GIS in secondary school geography', Available at: http://www.geography.org.uk/download/GA_CPDGISKeyStages.pdf [Accessed 4 February 2012].

Geographical Association (2011b) *Curriculum Consultation Full Report*, Available at: http://www.geography.org.uk/getinvolved/geographycurriculumconsultation/ [Accessed 12 April 2016].

Goodchild, M.F. (2006) 'The fourth r? Rethinking GIS education'ESRI ArcNews, Available at: http://www.esri.com/news/arcnews/fall06articles/the-fourth-r.html [Accessed 12 April 2016].

Goodchild, M.F. (2008) 'Whither VGI?', *GeoJournal*, 72, 239–244.

Goodchild, M.F. (2011) 'Looking forward: five thoughts on the future of GIS', *ArcWatch* (February). [500] 'Grounds for change': a public participatory GIS project, Available at: http://www.esri. com/news/arcwatch/0811/user-conference. html [Accessed 12 April 2016].

Gore, A. (1998) *The Digital Earth, Understanding our Planet in the 21st Century*, Speech given at the Californian Science Center, Los Angeles, California on 31 January 1998.

Herring, D. and Leopold, A. (2007) 'GIS and climate literacy', Paper presented at the Symposium for Digital Earth, Berkeley, California, June 2007.

Kerski, J. (2008) 'The role of GIS in digital earth education', *The International Journal of Digital Earth*, 1 (4), 326–46.

Koravec, N. (2002) 'GIS assessment of the vulnerability of a core tourist area in New Orleans to impacts of flood inundation during a hurricane event', *Trends in Cultural Geography* GEOG 7011 Cultural Landscapes, Spring 2002.

Lambert, D. (2011) 'Reviewing the case for geography, and the 'knowledge turn' in the English National Curriculum', *Curriculum Journal*, 22 (2), 243–64.

Malone, L. (2005) *Mapping our World: GIS Lessons for Educators*, Redlands, CA: ESRI Press.

Massey, D. and Clark, N. (2008) 'Introduction' in N. Clark, D. Massey and P. Sarre (eds.), *Material Geographies: A World in the Making*, London: Sage.

Mishra, P. and Koehler, M.J. 2006) TPACK model, Available at: http://www.tpck. org/ [Accessed 12 April 2016].

National Research Council (2006) *Learning to Think Spatially: GIS as a Support System in the K–12 Curriculum*, Washington, DC: The National Academies Press.

Ofsted (2011) *Learning to Make a World of Difference*, February 2011, Available at: www. ofsted.gov.uk/publications/090224 [Accessed 10 February 2012].

Openshaw, S. (1991) 'A view on the GIS crisis in geography, or using GIS to put Humpty Dumpty back together again', *Environment and Planning Part A*, 23 (5), 621–8.

O'Sullivan, D. (2006) 'Geographical Information Science: critical GIS', *Progress in Human Geography*, 30 (6), 783–91.

Pavlovskaya M. (2006) 'Theorizing with GIS: a tool for critical geographies?', *Environment and Planning Part A*, 38 (11), 2003–20.

Pickles, J. (ed.) (1995) *Ground Truth: The Social Implications of Geographic Information Systems*, New York: Guildford Press.

Scheepers, D. (2009) 'GIS in the geography curriculum', *Position IT*, July 2009, 40–5.

Schuurman, N. (2000) 'Trouble in the heartland: GIS and its critics in the 1990s', *Progress in Human Geography*, 24 (4), 569–90.

Schuurman, N. (2004) *GIS: A Short Introduction*, London: Blackwell.

Schuurman, N. (2009) 'Is the rubric "Critical GIScience" effective? An argument for theoretical GIScience', *Cartographica*, 44 (1), 10–11.

Sinton, D.S. and Bednarz, S.W. (2007) 'About that G in GIS', in D.S. Sinton, and J. Lund (eds.) (2007) *Understanding Place GIS and Mapping across the Curriculum*, Redlands, CA: ESRI Press.

Sinton, D.S. and Lund, J. (2007) *Understanding Place GIS and Mapping Across the Curriculum*, Redlands, CA: ESRI Press.

Turner, A. (2006) An introduction to neogeography, Available at: http://pcmlp.socleg.ox.ac.uk/sites/pcmlp.socleg.ox.ac.uk/files/Introduction_to_Neogeography.pdf [Accessed 12 April 2016].

Vaidhyanathan, S. (2010) *The Googlization of Everything (and why we should worry)*, Berkeley, CA: University of California Press.

Chapter 15

Geography and 'employability'

John Lyon

> Our latest research shows that businesses and schools are still worlds apart
> when it comes to getting young people ready for the world of work.
> (John Longworth, BCC Director General, 2015)

Introduction

As part of his response to the British Chamber of Commerce (BCC) findings
from its Business and Education Survey 2015,[1] John Longworth emphasised
'that secondary schools need to do more to help young people transition into
employment by ensuring that their students have the preparation that businesses
truly value'. The entry level skills reported as most valued by businesses in the
survey were communication (88 per cent), literacy (69 per cent), numeracy
(64 per cent), Information Technology (56 per cent) and team work (53 per
cent). Whilst schools focus on these 'key skills' and provide access to vocational
qualifications, careers advice and work experience, the quality of this provision
has come under close scrutiny (see Wolf, 2011; Ofsted, 2014; Parliament, House
of Commons, 2016). The need to close the 'employability gap' and provide
school leavers with the necessary skills to compete in a global economy remains
an educational priority (Morgan, N., 2014). It is within this wider context that
this chapter explores the ways in which geography education and geographers
can contribute to the development of knowledgeable citizens who are both skilful and employable.

It is worth reminding ourselves though that the relevance of geography to living and working in the twenty-first century is not a new discussion (see Stamp,
1960), and at times the very existence of geography as a curriculum entitlement
has been questioned (Morgan and Lambert, 2005). With regard to geography's
place in the curriculum, the Geographical Association's Manifesto (2009) justifies
it in the following terms:

> Geography serves vital educational goals: thinking and decision making with
> geography helps us to be, and live our lives, as knowledgeable *citizens*, aware
> of our own local communities in a global setting.

> Geographers are skilful: using maps and mediated images of people and place, numerical data and graphical modes of communication and getting to grips with the geographic information systems that underpin our lives, make geographers *skilful and employable.*
>
> (GA, 2009, p. 5)

To assert that the study of geography can develop knowledgeable citizens who are both skilful and employable is not new. In 1902, E.G. Hewlett noted how geography 'provides ... necessary information of a technical character to many vocations of life, such as commerce, politics or war, some provision of which must be made in school' (p. 104). This was geography teaching in part aimed at providing an educated workforce able to support and enhance Britain's position as a world power. Much later, Norman Graves presented the aims and objectives of geographical education as broadly serving a dual purpose 'for the development of mind and for the social, economic and political needs of society' (Graves, 1980, p. 9). However, he doubted whether pupils would fully understand the aims of geographical teaching, since most pupils are 'highly pragmatic in their attitude to school knowledge; they tend to look upon such knowledge as a means to an examination or to a job, even if incidentally they may become interested in what they are studying' (ibid.). One of the challenges facing teachers is to be responsive to pupils' pragmatic attitudes to learning, the future and career paths, whilst also keeping in mind broader educational aims for the subject.

With regard to the value of geography, teachers may face a range of questions from students: Who are geographers? What do they do? Does the geography I am doing now relate to a career I want to pursue? And the question every geography teacher should be ready for is: 'What use is geography to me when I leave school, will it get me a job?'

Geography and employability

A widely used definition of employability is 'the capability to gain initial employment, maintain employment and obtain employment if required' (Hillage and Pollard, 1998, p. 1). More detailed is the definition by ESECT (2003) of 'a set of achievements – skills, understandings and personal attributes – that make graduates more likely to gain employment and be successful in their chosen occupations' (p. 4). According to Darrel Sheinman, founder of Polestar, a global GIS satellite tracking company, 'There is no question that the understanding and skills that come from a study of geography are highly valued by employers' (RGS, 2008, p. 12). Several recent studies of graduates have demonstrated the employability of geographers. Esri UK, the leading Geographical Information Systems business, commissioned a survey of 200 business leaders across the UK public and private sectors. Published in 2010, it showed that the graduate skills/knowledge business leaders are looking for in future employees are 'critical thinking (78 per cent of businesses leaders), advanced analytical skills (76 per cent), understanding and interpreting complex data (71 per cent), advanced technology skills (57 per cent) and understanding socio-economic environments (54 per cent) – all of which are gained through the study of geography' (Esri UK, 2010). In 2016 the unemployment rates for geography undergraduates were among the lowest recorded, behind Sports Science and Civil Engineering (see Logan and Prichard, 2016).

However, the Royal Geographical Society with IBG (RGS-IBG) claims that the usefulness of geographical knowledge in the workplace, together with the unusually wide set of transferable skills that people learn through studying geography, is not always understood and that there is a need to make it more explicit to young people.

This orthodox position is not without its critics. For example, the late Rex Walford (2000) was not convinced. For him, geography itself is intrinsically interesting and stimulating and so is worthy of study on its own merits. Ron Johnston also strikes a note of caution. He makes the point that if learning how to learn is increasingly everything in ensuring employability skills in a changing world, and geography is everything, then surely geography must be well placed to respond. However, he notes that geography must continue to maintain the core identity and values of the traditional discipline, continuing to innovate in the curriculum while being wary of wholeheartedly jumping on short-term materialistic bandwagons driven by political decision makers (Johnston, 1997). He goes on to say, 'Geography is an academic discipline, not a profession, and one of its traditional strengths in British higher education is its use as a vehicle for the development of critical intellectual skills' (p. 245).

The report by the Expert Panel for the National Curriculum review (DfE, 2011) noted that 'the school curriculum should develop pupils' knowledge, understanding skills and attitudes to satisfy economic, cultural social, personal and environmental goals' (p. 16). Satisfying future economic needs for individuals and for the workforce as a whole is only one of five key aims in ensuring a balanced and broadly based curriculum. One issue for geography teachers then is deciding on the balance and relationship between subject knowledge, values, skills, and broader competences such as problem solving and independent learning, increasingly associated with developing capacities for future growth. A second issue is concerned with decisions about how geography teachers make connections between the subject and the workplace to enable students to more clearly see these opportunities.

We may see the value of learning geography as being of increasing importance as students are entering an employment market that has rapidly changing patterns in an increasingly uncertain world (Jenkins and Healey, 1995). There is an increased demand for employees to be able to solve environmental and spatial problems, which are essentially geographical issues. However, few of these employees, often drawn from geography graduates, will call themselves 'geographers' at work, which can be problematic, particularly when these are portrayed in the media, for example, as Town Planner, Coastal Engineer or Environmental Consultant, with the 'geography' effectively hidden. As career opportunities involving working with and solving such environmental and spatial problems are increasing, so raising awareness of these vocational pathways may be a course adopted to raise the perceived value of the subject. This applies to careers that are directly related to geography as well as careers that use skills developed through geographical learning. A range of techniques can be used to promote career pathways, including making direct reference to career opportunities related to the work being done in class, making field visits and inviting in adults who employ geographical skills significantly in their work, such as RGS 'Ambassadors'. These graduates may provide inspirational role models, demonstrating the value of geography for them to their further study and careers (see GA and RGS-IBG, 2011).

At the OECD Education Ministerial Meeting in November 2010 it was noted that:

> Today, education and training need to prepare learners at all levels for more rapid change than ever before, for jobs that have not yet been created, using technologies that have not yet been invented, to solve problems that cannot be foreseen.
>
> (OECD, 2010, p. 1)

Ministers highlighted the challenge to countries needing to develop 'flexible educational pathways through initial education; promote skill acquisition and equity of access to learning' (ibid., p. 6). They further noted that teachers are the key professionals on the front line facing these new demands and expectations.

How explicit might we make connections between the knowledge, skills and capabilities developed through geography with the workplace and the skills needed to live lives as knowledgeable *citizens*? Perhaps the largest and most thorough recent investigation into these issues is the *Nuffield Review, Education for All: The Future of Education and Training for 14–19 Year Olds* led by Richard Pring. The review posed the question: 'What counts as an educated 19 year old in this day and age?' The 'Summary, Implications and Recommendations' to the review argued for an understanding of education *for all* which would provide:

- the knowledge and understanding required for the 'intelligent management of life';
- competence to make decisions about the future in the light of changing economic and social conditions;
- practical capability – including preparation for employment;
- moral seriousness with which to shape future choices and relationships;
- a sense of responsibility for the community.

(Pring et al., 2009, p. 3)

The Review proposes that 'all learners will have to become more rounded, resilient, creative and social, if they are to help shape an increasingly unpredictable and demanding world' (ibid.). Therefore, what matters, as argued in the Review, is how essential knowledge, capabilities and qualities are translated into the learning experience of young people.

This need for workers to be agile and possess new skills and ways of understanding requires a response from geographers.

Geography and vocational programmes

Before looking at how geography and geographers have responded, it is worth briefly exploring what we mean by the term 'vocational education'. The Wolf Report (2011), a comprehensive review of vocational education, notes there is no formal definition of the term in England and that it is applied to wide-ranging and very different programmes. The report notes that:

> The many ways in which the term vocational is used, reflect the many different purposes which 14–19 education serves and its large and diverse student body. Some qualifications are highly specific, oriented to a particular occupation. Others are more general, and are referred to sometimes as vocationally-related or pre-vocational.
>
> (The Wolf Report, 2011, p. 23)

A further issue concerns the perceived parity between 'academic' and 'vocational' qualifications and students' choices and pathways, particularly as:

> The vocational strand has always been treated as inferior, with the consequence that students avoid training for careers which would be rewarding for themselves, as well as contributing to the UK economy, in favour of academic study for which they may not be suited, and which may not lead directly to employment
>
> (MacDonald Ross, 2009, p. 128)

The Wolf Report (2011) made ten recommendations of which one was designed to safeguard pupils' access to a common general core as a basis for progression, 'such that they can progress to a wide range of post-16 academic and vocational options; but also to ensure that academically successful pupils are given the chance to take practical courses' (p. 113). Government has responded to these recommendations (see DfE, 2015c) with changes to qualifications and status in performance tables; however it is in how schools and teachers present vocational options to students that can determine uptake.

In addition to geography teachers understanding vocational pathways, geography's focus on place, space and environment means they are well positioned to contribute to many vocational and pre-vocational courses. Over the years, geographers have successfully contributed to vocational courses such as the Technical and Vocational Education Initiative (TVEI) 1982–1997; General National Vocational Qualification (GNVQ) 1991–2007 and GCSEs in vocational subjects first launched in 2002. Geographers have more recently been involved in some of the short lived 14/19 Diplomas 2008–2013, notably construction and the built environment; environment and land-based studies and travel and tourism.

In many schools geographers become involved with vocational courses partly because aspects of the specifications can cover many of the contemporary issues taught in geography such as environment change, destination management, and human mobility. In particular, geography teachers have been involved with Leisure and Tourism in several guises, notably GNVQ Leisure and Tourism, Vocational Certificates of Education (VCE) courses in 'Leisure and Recreation' and 'Travel and Tourism', GCSE and GCE Travel and Tourism. However, while geographers have the subject knowledge, particularly in tourism development and impacts of tourism/sustainable tourism, other aspects such as marketing and customer service lie beyond most teachers' experience, and indeed the scope of geography. Ofsted (2004) reported that geographers teaching GCSE Leisure and Tourism found it challenging to 'teach this very different subject' (p. 20) and of schools not providing enough opportunity for practice in realistic environments such as simulated aircraft cabins or travel shops (Ofsted, 2009). To create conditions on vocational courses for learners to function as realistic practitioners, teachers need to move beyond classroom geography.

In May 2015, Government changes to the examination system and qualifications mean that only new qualifications accredited by the exams regulator Ofqual can be offered by awarding bodies in the future. Acting on recommendations in the Wolf Report (2011) 'poor quality qualifications and those covering specialist vocational content that was inappropriate for 14–16-year-olds, have been excluded from the list of non-GCSE qualifications recognised in the key stage 4 performance tables (DfE, 2015a, p. 4). New level 1 and level 2 qualifications called Technical Awards were introduced for 14–16-year-olds to 'equip students with applied knowledge and associated practical skills not usually acquired through general education' (DFE, 2015b, p. 10). At post-16, level 3 Applied Level Qualifications and Tech Levels were introduced. It remains to be seen how geography teachers may contribute to this latest set of vocational qualifications.

Applied geography

In their Curriculum Proposals and Rationale the Geographical Association (2011) looks at issues of pedagogy noting 'thinking geographically is a distinctive procedure … (it is) learned through exposure to, and direct experience of, high quality geographical enquiry which might include decision making or problem solving scenarios' (p. 2). This is essentially the approach of applied geography which can be seen as:

> The use of geographical knowledge as an aid to making choices from the many alternative courses open to us about how we use the planet and its

resources, how we distribute ourselves on the surface and how we relate to fellow men.

(Sant, 1982, p. 1)

As early as 1960, Dudley Stamp, a pioneer in the field of applied geography proposed:

> If the past 50 years have been spent in developing geographical method of survey and analysis, surely the time has now come to apply these methods towards understanding and interpretation of some of the features of the world of today and use these methods in helping towards the solution of some of the great world problems – the increasing pressure of population on space, the development of underdeveloped areas, or the attempt to improve living conditions which is the object of town and country planning.

(Stamp, 1960, pp. 10–11)

Towards the end of the 1970s and into the 1980s, geography needed to respond to governmental pressure, following the then Prime Minister, James Callaghan's speech in 1976 at Ruskin College, Oxford. He emphasised the need to make the curriculum more relevant to young people in preparation for their adult life. He was concerned about a disconnection between industry and education and that the school curriculum did not prepare young people for the demands of employment in a modern industrial society (Jamieson and Lightfoot, 1982). The speech refocused attention on the nature of the curriculum and the relationships between school and work. The Schools Council Industry Project (which became the School Curriculum Industry Partnership (SCIP), identified sets of overlapping pressures. The most relevant to geography were the pressures of the Industrial Society in general, which were related to calls for the school curriculum to be broader and less academically orientated, and to prepare young people more adequately for adult life (Corney, 1985, 1992).

One solution was to develop closer links between schools and industry. The Geography Schools Industry Project (GSIP) was one such response; established by the Geographical Association, its aims included the desire to forge school–industry links as a strategy in helping geography teachers contribute to their students' economic understanding. Building on the traditions of geographical education established by the Avery Hill, Bristol, and Geography 16–19 Projects, GSIP stressed an approach to teaching based on active student learning, assessment for learning and an emphasis on the economic dimension. Focusing on issues and questions deemed relevant to students, it employed a meaningful sequence of geographical enquiry through which students gained first-hand experience of workplaces, people at work and local communities. It allowed scope for the involvement of people from industry and the community in planning and implementing units of work. For many, this was a refreshing approach with its rich resources and relevant, topical units of work. Teachers were engaged with making their own curriculum, refreshing the subject matter and changing the way young people see the world. Others viewed it differently. For Huckle (1985) projects such as GSIP were concerned largely with the management of change as the state sought to restructure in the face of new challenges and with sectional interests of a community of educators rather than being progressive educational developments.

Government influence continued in 1985 when Sir Keith Joseph, the then Secretary of State, returned to this theme and posed the following set of questions to the Geographical Association:

> Is enough attention paid to the impact of political and economic processes and activities in geographical patterns and changes? ... is there not more scope for more effective cooperation between geography teachers and their colleagues in other disciplines to foster economic awareness and political understanding?
>
> (Joseph, 1985, p. 29)

Further emphasis entered the curriculum as Economic Understanding was one of the five major cross-curricular themes of the National Curriculum Council and Geography seemed well placed to contribute. The HMI view expressed in 'Geography from 5–16' was that 'geography can make a significant contribution to ... education in economic understanding ... and preparing young people for the world of work' (Bennetts, 1986, p. 302). For older students, the Geography 16–19 Project was in part an attempt to support this aim. The key to understanding the Project's approach to geography was that it was 'educational rather than strictly academic, enabling students to draw on geographical knowledge and theories in a meaningful way and to develop a wide range of skills and abilities' (Naish and Rawling, 1990, p. 61). In this way it offered a role for geography in the 16–19 Curriculum which had appeal and relevance for a large cross-section of students. Such an educational approach was felt to have possibilities in relation to some wider access courses in higher education. The 16–19 Project recommended that the study of geography should take place through enquiry-based teaching and learning, focusing on questions, issues, and problems arising from the interrelationship of people with their varied environments. An important emphasis was the development of students as responsible and competent individuals capable of playing a participatory role in society which incorporated the development of economic understanding and political literacy. However, the 16–19 Project was not overtly vocational in its approach, offering no real direct reference to specific vocations, but it certainly offered a wide set of transferable techniques and skills of value in a vocational context, could easily complement geography's presence in vocational courses such as Travel and Tourism and could be seen as an example of effective applied geography.

For Pacione (1999), applied geography involves problem-orientated research in both human and physical geography, and encompasses 'the fundamental philosophy of relevance or usefulness to society' (p. 4). An applied geographical approach, therefore, has the potential to illuminate the nature and causes of problems such as extreme natural events, for example, floods and drought; environmental concerns such as deforestation and disease; human issues such as crime and poverty; as well as inform the formulation of appropriate responses. Sant (1982) notes that such an approach is not, however, neutral in its application or in the choices that are made about reaping some personal or social advantage. These choices and decisions are made by someone, somewhere. Who makes these choices? Do they make these choices in a professional capacity? Are they geographers? And does it matter if they are not?

Of course, Stamp gave greater emphasis to land classification and evaluation and land-use planning than other forms of applied geography, reflecting his interests drawn from the First Land Use Survey of Britain which he set up and organised in the 1930s. By 1960 he noted that 'natural geographical factors are more important than they have ever been in the past. Man (*sic*) has not emancipated himself from these factors' (p. 194). It would be interesting to see how Stamp would have developed his thinking in response to new global challenges. Paul Crutzen, an atmospheric chemist, has begun to develop the idea that we now exist in the *Anthropocene*, where human activities are having an impact on the Earth's ecosystems so significant as to constitute a new geological era. Applied geography is well placed to address some of the issues this idea raises.

Conclusion

The nature and value of vocational and applied dimensions to the curriculum continue to exercise the Government as it presses ahead with its major reform agenda. With recent reform to geography at GCSE and A level occupying geography teachers' time, contributions to discussion and delivery of applied and vocational subjects may be limited but in their role as geography curriculum makers there will always be choices and decisions to be made.

One important choice concerns the potential for geography students to apply their knowledge and skills to causes and concerns of global importance. If we return to the GA *Manifesto*, we understand that geography

> *deepens understanding:* many contemporary challenges – climate change, food security, energy choices – cannot be understood without a geographical perspective which includes sound locational knowledge and understanding.
>
> (GA, 2009, p. 5)

Such matters concerning the future of the planet and its peoples have been taken up by John Morgan who argues

> We live in a time where there are serious questions about the ability of the planet to sustain current levels of economic development. Future generations

are likely to face a bleaker environmental future and will need to learn how to mitigate and adapt to the effects of climate change. However, despite the obvious importance of these issues most schooling continues with little direct engagement with questions of environmental change.

(Morgan, 2011, p. ii)

These are big issues involving some significant choices. The set of skills, knowledge and pedagogy that geography promotes offers significant opportunities for young people to explore how societal, economic and environmental change is likely to impact on all our futures and can enable them to better understand the world and their place in it. Geography itself is not a vocational subject but when taught thoughtfully, it offers powerful specialist knowledge, a skill set and an ability to understand issues from multiple perspectives that ensure geographers are highly sought after in the workplace. Within an applied context, geography teaching also has the potential to include detailed information about the people and jobs that will be involved in responding to crucial economic, social and environmental issues such as effective resource management or climate change.

I have tried to show in this chapter the long-standing debates over not only the nature of geography as an applied subject but also its role in relation to employability and vocational preparation. In the final analysis these are debates about geography, but also geography in a vocational setting. The value of geography would appear to be its contribution to a broad base of knowledge, perspectives on the world, and the development of practical and cognitive skills.

Key readings

1   Naish, M., Rawling, E. and Hart, C. (1987) *Geography 16–19: The Contribution of a Curriculum Development Project to 16–19 Education*, London: Longman for School Curriculum Development Committee. This book explores a complete philosophy about geography and applied approaches.
2   Rawling, E. (2001) *Changing the Subject: The Impact of National Policy on School Geography 1980–2000*, Sheffield: Geographical Association. In Eleanor Rawling's excellent account of school geography between 1980 and 2000, Chapter 7 covers the debate about the 14–19 curriculum and academic vocational divide.

Note

1   The BCC surveyed 3,552 businesses and educational institutions across the UK in July 2015 in order to learn what could be done to bridge the gap between schools and businesses.

References

Bennetts, T. (1986) 'Geography from 5 to 16: a view from the inspectorate', *Geography*, 70 (4), 299–314.

Corney, G. (ed.) (1985) *Geography Schools and Industry*, Sheffield: The Geographical Association.

Corney, G. (ed.) (1992) *Teaching Economic Understanding through Geography*, Sheffield: The Geographical Association.

Department for Education (DfE) (2011) *The Framework for the National Curriculum. A Report by the Expert Panel for the National Curriculum Review*, London: Department for Education.

Department for Education (DfE) (2015a) *Technical Awards For 14 To 16 Year Olds 2017 and 2018 Performance Tables: Technical Guidance for Awarding Organisations* Updated March 2015 (Annex D: 2018 Addendum added), London: Department for Education.

Department for Education (DfE) (2015b) *Key Stage 4 Performance Tables: Qualifications in the Technical Award Category July 2015* (replaces June 2015 version), London: Department for Education.

Department for Education (DfE) (2015c) *Review of Vocational Education, 2011 The Wolf Report: Recommendations Final Progress Report*, London: Department for Education.

Enhancing Student Employability Co-ordination Team (ESECT) (2003) *Briefings on Employability 2, Are your Students Employable?* Report from HEFCE's Enhancing Student Employability Co-ordination Team (ESECT), Available at: www.qualityresearchinternational.com/esecttools/esectpubs/B0E2%20Are%20your%20students%20 employable.pdf [Accessed 24 February 2012].

Esri UK (2010) Press release: UK Businesses Call For Advanced Technology Skills To Boost Economy. 17 November 2010, Available at: http://www.esriuk.com/aboutesriuk/pressreleases.asp?pid=647 [Accessed 25 July 2016].

Geographical Association (GA). (2009) *A Different View: A Manifesto from the Geographical Association*, Sheffield: Geographical Association.

Geographical Association (2011) *The Geography National Curriculum, GA Curriculum Proposals and Rationale,* Available at: http://geography.org.uk/get-involved/geographycurriculumconsultation/ [Accessed 24 August 2016].

Geographical Association and Royal Geographical Society (with IBG) (2011) *The Action Plan for Geography 2006–2011 Final Report and Evaluation,* Available at: http://www.geography.org.uk/download/GA_APGFinalReport.pdf [Accessed 24 August 2016].

Graves, N. (1980) *Geography Education in Secondary Schools*, Sheffield: The Geographical Association.

Hewlett, E.G. (1902) 'Aims and difficulties in the teaching of geography', *The Geographical Teacher*, 2, 104–7. London: Geographical Association/London Geographical Institute.

Hillage, J. and Pollard, E. (1998) *Employability: Developing a Framework for Policy Analysis*, London: Department for Education and Employment.

Huckle, J. (1985) 'Geography and schooling', in R. Johnson (ed.), *The Future of Geography*, London: Methuen.

Jamieson, I. and Lightfoot, M. (1982) *Schools and Industry; Schools Council Working Paper*, (3), London: Methuen.

Jenkins, A. and Healey, M. (1995) 'Linking the geography curriculum to the worlds of industry, commerce and public authorities', *Journal of Geography in Higher Education*, 19 (2), 177–81.

Johnston, R.J. (1997) '"Graduateness" and a core curriculum for geographers', *Journal of Geography in Higher Education*, 21 (2), 245–59.

Joseph, K. (1985) 'Geography in the school curriculum', *Geography*, 70 (4), 290–7.

Logan, E., and Prichard, E. (eds.) (2016) *What do graduates do?* Prospects/AGCAS, Available at: www.hecsu.ac.uk/assets/assets/documents/What_do_graduates_ do_2016.pdf [Accessed 30 November 2016].

Longworth, J. (2015) BCC: Businesses and schools 'still worlds apart' on readiness for work, Available at: http://www.britishchambers.org.uk/press-office/press-releases/bcc-businesses-and-schools-%E2%80%98still-worlds-apart%E2%80%99-on-readiness-for-work.html [Accessed 6 August 2016].

MacDonald Ross, G. (2009) 'The 14–19 diploma in humanities and social sciences', *Discourse*, 9 (1), 127–42.

Morgan, J. (2011) *Teaching Geography as if the Planet Matters*, London: Routledge.

Morgan, J. and Lambert, D. (2005) *Geography: Teaching School Subjects 11–19*, London: Routledge.

Morgan, N. (2014) Closing the skills gap and our plan for education, 19 November, American Enterprise Institute, Washington, DC, Available at: https://www.gov.uk/government/speeches/nicky-morgan-closing-the-skills-gap-and-our-plan-for-education [Accessed 5 August 2016].

Naish, M. and Rawling, E. (1990) 'Geography 16–19: some implications for higher education', *Journal of Geography in Higher Education*, 14 (1), 55–75.

Naish, M., Rawling, E. and Hart, C. (1987) *Geography 16–19: The Contribution of a Curriculum Development Project to 16–19 Education*, London: Longman for School Curriculum Development Committee.

Ofsted (2004) *Developing New Vocational Pathways: Final Report on the Introduction of New GCSEs*, London: HMI.

Ofsted (2009) *Identifying Good Practice: A Survey off College Provision In Leisure, Travel and Tourism*, London: Ofsted.

Ofsted (2014) *The Report of Her Majesty's Chief Inspector of Education, Children's Services and Skills 2013/14 Further Education and Skills*, London: Ofsted.

Organisation of Economic Co-operation and Development (OECD) 'Investing in Human and Social Capital: New Challenges', OECD Educational Ministerial Meeting, Paris, 4–5 November 2010, Available at: http://www.oecd.org/dataoecd/59/13/46253090.pdf [Accessed 20 August 2016].

Pacione, M. (ed.) (1999) *Applied Geography: Principles and Practice: An Introduction to Useful Research in Physical, Environmental and Human Geography*, London: Routledge.

Parliament. House of Commons. Sub-Committee on Education, Skills and the Economy (2016) *Careers Education, Information, Advice and Guidance*, Available at: http://www.publications.parliament.uk/pa/cm201617/cmselect/cmese/205/20508.htm#_idTextAnchor048 [Accessed 6 August 2016].

Pring, R., Hayward, G., Hodgson, A., Johnson, J., Keep, E., Oancea, A., Rees, G., Spours, K. and Wilde, S. (2009) *Education for All: The Future of Education and Training for 14–19 Year Olds in England and Wales:* Summary, Implications and Recommendations, Available at: http://www.nuffieldfoundation.org/14-19review [Accessed 9 August 2016].

Rawling, E. (2001) *Changing the Subject: The Impact of National policy on School Geography*, Sheffield: The Geographical Association.

Royal Geographic Society with Institute of British Geographers (RGS-IBG) (2008) *Going Places with Geography*, London: RGS-IBG.

Sant, M. (1982) *Applied Geography – Practice Problems and Prospects*, Harlow: Longman.

Stamp, L.D. (1960) *Applied Geography*, Harmondsworth: Penguin.

Times Educational Supplement (TES) (2011) Academy sponsor hit by riots plans skills schools for excluded, Available at: http://www.tes.co.uk/article.aspx?storycode=6109267 [Accessed 24 July 2016].

Walford, R. (2000) *Geography in British Schools 1850–2000*, London: Woburn Press.

Wolf, A. (2011) *Review of Vocational Education: The Wolf Report*, Available at: https://www.education.gov.uk/publications/eOrderingDownload/The%20Wolf%20Report.pdf [Accessed 3 August 2016].

Chapter 16

Handling controversial issues in geography

David Mitchell

> The more contemporary the issue the greater the problems for the teacher ...
> (Stradling, 1984, p. 3)

Introduction

In April 2016, the news in the UK reported migrants attempting to reach Britain from Syria and North Africa, the ongoing threat of extremist attacks in the cities of northern Europe and the referendum on British membership of the European Union. Geography teachers take pride in their ability to teach current topics like these, 'geographically'. Such events or issues seem 'relevant' to pupils by being current and newsworthy, and having resonance with pupils' lives (be that through their material lives, or thoughts and feelings). Stradling's quote reminds us that the more current the issue, the more controversial it is likely to be, making the teacher's role more difficult. Stradling points out the lack of hindsight, that primary sources of evidence are likely to be incomplete and biased, and that the criteria for valid 'evidence' may not yet be established. When dealing with the future, uncertainty is particularly great. Geography, we often claim, is 'relevant' to the present and has something to say about the future. Bonnett (2008) suggests that geography is a project with two purposes for humanity – first for survival and secondly for the understanding of one another. But, in undertaking such bold work, we deal in uncertainty and opinion about how the world is, how it ought to be and what part education should play. School geography is therefore 'shot through' with values (Slater, 1996) and, as Hopwood (2007) puts it, where values arise, controversy follows.

If we consider schooling and geography together, it emerges that school geography is not a neutral vehicle for the teacher to use as he or she wishes. Literature in the field of curriculum studies such as Apple (2004), Kelly (2009) and Fielding (2011) argues that the school curriculum has become dominated by a discourse of 'effectiveness' making it difficult for the teacher to tackle (or raise) controversy through deep engagement with the subject. J. Morgan (2011, 2012), through a historical analysis of the curriculum, argues that *school* geography has served a project, not so much for human survival and understanding, as for the interests of the corporate capitalist state.

Amidst such uncertainty, how should geography teachers handle controversial issues? And how does *geography*, the subject itself, help us to do so? This chapter discusses these questions, and the tensions and problems within literature which emerge. It can be argued, rather than seeking to diffuse or avoid controversy, pupils are better served by a school geography which raises controversy and poses problems.

What are controversial issues in geography education?

The 'Crick Report' (1998) defines a controversial issue as:

> an issue about which there is no one fixed or universally held point of view. Such issues are those which commonly divide society and for which significant groups offer conflicting explanations and solutions.
>
> (Advisory Group on Citizenship, 1998, p. 56)

Using this definition, geography is awash with controversial issues. Geography tends to deal with issues of super-complexity which defy clear 'proof' and definite 'clear-cut' answers (Lambert, 1999; Lambert and Morgan, 2005). Morgan (2006) uses the notion of 'wicked problems' to show how geographical issues become controversial. Wicked problems are difficult to define, are contested and have no clear cut answers. 'Answers' are value laden with 'better or worse' rather than 'right or wrong' solutions – climate change is a good example. A. Morgan (2011) argues that, unlike many non-humanities subjects, geography raises complex ethical and moral questions. It therefore becomes important for the geography teacher to develop 'ethical knowledge' to tackle the many 'geo-ethical' issues (such as environmental decay, terrorism, conflict and poverty). Coupled to this notion of super-complexity is that of instability. Barnett (2011) calls the world the student encounters 'radically unstable', radical, in that not only does the world change, but the very frameworks by which we understand the world (including subjects like geography, and institutions, such as schools) change too. This is a bewildering problem for the teacher. Not only does the world change, but the discipline of geography changes. Not only does the discipline change, but curriculum frameworks (like the National Curriculum and examination specifications) change, and simultaneously, schools change and young people change.

Making sense of controversial issues requires value judgement by learners and teachers – objective reasoning alone cannot result in certainty. Stradling (1984) made this link between values and controversy. Tackling controversy in geography teaching is closely linked to how we approach values. Halstead and Taylor (1996) define values as deep or fundamental convictions, stances, ideals or standards which guide or influence behaviour and are used as reference points in evaluating particular issues. Slater (1982) draws on Rokeach (1973) to emphasise the enduring nature of values over attitudes. Attitudes and opinions, however, are useful indicators. They can be expressive of the more deep-seated values (Slater,

1982). To use the example of migration, an opinion might be that all asylum seekers should be given shelter by the British state and legal representation. The attitude here is one of concern for the well-being of asylum seekers, but the deeper value is of social justice for all people.

Values become an important concern for geographers, encountered alongside the objective 'facts' of the world. But complicating matters further, there is doubt about whether there is any objective reality (the 'facts') at all. Depending on one's beliefs, the world (i.e. all geographical knowledge) is either more or less a social construct. So, for social constructivists who reject a realist view of knowledge, geography is constructed by people, and a matter of value judgement and interpretation, as well as power and control.[1] This makes all geography potentially controversial. A tension within the subject is reflected in different opinions in literature over how school geography should position itself in terms of fact versus value. Standish (2007, 2009) calls for a return to 'the facts', arguing that school geography has been diminished by the 'global dimension'. Marsden (1995) was wary of geography being used to promote 'good causes' and Lidstone and Gerber (1998) are concerned that geography is used to promote an environmental ethic. Such arguments have to be considered in light of critiques of the notion that school geography (and schooling itself) can be neutral. Teaching is always a political act, whether the political stance is open or hidden (Huckle, 1985; Apple, 2004; J. Morgan, 2011). Furthermore, Lambert (2008) argues that geographical knowledge cannot be reduced to 'facts' but is dynamic and changing and better understood as a conceptual framework.

Most geography educators accept some objective reality – that there are some objective 'facts' about the world, whilst recognising that some knowledge is socially constructed. This is as social-realist theory of knowledge (Wheelahan, 2010; Young and Muller, 2010).

The literature, thus, gives geography teachers two concerns to recognise in relation to controversial issues in geography. First, the curriculum is itself controversial by the selection of content. What is to be included and excluded is a value judgement and exposes the purposes of school geography as controversial. Secondly, school geography encounters issues which arouse strong emotion, personal differences of opinion and uncertainty. I now go on to explore these two concerns and the tensions in the literature relating to them.

Controversial purposes of school geography

The view of school geography as neutral knowledge about the world has been discredited. Recognition that the purposes of school geography are controversial helps teachers take a critical and morally careful approach to curriculum. In the 1970s, the 'new sociology of education' (Young, 1971) exposed knowledge and curriculum as matters of power and control. Claims to the possibility of 'rational curriculum planning' (Marsden, 1976), independent of political power, are therefore problematic. Drawing on the new sociology of education and Foucault's notion of the political economy of knowledge, radical geography educators, such as Huckle (1985) and J. Morgan (2011, 2012), give historical accounts to argue that school geography is not neutral, but serves the corporate capitalist state. An example of how value laden geography can be presented as 'fact' is through textbooks. The printed page carries an authority that can belie controversial views. From a right-wing perspective, Aldrich-Moodie and Kwong (1997) reported that textbooks in the UK and USA presented opinions about environmental value positions, for example, giving a message that recycling is good, before pupils understand what resources are, and how recycling fits into the economics of scarce resource use. Lambert and Balderstone (2000) argue that the 'morally careful' teacher is one who is conscious to help pupils distinguish values and opinions from facts.

Apple argues that schooling tends to see controversy as a bad thing, as it leads to conflict, and conflict is to be avoided, or quickly resolved. Yet, as Apple points out, controversy and conflict are the vital life blood of change and progress (in science and in society). Schools are teaching pupils to avoid conflict in order to reproduce human capital – willing workers and consumers, accepting of hierarchy, who will serve the economy and ensure profits and wealth for the elite. Schooling, therefore, is not neutral, but *ideological*. Controversy and conflict are essential to human progress, and a part of being human. They should therefore be welcomed, not diffused, if education aims to give hope, equal opportunity and the possibility of social change, Apple (2004) argues.

Radical school geography (seeking action and change) was losing ground by the 1990s. Neoliberal ideology has since been immersed in school geography, Morgan (2012) argues. This can be seen in the ways environment and environmentalism is handled. 'Ecological modernisation' has become accepted as 'common sense' (i.e. that sustainable development can be achieved within capitalist economic growth – alternatives are not given serious consideration, nor is capitalism itself seen as controversial). Lessons teaching children to behave in more 'green' ways, and to see the benefits of technological solutions, without challenging the system that creates the problem, exemplify 'ecological modernisation'. Thus, apparently well-meaning attempts to deal with issues such as fair trade in geography become more about helping the consumer construct their identity (as idealised 'ethical' consumer) than looking at possibilities for social justice. Thus, children are being taught to accept neoliberal consumerism as the only way to proceed (see Pykett, 2011). *Problem-solving* tends to validate and bolster the social and economic system, whereas *problem-posing* tends to expose and challenge its failures. Morgan (2012) suggests the former has become the focus of the handling of 'controversial' school geography, rather than the latter.

The political and economic landscape changed again in 2008 as global capitalism entered a crisis on a similar scale to that of the 1970s. Education and geography are now operating in a climate of increased scarcity in all aspects of life. The Coalition government of 2010 have heralded something of a 'knowledge turn'. The National Curriculum review is exploring a return to 'core knowledge' likely to reflect Hirsch's (1987) notion of 'cultural literacy' or a view that there can be transmission of 'the facts' of geography, and an avoidance of 'controversial' and value-laden geography. This may represent an elitist turn to school geography, which Young and Muller (2010) call 'knowledge of the powerful'. However, this moment also provides opportunities for school geography to become more 'problem-posing' using the subject to challenge the underlying causes and connections behind the problems of human–nature relations.

Historical analyses show that the geography curriculum is always controversial. It is ideological and linked to the social, economic and political agendas of the powerful. The 'morally careful' geography teacher must choose what and how to teach with critical consideration of underlying purposes. They must ask: *what is this geography for?*

Encountering controversial issues in the geography classroom

Earlier, in this chapter, I discussed the challenge of the 'super-complex' and 'radically unstable' world that students grapple with. Amidst such uncertainty, Barnett (2011) suggests that students may be inclined to give up on learning. In dealing with controversy and uncertainty about the future, he argues that students must have 'willingness to be changed as a result of one's learning' (p. 11). The will to learn is thus essential. Students must be open to being changed or 'becoming' who they are (Barnett, 2011).

Some aspects of geography are likely to arouse strong emotions and, at the same time, bring different opinions to light, based on different personal values. Issues such as race, cultural difference, immigration, housing, poverty, inequality, and questions about futures are examples which every geography teacher will encounter. The disagreement resulting may lead to debate, or argument. This can be a threat, with the risk of disorder in the classroom, anger or resentment amongst pupils. But it can also be an opportunity for values education through geography. There is substantial disagreement and tension in the literature over how values education and controversial issues should be handled.

Values education in geography – neutrality, balance or commitment?

Much of the literature on teaching of controversial issues deals with the question of how the teacher should present a value position or positions. Stenhouse (1975) emphasises the teacher's role as one of 'procedural neutrality', arguing that if the teacher had a personal value position they should not reveal it to the class. Each pupil should work out their own value position, rather than be influenced by the authority of the teacher. The pupil's values would therefore be more authentic and they would place more importance on that value, or opinion, than if it was passed on to them by the teacher (Halstead and Taylor, 1996).

Stradling (1984) suggests that complete neutrality is unrealistic and 'committed impartiality' is preferable, meaning that the teacher reveals their opinion without imposing it on others. The teacher's main role is to ensure fairness for debate, discussion and reasoning in a democratic setting. Oulton et al. (2004) and Cotton (2006) emphasise the need for the teacher to take a *balanced* position, whilst they also recognise the difficulty of remaining neutral. Another position is that of 'devil's advocate', which can enliven discussion. Each teaching approach (neutral, stated commitment, balanced and devil's advocate) can support the geography teacher, when used in the appropriate context, Stradling (1984) suggests.

The commitment to a democratic classroom, placing trust in the class to develop and clarify their own values, draws from Freire's (1970) critical pedagogy. This rejects the teacher as holder of authority and giver of knowledge, and encourages an emancipatory approach, by which the learners can find their own voice and realise their own authority. Freire's ideas were grounded in the context of Brazil in the 1960s and 70s, in which most lived in inescapable poverty and were taught obedience to religion and state, but Freire has influenced ideas about democratic, critical and emancipatory pedagogy elsewhere. The democratic classroom also draws from the child-centred tradition of education. Dewey (1916) emphasised the importance of the learner making sense through experience and activity. (Recent interest in young people's geographies reflects the child-centred tradition.) In the context of values, the child-centred approach gives weight to pupil voice and individual difference.

Socratic dialogue is an important principle to recognise in democratic approaches which use discussion. Ideas and opinions are tested with questions. Logic and reasoning lead to the development of robust, defensible value positions. Citizenship education, particularly, argues for the power of debate, discussion and dialogue (Hayward, 2007; Hess, 2009). Ultimately, though, there must be a moral judgement underlying the reasoning. When two or more values conflict, for example, a conflict between individual freedom and an equal society, the relative strength of values comes into play again relying on judgement and what A. Morgan (2011) calls 'ethical knowledge' of the subject.

The notion of the neutral teacher, child-centred education, the democratic classroom, and a strong 'pupil voice' is opposed by proponents of adult authority. The titles of work by these educationalists are evocative: *Wasted – Why Education Isn't Educating* (Furedi, 2009); *The Dangerous Rise of Therapeutic Education* (Ecclestone and Hayes, 2009); and *The Corruption of the Curriculum* (Whelan, 2007). The theme amongst these (drawn upon by the right-wing think-tank, Civitas) is that the curriculum must pass on the best adult knowledge, culture and values. Teaching must model adult authority. Failure to do so, they argue, is leading to education as 'therapy'. This is the result of a diminished view of children and a crisis of confidence in society, such that adults are not asserting their authority.

At the time of writing, the aftermath of the youth riots in 2011 have given fresh impetus to a debate about how best to approach values, education and (a perceived) 'moral decay'. It can seem like a straight choice between either pupil voice (democratic debate) or adult authority (transmission of values). But human rights education offers a perspective which may be able to reconcile the two. Basic human rights are universal; they apply to everyone, equally, adults and children alike. The protection of human rights is a collective responsibility, so the state has an important role in this. But human rights (as stated in the Universal Declaration of Human Rights, which all nations signed in 1948) are sometimes confused with the way human rights are applied. So, for example, everyone has the right to work (article 23), but this does not mean everyone has the right to an equal share of wealth. The political right sometimes portrays human rights education as part of a culture of entitlement and individualism. This misunderstands human rights education, which actively challenges such a destructive culture (Amnesty UK, 2009). Human rights education is as much about learning the importance of protecting other people's rights as it is realising one's individual rights. It is also noteworthy that human rights are deeply geographical in two ways. First, they are universal. Whilst cultural and political difference and national sovereignty are recognised, the Universal Declaration of Human Rights gives an integrating, global perspective to the governance of all people. Second, they are place-based, playing out locally by changing the environment and communities in which we live. Human rights, therefore, are a lens for geographers to tackle controversial issues, particularly when they arise across different cultural, political and national contexts (Mitchell, I., 2009).

Hopwood (2007) raises an important point with respect to pupil voice. In reviewing literature in geography education, he finds that, in dealing with controversial issues, much attention has been given to the teacher's role, but little to the pupil. Hopwood's own research into pupils' engagement with values education in geography shows that pupils generally feel the subject allows them to express a different view to others and that it teaches them to respect different viewpoints. However, they also feel that geography promotes a 'green' political position (Hopwood, 2004). Hopwood (2007) notes that there is a research gap in how *pupils* engage with values in their geography education. Literature on controversial issues in education is skewed towards the teacher's role.

There is an important difference between the teaching of values and teaching through values, which affects the question of how far the teacher should or can be neutral. The former suggests predetermined values to be transmitted to the pupil; the latter suggests more openness to a range of value positions which the pupil may develop. Lambert and Balderstone (2000) differentiate between five types of values education (see Figure 16.1).

The five approaches show that values education can take place within different ideologies and discourses of education. So, for example, values clarification sits easily with a child-centred ideology, values inculcation within a discourse of adult authority, and action learning with an ideology of education for social change. This does not mean such values approaches can only happen within those ideologies. But this shows that the processes of values education can themselves

Values inculcation	Has the objective that students will adopt a predetermined set of values.
Values analysis	Uses structured discussion and logical analysis of evidence to investigate values issues.
Moral reasoning	Provides opportunities to discuss reasons for value positions and choices with the aim of encouraging growth of moral reasoning ability.
Values clarification	Has the objective of helping students become aware of their own values in relation to their behaviour and that of others.
Action learning	Encourages students to see themselves as interacting members of social and environmental systems through having them analyse and clarify values with the intention of enabling them to act in relation to social and environmental issues according to their value choices.

Figure 16.1 Approaches to values education (from Lambert and Balderstone, 2000, p. 293).

indicate the educational values and beliefs of the teacher or values embedded in the school subject.

Deep in human value systems lie beliefs of what is morally right and wrong. Issues which raise questions of values usually raise moral questions too. Lambert and Balderstone (2000) see the geography teachers' role as a moral one. It is 'morally careless', they claim, to teach without helping pupils consider what is right and wrong. Sometimes, they suggest, it is unhelpful to tell pupils that there are 'no right or wrong answers', as this implies a vagueness to geography and moral ambivalence. There are occasions when something is clearly (in moral terms) either right or wrong. 'No clear-cut answers' is a better way to phrase the challenge of understanding the 'super-complex' world, they suggest. Marsden (1995) advocates 'moral reasoning' through discussion and debate. The view here is that moral questions can be dealt with *rationally* through appeal to reason and evidence. Fien and Slater (1981) advocate a similar process of rationality leading to defensible value judgements in their approach to values analysis; purported 'facts' are assembled and tested against value principles. Thus, pupils can both clarify their own values and understand the value principles behind the planning and decision-making process. Huckle (1981), however, argues that it is inappropriate to apply a diminished form of rationality and balance to values. This leads to acceptance of situations, he argues, and that powerful emotions should be embraced. This might encourage conflict, and thus lead to change.

Conclusion

Controversy arises both in the purpose and practice of school geography, and much of the literature deals with how best to handle or cope with controversial issues when they arise. However, geography offers a subject framework which can help us to make sense of (and even to seek out) controversial issues.

School geography offers a balanced approach to investigation of a subject grounded in both humanity and science. Thus, Maye (1984) provides a values-based framework for problem solving and decision making and Roberts (2003) shows how geographical enquiry provides a broad framework for making sense of the complexity world, which can be applied to both values and factual enquiry. Both Maye and Roberts take a 'rational' approach to the learning process, offering a framework for pupils based on logic and analysis of data, to draw conclusions. (Though as noted earlier, a rational approach to values issues is contested.)

Place, space and scale, concepts at the heart of geography, encourage a distinctive way of thinking about the world. Geographers thus have a distinctive way of approaching controversial issues, through a geographical lens. Jackson's (2006) 'thinking geographically' and Massey's (1991) 'global sense of the local' express this unique perspective, which can provide particular insight into controversial issues. The notion of 'living geography' (Mitchell, D., 2009) helps to express the relationship between the subject, controversial issues and relevance to everyday life. To give three examples from pupils' own localities: violations of human rights and loss of community can be examined through the concept of place and place-making; sustainability through the lens of integration (of society, economy and environment); and, the injustice of poverty through the lens of scale and connection of local to global.

Morgan (2011, 2012) draws on the concept of integration (social, economic and environmental) arguing that pupils can be helped to see through superficial causes and consequences to deeper, often hidden structures which reproduce life in the world. Thus, Morgan and Lambert (2001, 2003) suggest, school geography can challenge racism by showing how race and racism are constructed. There are opportunities, they argue, to deconstruct common and ideological representations of urban and rural, insider and outsider, established residents and newcomers. Morgan (2011, 2012) applies the same critical deconstruction to the controversy of the environment and sustainability. By helping pupils see that political economy produces and reproduces life in all respects, he argues that school geography can provide a deeper understanding of the world than the dominant neoliberal world view. This brings more hope for action and change. Morgan follows a radical tradition of school geography, such as Huckle (1985) and Fien and Gerber (1988), and radical curriculum critique more widely, such as Apple (2004). Radical school geography seeks to awaken pupils to social injustice and how the capitalist world fails people and nature. School geography makes full use of the powerful concept of integration (and interconnectedness) when it accepts that this will pose problems for young people, rather than reassure with solutions. Geography thus offers teachers a conceptual framework to embrace controversy.

However, not all teachers will take such a radical position. There are different educational traditions (sometimes described as philosophies, beliefs or ideologies) in school geography and no tradition can claim superiority over another (because the purposes of education are a matter of values).[2] Radical geography (seeking to change the world, or 'social reconstruction') is one tradition, but others include child-centred education, academic scholarship, cultural heritage and for social/economic 'efficiency'. Teachers tend to hold a mix of these traditions and beliefs about education. But geography teachers (and departments) can vary substantially in their views over the purpose of geographic education. This affects the approach to controversial issues in geography. So, for example, a child-centred focus may use geography to support pupils clarifying their own values, a social/economic efficiency focus might use problem-solving geography a great deal, and an academic scholarship focus might be expected to make strong use of knowledge-based reasoning. School geography therefore presents much opportunity for teacher and pupil to engage with controversial issues, though the 'educational' outcomes of the engagement may be very different depending on the department. This makes controversial issues a matter worthy of the geography teacher's planning, reflection and research.

Key readings

1   Stradling, R., Noctor, M. and Baines B. (eds.) (1984) *Teaching Controversial Issues*, London: Edward Arnold. The introductory chapter by Stradling, 'Controversial Issues in the Classroom' provides an excellent argument for why controversial issues are educationally important, and considers the strategies for the teacher handling controversial issues.
2   Slater, F. (1982) *Learning through Geography*, London: Heinemann. In this book, chapter 4, 'Interpreting and analysing values and attitudes' is very helpful in illuminating how values arise from geographical learning.

Notes

1   For an account of the controversial nature of geographical knowledge and challenges to the authority of science, see Unwin (1992). For theories of the relationship between curriculum, knowledge and power see (Young 1971) and Young and Muller (2010).
2   For a discussion of educational traditions and 'ideologies' in geography, see Walford (1981) and Rawling (2001). For more general analysis of different educational ideologies, see Schiro (2008) and Taylor and Richards (1985).

References

Advisory Group on Citizenship (1998) *Education for Citizenship and the Teaching of Democracy in Schools: Final Report of the Advisory Group On Citizenship*, Available at: http://dera.ioe.ac.uk/4385/1/crickreport1998.pdf [Accessed 2 August 2016].

Aldrich-Moodie, B. and Kwong, J. (1997) *Environmental Education*, London: Institute of Economic Affairs.

Amnesty UK (2009) *Making Human Rights Real: Teaching Citizenship through Human Rights*, London: Amnesty, Available at: https://www.amnesty.org.uk/sites/default/files/book_-_making_human_rights_real.pdf [Accessed 12 August 2016].

Apple, M. (2004) *Ideology and Curriculum* 3rd edn, New York: RoutledgeFalmer.

Barnett, R. (2011) 'Learning about learning: a conundrum and a possible resolution', *London Review of Education*, 9 (1), 5–13.

Bonnett, A. (2008) *What is Geography?* London: Sage.

Cotton, D. (2006) 'Teaching controversial environmental issues: neutrality and balance in the reality of the classroom', *Educational Research*, 48 (2), 223–41.

Dewey, J. (1916) *Democracy and Education: An Introduction to the Philosophy of Education*, New York: Macmillan.

Ecclestone, K. and Hayes, D. (2009) *The Dangerous Rise of Therapeutic Education*, London: Routledge.

Fielding, M. (2011) *Radical Education and the Common School: A Democratic Alternative*, London: Routledge.

Fien, J. and Gerber, R. (1988) *Teaching Geography for a Better World*, Edinburgh: Oliver & Boyd.

Fien, J. and Slater, F. (1981) 'Four strategies for values education in geography', *Geographical Education*, 4 (1), 39–52.

Freire, P. (1970) *Pedagogy of the Oppressed*, New York: Continuum.

Furedi, F. (2009) *Wasted: Why Education isn't Educating*, London: Continuum Press.

Halstead, J.M. and Taylor, M.J. (eds.) (1996) *Values in Education and Education in Values*, London: Falmer Press.

Hayward, J. (2007) 'Values, beliefs and the citizenship teacher', in L. Gearon (ed.), *A Practical Guide to Teaching Education in the Secondary School*, London: Routledge.

Hess, D. (2009) *Controversy in the Classroom: The Democratic Power of Discussion*, London: Routledge.

Hirsch, E.D. (1987) *Cultural Literacy*, New York: Houghton Mifflin.

Hopwood, N. (2004) 'Pupils' conceptions of geography: towards an improved understanding', *International Research in Geographical and Environmental Education*, 13 (4), 348–61.

Hopwood, N. (2007) Values and controversial Issues. *GTIP Think Piece*, Available at: http://www.geography.org.uk/gtip/thinkpieces/valuesandcontroversialissues/ [Accessed 2 August 2016].

Huckle, J. (1981) 'Geography and values education', in R. Walford (ed.), *Signposts for Geography Teaching*, Harlow: Longman.

Huckle, J. (1985) 'The future of school geography', in R. Johnston (ed.), *The Future of Geography*, London: Methuen.

Jackson, P. (2006) 'Thinking geographically', *Geography*, 91 (3), 199–204.

Kelly, A. V. (2009) *The Curriculum: Theory and Practice*, 6th edn, London: Sage.

Lambert, D. (1999) 'Geography and moral education in a super complex world: the significance of values education and some remaining dilemmas', *Philosophy and Geography*, 2 (1), 5–18.

Lambert, D. (2008) 'Review article: the corruption of the curriculum', *Geography*, 93 (3), 183–5.

Lambert, D. and Balderstone, D. (2000) *Learning to Teach Geography in the Secondary School*, London: RoutledgeFalmer.

Lambert, D. and Morgan, J. (2005) *Geography:Teaching School Subjects 11–19*, London: Routledge.

Lidstone, J. and Gerber, R. (1998) 'Theoretical underpinnings of geographical and environmental education research: hiding our light under various bushels', *International Research in Geographical and Environmental Education*, 7 (2), 87–9.

Marsden, W.E. (1976) *Evaluating the Geography Curriculum*, Edinburgh: Oliver and Boyd.

Marsden, W.E. (1995) *Geography 11–16: Rekindling Good Practice*, London: David Fulton.

Massey, D. (1991) 'A global sense of place', *Marxism Today*, June 1991, Available at: http://www.aughty.org/pdf/global_sense_place.pdf [Accessed 18 August 2011].

Maye, B. (1984) 'Developing valuing and decision making skills in the geography classroom', in J. Fien, G. Gerber and P. Wilson (eds.), *The Geography Teacher's Guide to the Classroom*, Melbourne: Macmillan.

Mitchell, D. (ed.) (2009) *Living Geography*, London: Optimus.

Mitchell, I. (2009) 'Living with rights: a human rights approach to geography', in D. Mitchell (ed.), *Living Geography*, London: Optimus.

Morgan, A. (2006) 'Argumentation, geography, education and ICT', *Geography*, 91 (2), 126–40.

Morgan, A. (2011) 'Morality and geography education', in G. Butt (ed.), *Geography Education and the Future*, London: Continuum.

Morgan, J. (2011) 'What is radical school geography today?' *Forum*, 53 (1), 116–28.

Morgan, J. (2012) *Teaching Secondary Geography as if the Planet Matters*, London: Routledge.

Morgan, J. and Lambert, D. (2001) 'Geography, 'race' and education', *Geography*, 86, (3), 235–46.

Morgan, J. and Lambert, D. (2003) *Race, Place and Geography Teaching*, Sheffield: Geographical Association.

Oulton, C., Day, V., Dillon, J. and Grace, M. (2004) 'Controversial issues: teachers' attitudes and practices in the context of citizenship education', *Oxford Review of Education*, 30 (4), 489–507.

Pykett, J. (2011) 'Teaching ethical citizens' in G. Butt (ed.), *Geography, Education and the Future*, London: Continuum.

Rawling, E.M. (2001) *Changing the Subject: The Impact of National Policy on School Geography 1980–2000*, Sheffield: Geographical Association.

Roberts, M. (2003) *Learning through Enquiry; Making Sense of Geography in the Key Stage 3 Classroom*, Sheffield: Geographical Association.

Rokeach, M. (1973) *The Nature of Human Values*, London: Free Press.

Schiro, M. (2008) *Curriculum Theory: Conflicting Visions and Enduring Concerns*, London: Sage.

Slater, F. (1982) *Learning through Geography*, London: Heinemann.

Slater, F. (1996) 'Values: towards mapping their locations in a geography education', in A. Kent, D. Lambert, M. Naish and F Slater (eds.), *Geography in Education: Viewpoints on Teaching and Learning*, Cambridge: Cambridge University Press.

Standish, A. (2007) 'Geography used to be about maps', in R. Whelan (ed.), *The Corruption of the Curriculum*, London: Civitas.

Standish, A. (2009) *Global Perspectives in the Geography Curriculum*, London: Routledge.

Stenhouse, L. (1975) *Introduction to Curriculum Development*, London: Heinemann.

Stradling, R. (1984) 'Controversial issues in the classroom', in R. Stradling, M. Noctor, and B. Baines (eds.), *Teaching Controversial Issues*, London: Edward Arnold.

Taylor, P.H. and Richards, C.M. (1985) *An Introduction to Curriculum Studies* 2nd edn, Windsor: NFER-Nelson.

Unwin, A. (1992) *The Place of Geography*, London: Longman.

Walford, R. (1981) 'Language, ideologies and geography teaching', in R. Walford (ed.) *SignPosts for Geography Teaching*, London: Longman.

Wheelahan, L. (2010) *Why Knowledge Matters in Curriculum: A Social Realist Argument*, London: Routledge.

Whelan, R. (ed.) (2007) *The Corruption of the Curriculum*, London: Civitas.

Young, M. (1971) *Knowledge and Control: New Directions for the Sociology of Education*, London: Collier-Macmillan.

Young, M. and Muller, J. (2010) 'Three educational scenarios for the future: lessons from the sociology of knowledge', *European Journal of Education*, 45 (1), 11–27.

Part III

Subject debates

Chapter 17

The Anthropocene and the global

Charles Rawding

> Change is a normal part of geological history; the most recent was the Earth's move from the long period of glaciation to the present warmish interglacial. What is unusual about the coming crisis is that we are the cause of it, and nothing so severe has happened since the long hot period at the start of the Eocene, fifty five million years ago.
>
> (Lovelock, 2007, p. 7)

Introduction

The ongoing discussions about whether to designate the latest period in the geological history of the Earth as the Anthropocene presents both an immense challenge and an enormous opportunity for geography education. By arguing, as James Lovelock does, that humans are now having such an impact on the formation of the earth that they require recognition in geological terms, represents clear evidence of the growing interconnections between human geographies, physical geographies and geologies. For the geologist, the key challenge is to determine to what extent humanity influences the development of the planet, and when this influence became such that it began to affect the Earth's physical systems, while for the geographer the increasing inseparability of the human and the natural points towards an increasing integration of an academic discipline that at times can be criticised for having become too fragmented.

There is a long standing discussion in geography about the nature of the subject *as a whole* both in terms of the academic discipline (Livingstone, 1992; Matthews and Herbert 2004; Cresswell, 2013) and the school subject (Rawding, 2013a). The diverse nature of the subject and its ability to synthesise is a frequent theme in such discussions. Indeed, when referring to the origins of modern geography at the end of the nineteenth and beginning of the twentieth centuries, Livingstone (1992) was able to state: 'geography was the integrating subject *par excellence* that kept the study of nature and culture under one disciplinary umbrella' (p. 354). However, he felt much less confident of making such an assertion about more recent trends within the discipline:

> Now it seems, cultural and epistemological pluralism are inevitable. Fragmentation of knowledge, social differentiation and the questioning of scientific rationality have all coalesced to reaffirm the importance of the particular, the specific, the local.
>
> (Livingstone, 1992, p. 358)

Concerns over fragmentation and calls for unity can be traced throughout the history of the discipline. This chapter aims to offer a unifying approach to contemporary geography based on two key ideas: the Anthropocene and the global. The first section looks at the debate surrounding the Holocene/Anthropocene boundary. The second section considers how geographers have viewed issues relating to the environment over the last 50 years or so before considering approaches to nature. The third section considers the conceptual framework of the Anthropocene before moving on to a discussion of how the concept might be incorporated within studies of the global. The final section provides illustrations of how holistic approaches might be tackled within the secondary geography curriculum.

The Holocene and the Anthropocene

The Holocene is a geological epoch (following the Pleistocene) within the Quaternary period covering the time since the last major glacial retreat and representing the beginning of a warmer period in Earth's history, this is effectively the last 11,000 years.[1] As such, the Holocene also covers the entirety of written human history and a time during which human impacts on the planet as a whole have rapidly increased. The Anthropocene relates to a proposed geological epoch that follows on from the Holocene, reflecting the increased impact of humanity on the planet in its entirety. The timing of the shift from the Holocene to the Anthropocene is somewhat contentious. Authors such as Ruddiman (2007) would place the origins of such impacts at the time of the first agricultural revolution (thereby almost replacing the Holocene by the Anthropocene) and argue for a progressive increase from pre-historic times through to the present, while others (e.g. Crutzen, 2002) have suggested the onset of the Industrial Revolution and the rapid increase in the use of fossil fuels is a more realistic time-frame. Given the significant time differences in terms of adoption and diffusion around the world for both of these 'revolutions', it becomes clear that identifying the start of the Anthropocene is far from straightforward.

Geologists tend to identify breaks between epochs through interruptions in the stratigraphic record. Interestingly, in their discussion of whether we are now living in the Anthropocene, Zalasiewicz et al., (2008) point to the difficulties of identifying such a clear break before suggesting two possibilities:

> From a practical viewpoint, a globally identifiable level is provided by the global spread of radioactive isotopes created by the atomic bomb tests of the 1960s; however, this post-dates the major inflection in global human activity.

Perhaps the best stratigraphic marker near the beginning of the nineteenth century has a natural cause: the eruption of Mount Tambora in April 1815, which produced the "year without a summer" in the Northern Hemisphere and left a marked aerosol sulphate "spike" in ice layers in both Greenland and Antarctica and a distinct signal in the dendrochronological record.

(Zalasiewicz et al., 2008, p. 7)

These suggestions complicate discussions further by introducing an extreme physical event (the volcanic eruption) and an extreme human event (the atom bomb) into a process which surely needs to be considered as a rather more gradual process. Having discussed the problematic geological issues surrounding definitions of the Anthropocene, it is now time to turn to how geographers have addressed environmental issues over time.

A changing approach to environmental issues

Studying the environment has always been central to geography. The impact of humans on the natural environment has long been recognised, particularly in those areas of the world that experienced industrialisation from the eighteenth century onwards. Such economic developments have been able to transform local and even regional environments. Until the 1960s, such developments were generally viewed with a relatively uncritical eye, perhaps reflecting prevailing ideas of economic growth at the time (Rostow, 1960).

However, by the late 1960s, a range of environmental issues had become a focus of attention for geographers. Population increase, economic growth and mass consumption were seen to be having a profound effect on the availability of natural resources and on the integrity of ecosystems (Castree, 2005, p. 72). This was reflected in a range of texts aimed at raising general awareness of environmental problems facing the planet. Rachel Carson's 1965 text *Silent Spring* highlighted the dangers to ecosystems from modern farming techniques, while academics such as Paul Ehrlich (1968) highlighted the impact of increasing population on the resources of the planet. In many ways, the culmination of this work was the neo-Malthusian text, *The Limits to Growth* (Meadows et al., 1972), although related discussions have continued to the present (Foster et al., 2010; Dalby, 2013).

In the latter half of the twentieth century, the use of the term ecosystem became mainstream, while new ideas and terminology developed as ecologists and biogeographers discovered and wrote about planetary scale systems. The highly influential work of James Lovelock (1989, 2007) went much further in discussing how life on Earth exerts control over atmosphere, lithosphere and hydrosphere, seeing Earth as a self-stabilising mechanism, regulating atmospheric chemistry, which may even render the planet inhabitable, at least for human beings. This view of the earth's biosphere as a planetary ecosystem is important, particularly because it strongly conveys the impression of living flora and fauna interacting with and regulating their physical environments.

In the latter stages of the twentieth century, the pre-occupation with resource depletion and over-population was replaced by a focus on anthropogenic environmental change – global warming, ozone thinning, acid rain and desertification (Kemp, 1994; Castree, 2015). Such a focus emphasised the shift towards analysis at the global scale, as there was a growing awareness of the impact of humanity on the entire planet. Such developments resulted in the development of the idea of the Anthropocene (Crutzen, 2002), which Castree defines as:

> The first geological epoch where a step-change in Earth surface conditions has been caused, albeit unintentionally, by people's combined activities. The Anthropocene concept thus includes, but also transcends, the idea of anthropogenic climate change.
>
> (Castree, 2015, p. 66)

How natural is the natural?

While it is relatively straightforward to outline a history of approaches to environmental issues in geography, geographical understandings of what constitutes 'nature' and 'the natural' are rather more complex. Williams (1988) notes that 'nature is perhaps the most complex word in the language' (p. 219). In a wide-ranging and thought-provoking discussion of the subject, he highlights the emotive aspects of the concept such as the 'persistent personification of nature – 'mother nature,'' (Williams, 1988, p. 221) and also its use in 'the selective sense of goodness and innocence. Nature has meant the countryside, unspoilt places, plants and creatures other than man. The use is especially current in contrasts between town and country' (ibid., p. 223). Macnaghten and Urry (1999) conclude that 'there is no singular nature as such, only natures. And such natures are historically, geographically and socially constituted' (p. 15).

Rural geographers have questioned the view that the countryside is more inherently natural than the towns (Castree, 2015, p. 167) while Harvey (2015) notes that 'many organisms actively produce a nature conducive to their own reproduction and humans are no exception' (p. 247). Indeed Harvey goes further, stating:

> [T]here is nothing unnatural about species, including ours, modifying their environments in ways that are conducive to their own reproduction. Ants do it, bees do it, and beavers do it most spectacularly. In the same way that there is nothing unnatural about an ant hill, so there is, surely, nothing particularly unnatural about New York City.
>
> (Harvey, 2010, p. 85)

In many ways, the concept of the Anthropocene attempts to integrate human and non-human elements by emphasising the impacts of human-induced changes to the Earth's biosphere while highlighting how this is now expressed in the recent fossil and sedimentological record. Only one-quarter of the Earth's ice-free surface now represents 'natural' wilderness, and by measures such as climate change and distribution of pollutants, large-scale biodiversity loss and landscape transformation, there is no place on Earth that has not been altered by humans (Dalby, 2013; Williams et al., 2015).

The impact of human activity has been further emphasised with the introduction of the concept of 'neobiota' to refer to those species that have changed their spatial ranges and moved into new territories as a result of human intervention (either deliberate or accidental). A species is considered neobiotic only in its new range (not in its prehistoric range, that is, the range it occupied before human-influenced range alterations). Neobiota is a more neutral term than 'invasive species' or 'exotic species', which have also been used. Along with neobiota, the term 'anthrome' has been coined to refer to *anthropogenic biomes* which represent the global ecological patterns created by sustained direct human interactions with ecosystems. (Williams et al., 2015).

Some neobiota have large-scale negative effects for other species. Domestic cats have spread across the planet with the help of European settlers, as have brown rats. Many of Earth's 179,000 islands now possess one or both of these highly invasive species. The toll on native species can be heavy. In the USA alone, cats now kill between 1.4 billion and 3.7 billion birds, and 6.9 billion and 20.7 billion mammals annually (Loss et al., 2013). Such depredations have additional impacts. For instance, the Brown Tree Snake, which arrived on the Pacific Island of Guam after the Second World War, decimated local bird populations and disrupted the propagation of local tree species that rely on birds for seed dispersal (Williams et al., 2015, p. 9).

Integrating the Anthropocene and the global

The concept of the Anthropocene suggests that the world is no longer characterised by 'natural' ecosystems (e.g. lacking significant anthropogenic influence) with humans disturbing them, but rather is characterised by a combination of human engineered and used ecosystems and more or less modified novel ecosystems. This is not to suggest, however, that all anthromes are biologically impoverished. Landscapes strongly influenced by humans can be managed in a way that preserves or even expands biological diversity compared with a Holocene baseline (Williams et al., 2015).

The Anthropocene is an holistic concept. It is a way of bringing together a range of anthropogenic environmental changes. "The Anthropocene' concept deliberately alerts us not only to coincident changes in everything from ocean acidity to species diversity; it further suggests causal connections between induced changes in one biophysical domain and another' (Castree, 2015, p. 70). As such the concept is profoundly geographical, linking humanity to the non-human world at all scales from local to global, breaking down the barriers between the world of nature and the world of people. In this way, it emphasises the bridges between human and physical geography (Castree, 2015).

It is in this context that it is possible to see the Anthropocene as part of a globalised world. As Massey (2014) states:

> When the twenty-first century is so utterly globalised, when the term global is part of every-day speech; economic transactions, cultural influences, globe-spanning new technologies, global climate change and the simple fact that we have seen pictures of our planet as a whole: all confirm that we live on an earth that is both one and thoroughly interconnected. It is part of popular consciousness, to which students need to be introduced. And geography is one of the few disciplines that has the potential to bring together some of this complexity, to address this dynamic interdependent world and, indeed, to address the very question of what we mean by global.
>
> (Massey, 2014, p. 36)

However, it is important here that we remain aware of the variations in impacts both in terms of physical and human geographies. Again, to cite Massey:

> 'global' does not imply total coverage; it means that these processes have trans-planetary reach. Even the financial system that is so central to the globalised economy may not reach to every single part of the world, but there is no doubt that it is global. The same is evidently true of many physical geographical processes, including ocean currents, pressure systems and winds, and the constant movement of tectonic plates.
>
> (ibid.)

Although it would be wrong to suggest that the global and the Anthropocene are both recent phenomena, it is the case that over the last 50 years:

> The globalisation of the world economy has developed and intensified in ways that were qualitatively very different from those of earlier periods. In the process, many of the things we used in our daily lives became derived from an increasingly complex geography of production, distribution and consumption, whose geographical scale became vastly more extensive and whose choreography became increasingly intricate.
>
> (Dicken, 2015, p. 1)

In the same way that the development of anthromes might be considered to vary across the planet according to the scale and impacts of human involvement, so the geographies of capitalism in the global economy are highly variegated. As Peter Dicken rightly states: 'Capitalism is emphatically not the same everywhere' (p. 53). Globalisation can be seen as a somewhat abstract concept, yet:

> The effects of globalizing processes are felt not at the global or the national level but at the *local* scale: the communities within which people struggle

to meet the needs of their daily lives. It is at this scale that most people make their living and create their own family, household and social communities.

(ibid., p. 305)

The local can be seen as a product of the global. Yet at the same time, local actions and events can help produce the global. For instance, Massey (2014) suggests that:

> In physical geography one might point to the weather effects of the eruption of Krakatoa. In human geography one might point to the implosion of the finance sector from the year 2007 onward. The latter's trigger was in a particular place – here the southern states of the USA was the local place where the system blew. Moreover, the financial system itself, although global, also had local origins – especially the City of London and Wall Street. From here both the financial system and its implosion reverberated around the world creating new global conditions. Hence 'the global' can be a product of the local; and geography can be at the forefront of understanding this constant (dynamic) interplay, through its rigorous grasp of space and place.
>
> (Massey, 2014, pp. 38–39)

Seemingly similar events may also have markedly different consequences depending on circumstances. For instance, the massive eruption of Laki on Iceland in 1783 (Witze and Kanipe, 2014) appears to have been a major contributor to harvest failure across Europe, while the 2010 eruption of Eyjafjallajökull resulted in the grounding of airplanes across the northern hemisphere (Rawding, 2015). Integrating the physical and the human, the local and the global, enables a more holistic approach to be developed. The overarching concept of the Anthropocene encourages such holistic thinking.

Approaching holistic thinking in the classroom

In relation to how such integrated approaches might be considered in the classroom, I have discussed holistic geographies elsewhere (Rawding, 2013a, b, 2014). In this section, I aim to develop some of these ideas further discussing two 'messy' examples that illustrate surprising linkages that can be used with students to demonstrate how the human and the physical, nature and capitalism, the global and the Anthropocene are inextricably interlinked within the complexities of the modern world. Such approaches should encourage relational thinking (Renshaw and Wood, 2011) and geographical thinking (Jackson, 2006; Massey, 2008).

In illustrating the complexity and unpredictability of human/physical, nature/ capital relations, Castree (2005) discusses the case of an abandoned oil terminal on Canvey Island, England, which was found to contain numerous plant and animal species, many of which were endangered and some were thought to be extinct. This rather curious environmental development had occurred as a result of a series of decisions taken some 30 years previously by the Occidental Petroleum Corporation to dredge thousands of tons of silt from the Thames Estuary to prepare land for a new oil terminal that in the end was not built. The abandoned site was subsequently played on by children and bikers which resulted in the soils being regularly disturbed, thereby preventing trees from taking root and allowing grasses, wildflowers and shrubs to prosper. The result of all this was an environment where significant numbers of rare species of animals and insects were able to prosper (Castree, 2005, pp. 2–3).

Castree suggests that the site should be seen as a network rather than as a place where nature and society come together, thereby emphasising the links and how the actions and effects of one phenomenon are part of the others in the network. Focusing on any form of society-nature dualism, simplifies a world that is in reality far messier than such over-simplistic conceptualisations would suggest. Such an approach renders any natural/unnatural dichotomy irrelevant, while effectively illustrating the influences that human activity (and inactivity) can have on the development of an area. Such examples illustrate the conceptual importance of the Anthropocene at a local level while clearly referencing the global influences that led to the actions of Occidental Petroleum.

A second, rather curious example of anthropogenic influences on environmental processes can be seen in the case of Sheffield's fig trees (Jones, 2008). In this instance, the banks of the River Don were colonised by wild fig trees. It appears that the trees grew from seeds carried downstream in human sewage or waste from food factories. Their germination in the rather cool location of South Yorkshire has been attributed to the effect of the steel industry on the waters of the River Don. The river waters were used for cooling purposes, thereby raising the ambient temperature in the river, and maintaining a steady temperature of 20°C, which was warm enough for Mediterranean species to germinate. However, a combination of stricter controls on industrial usage of the river and the decline of the steel industry has meant that no new trees have grown as river temperatures have cooled. Nevertheless, a successful campaign by locals to protect the trees, now regarded as an integral part of the local landscape, highlights an intriguing local attachment to an 'invasive species'. In this instance, the environmental consequences of industrial development had specific local effects that, in turn, led to local responses as circumstances changed.

Along with sometimes unexpected local consequences of complex processes, it is also possible to highlight global links and to connect these ideas to the overarching concept of the Anthropocene. Not only did the closure of steelworks in Sheffield impact on river ecology and subsequent fig tree propagation, but also as 'the steel mills of Sheffield and Pittsburgh close down ... the air quality miraculously improves in the midst of unemployment, while the steel mills of China open up and contribute massively to the air pollution that reduces life expectancies there' (Harvey, 2015, p. 258).

Conclusion

The use of such 'messy' examples enables the student to come to terms with, and understand the interconnectedness of the human and the physical, while effectively dispensing with what might now be considered an unhelpful binary. In this context, it might be useful to consider the Anthropocene as a threshold concept (Meyer and Land, 2003) which, 'if properly understood, can transform the understanding of the subject by students' (Renshaw and Wood 2011, p. 373). Clearly, the very essence of the idea of the Anthropocene is that of interdependence between humanity and the planet's physical systems that emphasise a unity which should be at the very core of geographical understanding.

If the physical environment is being affected to such an extent that we have moved into the Anthropocene, then understanding the concept of the Anthropocene must be considered as not only a threshold concept in geography, but also as a fundamental underpinning for the geography curriculum. It is clearly the role of the geography teacher to provide a framework to enhance student understanding of the key linkages between the way in which our planet behaves and the impacts that the human race has on that behaviour.

Key readings

1   Castree, N. (2015) 'The Anthropocene: a primer for geographers', *Geography*, 100 (2), 66–75. This journal article provides an effective summary for geographers of current considerations relating to the Anthropocene.
2   Williams, M., Zalasiewicz, J., Haff, P.K., Schwägerl, C., Barnosky, A.D. and Ellis, E.C. (2015) 'The Anthropocene biosphere', *The Anthropocene Review* 1–24. This provides an accessible overview of the wide variety of elements contributing to the development of the Anthropocene.

Note

1   For an overview of geological periods and epochs see: http://www.ucmp.berkeley. edu/help/timeform.php

References

Carson, R. (1965) *Silent Spring*, Harmondsworth: Penguin.
Castree, N. (2005) *Nature*, London: Routledge.
Castree, N. (2015) 'The Anthropocene: a primer for geographers', *Geography* 100 (2), 66–75.
Cresswell, T. (2013) *Geographic Thought: A Critical Introduction*, Chichester: Wiley-Blackwell.
Crutzen, P. (2002) 'Geology of mankind', *Nature*, 415 (3), 23.
Dalby, S. (2013) 'Biopolitics and climate security in the Anthropocene', *Geoforum*, 49, 184–192.

Dicken, P. (2015) *Global Shift* 7th edn, London: Sage.

Ehrlich, P. (1968) *The Population Bomb*, San Francisco: Sierra Club.

Foster, J. B., Clark, B. and York, R. (2010) *The Ecological Rift: Capitalism's War on the Earth*, Monthly Review Press, New York.

Harvey, D. (2010) *The Enigma of Capital and the Crises of Capitalism*, London: Profile.

Harvey, D. (2015) *Seventeen Contradictions and the End of Capitalism*, London: Profile.

Jackson, P. (2006) 'Thinking geographically', *Geography*, 91 (3), 199–204.

Jones, O. (2008) 'Of trees and trails: place in a globalised world', in N. Clark, D. Massey and P. Sarre (eds.) *Material Geographies: A World in the Making*, London: Sage.

Kemp, D.D. (1994) *Global Environmental Issues: A Climatological Approach* 2nd edn, London: Routledge.

Livingstone, D.N. (1992) *The Geographical Tradition*, Oxford: Blackwell.

Loss, S.R., Will, T. and Marra, P.P. (2013) 'The impact of free-ranging domestic cats on wildlife of the United States', *Nature Communications* 4, 1396.

Lovelock, J. (1989) *The Ages of Gaia: A Biography of Our Living Earth*, Oxford: Oxford University Press.

Lovelock, J. (2007) *The Revenge of Gaia*, New York: Basic Books.

Macnaghten, P. and Urry, J. (1999) *Contested Natures*, London: Sage.

Massey, D. (2008) 'Thinking geographically' *GA Magazine*, Spring, p. 5.

Massey, D. (2014) 'Taking on the world', *Geography* 99 (1), 369.

Matthews, J.A. and Herbert, D.T. (2004) *Unifying Geography: Common Heritage, Shared Future*, London: Routledge.

Meadows, D.H., Meadows, D.L., Randers, J. and Behrens, W.W. (1972) *The Limits to Growth: A Report for the Club of Rome's Project on The Predicament of Mankind*, New York: Universe Books.

Meyer, J.H.F. and Land, R. (2003) 'Threshold concepts and troublesome knowledge: linkages to ways of thinking and practising' in C. Rust (ed.) *Improving Student Learning – Theory and Practice Ten Years On*, Oxford, Oxford Centre for Staff and Learning Development (OCSLD).

Rawding, C. (2013a) *Effective Innovation in the Secondary Geography Curriculum: A Practical Guide*. London: Routledge.

Rawding, C. (2013b) 'Challenging assumptions: the importance of holistic geographies' *Geography*, 98 (3), 157–9.

Rawding, C. (2014) 'The importance of teaching 'holistic' geographies' *Teaching Geography* 40 (1), 10–13.

Rawding, C. (2015) 'Marie Antoinette and Heathrow Airport: holistic geographies' *Teaching Geography* 41 (1), 32–3.

Renshaw, S. and Wood, P. (2011) 'Holistic Understanding in Geography Education (HUGE): an alternative approach to curriculum development and learning at Key Stage 3' *The Curriculum Journal*, 22 (3), 365–79.

Rostow, W.W. (1960) *The Stages of Economic Growth: A Non-communist Manifesto*, Cambridge, Cambridge University Press.

Ruddiman, W.F. (2007) *Plows, Plagues and Petroleum*, Woodstock: Princeton University Press.

Williams, R. (1988) *Keywords*, London: Fontana.

Williams, M., Zalasiewicz, J., Haff, P.K., Schwägerl, C., Barnosky, A.D. and Ellis, E.C. (2015) 'The Anthropocene biosphere', *The Anthropocene Review*, 1–24.

Witze, A. and Kanipe J. (2014) *Island on Fire*, London: Profile.

Zalasiewicz, J., Williams, M., Smith, A.G., Barry, T.L., Coe, A.L., Bown, P.R., Brenchley, P., Cantrill, D., Gale, A., Gibbard, P., Gregory, F.J., Hounslow, M.W., Kerr, A. C., Pearson, P., Knox, R., Powell, J., Waters, C., Marshall, J., Oates, M., Rawson, P. and Stone, P. (2008) 'Are we now living in the Anthropocene?', *GSA Today*, 18 (2), 4–8.

Chapter 18

Geography's identity as an academic discipline

Nick Clifford

> There is no single history of 'geography', only a bewildering variety of different, often competing versions of the past.
>
> (Heffernan, 2009, p. 3)

Introduction

Since its emergence as a formal academic discipline in Western universities in the middle-to-late nineteenth century, geography has had recurrent crises of identity and status. In simple terms, the problem has been one of 'breadth versus depth' – as an elementary or foundation subject, it is an ideal provider of essential general knowledge and a transferrable skill set; but its distinct intellectual contribution and critical theoretical core has been difficult to pin down, or gain consensus between its many advocates and adherents. Over more than a century of academic development, the boundaries of geography have pushed ever wider, but its focus and its centre have become correspondingly less clear. Universities wrestle with how to place it in a traditional faculty structure – is it in the sciences, arts or humanities? Some departments have split between physical and human; and increasingly, other, often newer fields of study, recognising the need for integrated, multi-disciplinary study, encroach on territory hitherto the domain of geography, with new programmes such as earth systems science, development and sustainability studies. Taken to the extremes, this ultimately questions whether the idea of a 'discipline' can capture what geography and geographers do, and indeed, why we would want to do this.

Yet, the subject remains immensely popular and essential in schools and universities, and it does seem otherwise well placed to address increasingly complex and important questions of the grand challenges facing environment-society interactions. Faced with enduring challenges to its identity, yet in the context of enormous opportunities to progress, it is once more timely to revisit some of the dimensions of geography's identity challenge, whether historical, contemporary or future-facing. A series of historiographies emerge, in which institutional arrangements in schools and universities channel funding and provide administrative arrangements and hierarchies, but which frequently seem arbitrary or at least, inconsistent, and which are increasingly out of step in a post-disciplinary world. It should be noted that nearly all such writings concentrate on Anglo-American, and occasionally European *human* geography, and with this, inevitably reinforce only particular identities at the expense of others – whether geographical in themselves (e.g. Kitchin, 2005) or gendered (Rose, 1993). Physical geography rarely appears in such discourse, but an up-to-date, readable and authoritative discussion of ideas, disciplinary identity and shifts in aims, methods and techniques relating to physical geography can be found in Gregory's *The Earth's Land Surface* (Gregory, 2010, pp. 17 – 40).

Definitions, components and histories

Most straightforward and high level definitions of geography derive from its core component words: geo (earth) and graphos (writing) – to yield such basic definitions as:

> The study of the ways in which space is involved in the operation and outcome of social and biophysical processes.
>
> (Gregory, 2009, p. 288)

Unpacking such an abstraction is where identity debates often begin. It is possible, for example, to identify the roots and subsequent developments of the subject in different ways. Perhaps the most enduring and authoritative traces a cartographic tradition through the ancient civilizations, building on this key knowledge set through the Enlightenment into the service of modern European empires, where accurate navigation, the charting, allocation and analysis of natural and manufactured goods required a new kind of academic and applied knowledge which the subject readily filled. The classic and most comprehensive such account is that of Livingstone (1992). That said, there are important critiques and alternatives, which span those who see the subject more as a derivative of the natural and biological sciences (for an entertaining and quirky account see Stoddart, 1986); those which point to non-Western geographies or schools of thought and those which pay more attention, for example, to critical aspects, such as gender and race (Domosh, 1991; Rose, 1993). The very historiography of the subject, therefore, is one of contested debate.

Constraining the time period considered in the formation of the subject offers little help in resolving contests, either. Peter Haggett, one of the foremost geographers of the twentieth century, was one of the key figures in geography's 'Quantitative Revolution', a mid-century explosion in data provision, analysis and representation, and an interest in systematic quantification and modelling of spatial phenomenon (see Barnes, 2014). Haggett's diagrammatic representation of 'Links between Geography and supporting fields', which was published in 1983 (Haggett, 1983, fig. 25.8, p. 616), showed no fewer than 18 sub-divisions of Anglo-German geography from the later eighteenth to the later twentieth centuries; sub-divisions included quaternary studies, biogeography, population geography, regional economics and urban sociology.. Within a decade of his diagram's production, the subject had undergone its 'cultural turn', where humanistic and qualitative methodologies, a concern for ethnographic methods and a reaction to scientific or 'positivist' thinking had occurred (see Graves, 1979, for a discussion of this period from a geography educationist's point of view). To update the diagram in post-Millennium times would necessitate even more to be added, such as development and sustainability studies and nexus studies, together with areas connecting much more to the humanities. Clifford et al, (2016) provide a very brief introduction to the last fifty years of the subject, and to the methodological contrasts and techniques used, some of which are touched upon below.

The point here is simple. Whether viewed historically or in contemporary terms, geography has continued both to extend and to blur its own boundaries, and to compete on territory occupied by other disciplines. It has adopted a plethora of techniques and methods to allow it to range so widely, to such an extent that it is impossible to claim any epistemological or ontological position which is uniquely its own. In Hagget's representation for example, geography itself is neither prominent nor is it at the *centre* of a network of connections. Philosophical, methodological and substantive pluralism characterise contemporary geography, provoking such fundamental binaries as the scientific (or positivist) and humanistic, and the quantitative vs. qualitative. Methodological pluralism, itself open to further exploration, is increasingly being championed in the subject (DeLyser

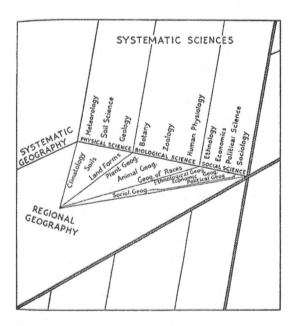

Figure 18.1 The geographical plane. Figure 1.4 from Haggett (1990), p. 12.
Original source: Hartshorne (1939), figure 1, p. 147.

and Sui, 2014). Such calls are as much a recognition of the changing world *around* the subject as it is any commitment to change *within* it. Geography now embraces a range of philosophical approaches to knowledge, from positivism to post-structuralism. It studies human behaviour, built and (increasingly) imagined worlds, the physical environment extending to biological, ecological and geo-physical systems, and to the intersections between these. As such, it is involved with the representation, interpretation and explanation of social and physical rela-tionships and also the experiences and the practices which embody these (Clifford et al, 2016). But for those looking for safety and simplicity in geography's iden-tity, its core could lie anywhere, and hence nowhere, or as I have said elsewhere, 'the whole is less than the sum of its parts' (Clifford, 2002).

Interestingly, in trying to make sense of the plethora in his 'Links between Geography and Supporting fields', Haggett distils three essential qualities which define and span Geography and its constituent parts:

> an emphasis on location, patterns and variations, whether technical or descrip-tive, and whether dealing with human or physical attributes of the world;
> land-people interactions at all scales from the local to the global;
> and regional synthesis which integrates or fuses sub-disciplinary fields to explain within- and between region characteristics and linkages.
>
> (Haggett, 1990, p. 10)

The use of regional synthesis is, at least historically, perhaps the most important of these qualities, and the role of the region as a focus for geography is powerfully encapsulated in a classic representation in Figure 18.1. This figure originates from a seminal examination of the nature of geography, by Richard Hartshorne in the mid-twentieth century (see Alex Standish's chapter in this volume). Essentially, there are two intersecting planes: the vertical representing the systematic sci-ences; and the horizontal, representing geography. Geography as a subject occurs on different planes of interconnection with other subjects: it has its systematic elements, which reflect traditions, methods and subject of enquiry (part) shared with the other 'sciences'; but these uniquely come together – they achieve focus in a distinct geography – when they are applied to describe, interpret and under-stand physical and human phenomenon at the *regional* scale.

Hartshorne's identification of a focusing or fusing device in the region is criti-cal to debates. Arguably, it is the loss of such a focus which is responsible for seemingly endless, repetitive and inconclusive forays into the nature, future and status of the discipline. The region is a truly powerful and enabling conceptual device, but regional geography ceased to be such a focus in the later twentieth century. This occurred in part as a response to the effects of globalisation; in part, as a result of the intensification of fragmentation in the subject. In human geogra-phy, the rise of cultural theory both extended and questioned such terms as 'social science' or the purpose of general explanations. In physical geography, there was a kind of upward or outward pull from geography *into* the other sciences, as physical geographers deployed increasingly complex technologies and the language and cultures of the sciences. Whereas geography's whole *should be* more than the sum of its parts, the history of the discipline post regional geography tends to make it, paradoxically, less so. A very clear indicator of this in the UK, for example, can be found in the analysis of publication cultures post the 2008 'Research Excellence Framework'[1] (Richards et al, 2009). Physical and human geography accounted for a rough proportionate balance in the outputs assessed, but it was noted that physical geography was clearly lacking in major conferences and outlets associated with the discipline's main learned society meetings, the RGS-IBG and the AAG: there is no balanced identity in geographical *practice* or culture, therefore. Moreover, the total number of academic journals in which publications were returned numbered over 700 (no misprint: *seven hundred* journals have carried scholarly articles from geographers). As Richards et al. (2009, p. 235) put it:

> The evidence of such a wide range of journals …. may be read in two opposing ways. It can be taken to be clear evidence of a vibrant and interdisciplinary field, willing to present its contributions to research and scholarship across a wide range of publishing outlets in cognate …. and to contribute to other host communities. The less benign opposing interpretation is that not all of these are journals that habitually publish world-leading outputs, and that to some degree the promiscuity on display here may be viewed as something of an indulgence.

The present and future identity

In his short, but exceptional, synthesis defining geography, Gregory (2009, pp. 287–95) provides an envelope in which to contain its multiple and contested identities. Beyond simple definitions, he identifies a subject where writing *about* the world through description, representation and representing exists in an inescapable coupling with a more active *writing of* the world – that is making, shaping and transforming. There is a continually changing set of situated practices: geography is made by its practitioners for particular purposes, reflecting different knowledge sets, methodologies, and crucially, power relations at all levels. Exploring this duality of writing and doing, he summarises a body of historical and much more contemporary work, suggesting six observations as starting points for discussion and thus providing the context for understanding an *essential* contested identity for geography. In brief, these are:

Geography is a formal body, or field of intellectual enquiry, describing knowledge of the earth; but it also a material property of the earth – there are geographies of countries, of people, and of processes, whether social or physical.

There is no single paradigm which describes or accounts for the many ways in which space and processes are linked, and, too, the way in which geographers have and do approach this. There are geographies of Geography, reflecting intellectual and regional/cultural traditions, and the plurality of approaches are an intrinsic effect of so many intersections or conversations between geography and related or supporting fields of enquiry, and indeed, objects of that enquiry.

In using space as a focal or foundational concept, due regard should be given to place, regions and landscape – all of which have theoretical adherents and which have been the source of contestation and debate in their own right. Very powerfully, it is possible to see the identity of geography shaped and changed as technologies and capacity to make sense of the Earth at multiple, and now simultaneous, scales, evolves. The emergence of critical GIS (e.g. Elwood et al., 2011) or virtual geographies (Crang and Mohamad, 2016) provide good examples of this.

There is a pervasive and increasingly important concern for process – for theoretically informed description and explanation, not content with gazetteer-type descriptions and the concentration on 'outcomes'. Whether social or physical, process based explanations are readily taken-up in a world which is so concerned with the occurrence and effects of 'change'. This also applies to those in a critical tradition whether Marxist, feminist, radical or something else; and those who increasingly see a role in shaping public debate: a transformative and engaged approach. We need to know not simply the what and the where, but the why and the how – and now, perhaps, the what *should* or *could* there be instead?

One way of further explaining, or even accepting ways of embracing such a varied identity, has been suggested by Vernon who, in a short article, has helpfully explored the nature of geography from a teacher-practitioner perspective (Vernon, 2016). Her suggestion is to use educational theory to reconceptualise geography as a subject whose identity is necessarily multiple and contested. Vernon deploys a basic typology of knowledge (Bernstein, 1999) which distinguishes between 'vertical' (largely scientific) knowledge, where progress is hierarchical through increasing abstraction and explanatory laws; and 'horizontal' knowledge, where new questions, requiring different languages of explanation exist side-by-side. Whereas vertical subjects have strong 'grammar' – they have clear, and clearly articulated, rules of explanation, description – a horizontal one is less ordered, and potentially lacks clarity and coherence. Additionally, whereas vertical subjects have cumulative, or successive and hierarchical growth in knowledge; horizontal subjects grow by accumulation, often revisiting and reinterpreting pervious knowledge. Such distinctions might, Vernon suggests, manifest in geography as the difference between traditional 'naming' and fact-based approaches, or even by the abstraction and reduction of areas of geographical enquiry such as 'post-colonial'; rather than knowledge which constantly questions, creates tensions or requires a thinking through of subjects and a non-progressive stance. Figure 18.2 (especially Q 5) details opportunities to characterise geography as a horizontal subject, and *hence to make sense of its diverse identity and practice.*

Q3 and Q4 in the table reflect a further, and historic, component of geography's identity debates – the way in which its essential character is shaped or learned in schools. In the simplest terms, and as long ago as the late nineteenth

Questions that arise from Bernstein's theory	Why they may be useful to pursue
Q1: To what extent can our understanding of knowledge structure help us know what knowledge looks like at different 'levels' (e.g. between school and university)?	What (if anything) structurally changes with increased depth? How does 're-contextualizing' geography as a school subject necessitate transformation of the knowledge? Such questions might help us better understand and articulate the desired relationship between the discipline and the school subject, as well as what we mean by progression in learning within these categories.
Q2: Are there evident dimensions of verticality within geography (both physical and human geography)?	Would it be helpful to explore a social realist approach to geographical knowledge (see Firth, 2013; and Young et al., 2014)? This might help us better understand what progression in geography looks like.
Q3: Can Bernstein's insights help us better conceive what 'good geography' is at age ... 11? ... 16? ... 18? ... 21? ...26? ... . 66?	A theoretically strong concept of good geography might help us better understand the relationship between epistemology and pedagogy thus affording both greater intellectual integrity and the scope to select more 'powerful knowledge' to be represented in the curriculum. More, it could adjudicate what is 'better' knowledge to pursue and build on within the discipline.
Q4: What might help us achieving integrity in the classroom?	For example, in the kinds of 'texts' that are used and the way they are used – do they afford the possibility of appreciating the developmental nature of geographical knowledge? Does it allow the students to think critically about the production and justification of knowledge claims? Does it position them? In other words, does it, as Firth argues, enable students to 'make sense of how geography helps them make sense of the world' (2007, p. 19; author's emphasis added)?
Q5: To what degree and in what ways can we (or should we) represent geography-as-philosophy in the classroom (i.e. as a 'way of thinking')?	To do so might help us better understand the role 'big concepts' (such as place, space, scale and environment) should play in the classroom. This might help us show that concepts such as place or scale can be interpreted differently according to distinct intellectual traditions (re Bernstein's 'languages'); these traditions in turn ascribe value very differently to different objects of study. An example is the role we place on the author, the historical context and the intellectual paradigm they are reasoning through – should A-level students be equipped with a basic grounding in particular authors and paradigms?

Figure 18.2 Potential areas of enquiry into the coherence of Geography. Reproduced from Vernon (2016, p. 102, figure 2).

century, leading figures in the academic discipline have identified inconsistencies, or at least, some limitations in approaching the subject as a series of skills, as opposed to the critical concepts or theories. Marsden (1997) has a very accessible historical review of such debates, which is neatly summarised in the idiosyncratic 1954 presidential address to the GA (Wooldridge, 1955):

> British geography is rather too prone to certain fissiparious tendency.
>
> (p. 73)

and the rhetorical question he posed: *to teach Geography or to teach George?*

Teaching George was, he suggested, characterised school level Geography, but did not provide for a distinct analytical or thinking style associated with a cognate university or academic discipline: an identity question was thus inherent in the way the discipline was configured at the different levels.

Intriguingly, the style and content of learning and teaching is now in renewed debate. This is not simply a matter of pedagogic educational theory and discourse, but is partly a response to wider societal debates and revaluing of 'academic' versus 'practical' subjects, and the role of university education in a market-based system. Most notably, this is reflected in the different perspectives between advocates of more 'active' learning styles and the promotion of issue-based learning (which is assumed to have more relevance to humans and thus is part of a more general questioning), or those who believe in the importance of subject-based knowledge, fact and concepts as a critical step in being able to fully appreciate and analyse such issues. An argument runs that, through geography's engagement with 'issues', and through a period of internal questioning of scientific, positivist methods and its adoption of a human-focussed, radical or critical stance, its teaching has been pushed in one direction (Birnie, 1999). The principal casualty has not simply been geographical theory and identity, (see Q1 and Q3 in Figure 18.2), but most often, the dominance of human geography and arguably the disappearance of physical geography within schools (for a brief review and synopsis, see Clifford and Standish, 2017, and Duncan Hawley in this volume). In this way, a partial, unbalanced, and perhaps less enabling, identity for the subject has almost inadvertently been created in the last generation of so. A fuller analysis is awaited, but it maybe that the notion of 'epistemic ascent' (Winch, 2013) could be particularly useful in achieving some closure on such debates. The idea seeks to trace the development of disciplinary practitioners from novice to expert, both by identifying knowledge types (from formal propositions, 'know how' and 'know that' and knowledge by acquaintance; Hirst, 1975), and determining the rationale for their different positions in a curriculum hierarchy (Winch, 2013). Returning to Wooldridge's anecdote, such an analysis might just take us *from* George *to* geography, identifying both the subject and its contents along the way!

Identity in a post-disciplinary world

The Anthropocene is now a widespread term to define an epoch of human-influenced environmental change, as well as a period in which the technical, economic and now cultural change has emerged to drive this (see Charles Rawding's chapter in this volume). If geography's boundaries are naturally broad, and if its tendencies are naturally integrative, then it should be ideally situated to contribute to a rapidly-emerging collection of Anthropocene-type studies. Castree (2015) provides a short review of the relations this concept might have for the disciplines identity and practice, and Clifford and Standish (2017) provide short accounts of key components of this, namely sustainability studies, nexus studies and earth system science in relation to the teaching of physical geography. All of these can, of course, be seen as 'threats' to the integrity and identity of the more traditional subject, as new knowledge claims and examples of interest subsume older concerns. At the same time, the emergence of new society-environment questions alongside the more traditional diet of geography is also paralleled by the now commonplace of huge amounts of digital data, supported with an array of computing and networking power to represent, analyse and communicate results. There has been an accompanying societal shift in our ability not just to access these data, but also to participate in data, problem and solution creation: whether this is through more familiar citizen science and its embrace of new technologies to upload, share and use information; or whether in new forms of communication and exploration. Geography neither is, nor should be, immune to the Big Data revolution, or to new possibilities this creates in revisiting more familiar themes and methods (Graham and Shelton, 2013; Kitchin, 2014; Wyly, 2014). Twenty years on from the network revolution (Castells, 1996), the phenomenon of globalisation and its attendants pose some fundamental re-conceptualisations of more traditional questions relating to nature, culture and society, and to questions of the scale of enquiry (Richards and Clifford, 2008; Clifford, 2009), and hence, once more, to the identity of the subject of geography.

On the one hand, geographers have recognised that the scope, scale and pace of human-environment interactions, which are increasingly complex and poorly defined, requires academic subject to adapt and embrace essential hybridities, and new discourses of enquiry (Whatmore, 2002; Lorimer, 2012; Johnson and Moorhouse, 2014; Castree, 2014). On the other, pushing at these limits, however, there is a wholesale move to redefine traditional research as *both* practice and theory – or both analysis and application – which leads to a fundamental questioning of the need for, and character of, strong disciplinary identities. More familiar calls for multi-disciplinary working (where views from different subjects are considered in relation to one another) and inter-disciplinary perspectives (with a stronger integration of aims, methods and goals of enquiry) are now accompanied by the promotion of *transdisciplinarity*. In the article by Stock and Burton (2011) transdisciplinarity involves multiple academic perspectives and participants, including non-academics as part of the research process. The aim is explicitly goal-orientated: to generate (social) scientific work and decision-making capabilities. As a result, transdisciplinarity focuses on the problem *rather than the discipline involved*, and bridges across experts and lay participants, and science and non-science contributions. As such, transdisiplinarity questions hitherto accepted notions of 'expert' and 'lay' and of the distinctiveness, and even desirability of strong disciplinary identities.

Returning to perspectives on the history and identity of the subject – and remember, as Gregory asserts, geography's identity has always been defined by a series of embedded social practices – then the implications of transdisciplinary study are that the identity question will become increasingly difficult to interpret and perhaps, even less relevant. In some respects, strong disciplinary identity at some levels or stages of study may still be vital to appreciate and define the very multiple perspectives that transdisciplinarity supports (Lang et al, 2012). In other respects, the different faces, personas and practices of the subject will, in the future, be desirable and flexible for the next set of challenges and the next generation of students, provided we are no longer so caught-up in our own identity crises!

Conclusion

Geography is a discipline with a very long history, and it encompasses a very broad range of intellectual traditions spanning the human and physical sciences, and increasingly, the arts and humanities. Not surprisingly, geography as a formal discipline is also 'contested': whether viewed historically, in the present, or in looking to the future, it is clear that geography does not fall neatly within a single identity narrative. There is no single, universally-accepted historiography of the subject, and its range and diversity of subject matter is matched by a similar diversity (and often incommensurability) of methods, philosophies and purposes. Simple distinctions between human and physical geography are commonplace, but do no justice to the many long-standing subdivisions and supporting disciplines of the subject; nor too, an increasing commitment to integration across disciplinary subdivides. Moreover, the subject is still evolving, whether as a response to 'internal' educational and academic debates, or the external factors of socio-economic and environmental challenge.

In some senses, it is futile to attempt to impose a definition of the core of geography (as John Morgan argued in this book in its 2013 edition). One thing that a continuing identity debate can do, however, is to help inform those who teach and those who study geography to account for the nature and also the value of geographical perspectives/understandings. There is, then, a value in continuing analysis and awareness of geography's contested identity, both to define the essentials of a geographical perspective and a geographical education, and also to help attach the subject to new and emerging social and environmental questions. Looking ahead, an emphasis on inter- and trans-disciplinarity in academic study, and on socio-economic impact of academic research and education, offers productive and positive grounds for revisiting and reinterpreting identity debates and traditions in the subject. Similarly, contemporary debates in the education literature regarding geography as a 'horizontal' rather than 'vertical' subject also offer helpful frameworks for making sense of the concerns regarding geography's identity, and the concept of 'epistemic ascent' may, in the future, be applied to understanding the practice of Geography as a subject.

In short, some idea of the evolving history of the subject is now more important than ever, as we experience increasing change in a globalised world, and as geography as a subject needs to take its part in addressing complex questions at the interface of society and environment. Without this, teaching geography will all too often default to a lot of 'knowing that' at the expense of 'knowing how', and both the subject and its students will be much less well placed to make the kind of contributions that otherwise seem so obvious given both its breadth and its depth of enquiry.

Key readings

1   Marsden, B. (1997) 'On taking the geography out of geography education; some historical pointers', *Geography*, 82 (3), 241–52. This is an important article and a precursor of the critical stance taken by Alex Standish (2009) and others on the undermining of geographical subject knowledge in the school curriculum. He shows that historically the disciplines (including geography) are important in education, not least to guard against indoctrination and government meddling. But he also shows that subjects are always under threat by other priorities, including those of progressive educationists (who would integrate subjects) and 'good causes' such as environmentalism and citizenship. The article provides an excellent framework, then, for considering subject identities within both a historical and an educational context.

2   Gregory, D.J. (2009) 'Geography', in D.J. Gregory, R.J. Johnson, G. Pratt, M.J. Watts and S. Whatmore (eds) *The Dictionary of Human Geography*, 5th edn, Chichester: Wiley-Blackwell, pp. 287–95. This is a short, but deeply considered 'definition' of Geography and as a subject. It addresses some areas of subject content, and provides background to the various ways in which others have traditionally made sense of the subject's identity. It also makes a compelling case that Geography is necessarily defined with respect to a set of contested practices, many of which are historically as well as culturally/geographically determined. There is thus no simple definition of the subject, and perhaps there can, or should, never be one.

Note

1   This refers to the process, which takes place every six or seven years, by which universities are evaluated and judged for their research output.

References

Barnes, T. (2014) 'What's old is new, and new is old: history and geography's quantitative Revolutions', *Dialogues in Human Geography*, 4 (1), 50–3.

Bernstein, B. (1999) 'Vertical and horizontal discourse: an essay', *British Journal of Sociology of Education*, 20 (2), 157–73.

Birnie, J. (1999) 'Physical geography at the transition of higher education: the effect of prior learning', *Journal of Geography in Higher Education*, 23, 49–62.

Castells, M. (1996) *The Rise of the Network Society, The Information Age: Economy, Society and Culture*, Oxford: Blackwell.

Castree, N. (2014) 'The Anthropocene and the environmental humanities: extending the conversation', *Environmental Humanities*, 5, 233–60.

Castree, N. (2015) 'The Anthropocene: a primer for geographers', *Geography*, 100, 66–75.

Clifford, N.J. (2002) 'The future of *geography*: when the *whole* is less than the sum of its *parts*', *Geoforum*, 33, 431–36.

Clifford, N.J. (2009) 'Globalisation: a physical perspective', *Progress in Physical Geography*, 33, 5–16.

Clifford, N.J., Cope. M., Gillespie, T., French, S. and Vallentine, G. (2016) 'Getting started in geographical research' in N.J. Clifford, M. Cope, T. Gillespie and S. French (eds.) *Key Methods in Geography*, 3rd edn, London: SAGE.

Clifford, N. And Standish, A. (2017) 'Physical geography' in Jones, M. (ed.) *The Handbook of Secondary Geography*, Sheffield: Geographical Association.

Crang, M. and Mohamad, S.M.H. (2016) 'Researching virtual communities', in N.J. Clifford, M. Cope, T. Gillespie and S. French (eds.) *Key Methods in Geography*, 3rd edn, London: SAGE.

DeLyser, D. and Sui, D. (2014) 'Crossing the qualitative-quantitative chasm III: Enduring methods, open geography, participatory research and the fourth paradigm', *Progress in Human Geography*, 38, 294–307.

Domosh, M. (1991) 'Toward a feminist historiography of geography', *Transactions Institute of British Geographers*, 16 (1), 95–104.

Elwood, S., Schuurman, N. and Wilson, M. W. (2011) 'Critical GIS', in T. Nyergers, H. Couclelis and R. Mcmaster (eds.), *The SAGE Handbook of GIS & Society*, London: SAGE.

Graham, M. and Shelton, T. (2013) 'Geography and the future of big data, big data and the future of geography', *Dialogues in Human Geography* 3 (3), 255–61.

Graves, N. (1979) 'Contrasts and contradictions in geographical education', *Geography*, 64 (4), 259–67.

Gregory, D.J. (2009) 'Geography', in D.J. Gregory, R.J. Johnson, G. Pratt, M.J. Watts and S. Whatmore (eds.) *The Dictionary of Human Geography* 5th edn, Chichester: Wiley-Blackwell, pp. 287–95.

Gregory, K.J. (2010) *The Earth's Land Surface*, London: SAGE.

Haggett, P. (1983) *Geography, A Modern Synthesis*, 3rd revised edn, New York: Harper and Row.

Haggett, P. (1990) The *Geographer's Art*, Oxford: Blackwell.

Hartshorne, R. (1939) *The Nature of Geography: A Critical Survey of Current Thought in the Light of the Past*, Lancaster, Penn.: Association of American Geographers.

Heffernan, M. (2009) 'Histories of geography', in N.J. Clifford, S.L. Holloway, S.P. Rice and G. Valentine (eds.), *Key Concepts in Geography*, 2nd edn, London: Sage.

Hirst, P. (1975) *Knowledge and the Curriculum: A Collection of Philosophical Papers*, London: Routledge and Kegan Paul.

Johnson, E. and Morehouse, H. (2014) 'Introduction: toward a politics for the Anthropocene', a forum special issue on the politics of the Anthropocene, E. Johnson and H. Morehouse (eds.), *Progress in Human Geography*, 38 (3), 439–41.

Kitchin, R. (2005) 'Disrupting and destabilising Anglo-American and English-language hegemony in geography', *Social and Cultural Geography*, 6, 1–16.

Kitchin, R. (2014) *The Data Revolution: Big Data, Open Data, Data Infrastructures & Their Consequences*, London: SAGE.

Lang, D.J., Wiek, A., Bergmann, M., Stauffacher, M., Martens, P., Moll, P., Swilling, M. and Thomas, C. J. (2012) 'Transdisciplinary research in sustainability science: practice, principles, and challenges', *Sustainability Science*, 7 (Supplement 1), 25–43.

Livingstone, D.N. (1992) *The Geographical Tradition*, Oxford: Blackwell.

Lorimer, J. (2012) 'Multinatural geographies for the Anthropocene', *Progress in Human Geography*, 36 (5), 593–612.

Marsden, W.E. (1997) 'On taking the geography out of geographical education', *Geography*, 82 (3), 241–52.

Richards, K.S. (et al) (2009) 'The nature of publishing and assessment in geography and environmental studies: evidence from the research assessment exercise 2008', *Area*, 41 (3), 231–43.

Richards, K.S. and Clifford, N.J. (2008) 'Science, systems and geomorphologies: why *LESS* may be more', *Earth Surface Processes and Landforms*, 33 (9), 1323–40.

Rose, G. (1993) *Feminism and Geography: The Limits of Geographical Knowledge*, Cambridge: Polity Press.

Standish, A. (2009) *Global Perspectives in the Geography Curriculum*, London: Routledge.

Stock, P. and Burton, R.J.F. (2011) 'Defining terms for integrated (Multi-Inter-Trans-Disciplinary) Sustainability Research', *Sustainability*, 3 (8), 1090–113.

Stoddart, D.R. (1986) *On Geography and its History*, New York: Blackwell.

Vernon, E. (2016) The structure of knowledge: does theory matter? *Geography*, 101 (2), 100–4.

Whatmore, S. (2002) *Hybrid Geographies: Natures Cultures Spaces*, London: SAGE.

Winch, C. (2013) 'Curriculum design and epistemic ascent', *Journal of Philosophy of Education*, 47, 128–46.

Wooldridge, S.W. (1955) 'The status of geography and the role of fieldwork', *Geography*, 40, 73–83.

Wyly E. (2014) The new quantitative revolution, *Dialogues in Human Geography* 4 (1), 26–38.

Chapter 19

Understanding the gap between schools and universities

Graham Butt and Gemma Collins

> A chasm has developed between those who teach at school and those who teach in universities.
>
> (Goudie, 1993, p. 338)

Introduction

The current 'state of play' concerning the health of geography education in English state schools and universities is intriguing. On the one hand, geography remains a popular option in many English schools, experienced positively by large numbers of students who ultimately perform well in public examinations. In these schools, standards of teaching on examination courses remain high, with pleasing numbers of students progressing onto geography (or geography-related) courses as undergraduates – where their experiences are also generally positive (Butt, 2008, 2011). The launch of an English Baccalaureate in 2010, in which students are expected to achieve 'good' GCSE grades (at level C or above) in a number of subjects – including either geography or history – has also provided a substantial fillip to the numbers opting for geography (geography is now the eighth most popular GCSE after substantial rises in candidate numbers in recent years). Geography remains a subject of real relevance to many young people in our rapidly changing world, capable of addressing aspects of space, place and environment that will affect their future lives.

On the other hand, geography is under pressure. For example, there are challenges recruiting qualified teachers to teach high quality geography in secondary schools. And just as geography departments in schools have faced pressures, so too have those in universities, as outlined by Castree (2011).

This constitutes a backdrop to the current policy shifts affecting geography education (see Gardner in this volume). In his GA Presidential lecture Andrew Goudie (1993) bemoaned the lack of involvement of academic geographers both in the Association and in schools, stating 'a chasm has developed between those who teach in schools and those who teach in universities' (p. 338). However, this begs the question of how best to conceptualise the relation between the school subject and the wider academic discipline. They are different, with different priorities and different purposes. Maybe we should perhaps *expect* a 'gap'.

Eroding the links between university and school geographies

All school subjects have a 'curriculum story', and probably all subjects experience periods of uncertainty about their status and appeal. For school geography, the rise of humanities teaching in many schools in the 1960s and 1970s, the debate over whether geography would be included in the National Curriculum in the late 1980s (see Bailey and Binns, 1987), and the increased focus on vocational education from the 1990s, all feature as pressure points. Essentially, school geography has always been affected, to a greater or lesser extent, by:

> the prevailing philosophies of education, the existing paradigm of geography in higher education, the economic climate and the political complexion of the government of the day.
>
> (Butt, 2002, p. 17)

The comprehensivisation of state secondary schools from the mid-1960s meant that many secondary school teachers in England found themselves teaching a different student clientele. This led significant numbers of geography educators towards curriculum development, driven primarily by the educational needs of a 'new' student group. Graves (1975) refers to this period as one of 'crisis in geographical education in Britain' (p. 61), a consequence of conceptual shifts in academic geography, advances in education theory and the restructuring of secondary schools. Marsden (1997) echoes these observations, referring to the 'unhealthy stresses' between school and university geography which developed from this time.

For Naish (2000), the period from the late 1960s to the early 1980s was one of 'laissez faire' in geography curriculum development, when considerations of the broader aims, objectives and purposes of education came to the fore. One of the consequences of this increased '*educational focus*' was that many geography teachers, according to Naish, stepped back from considering the primacy of geography's academic subject content. The Schools Council, founded in 1964, actively supported curriculum reform and development, sponsoring three major geography curriculum development projects in the 1970s: Geography for the Young School Leaver (GYSL); Geography 14–18 (Bristol Project) and the Geography 16–19 Project. Geography curriculum development was also influenced by a project from abroad – the American High Schools Geography Project (HSGP, 1971) – which instructed teachers how to incorporate new ideas, content and techniques from the 'quantitative revolution' in academic geography into their schemes of work. However, most curriculum development projects focused more on how geography could contribute to the fulfilment of the needs of young people, than on considerations of academic subject content. The Geography 16–19

Project, examined at A level from 1982, achieved great popularity, experiencing a near-exponential growth in student numbers during the 1980s. This project had an impact on the teaching of geography within universities – for incoming undergraduates who had studied 16–19 Geography had been taught through a 'route to enquiry' approach, acquiring geographical content, skills, techniques and values very different from those provided by more 'traditional' geography syllabuses. The change was not universally welcomed by university geographers, many of whom criticised the (supposed) superficiality of content covered by the 16–19 syllabus, particularly of physical geography. Although these curriculum development projects offered some connection with academic geographers and their research, the 16–19 Project team stated that there was 'no requirement that all new academic developments necessarily be translated into the school context' (Naish et al., 1987, pp. 26–7).

The geography curriculum development projects were based within higher education institutions (HEIs) – predominantly in departments of education, not geography – with each project team emphasising the need for geography teachers to be involved (Boardman, 1988). The resultant curricula reflected *some* of the changes from the academic frontiers of the subject, often mediated by teacher educators, but also incorporated (and valued highly) the application of innovative curriculum theory. During the late 1970s, university geography departments saw humanistic, behavioural, welfare and radical geographers reacting against the narrowness of the positivistic, quantitative approaches developed at least a decade earlier. This plurality of approaches may have proved confusing for school geographers, making the application of new ideas in schools problematic. A further, practical issue when considering the connections between schools and universities is the time lag between developments in universities and their adoption in schools, as there is an understandable conservatism about swapping syllabuses.

The 1980s saw increasing centralisation and politicisation of the school curriculum, culminating in the passing of the Education Reform Act (1988) and the establishment of a National Curriculum in English and Welsh schools. The first iteration of the Geography National Curriculum (GNC) (DES, 1991) has been seen as a 'restorationist' curriculum (Rawling, 2001). As Lambert (2011) succinctly observes:

> The Schools Council projects introduced the idea that subject knowledge was not an end point in education, but a vehicle contributing towards educational ends (geography as a 'medium of education'). The 1991 National Curriculum can be interpreted as an attempt to restore subject knowledge.
>
> (p. 248)

Morgan (2008) has outlined the development of school geography curricula since the 1970s, highlighting an uncoupling of school and university geography during this period. He notes the limited involvement of academic geographers in the development of the GNC – just two were chosen to sit on the Geography

Working Group, and few made significant submissions to the curriculum-making process. This reflects the declining influence of university geographers in shaping the content of geography taught in schools over the past forty years. By the late 1990s, few academic geographers crossed the school–university divide. From the mid-1980s numbers of geography undergraduates were increasing rapidly, with commensurate pressures on university class sizes, teaching and research quality, funding and research outputs. Just as schools have endured huge changes in policy and practice, higher education has also been subject to increased bureaucratisation, marketisation and rising accountability. The limited involvement of most academic geographers in debates about the content of public examinations in geography, their general unwillingness to write for school teachers and students, and their lack of engagement in the professional development of teachers may be attributable to their need to publish high-quality research and on preparing high-stakes audits (QAA) (see Castree et al., 2007).

The 'divide' between school and university geography – retrospect and prospect

The first of the famous Madingley conferences in 1963, creating what Rex Walford called the 'new model army' (Walford, 2001, p. 158), gave academic geographers and (some) teachers opportunities to discuss developments in their subject, under the direction of a couple of exciting and ambitious young Oxbridge geographers, Richard Chorley and Peter Haggett (see Haggett, 2015). The tone of these conferences was to some practitioners somewhat paternalistic, given that academic geographers were largely handing down research findings and techniques to those teachers present – who Rawling refers to as 'junior partners in this relationship' (Rawling, 1996, p. 3). Nonetheless, Unwin (1996) comments positively on the influence of Chorley and Haggett's ideas on 'a generation of geography teachers', noting how their emphasis on quantitative approaches, modelling and theory building subsequently 'filtered down into school textbooks and examination syllabuses' (p. 21). Although sceptical about the extent of these impacts across the majority of schools, Unwin (1996) asserts that a minority of geography teachers remained heavily influenced by the research agendas of university geographers in the 1970s and early 1980s.

Whilst it would be a misjudgement to visualise the 1960s and early 1970s as some kind of 'golden age' of interaction between school and university geographers, there is evidence of pockets of influential engagement with regard to examinations and professional development. This gradually changed from the mid-1970s, as the sectors began to grow further apart. One reason for this, according to Bradford (1996), was that:

> During the 1980s and 1990s there has not been one major trend affecting as many areas of the subject as did either the scientific revolution of the 1950s and early 1960s, or the radical geography movement of the early 1970s. The

absence of such major changes may partly account for the reduced impact of higher education on the geography taught in secondary education.

(p. 282)

Michael Bradford's view of the school–HE interface as 'presenting a gap or discontinuity in methods and content' (1996, p. 277), has held true for much of the following 15 years, despite attempts to bridge the gap, notably by the Council for British Geography (Cobrig) and its seminars of the mid 1990s (see Daugherty and Rawling, 1996). In fact, it seemed like a decision needed to be made about whether 'there should be uniformity or diversity in what is learned' (p. 277) in schools and universities. This is a fundamental issue, at the very heart of our consideration of the connections between the geographies taught within schools and universities. It hints at a basic epistemological divide between the aims, rationale and scope of the work of academic and school geographers, with respect to both teaching and research. Essentially, when considering geography either as an academic discipline or as a school subject, there will always be differences and divides. Put crudely, geography in the academy is afforded the opportunities to develop in innovative, experimental, tentative and uncertain ways – the very nature of 'cutting edge' academic research work makes this so. Here we are at the forefront of knowledge creation, which is a piecemeal, painful and 'backwards and forwards' process, often leading down blind alleys or, at best, revealing findings that are contingent and relational. The geography taught in schools probably cannot be of this nature. It is certainly *informed* by the advances in knowledge achieved by academic geographers, but requires more stability and clarity about the content[1] it conveys (not least as it is taught by teachers who are not specialist geographers). The selections of geography to be taught in schools need to serve in an educational rather than research oriented context. A divide will therefore always exist between academic and school geography. This will not be 'closed' by seeking to align both geographies (an impossible, Sisyphean task) but bridged by achieving a better understanding of their differences. Roger Firth (in this volume) has explored this issue in depth – and there are others: see Maude (2016) and Esther Vernon (2016), a practising teacher who sees the need to theorise the question of how new knowledge is 'recontextualised' for the school curriculum.

Bridging the divide – ways forward

We have seen that the issue of a 'chasm', 'gap', 'border' or 'discontinuity' between geography education in schools and universities is persistent (see Goudie, 1993; Machon and Ranger, 1996; Bradford, 1996; Marsden, 1997; Bonnett, 2003; Butt, 2008; Johnston, 2009; Hill and Jones, 2010), although some geographers have recently attempted to build bridges between the two sectors. The need for further dialogue (Jeffrey, 2003; Stannard, 2003), hopefully followed by rapprochement (Yarwood and Davison, 2007; Pykett and Smith, 2009), is generally acknowledged.

Table 19.1 Bridging the divide – energising school geography

Activity	Agents
Professional development conferences and events	Professional associations (e.g. GA and GA branches, RGS-IBG and GA conferences)
Academic conferences and events	Academic geographers and initial teacher educators (with some geography teachers) (e.g. COBRIG, Association of American Geographers Conference, IGU, ESRC 'Engaging Geographies' seminar series, RGS-IBG and GA conferences)
Producing textbooks/ journal articles for school students/ geography teachers	Geography teachers, academic geographers and/or initial teacher educators (in schools and universities) (e.g. *Teaching Geography, Geography Review, Geography*)
Producing scholarly/ research texts	Academic geographers and/or initial teacher educators (in schools and universities) (e.g. GEReCo, Rawling and Daugherty (1996), Kent (2000), Butt (2011))
Research projects	Geography teachers in association with academic geographers and/or initial teacher educators (in schools and universities) (e.g. Young People's Geographies Project)
Curriculum Development Projects	Notably subject associations (e.g. see under 'projects' on geography.org.uk
'Mediation'	'Mediators' and 'Ambassadors' working in/with geographers in schools (e.g. GA Chief Executive/ Professor of Geography Education; RGS-IBG subject officers; key geography academics; initial teacher educators in geography; geography undergraduates in schools; A level geography students attending day 'outreach/widening participation' courses in university geography departments).
Special Interest Groups	As represented in professional associations (IGU, GA, RGS-IBG, etc.)
Political lobbying for government funded initiatives	Professional associations (GA, RGS-IBG) (e.g. Action Plan for Geography); 'mediators'
Award bearing courses/ CPD (Masters, EdD, PhD in geography education)	University Schools of Education
Initial Teacher Education	New geography teachers, with geography educators (e.g. PGCE and PGDipEd courses)
Development and review of examination specifications[2]	Awarding bodies in association with academic geographers (see Evans, 2015), teacher educators and geography teachers

We outline above (Table 19.1) ways in which academic geographers, initial teacher educators, professional associations, awarding bodies and geography teachers can connect to develop the content of school geography. There are obvious overlaps between many of the suggested 'activities' and 'agents' – the key is achieving stronger, more frequent and clearer lines of communication between the academy and schools. Often this will occur through the actions of particular 'mediators' and 'ambassadors' interested in the wider development of geography content and pedagogy.

Each year new cohorts of geography graduates train to become geography teachers through programmes of initial teacher education (ITE), be they school or university based. Each trainee must make their own attempt to bridge the 'gap' between university and school geography, striving to translate or transform their recently gained geographical knowledge, understanding and skills to the classroom. This is not an easy process as 'students are recruited to teacher education courses with wildly different concepts of the nature of geography' (Marsden, 1997, p. 250; also see Barratt Hacking, 1996; Walford, 1996; Brooks, 2010). In some sense each ITE student acts as a conduit, bringing aspects of recently acquired geography content from their university courses into schools – a process extended by the growing cohort of geography teachers who go on to study for a Master's degree, EdD or PhD in geography education.

The 'knowledge turn'

We have largely focused this discussion on the connections between geography in schools and in Higher Education. We choose to end our deliberations by concentrating on the recent 'knowledge turn' in school geography:

David Lambert (2011) shows that the direction of travel taken by the Schools White Paper, *The Importance of Teaching* (DfE, 2010), encourages (geography) teachers to engage more deeply with the question of 'what to teach?' Whether this is a question solely about 'school geography' or whether the impetus is for geography teachers to engage with developments in their subject discipline is unclear. Lambert welcomes a re-focusing of geography teachers' attention on their subject, arguing that this has been neglected during a period of overemphasis on aspects of pedagogy. David Mitchell (2011; see also Mitchell and Lambert, 2015) similarly refers to an 'emptying of subject knowledge', and is concerned about the 'weak' geographical content taught in schools – a consequence of the extent to which pedagogy (how to teach) has come to dominate curriculum (what to teach). This serves to exacerbate the 'great divide' between university and school geographies as the relevance of the discipline to raising achievement becomes questionable on a practical level. John Morgan (2009), Margaret Roberts (2010, 2012) and Ruth Totterdell (2012) each explore the issue of what makes geography teachers, and their lessons, 'good' – concluding that the focus should be as much on the geography taught (and learned) as on the process of teaching. Mitchell (2011) implies the need to develop a more theorised and sophisticated understanding of perspectives on knowledge, incorporating an appreciation of Young's conceptions of 'powerful knowledge' (Young, 2008; Maude, 2016), Hirsch's notions of core knowledge and cultural literacy (Hirsch, 1987, 2007) and possibly the 'capability approach' to geography[3] (Lambert and Morgan,

2010; Lambert et al., 2015), which stresses the role of 'powerful disciplinary knowledge' in education.

In these scenarios, geography teachers are visualised as 'independent, autonomous, knowledge workers' (Mitchell, 2011), as well as 'curriculum makers' (Lambert and Morgan, 2010), and of course, this is distinctive and results in a very particular form of geography: that is, geography in education (rather than geography as an independent discipline). The prospects of bridging the gap between schools and universities are not necessarily dimmed by making such a distinction, but we may have to work hard at working out what the links are, or should be. For example, as Peter Jackson (2006) has argued, we could stress that 'thinking geographically', allowing us to apply geographical knowledge and conceptual understanding to different settings, is a uniquely powerful way for students to see the world and make connections. Conceptualising geography in this way may help us build bridges. We do not need to unify for, as Noel Castree reminds us, 'students will only come to university to read for a geography degree if they've first been inspired by their geography teachers – teachers who often present a very different sort of geography to that most university academics teach' (Castree, 2011, p. 3). But, we might add, it does need to be geography.

Reforms to the school geography curriculum, and to public examinations, inevitably affect both schools and higher education – altering the nature of cross-phase collaboration and shifting the drivers responsible for the creation of geography subject knowledge. The most recent reviews of the National Curriculum, GCSE and AS/A level geography examinations in England have been 'knowledge-led' and more inclusive of contributions made from higher education. The work of the A-level Content Advisory Board (ALCAB) resulted, despite some inevitable disappointments, in 'a degree of reconnection of HE with A level content' (Evans, 2015) with concomitant alterations of specifications for the teaching and assessment of geography.

However, the radical reform of initial teacher education – which has now emphatically shifted location, both physically and intellectually, away from university-led provision to school-based training – is having a significant impact on both the quality of preparation of new entrants to the profession, and on geography curriculum development in schools (Butt, 2015). Recent policy statements from each of the main political parties firmly position the future of teacher education and training in schools, largely ignoring the contributions made previously to England's 'world class teaching profession' by higher education institutions (HEIs). The role of the specialist geography educator in ITE is therefore sadly disappearing. Given the significant decline in numbers of trainee geography teachers based in HEIs, and the increasing placement of trainee teachers on school-based routes, this is likely to lead to narrower forms of teacher preparation and the loss of subject specialisms. This will inevitably have far reaching effects on research and scholarship in geography education and ultimately on the quality of geographical knowledge experienced by students in schools (Tapsfield et al., 2015).

Conclusion

One important purpose of school is to introduce disciplinary knowledge to young people. More prosaically, universities will continue to supply new geography graduates to be trained as geography teachers and there must be a shared commitment both to, and for, the geographical education of young people. This symbiosis, borne from the mutual needs of both sectors, should encourage the creation of closer ties. Or, if not closer ties, links and connections that are better understood. More modestly, we encourage a deeper appreciation of the geography taught in schools and universities, and how collectively this may contribute to 'thinking geographically' (see John Morgan and Nick Clifford in this volume). This is not to create uniformity, or an overly regimented continuity and progression of geographical themes, but to achieve a mutual, coherent and agreed understanding of the subject, recognisable by both sectors.

Key readings

1   Rawling, E. and Daugherty, R. (eds.), (1996) *Geography into the Twenty-First Century,* Chichester: Wiley. Eleanor Rawling and Richard Daugherty's edited work provides a good historical account of how school and university geographies have progressed up to the mid-1990s.
2   Butt, G. (ed.) (2011) *Geography, Education and the Future,* London: Continuum. To take these debates forward, read selected chapters from Graham Butt's (2011) edited work.

Notes

1 We cannot escape the sustained influence of the awarding bodies on the content of geography taught in schools and the pressure felt by many teachers to teach only the 'content' which they believe will be credited by the examiners.
2 www.geocapabilities.org
3 Castree (2011) estimates that some 80 (of 140) English higher education institutes (HEIs) offer single or joint honours degrees in geography, to around 15,000 students in 2008–9. Similar numbers are currently studying for degrees in mathematics, and economics.

References

Bailey, P. and Binns, T. (eds.) (1987) *A Case for Geography,* Sheffield: Geographical Association.
Barratt Hacking, E. (1996) 'Novice teachers and their geographical persuasions', *IRGEE,* 5, 77–86.
Boardman, D. (1988) *The Impact of a Curriculum: Project Geography and the Young School Leaver,* Birmingham: Educational Review Publications.
Bonnett, A. (2003) 'Geography as the world discipline: connecting popular and academic geographical imaginations', *Area,* 35 (1), 56–63.

Bradford, M. (1996) 'Geography at the secondary/higher education interface: change through diversity', in E. Rawling, and R. Daugherty (eds.), *Geography into the Twenty-First Century*, Chichester: Wiley.

Brooks, C. (2010) Developing and reflecting on subject expertise', in C. Brooks (ed.), *Studying PGCE Geography at M Level: Reflection, Research and Writing for Professional Development*, London: Routledge.

Butt, G. (2002) *Reflective Teaching of Geography 11–18*, London: Continuum.

Butt, G. (2008) 'Is the future secure for geography education?', *Geography*, 93 (3), 158–65.

Butt, G. (ed.) (2011) *Geography, Education and the Future*, London: Continuum.

Butt, G. (2015) *What Impact will Changes in Teacher Education have on the Geography Curriculum in Schools?* Presentation at RGS-IBG Annual International Conference, University of Exeter, 3 September 2015.

Castree, N. (2011) 'The future of geography in English universities', *The Geographical Journal*, 136, (4), 512–19.

Castree, N., Fuller, D. and Lambert, D. (2007) 'Geography without borders', *Transactions of the Institute of British Geographers*, 32, 129–32.

Daugherty, R. and Rawling, E. (1996) 'New perspectives for geography: an agenda for action', in E. Rawling, and R. Daugherty (eds.), *Geography into the Twenty-First Century*, Chichester: Wiley.

DES (1991) *Geography in the National Curriculum (England)*, London: HMSO.

DfE (2010) *The Importance of Teaching: The Schools White Paper*, London: The Stationery Office.

Evans, M. (2015) *Reconsidering Geography at the Schools-HE boundary; the ALCAB experience*, Presentation at RGS-IBG Annual International Conference, University of Exeter, 3 September 2015.

Goudie, A. (1993) 'Schools and universities – the great divide', *Geography*, 78 (4), 338–9.

Graves, N. (1975) *Geography in Education*, London: Heinemann.

Haggett, P. (2015) 'Madingley: half century reflections on a geographical experiment', *Geography*, 100 (1), 5–12.

Hill, J. and Jones, M. (2010) '"Joined-up geography": connecting school-level and university-level geographies', *Geography*, 95 (1), 22–32.

Hirsch, E.D. (1987) *Cultural Literacy: What every American needs to know*, Boston, MA: Houghton Mifflin Co.

Hirsch, E.D. (2007) *The Knowledge Deficit*, Boston, MA: Houghton Mifflin Co.

HSGP (1971) *American High School Geography Project. Geography in an Urban Age*, Toronto, Ont., Canada: Collier-Macmillan.

Jackson, P. (2006) 'Thinking geographically', *Geography*, 91 (3), 199–204.

Jeffrey, C. (2003) 'Bridging the gulf between secondary schools and university-level geography teachers: Reflections on organising a UK teachers' conference', *Journal of Geography in Higher Education*, 27, 201–15.

Johnston, R. (2009) 'On geography, geography and geographical magazines', *Geography*, 94 (3), 207–14.

Kent, A. (ed.) (2000) *Reflective Practice in Geography Teaching*, London: Paul Chapman Publishing.

Lambert, D. (2011) 'Reviewing the case for geography, and the 'knowledge turn' in the English national curriculum', *The Curriculum Journal*, 22 (2), 243–64.

Lambert, D. and Morgan, J. (2010) *Teaching Geography 11–18: A Conceptual Approach*, Maidenhead: Open University Press.

Lambert, D., Solem, M. and Tani, S. (2015) 'Achieving human potential through geography education: a capabilities approach to curriculum making in schools', *Annals of the Association of American Geographers*, 105 (4), 723–35.

Machon, P. and Ranger, G. (1996) 'Change in school geography', in P. Bailey and P. Fox (eds.), *Geography Teacher's Handbook*, Sheffield: Geographical Association.

Marsden, W. (1997) 'On taking the geography out of geographical education – some historical pointers on geography', *Geography*, 82 (3), 241–52.

Maude, A. (2016) 'What might powerful knowledge look like?', *Geography*, 101 (2), 70–6.

Mitchell, D. (2011) 'A "knowledge turn" – implications for geography initial teacher education (ITE)', Paper presented at the IGU-CGE conference, Institute of Education, University of London, April 2011.

Mitchell, D. and Lambert, D. (2015) 'Subject knowledge and teacher preparation in English secondary schools: the case of geography', *Teacher Development*, 19 (3), 365–80.

Morgan, J. (2008) 'Curriculum development in "new times"', *Geography*, 93 (1), 17–24.

Morgan, J. (2009) 'What makes a "good" geography teacher?', in C. Brooks (ed.), *Studying PGCE Geography at M Level*, London: Routledge.

Naish, M. (2000) 'The geography curriculum of England and Wales from 1965: a personal view', in D. Lambert and D. Balderstone (eds.), *Learning to Teach Geography in the Secondary School*, London: RoutledgeFalmer.

Naish, M., Rawling, E. and Hart, C. (1987) *Geography 16–19: The Contribution of a Curriculum Project to 16–19 Education*, London: Longman.

Pykett, J. and Smith, M. (2009) 'Rediscovering school geographies: connecting the distant worlds of school and academic geography', *Teaching Geography*, 34 (1), 35–8.

Rawling, E. (1996) 'Madingley revisited?', in E. Rawling and R. Daugherty (eds.), *Geography into the Twenty-First Century*, Chichester: Wiley.

Rawling, E. and Daugherty, R. (eds.) (1996) *Geography into the Twenty-First Century*, Chichester: Wiley.

Rawling, E. (2001) *Changing the Subject: The Impact of National Policy on School Geography 1980–2000*, Sheffield: Geographical Association.

Roberts, M. (2010) 'Where's the geography? Reflections on being an external examiner', *Teaching Geography*, 35 (3), 112–13.

Roberts, M. (2012) What makes a good geography lesson?, Available at: www.geography.org.uk/projects/makinggeographyhappen/teachertips [Accessed 12 December 2011].

Stannard, K. (2003) 'Earth to academia: on the need to reconnect university and school geography', *Area*, 35, 316–32.

Tapsfield, A., Roberts, M. and Kinder, A. (2015) *Geography Initial Teacher Education and Teacher Supply in England*. Sheffield: Geographical Association.

Totterdell, R. (2012) 'What makes a geography lesson "good"?', *Teaching Geography*, 37 (1), 35.

Unwin, T. (1996) 'Academic Geography; the key questions for discussion', in E. Rawling and R. Daugherty (eds.), *Geography into the Twenty-First Century*, Chichester: Wiley.

Vernon, E. (2016) 'The structure of knowledge: does theory matter?', *Geography*, 101 (2), 100–4.

Walford, R. (1996) '"What is geography?" An analysis of definitions provided by prospective teachers of the subject', *IRGEE*, 5, 69–76.

Walford, R. (2001) *Geography in British Schools 1850–2000*, London: Woburn Press.

Yarwood, R. and Davison, T. (2007) '"Bridges or fords?" Geographical Association branches and higher education', *Area*, 39, 544–50.

Young, M. (2008) *Bringing Knowledge Back in: From Social Constructionism to Social Realism in the Sociology of Education*, London: Routledge.

Chapter 20

Recontextualising geography as a school subject

Roger Firth

> How a society selects, classifies, distributes, transmits and evaluates the educational knowledge it considers to be public, reflects both the distribution of power and the principles of social control.
>
> (Bernstein, 1971, p. 47)

Introduction

This chapter reflects on the usefulness of Basil Bernstein's theory of the *pedagogic device* and the *structure of knowledge*. It asks: to what extent and in what ways the theory assists in describing disciplinary knowledge, its recontextualisation as a school subject and subsequent acquisition[1] in the geography classroom? It goes on to argue that although Bernstein's theory of the pedagogic device and his model of knowledge structures (as well as the development of his work in the past few years by a number of theorists advancing a 'social realist' approach to educational knowledge) are useful, the ideas are not specialised enough to engage specifically with the socio-epistemic nature of students' engagement with disciplinary knowledge. The chapter starts from the premise that the distinction between the academic discipline and the school subject is a significant one and teaching disciplinary knowledge is important: disciplinary knowledge allows students to develop the capacity to engage in the distinctive modes of investigation and analysis through which human experience and society is understood. It gives emphasis to the significance of the teacher's role in the recontextualisation and acquisition of knowledge.

The theoretical project of Bernstein, a British sociologist internationally known for his work in education, is of enormous significance to a sociological analysis of the production and reproduction of knowledge and issues of inequality. In his later work, Bernstein turned his attention to the ways in which discourse functions in society, especially discourse concerned with education (1990, 1996, 2000). His work over four decades was committed to researching what constituted barriers to upward social mobility. He sought to link microprocesses (language, transmission, and pedagogy) to macroforms – to how cultural and educational codes[2] and the content and process of education are related to social class and power relations' (Sadovnik, 2001, p. 5).

The chapter has two distinct, interrelated parts. The main part of the chapter details Bernstein's ideas about knowledge *structures* and the recontextualisation of knowledge, which is encapsulated in his concept of the *pedagogic device*. The pedagogic device is a theoretical framework that describes the principles regulating the organisation, distribution and structuring of knowledge and the conversion of knowledge into pedagogic communication. It begins to explicate the inner logic of pedagogic discourse and practices. Recontextualisation happens at different levels of decision making, where various agents are involved in the *what* and *how* of curricular and pedagogic content. The teacher's role in turning knowledge as originally generated (here, disciplinary knowledge) into educational or school knowledge is shown up. Most importantly, it emphasises that not only are teachers recipients of recontextualised knowledge, but they also are recontextualisers of knowledge. Curriculum and pedagogy can be understood as interrelated stages of such recontextualisation. How disciplinary knowledge is turned into recontextualised school knowledge, geography included, is central to any pedagogic theory that looks at curriculum and teaching and learning in the context of subject matter.

Having emphasised the significance of a Bernsteinian and social-realist approach to theorising educational knowledge, the chapter ends with some thoughts about its limitations as an overarching theory for educational purposes. This revolves around the extent to which it recognises the socio-epistemic relations *between* educational and disciplinary contexts, the nature of epistemic communities and the nature of disciplines themselves. It is argued that engagement with such issues is necessary if teachers are to support the cumulative acquisition of knowledge and how students develop what Baldwin (2010) has termed a *relationship* with disciplinary knowledge, and I have described as a *disposition* towards disciplinary knowledge (Firth, 2011). These terms highlight a concern with how students experience the acquisition of disciplinary knowledge and how such knowledge becomes meaningful. It is to emphasise the importance of the socio-epistemic nature of students' engagement with disciplinary knowledge and the role of the teacher in that process (Baldwin, 2010, p. 9).

Knowledge in theory

In the last few years, there has been a growing interest and debate concerning the 'issue of knowledge' within the geography education community as part of a wider educational challenge of bringing knowledge back in to education (Young, 2008a), and as the community continues to grapple with ongoing debates about the what and how of teaching geography and its impact on student learning. In doing so, there has been engagement with the work of Bernstein and with theoretical work building on his ideas that has come to be known as social realism.

A number of theorists have developed Bernstein's work, advancing what has come to be termed a 'social-realist' approach to educational knowledge (Muller, 2000; Moore, 2004; Young, 2008a; Wheelahan, 2010; Maton, 2014). This theoretical position 'puts knowledge as an object centre-stage in thinking about education' (Maton and Moore, 2010, p. 2). It has challenged the idea prevalent in many education systems 'that knowledge should be seen as a 'process' rather than as an 'object' and that it is co-constructed in the interactions between teacher and students' (Morgan, 2014, p. 136). Social realism is a challenge to the scepticism towards knowledge and at the risk of oversimplifying, of characterising any educational event 'that has the learning of knowledge as the basic objective – [as] a questionable aim for teaching' (ibid.). Like social constructivism, social realism calls attention to the social nature of knowledge, but unlike social constructivism, it argues knowledge '*also* requires warrant independent of social interests and the related dynamics of power' (Lauder, 2008, p. xi; emphasis added). Acknowledgement of these epistemic standards of disciplinary knowledge is central to the social-realist endeavour to establish an educational discourse 'whereby a knowledge-based curriculum [and pedagogy] can be supported for educationally progressive purposes' (Moore, 2004, p. 173).

It is important to recognise, however, 'the extent to which arguments 'for knowledge' are out of kilter with the recent direction of cultural and educational change' (Morgan, 2015, p. 16). Having said this, the opposite trend is the situation in England. This is not to suggest, however, that the education policies of the Coalition and subsequent Conservative government (DfE, 2010, 2016) are in alignment with a social realist conception of knowledge.

The pedagogic device

The pedagogic device provides an analytical description of a general process – 'how knowledge is recontextualised as it moves from outside to inside the school' (Ivinson and Duveen, 2009, p. 110). It describes a series of principles or rules that 'regulate the pedagogic communication it makes possible' (Davies, 2006, p. 4) and 'via which knowledge is converted into classroom talk and curricula' (Singh, 2002, p. 571). For Bernstein the pedagogic device makes the transformation of power into differently specialised subjects possible. It provides researchers and educators with explicit criteria/rules and terminology to describe the structuring of knowledge, 'and in particular the generative relations of power and control constituting knowledge' (ibid.). Thus, 'Curriculum and pedagogic debates, seen in this light, are, in large measure, struggles for cultural dominance' (Wright and Froehlich, 2012, p. 215). To explain the internal and the external features of the pedagogic device Bernstein outlined the hierarchical relation between three sets of rules – distributive, recontextualising and evaluative.

Distributive rules govern the way in which different forms of knowledge are distributed: what can legitimately be taught in schools, who may legitimately take on the role of teacher or learner and the conditions under which teaching-learning processes take place (Ashwin 2009, p. 91). Distributive rules provide the means to create hierarchically-ordered social groups who have access to different types of knowledge, consciousness and degrees of power. Increasingly controlled by the state in many societies, the rules regulate who is allowed to produce knowledge and how such knowledge is grouped into disciplines. The distributive rules recognise three specific fields of activity: production, recontextualisation and *reproduction*. The field of production is where new knowledge is constructed 'and decisions are made about how knowledge can be produced and by whom. The field of production is regulated by a set of distributive rules which can be defined as the ordered regulation and distribution of the "worthwhile" knowledge in a field' (Vorster and Quinn, 2012, p. 53). This is mainly, but not exclusively, the university.

Recontextualising rules regulate the process by which knowledge is removed from its original site of production and turned into something else: the school subject. The field of recontextualisation is where discourses from the field of production are selected, appropriated and transformed to become 'educational' knowledge. The field of reproduction is where pedagogic transmission and acquisition (teaching and learning) take place (with differential results) and is regulated by evaluative rules. It is the field 'where students come to understand the criteria by which they will be evaluated/assessed... [and] come to understand what constitute legitimate knowledge, as well as how this knowledge can be articulated' (Vorster and Quinn, 2012, p. 54). While these rules legitimise knowledge recontextualization, Bernstein (1996) noted what he termed 'the discursive gap' (p. 30), which is a space for ideology to play; for Bernstein no discourse ever moves without ideology at play. These rules are a specific focus of this chapter (see later).

Finally, *evaluative* rules relate to pedagogic practices and regulate recognition of the acquisition of curricular content and regulative dispositions for learning (e.g. social conduct, character, engagement). Evaluative rules are 'the key to pedagogic practice' (Bernstein, 1996, p. 47). They are in operation throughout all levels of the pedagogic device and have increasingly been appropriated by the state. They are particularly evident in assessment regimes which send strong messages about what counts as legitimate knowledge and knowing (Maton, 2006). Teachers, too, 'employ evaluative rules by stressing what, in [their] own mind, is or is not important for their pupils to learn' (Wright and Froehlich, 2012, p. 215). Together they describe the process of the transformation of knowledge from the field of production of knowledge, to the field of recontextualisation, to the field of reproduction in the classroom. It is in the classroom that teachers interpret and recontextualise the official curriculum message through their pedagogic and assessment practices.

Bernstein's notion of the 'pedagogic device' has been extended by Maton (2014). He has made some adjustments to the framework, systematising and extending it. This is illustrative of the efforts of social-realist theorists to develop the work of Bernstein. The pedagogic device 'was an ambitious attempt to capture the role of education in the sociological big picture, reaching from social structure to individual consciousness' (Hoadley and Muller, 2010, p. 74). It helps describe 'in nuanced ways the substance and nature of the message carried by the curriculum and the ways in which the policy message is re-fashioned, recontextualised and re-interpreted as it moves through various levels of the education system' (Bertram, 2012, p. 5). In this process the original discourse undergoes 'an ideological transformation' (ibid.). It is therefore possible to agree with Moore (2004) that the pedagogic device is not straightforward and cannot be taken for granted.

Recontextualisation

As we have seen, this is the principle that governs the way in which knowledge is selected from the field in which it was produced and transformed for the purpose of acquisition in schools. The process of recontextualisation is regulated by two sets of recontextualising rules which Bernstein (1990, 2000) terms the *regulative discourse* and the *instructional discourse*. The regulative discourse refers to a society's moral order – the values and social order on which the curriculum and pedagogy are based, whereas the instructional discourse refers to pedagogic practices, such as the selection, sequencing, pacing and assessment (Vorster and Quinn, 2012, p. 54). These discourses create the knowledge and skills within the school subject. The important point is that Bernstein did not draw this analytical distinction simplistically to fragment the transmission of knowledge and skills and values. For Bernstein there was only one discourse: the pedagogic discourse. By their very nature, all curricula and pedagogy have a values orientation, whether this is explicitly articulated or not. Bernstein argues that the regulative discourse is always dominant; the instructional discourse is embedded within the regulative framework. Regulative discourse controls relations between all actors, creating social order and constructing identities. Regulative discourse dominates instructional discourse: thus, while the curriculum increases a student's knowledge, more importantly, it moulds a student's attitude towards reality. It operates therefore as a form of control.

Bernstein differentiated between two sub-fields in the field of recontextualisation and emphasised the interplay between the two: the *official* recontextualising field (ORF) and the *pedagogic* recontextualising field (PRF). The ORF is created and dominated by the state, its agencies and its official statements of curriculum, such as the national curriculum programmes of study and examination specifications. The PRF consists of teacher educators in university departments of education and schools, subject associations, private research groups, and textbook publishers.

Interestingly, Bernstein does not include teachers, although teachers are inevitably part of the process. The ORF and the PRF struggle to control education by selecting knowledge, sequencing subject content and the pacing of instruction. A review of the ORF in relation to curriculum and pedagogy in England over the last three decades would suggest that it has become increasingly influential in relation to classroom practice, as Eleanor Rawling (2001) and others have shown.

The process of creating new knowledge is described by Bernstein as knowledge production: 'The production of knowledge is distinctively different to the process of making such knowledge available to others who do not have access to it' (Brooks, 2016, p. 52). This conceptualisation acknowledges that disciplinary discourses are only fully meaningful in their own contexts and 'in taking knowledge from the disciplines and making it available for students, it is subjected to transformation' (ibid.). It also raises questions about the relations between discipline and school subject and the challenge in bridging the meaning that is made between participants in the different contexts (the field of production and the field of recontextualisation). It is useful here to refer to Bernstein's concept of the structure of knowledge (see next section). Clearly, 'knowledge as taught is different from knowledge as created' (ibid., p. 35).

Teachers act as 'recontextualising agents' for appropriating and repositioning official curriculum specifications through the design of school curricula, pedagogising subjects and developing and drawing upon published materials and resources, the organisation of teaching and the ordering and sequencing of learning and assessment in geography departments and classrooms. This complex process has been called 'curriculum making' (see Biddulph in this volume; Lambert, 2016), and Lambert (2017) discusses this as a *responsibility* that falls to teachers. Although the teacher is a key focus of knowledge in any classroom, 'guiding, selecting and representing knowledge from their particular discipline' (Brooks, 2016, p. 51), the pedagogic device and the process of recontextualisation show that educational practices are not personal choices alone. Further, as Ball (2006) has observed, the 'roll-out' of a curriculum is rarely smooth and teachers will not easily adopt all the requirements of an official policy. 'Policy fractures' (Davies and Hughes, 2009) are always likely to occur 'as there are disjunctures between the espoused, the enacted and the experienced curriculum' (Bertram 2012, p. 2).

Structures of knowledge

The pedagogic device also introduces a number of important issues that had been somewhat neglected in Bernstein's earlier work. A key issue was 'the question of what knowledge was: its structure and social base' (Hoadley and Muller, 2010, p. 74). In his later work Bernstein introduced a theory of knowledge, one indebted to the French sociologist Emile Durkheim, in arguing that all societies distinguish between what he termed esoteric knowledge on the one hand, and mundane knowledge on the other. Esoteric knowledge is theoretical and conceptual knowledge, mundane knowledge is everyday knowledge. As Bernstein (1999) reasons, it is educationally essential to be clear about the difference between these two discourses. It is important to grasp that this is not, however, to ascribe a difference in *value*, but rather a difference in *role*.

Bernstein elaborated Durkheim's distinction between esoteric and mundane knowledge through his exploration of the structures of knowledge in each case, and the social relations they are based on. He described esoteric knowledge as a form of vertical discourse, whereas mundane or everyday knowledge is a form of horizontal discourse, with different social relations underpinning each. In horizontal discourse, there is a direct relation between meanings and a specific material base. The principle through which knowledge is selected and applied is relevant to the local context. Horizontal discourse is thus tied to specific contexts and largely only meaningful within that context (knowledge is context specific). By contrast, vertical discourse requires systematic ordering principles for the generation and integration of meanings. Knowledge segments fit together in a time and space not given by relevance to specific contexts (knowledge is context-independent).

Within vertical discourse, Bernstein distinguishes between two kinds of knowledge structure: hierarchical and horizontal. It was a way of conceptualising the underlying principles that generate different forms of knowledge and how they develop over time. Hierarchical and horizontal knowledge structures differ in two ways: in their 'verticality' and 'grammaticality'. Verticality has to do with how a theory develops internally: 'the capacity of theory to progressively integrate and subsume knowledge at increasing levels of generality and abstraction' (Moore et al., 2006, p. 2) with ever more explanatory sophistication. Grammaticality is 'the capacity of a theory, through its concepts, to engage with the world – to produce an external language of description that specifies the manner in which we would recognise the world and the kinds of things the theory posits as existing there' (ibid.). The stronger the grammar of a language, the better able it will be to progress through worldly (empirical) validation.

Bernstein's typology of knowledge sits within broader historical and philosophical debates concerning the possibility of progress in knowledge. It can be criticised for offering dichotomous ideal types whose differences are too strongly drawn (Young, 2008a, p. 210) based on his preference for a realist ontology and an empiricist epistemology as the ideal (Luckett, 2009). Social realism 'addresses in more detail the problems highlighted by Bernstein, namely the problem of the interface or articulation between horizontal and vertical discourse and the place of these forms of knowledge in the curriculum' (Baldwin, 2010, p. 99). In summary, a social realist approach provides the means to adopt a realist view of knowledge in contrast to a postmodern approach, which regards knowledge as relativist. Social realism is also in contrast to a foundationalist model of knowledge, which is premised on the notion that knowledge is somehow 'given'. In emphasising the sociality of knowledge as grounds for *the basis of its objectivity*, it thus provides an argument for the status of disciplinary knowledge as powerful and context-independent knowledge within the school curriculum (Young, 2008b). It is argued that because constructivist or progressive approaches to curriculum and pedagogy do not have a robust theory of knowledge, they fail to recognise the importance of students' access to what Young calls 'powerful knowledge' (Young and Lambert, 2014).

Teachers will understand the difference and the relationship (Stengel, 1997) between the academic discipline and the school subject in various ways from their experiences as school students, undergraduates and teacher trainees (see chapters by Butt and Collins, and Clifford both in this volume). A teacher's relationship with a discipline has both an ethical and a knowledge perspective which will influence how they select content, their preferred methods of enquiry and how they recontextualise the discipline. It is important to point out that Bernstein's theory of vertical and horizontal knowledge structures is not specific enough to provide an understanding of the nature of geography as a specialised discipline and its recontextualisation as a school subject. There is an important difference between discussion in the abstract compared with an exploration of the actual discipline. Thus, although analysis of knowledge structures are a starting point, they are not sufficient to interrogate geography as a specialised discipline (see Firth, 2011 for a more detailed discussion of this issue).

The nature of different epistemic communities

The socio-epistemic perspectives offered by Bernstein and other social realist theorists are limited to the field of knowledge production and the knowledge structure of academic disciplines themselves. Similar scrutiny is not given to the fields of recontextualisation or reproduction. In consequence the different epistemic communities and contexts and forms of knowledge within them are not considered. However, as Vernon (2016) illustrates in her discussion of Bernstein's theory of knowledge structures, what teachers can draw from general theory is useful.

Important to the discussion here are the subject-matter knowledge of the teacher that relates to the 'school community', and the 'everyday knowledge' of the student, based in the 'general community'. There has been a neglect in educational studies (and in teacher training) of the distinction between knowledge and epistemic communities and also the distinction between these different epistemic communities. These communities and forms of knowledge are important to a theory of knowledge for education.

Here the idea of 'owned knowledge' (Paechter, 1998) takes on relevance. Paechter used the concept in consideration of the relationship between 'school' and 'non-school' knowledge, that is, the knowledge that students bring to school. The concept can be extended to recognise and identify teachers' owned knowledge, such knowledge is learned 'in a context and for a purpose' (Paechter, 1998, p. 172). In terms of the recontextualisation of knowledge, teachers' owned knowledge becomes significant. Recontextualisation involves the complex interplay of official and pedagogic agents (particularly teachers), which emphasises that although formal school knowledge is based upon specified curriculum formulations, it is also made in that context, and acted upon by teachers (and students). It raises questions about how formal school knowledge becomes owned knowledge and how owned knowledge – the geography that teachers teach – relates to disciplinary knowledge. Bernstein and social realist theorists point to the importance not only of adequate subject knowledge, but that this subject knowledge is located within the 'cosmology' of the discipline. The work of Brooks (2016) points to the fact that teachers develop a personalised view of the subject, and their geographical expertise is seen as a guiding principle, which influences their practice and their decision making, but that disciplinary knowledge plays only a part in this owned knowledge. In other words, the school subject as taught and learned cannot be simply seen as a transformation of pre-existent disciplinary knowledge. Paechter's (1998) idea of owned knowledge is also significant when thinking about the kind of knowledge students bring to school. How teachers *and students* understand the discipline-school subject-everyday knowledge relationship is thus highly significant.

Conclusion

Bernstein and social realism provide a theoretical basis for the place of disciplinary knowledge in the school curriculum. Recontextualisation draws attention to the curriculum and pedagogising work undertaken by teachers as part of a larger process of transforming knowledge for educational purposes. It seems productive to view the process of classroom practice as, in part, a product of the recontextualisation and reproduction of disciplinary knowledge. In viewing geography education through Bernstein's theoretical lens, questions are raised concerning *how* and by *whom* disciplinary knowledge is selected and recontextualised to become the subject matter of the school subject. These questions reach back to issues of policy and politics; but they also reach into teachers' culture and the nature of teachers' subject identity and expertise (Brooks, 2016), both of which carry values and cultural preferences.

Extending Bernstein's concept of recontextualisation, raises the possibility of seeing curriculum and pedagogy as a space of interaction between the different *epistemic communities* (discipline, teacher and student). These are spaces where learning is as much about learning to navigate and negotiate knowledge and its communities and practices, and its ways of constructing objects/subjects as it is about learning particular subject concepts and processes. The accentuation of epistemic communities and in this sense the performance of disciplinary ways of thinking – a view of disciplinary knowledge in use – clearly gives a more active, interpretive role to both teachers and students. It is in such spaces that the educational aim of developing students' disposition towards disciplinary knowledge is likely to be most fully accomplished (Firth, 2011, p. 307).

Key readings

1   Wright, R. and Froehlich, H. (2012) 'Basil Bernstein's Theory of the Pedagogic Device and Formal Music Schooling: Putting the Theory Into Practice', *Theory Into Practice*, 51 (3), 212–220. The theoretical work of Bernstein has been put to work worldwide in the study of education, though to a very limited extent in geography education. This is why Ruth Wright

and Hildegard Froehlich's article is included as a key reading; they describe Basil Bernstein's theory of the pedagogic device as applied to school music education in the United States. The article describes how education functions as a vehicle for social reproduction; however, emphasis is given to teachers as recontextualisers of knowledge, and in this role, they argue, there is some scope for teachers to attempt to transform the rules which shape the pedagogic device and, by extension, the social order.

2   Ivinson, G. and Duveen, G. (2009) 'Children's recontextualisations of pedagogy', in R. Moore, M. Arnot, J. Beck and H. Daniels (eds.) *Knowledge, Power and Educational Reform*, London: Routledge, pp. 109–26. Gabrielle Ivinson's and Gerard Duveen's study focuses on the recontextualisation of knowledge that takes place between the education institution and the children within it through different types of pedagogic practice. It draws attention to the interplay of voice, identity and pedagogic discourses and the fact that there is a further level of mediation of knowledge, which has been given little attention, that is the constructive activities of children themselves. It illustrates how Bernstein's concepts can be used to collect and analyse data and understood theoretically an educational state of affairs.

Notes

1 Acquisition is commonly associated with the idea of education as the transmission of knowledge and a passive model of learning, which has rightly been heavily criticised by educationalists. The use of the word by social realist scholars and in this article has a different meaning; it explicitly presupposes the active involvement of the learner in the process of acquiring knowledge.

2 Code refers to the principles regulating meaning systems; the general principles underlying the transformation of knowledge.

References

Ashwin, P. (2009) *Analysing Teaching-learning Interactions in Higher Education: Accounting for Structure and Agency*, London: Continuum.

Baldwin, S. (2010) 'Teachers' and students relationship with knowledge': an exploration of the organisation of knowledge within disciplinary and educational contexts, Unpublished PhD thesis: Lancaster University.

Ball, S. J. (2006) *Education Policy and Social Class. The Selected Works of Stephen J Ball*, London and New York: Routledge.

Bernstein, B. (1971) 'On the classification and framing of educational knowledge', In M.F.D. Young (ed.) *Knowledge and Control: New Directions for the Sociology of Education*, London: Collier MacMillan.

Bernstein, B. (1990) *The Structuring of Pedagogic Discourse*, London: Routledge.

Bernstein, B. (1996) *Pedagogy, Symbolic Control and Identity: Theory, Research, Critique*, London: Taylor & Francis.

Bernstein, B. (1999) 'Vertical and horizontal discourses: an essay', *British Journal of Sociology of Education*, 20 (2), 157–73.

Bernstein, B. (2000) *Pedagogy, Symbolic Control and Identity* 2nd edn, Oxford: Rowman and Littlefield.

Bertram, C. (2012) 'Bernstein's theory of the pedagogic device as a frame to study history curriculum reform in South Africa', *Yesterday & Today*, 7, 1–22.

Brooks, C. (2016) *Teacher Subject Identity in Professional Practice: Teaching with a Professional Compass*, London: Routledge.

Davies, B. (2006) 'Understanding policy, understanding pedagogic discourse', in J. Fitz, B. Davies and J. Evans (eds.) *Educational Policy and Social Reproduction Class Inscription and Symbolic Control*, London: Routledge.

Davies, P. and Hughes, J. (2009) 'The fractured arm of government and the premature end of lifelong learning', *Journal of Education Policy*, 24, 595–610.

Department for Education (DfE) (2010) *The Importance of Teaching: Schools White Paper*, Norwich: The Stationery Office.

Department for Education (DfE), 2016 *Educational Excellence Everywhere*: Schools White Paper, Norwich: The Stationery Office.

Firth, R. (2011) 'Making geography visible as an object of study in the secondary school curriculum', *Curriculum Journal*, 22 (3), 289–316.

Hoadley, U. and Muller, J. (2010) 'Codes, pedagogy and knowledge advances in Bernsteinian sociology of education', in M. W. Apple, S. J. Ball and L. A. Gandin (eds.) *The Routledge International Handbook of the Sociology of Education*, London: Routledge.

Ivinson, G. and Duveen, G. (2009) 'Children's recontextualisations of pedagogy', in R. Moore, M. Arnot, J. Beck and H. Daniels (eds.) *Knowledge, Power and Educational Reform*, London: Routledge.

Lambert, D. (2016) 'Geography', in D. Wyse, L. Hayward and J. Pandya. (eds.) *The Sage Handbook of Curriculum, Pedagogy and Assessment*, London: Sage Publications.

Lambert, D. (2017) 'The road to future 3: the case of geography', in D. Guile, D. Lambert and M. Reiss. (eds.) (2017) *Sociology, Curriculum Studies and Professional Knowledge: New Perspectives on the Work of Michael Young*, London: Routledge.

Lauder, H. (2008) Foreword, in M.F.D. Young (ed.), *Bringing Knowledge Back in: From Social Constructivism to Social Realism in the Sociology of Education*, London: Routledge.

Luckett, K. (2009) 'The relationship between knowledge structure and curriculum: a case study in sociology', *Studies in Higher Education*, 34 (4), 441–53.

Maton, K. (2006) 'On knowledge structures and knower structures', in R. Moore, M. Arnot, J. Beck, and H. Daniels (eds.) *Knowledge, Power and Educational Reform: Applying the Sociology of Basil Bernstein*, London: Routledge.

Maton, K. (2014) *Knowledge and Knowers: Towards a Realist Sociology of Education*, London: Routledge.

Maton, K. and Moore, R. (eds.) (2010) *Social Realism, Knowledge and the Sociology of Education Coalitions of the Mind*, London: Continuum.

Moore, R. (2004) *Education and Society: Issues and Explanations in the Sociology of Education*, Cambridge: Polity Press.

Moore, R., Arnot, M., Beck, J. and Daniels, H. (2006) 'Introduction' in R. Moore, M. Arnot, J. Beck, and H. Daniels (eds.) *Knowledge, Power and Educational Reform: Applying the Sociology of Basil Bernstein*, London: Routledge.

Morgan, J. (2015) 'Michael young and the politics of the school curriculum', *British Journal of Educational Studies*, 63 (1), 5–22.

Morgan, J. (2014) 'Neither existence nor future': the social realist challenge to school geography, in B. Barrett and E. Rata, (eds.) *Knowledge and the Future of the Curriculum: International Studies in Social Realism*, Basingstoke: Palgrave Macmillan.

Muller, J. (2000) *Reclaiming Knowledge: Social theory, Curriculum and Education Policy*, London: RoutledgeFalmer.

Paechter, C. (1998) 'School and the ownership of knowledge', *Pedagogy, Culture and Society*, 6 (2), 161–76.

Rawling, E. (2001) *Changing the Subject: The Impact of National Policy on School Geography 1980–2000*, Sheffield: Geographical Association.

Sadovnik, A. (2001) 'Basil Bernstein (1924-2000)', *Prospects: The Quarterly Review of Comparative Education*, Paris, UNESCO: International Bureau of Education), 31 (4), 687–703.

Singh, P. (2002) 'Pedagogising knowledge: Bernstein's theory of the pedagogic device', *British Journal of Sociology of Education*, 23 (4), 571–82.

Stengel, B. S. (1997) 'Academic discipline' and 'school subject': contestable curricular concepts, *Journal of Curriculum Studies*, 29 (5), 585–602.

Vernon, E. (2016) 'The structure of knowledge: does theory matter?' *Geography*, 101 (2), 100–4.

Vorster, J. and Quinn, L. (2012) 'Theorising the pedagogy of a formal programme for university lecturers, in L. Quinn (ed.) *Reimagining Academic Staff Development: Spaces for Disruption*, Stellenbosch: Sun Press.

Wheelahan, L. (2010) *Why Knowledge Matters in Curriculum: A Social Realist Argument*, London: Routledge.

Wright, R. and Froehlich, H. (2012) 'Basil Bernstein's theory of the pedagogic device and formal music schooling: putting the theory into practice', *Theory into Practice*, 51 (3), 212–20.

Young, M.F.D. (2008a) *Bringing Knowledge Back In: From Social Constructivism to Social Realism in the Sociology of Education*, London: Routledge.

Young, M.F.D. (2008b) 'From constructivism to realism in the sociology of the curriculum', *Review of Research in Education* 32 (1), 1–28.

Young, M. and Lambert, D. (with Roberts, C. and Roberts, M.) (2014) *Knowledge and the Future School: Curriculum and Social Justice*, London: Bloomsbury Academic.

Chapter 21

Are we thinking geographically?

John Morgan

> On holiday once in Svalbard I spent some time collecting rubbish from the beach. It was stuff that had, apparently, been discarded in Florida and which had travelled there on the North Atlantic Drift ... Just picking it up – and given a geographical imagination that began in my schooldays – evoked a real sense of locatedness on the planet.
>
> (Doreen Massey, 2014, p. 39)

Introduction

It is a truth universally acknowledged that geography is a subject that gets students to 'think'. It would be hard to imagine any geography teacher admitting otherwise! However, it is not always self-evident what we mean by *thinking geographically*. This chapter adopts a social-historical approach which is not that common in discussions of geographical education. This approach is based on the belief that is there is a tendency to imagine that teaching these days is 'better' or 'worse' or more or less based in knowledge about learning than it used to be. Taking a longer view provides a different way of approaching the problem.

This chapter is a second-take at the question: 'what does it means to think geographically? My first take was published in the first edition of *Debates in Geography Education* (Lambert and Jones, 2013) and took the form of a discussion of various attempts to define what it means to think geographically. This chapter serves as a 'prequel': in what follows, I want to explain why it is that we have come to be interested in the question of what it means to think geographically.

The education revolution

In *The Schooled Society* the sociologist David Baker (2014) sets out to demonstrate that the values and practices associated with education have come to dominate an increasingly large part of the globe. This, he argues, is an extraordinary development: in little over 200 years the values and assumptions of education (e.g. truth, reason, explanation etc.) have come to inform a wide range of institutions and organisations. One of the effects of this is the spread of what Baker terms a culture of cognition. He notes that the

> growth and intensity of science, rationalized inquiry, theory, empirical methods, all influenced and reinforced by an overarching cognitization of academic intelligence understood as empowering the educated to think more abstractly and assertively, are at the core of the epistemological revolution brought on by the education revolution.
>
> (pp. 190–91)

What this means is that 'traditional' mental skills such as recitation, disputation, memorisation, formalistic debate, formulae application, rote accuracy and authoritative text reading have been pushed aside as 'mental problem-solving, effortful reasoning, abstraction and higher-order thinking, and the active use of intelligence take centre stage' (ibid., p. 190). We have reached the point where it is assumed that from the youngest ages 'the student is an individual empowered to know, use, and even create knowledge' (ibid., p. 207).

On one level, it is possible to see geography education as an important and central element of this culture of cognition. Thus, traditional forms of geographical thinking, based on the rote memorisation and recall of facts and statistics have, over time, been replaced by approaches that favour synthesis, problem solving and reasoning. However, as I will argue in what follows, there is a paradox in that *as the culture of cognition has developed, geography educators have raised concerns that the specific nature of geographical thinking has been neglected or assumed to have become less important than more generic thinking skills.* This has led to calls by those in geographical education to more clearly define what it means to think geographically (e.g. Jackson, 2006).

The end of tradition

In his account of the making of human geography, Cox (2014) argues that the first half of the twentieth century can be seen as 'the quiet half century'. In that period, school geography was largely uncontroversial, sought to provide an accurate (if simplified) representation of the world, focused on human activity in its physical setting, avoid questions of morality, and offered limited reflection on aspects of political and social organisation. The textbook descriptions offered to pupils were framed within a broad narrative of human development and progress. This was 'traditional' geography. The subject was a popular option in schools, though not one that enjoyed particularly high status. It was based on a particular view of learning. As Hall wrote in 1989:

> Until the 1960s, learning in the geography classroom was the memorization of facts for their own sake ... as the mind was seen as a bucket, students were the recipients of second-hand information. Some buckets might be bigger

than others and less prone to leakage (memory failure): the best could not only store large quantities of it but sort and retrieve it in conversation or quiz questioning.

(Hall, 1989, p. 11)

A 'good' geography lesson was received by a quiet, attentive class. The teacher 'got through' a lot of material and ensured efficient coverage of the syllabus so that students were able to demonstrate knowledge in written tests.

The spatial and quantitative revolution

The 1960s were a period of curriculum innovation. The successful launch, by the Soviet Union, of the Sputnik satellite had prompted concern that Western nations were falling behind and that new investments in science and technology were required. Simultaneously, the post-war period had seen the growth and specialisation of knowledge which demanded curriculum reform, and new insights emerging from psychology suggested the need for changes in teaching and learning. As an academic discipline, geography was not immune to these influences, and the 'paradigm shift' from a regional (descriptive) approach to a systematic (scientific) approach meant it likely that new teachers – equipped with the new models and techniques- would seek to introduce these new ideas and methods to school geography.

The 'new geography' was a conceptual geography, as this statement from the introduction to one of the key texts of the new geography – *Settlement Patterns* – explained:

Teachers are beginning to realize that much of what is taught in our schools is purely repetitive and lacks intellectual stimulus and challenge to the student. Basic to these changes, we feel, is an ability on the part of student to appreciate fundamental concepts in geography: those concerned with space, location and interactions through time.

(Everson and Fitzgerald, 1969, p. 1)

The new geography in schools was aided by state-sponsored curriculum development, itself a response to the perceived need to develop a more skilled and scientifically literate population to meet the needs of a rapidly changing society. In school geography, what Biddle (1985, p. 27) had called 'serious concerns' about the quality of geographical education, were reflected in governmental publications that sought to argue for, and introduce, the new approaches to teachers. The Schools Council funded a series of curriculum development projects that sought to raise the professional status of geography teaching and bring the subject into line with the requirements of a modern, rational, technological society. In the process, insights from the newly dominant psychology of education were influential in schools. Rather than being a simple transmission of knowledge from the teacher to the pupil, learning was linked to complex processes of development. The key figures here were Piaget and Bruner, both of whom saw the development of the individual child in interaction with the learning environment. Learning was to be structured logically. There seems little doubt that, where these ideas were taken up, the quality of thinking in geography lessons was greatly improved.

All these developments were taking place under conditions of educational expansion. The idea that all children should stay in school for longer required new schools and more and better trained teachers, and it is no coincidence that the founding texts of 'modern' geography education – by David Hall (1976), Norman Graves (1975) and Bill Marsden (1976) – were all published in the aftermath of the James Report (DES, 1972), which recommended that teaching should be a graduate profession, leading to the establishment of university departments of education. These books repay careful study, and remain the best examples we have of how the ideas of developmental psychologists can be applied to geographical teaching and learning.

The emergence of a distinct field of study known as 'geography education' represented an important shift in control of the nature of geography teaching from university geography departments to education departments. In Britain, the central debates about schooling from the mid-1960s were concerned with whether or not increased educational provision was leading to greater levels of social equality. The main focus of these debates was between sociologists and language experts at the University of London's Institute of Education. In the mid-1960s, Basil Bernstein studied and documented the speech patterns and codes of children in different parts of London. He developed the idea – subsequently transmitted to generations of school teachers – of the 'elaborated' and 'restricted' codes. Bernstein's work was controversial, especially in the eyes of influential teacher educators such as Harold Rosen, who argued that Bernstein's work led to a pessimistic assessment of the possibilities of social mobility based upon a deficit view of childhood. Rosen and colleagues worked with ideas developed from Lev Vygotsky, who stressed the intimate relation between language and thought. It is important to remember that Vygotsky was also a psychologist, but his work developed from Piaget to include the notion that a child's intellectual development could be accelerated through careful structuring of the pedagogical environment – notably the idea of the ZPD (the Zone of Proximal Development). The important point was that children from working-class homes possessed a particular linguistic repertoire which should be seen as the starting point for educational development, and certainly not as an inhibitor. This work developed around language in classrooms, notably that of Douglas Barnes and colleagues and which was given official recognition in the Bullock Report of 1975 – *A Language for Life*. Though geography educators were not centrally involved in these debates, the subsequent 'language across the curriculum' projects involved geography educators such as Michael Williams, Margaret Roberts, and Frances Slater.

Thus, by the end of the 1970s, the nature of geography teaching in schools had radically changed. Indeed, at the end of two decades of curriculum modernisation,

Leslie Jay portrayed, with a touch of regret, the changing scene of geography teaching in schools:

> In the days when pupils were expected to be docile recipients of information conveyed by their teachers the fashionable mode of instruction was to enforce the learning by heart of geographical locations and resources country by country ... In recent years, however, the teaching of geography has undergone a conceptual revolution and the current vogue is for problem-solving and hypothesis testing ... Associated with the emergence of these new concepts and skills is a changed relationship between teachers and pupils, less formal than before, in which children are more vocal in expressing their opinions and preferences.
>
> (Jay, 1980, pp. 129–30)

The retreat from reason

So far, this story is one of gradual progress in how geography teachers encourage geographical thinking. The developments described above are in line with Baker's notion of the culture of cognition associated with the education revolution. It is away from traditional forms of thinking and towards abstraction – expressed in the idea that geography teaching should be concerned with concepts. However, there are other layers of complexity that need to be woven into this account.

At the same time that geography educators in university departments of education were discovering psychology and rational curriculum planning as the basis for teaching in schools, geography as an academic discipline was changing. The so-called 'new geography', with its focus on generalisation, scientific models and measurable facts, was challenged by the rise of humanistic and radical philosophies, which rejected the notion that there existed one single approach to geographical material. It was recognised that places and landscapes were imbued with meaning, and indeed were a reflection of human values. Geographical issues were based around conflicts and political viewpoints. This required new types of thought: it was not simply a case of examining the facts and evidence and reaching the best decision, but about understanding people's (both individual and social groups) values. This gave rise to the introduction of values analysis into school geography. This was a key moment of change in the nature of geographical thinking, one that is best expressed in Frances Slater's (1983) *Learning through Geography*. More than any other text in the Anglo-speaking geographical education, Slater's book centres on the tension between objective and subjective ways of seeing the world:

> 'geography as science' and 'geography as personal response' to the environment both have a part to play in developing student understanding ... both logical positivism and humanism have a contribution to make to geography.
>
> (Slater, 1983, p. 1)

Significantly, Slater's book was one of the first to draw upon the early ideas about language and learning and developed one of the clearest accounts of enquiry learning. In terms of learning, Slater was making an early argument for a social constructivist view of learning. Constructivism was associated with the psychologists she cited in the index to *Learning through Geography* (Piaget, Bruner, Ausubel and Gagne), but the model of enquiry that she developed is much more rooted in a form of social constructivism – though at this point Vygotsky is not mentioned.

Taken together, the notion that learning is a process of construction and that geographical knowledge is relative, have emerged as the key elements of any contemporary answer to what it means to 'think geographically'. Whilst Frances Slater's book is full of geographical knowledge and examples, it represents a 'text of the break': in future, there would be more emphasis on 'thinking', and less on the 'geography'.

Thinking through geography or just thinking?

In 1997, geography educator David Leat wrote that:

> I would argue that there is a particularly serious problem in some geography teaching. Essentially, there is too much concern with teaching and not enough with learning, too much emphasis on substantive aspects of geography and not enough on the intellectual development of pupils.
>
> (Leat, 1997, p. 143)

Leat outlined a series of problems he saw as befalling geography teaching in the mid-1990s, before arguing for an approach based on different assumptions. He argued that intelligence is not fixed and can be developed and that the curriculum for lower-achieving pupils should be aimed at changing the characteristics of the learners. The evidence for this came from various cognitive acceleration projects that were taking place in Mathematics and Science education (Adey and Shayer, 1994). Leat's arguments resonated with many geography teachers in schools, and his ideas were aided by an effective programme of professional development so that, by the year 2000 when I was visiting student teachers in Bristol and its region, it was rare to find a geography department where the activities in *Thinking through Geography* (Leat, 1998) and *More Thinking through Geography* (Nichols, 2001) were not being adopted.

Thinking through Geography was based on a distinctive theory of what it meant to 'think', explained under the headings of 'constructivism', 'challenge', 'talk between pupils and between teacher and pupils', 'concept elaboration', 'debriefing', 'metacognition', 'transfer', and 'appealing to all the senses'.

Although this seems like a clear statement, it is now clear that (intentionally or not) the activities were more likely to prompt 'thinking about thinking' than about what it means to 'think geographically'. An example is the activity in

More Thinking through Geography where students are presented with a structured decision-making exercise in which a male worker is offered a job in the north-east of England. This means the family will have to move house and the students have to decide what is the 'best option' for the family, based on a range of data. Once they have made their decision, the teacher complicates the situation by providing more information about the wants and feelings of the family members. Invariably this led to a rethinking of the original decision. This is an interesting activity, but the question remains: are students thinking geographically? If they are, it is within a limited positivist and behaviourist view of the housing market and its geographies. *Really* thinking geographically about this might involve understanding something of the historical and regional development of the job market (e.g. male and female labour, job mobility) and the geographies of the housing market (tenure, quality, politics of provision etc.) The point I want to emphasise is that an influential model of *thinking* did not deem it necessary to develop complex *geographical thought* (though no doubt some skilled teachers would have sought to do this).

Expansive education

In retrospect, *Thinking through Geography's* approach was indicative of a wider set of ideas about learning associated in the late 1990s and 2000s with the drive to 'raise standards' and modernise 'pedagogy'. Indeed, the approach became an important element in the National Key Stage 3 'strategies' and the popular adoption in schools of the ideas of 'learning styles' and 'learning to learn', and Howard Gardner's notion of 'multiple intelligences', and, later Carol Dweck's (2006) idea of 'mindsets'. These ideas were popularised by enterprising commentators such as Guy Claxton, who suggested that they amounted to nothing less than the need to redefine 'the point of school':

> Education is above all a preparation for the future. Its core purpose is to give all young people the confidence and capacity to flourish in the world they are going to inhabit.
>
> (Dweck, 2006, p. 3)

For Lucas et al., (2013) expansive education:

> takes us beyond the realms of knowledge, understanding and even of skills. Resourcefulness, discernment, fortitude and friendship are not mere skills: they are composed of attitudes, values, interests and habitual ways of meeting the world.
>
> (p. 70)

These statements, whilst in line with Baker's optimistic view of the culture of cognition, are generic and offer little in the way of helping teachers answer the question of what it means to 'think geographically'. The problem for many geography educators is that at the same time as there is a desire to focus on 'learning', there is little incentive to develop an understanding of what it means to think geographically.

The return to knowledge?

It is in this context that there have, in recent years, been calls for a return to 'knowledge' in discussions of school geography, countering the view, promoted by influential writers such as John Hattie, that learning is essentially a 'visible' (i.e. measurable and replicable) process (Hattie, 2009). The most prominent voice in this debate in school geography is David Lambert, who, in a series of articles and chapters published in the last decade, has argued that school geography would benefit from agreement about what would constitute a curriculum of core knowledge. In his inaugural professorial lecture at the University of London Institute of Education, Lambert (2009) described the retreat from the idea that school subjects provide the basic 'knowledge and understanding' that underpin the curriculum. Against this, curriculum policy is increasingly based on the assumption that advanced Western economies are moving towards a 'knowledge-based economy' where the skills of information literacy and 'learning how to learn' are more important than the content of learning. Lambert argues that one of the contemporary challenges for geography teachers, as curriculum makers, is to work out the nature of their relationship with the discipline of geography, based on the proviso that, since, 'Geography is a moving, changing and sometimes restless idea' there can be no easy return to a 'traditional' definition of the subject. Lambert is acutely aware of the importance of metaphors and how they help to construct geography teachers' understanding of their work. During his tenure as Chief Executive of the Geographical Association between 2001 and 2012, Lambert sought to make a strong case for geography as 'the curriculum resource, *par excellence*'. The first aspect of this was the argument that geography education should allow students to 'think geographically', or to 'apply knowledge and conceptual understanding to new settings'. The second metaphor that has gained some currency is the idea of 'Living geography' which seeks perceptive and deep description of the real world and which 'seeks explanations about how the world works and helps us to think about alternative futures' (Geographical Association, 2009).

At present these are more aspirational labels than fully developed approaches (though see Lambert's recent work with others on www.geocapabilities.org). They attempt to develop a view of school geographical knowledge which avoids the pitfalls of 'traditional' approaches and also the process-based pedagogy which denies the centrality of knowledge. The aim is to counter a discourse which over-emphasises learning as constructivist, learner-centred and technology based to the extent that knowledge becomes a means to an end, rather than an end in itself. Lambert seeks to establish the 'core' knowledge that could become the basis for the school curriculum, but one that is based on 'concepts' that can enable students to 'think geographically'.

A forlorn hope?

Such calls for a return to geographical thinking are brave and principled. However, I am not optimistic that they are likely to be realised any time soon. I have never been one for those slogans that tell us 'geography is everywhere', or 'without geography, you're lost'. Instead, I am taken by John Pickles' argument, way back in 1985 that 'society gets the kind of geography it deserves'. If there has been a long-term decline in the importance of geographical thinking, then this reflects something of what society thinks is valid. It may be that we are seeing the 'cultural production of geographical ignorance' (Morgan, forthcoming). Now, it may be that ignorance is not always a bad thing; the interesting question is why it has come about that certain forms of knowledge are not important anymore? What are the circumstances that lead to loss or forgetting of certain forms of geographical knowledge?

In this chapter, I have begun to sketch something of an answer to this question. Prior to the Second World War, those who went to school could expect to be provided with a relatively detailed world geographical knowledge (of a particular kind). The expansion of schooling in the post-war period presented a challenge to this vision, where internationally there were moves towards social studies and subject integration. School Geography resisted this tendency, and instead aligned itself with developments within the academic discipline which were becoming increasingly based on abstraction and models. However, as the pace of social changed quickened, these had limited appeal to many students, especially as the world outside the classroom seemed beset by more urgent problems, and geographers themselves became interested in political issues and values. The 'long march' away from knowledge was perhaps prefigured in Frances Slater's fine book *Learning through Geography*, but by the 1990s handbooks that promised advice on 'learning to teach geography' were more about just 'learning to teach'. These changes coincided with important shifts in the knowledge landscape, including the rise of commercial forms of knowledge, the validation of popular or everyday knowledge(s), and the heightened interest in 'other' (previously marginalised) geographies. Teacher education became increasingly dominated by forms of constructivism, which held that knowledge was relative and 'produced' rather than 'transmitted'. The advent of newer technologies and the reinvention of psychology under conditions that are obsessed with therapeutic ideas of the social and emotional aspects of learning, and with notions of 'learnable intelligence' have further consolidated the moves away from 'disciplined' thinking. Geography education, lacking a long tradition and culture of research, has been particularly susceptible to this process. I hope this chapter will encourage readers to reflect on the paradox at the heart of this process.

Key readings

1   Dorling, D. and Lee, C. (2016) *Geography*, London: Profile. This short book provides a 'case for geography' as the subject most able to help us make

sense of a rapidly changing and interconnected world. It suggests that the concepts of globalisation, sustainability, equality and futures are central to the discipline.

2   Lambert, D. (2017) 'Thinking Geographically' in M. Jones (ed.) *The Handbook of Secondary Geography*, Sheffield: Geographical Association. This chapter provides an accessible synthesis of perspectives on how to express what it means to 'think geographically'. It draws on several sources (including Morgan, 2013).

References

Adey, P. and Shayer, M. (1994) *Really Raising Standards: Cognitive Intervention and Academic Achievement*, London: Routledge.

Baker, D. (2014) *The Schooled Society: The Educational Transformation Of Global Culture*, Stanford CA: California University Press.

Biddle, D. S. (1985) 'Paradigms and geography curricula in England and Wales 1882–1972' in D. Boardman (ed.) *New Directions in Geographical Education*, Lewes: The Falmer Press, 11–33.

Cox, K. (2014) *Making Human Geography*, New York: Guilford Press.

Department of Education and Science (DES) (1972) *Teacher Education and Training. Report by a Committee of Inquiry appointed by the Secretary of State for Education and Science, under the Chairmanship of Lord James of Rusholme*, London: HMSO.

Dweck, C. (2006) *Mindset: The New Psychology Of Success*, New York: Ballantine Books.

Everson, J.A. and Fitzgerald, B.P. (1969) *Settlement Patterns*, London: Longman.

Geographical Association (2009) *A Different View: A Manifesto from the Geographical Association*, Sheffield: Geographical Association.

Graves, N. (1975) *Geography and Education*, London: Heinemann.

Hall, D. (1976) *Geography and the Geography Teacher*, London: George Allen and Unwin.

Hall, D. (1989) 'Knowledge and teaching styles in the geography classroom' in J. Fien, R. Gerber and P. Wilson (eds.) *The Geography Teacher's Guide To The Classroom* (2nd edn), South Melbourne: Macmillan Education Australia, pp. 10–21.

Hattie, J. (2009) *Visible Learning*, London: Routledge.

Jackson, P. (2006) 'Thinking geographically', *Geography*, 91, (3), 199–204.

Jay, L. (1980) *Geography Teaching – With A Little Latitude*, London: George Allen.

Lambert, D. (2009) *Geography in Education: Lost in the Post?* Inaugural Lecture, London: Institute of Education, University of London.

Lambert, D. and Jones, M. (eds.) *Debates in Geography Education*, London: Routledge.

Leat, D. (1997) 'Cognitive acceleration in geography education', in D. Tilbury and M. Williams (eds.), *Teaching and Learning Geography*, London: Routledge.

Leat, D. (1998) *Thinking through Geography*, Cambridge: Chris Kington Publications.

Lucas, B., Claxton, G. and Spencer, E. (2013) *Expansive Education: Teaching Learners for the Real World*, Victoria AU: ACER.

Massey, D. (2014) 'Taking on the world', *Geography: An International Journal*, 99 (1), 36–9.

Marsden, W. (1976) *Evaluating the Geography Curriculum*, Edinburgh: Oliver and Boyd.

Morgan, J. (2013) 'What do we mean by thinking geographically?' in D. Lambert and M. Jones (eds.) *Debates in Geography Education*, London: Routledge.

Morgan, J. (forthcoming) 'The making of geographical ignorance', *Geography* 102, xx, yy–zz.

Nichols, A. (2001) *More Thinking through Geography*, Cambridge: Chris Kington Publications.

Slater, F. (1983) *Learning through Geography*, London: Heinemann Educational Books.

Chapter 22

Evidence-based practice and research in geography education

Roger Firth and Clare Brooks

The idea that professional practices such as education should be based upon or at least be informed by evidence continues to capture the imagination of many politicians, policy makers, practitioners and researchers. There is growing evidence of the influence of this line of thought. At the same time there is a growing body of work that has raised fundamental questions about the feasibility of the idea of evidence-based or evidence informed practice.

(Biesta, 2010, p. 491)

The relationship between research, policy and practice has been high on the agenda in education for a number of years now. Within this agenda the idea that teaching should develop into a so-called 'evidence-based' profession with a strong emphasis on student outcomes 'has become influential in many countries around the world' (Biesta, 2010, p. 491). Hammersley (2001), as Biesta, provides a critique of evidence-based practice, analysing it as a neoliberal managerialist strategy, and points out that

the movement for evidence-based practice, for enhanced use of research evidence in the work of the professions, started in medicine in the early 1990s. It has grown in influence there, and spread across a number of other fields, including education.

(Hammersley, 2001 p. 1)

In response to government policy (DfE, 2013a, b, 2014) and the establishment of a more devolved and autonomous education system in England, there has been ever more emphasis to make the best use of evidence about 'what works' in improving educational outcomes for all young people 'in a context where policy makers claim to be no longer bound by ideology and thus free to act on the basis of the best available evidence' (Ozga, 2004, p. 2). As a result of the recent establishment of 'Teaching Schools' and 'Teaching School Alliances', which are a central part of the government's aim to give schools a central role in raising standards by developing a self-improving, evidence-based sustainable school-led system, there are signs of an emerging infrastructure for research development and engagement in schools. The increasing emphasis of impact on change as a purpose of research raises questions about appropriate research methodologies (set-up, design and evaluation).

A significant motivation for the initiation of a national 2-year research programme in 2014, *Closing the Gap: Test and Learn*,[1] framed within externally set parameters through the National College for Teaching and Leadership (NCTL) and in association with Teaching Schools and Alliances, was to stimulate schools involvement with and in research. The programme brought together the Coalition government's commitment to close the attainment gap for disadvantaged pupils and the policy priority of developing teaching into a research and evidence-informed profession – a policy priority since 1997. The government's intention was both to focus on impact and to strengthen the 'scientific assurance' of teachers' use of research and evident knowledge for professional practice and to stimulate 'robust' school-led research and development headed by outstanding schools. The programme involved the large scale trialling of seven pedagogic interventions simultaneously across over 700 schools using randomised control trials (RCTs). Alongside this, teachers were trained to design and conduct their own small-scale RCTs, which were funded by 'early-adopter' grants (50 were developed).

Teachers, needless to say, need to be convinced about having a sound evidence base for pedagogical practice. 'We know that teachers' opinions and values about research are the most important predictor of their evidence use' (NFER, 2014, p. 19); but given what Nieveen and Kuiper (2012) describe as 'output regulation' manifested through high levels of external accountability, teacher engagement in, and with research, is experiencing a strong pull towards school improvement approaches related to the dictum 'what works'.[2] It is illustrative of the way teachers' professional knowledge has become a matter of public and political interest.

The chapter is an upshot of government attempts to 'support' and 'enable' school-led research, the emerging school infrastructure for research development and engagement, the recent BERA-RSA Inquiry into *Research and the Teaching Profession* and Morgan's (2015) criticisms of research in geography education. In addition, the authors' reviews within their respective universities of Masters-based teacher research in geography education and its contribution to professional learning inform the discussion. Both courses reflect a commitment to teacher research which stems from Stenhouse's (1981) ideas of the 'teacher as researcher' and professional learning.[3]

The chapter takes a critical look at the idea of evidence-based practice and its significance for teachers understanding of educational research. It discusses a number of assumptions that inform the ways in which government has promoted and implemented the idea of evidence-based practice. It argues the need for a broader articulation of school/teacher-led research less closely aligned to government policy and particular forms of practice. Of central relevance to the contemporary evidence-based practice debate is the broader debate about the kind of epistemologies that might be appropriate for an adequate understanding of the role of knowledge in professional action.

Recent debate

Doubts about the quality and value of educational research to inform practice and policy in education and teacher education are not new, and neither is the debate about the need for an evidence-based teaching profession. These were highlighted throughout the 1990s and diverse perspectives on educational research were thrown into sharp relief. These doubts 'were not only raised by policy makers and educational practitioners ... they also came from within the educational research community itself' (Biesta, 2007, p. 1). The 1996 lecture to the Teacher Training Agency by David Hargreaves, an educational researcher himself, is regarded by many as the prompt that sowed the seeds for the 'evidence into education' movement (NFER, 2014, p. v). A number of other damning and controversial criticisms and reports followed, including Tooley and Darby (1998) for the Office for Standards in Education (OfSTED) and Hillage et al. (1998) for the Department for Education and Employment (DfEE). It became a particular issue for the New Labour Government of the time 'with its proclaimed commitment to evidence-informed policy and its emphasis on finding out and disseminating what works' (Whitty, 2006, p. 159). 'Many argued that in the 1990s the critiques of research smoothed the way for values such as performative accountability, "what works" and "value for money"' (Oancea, 2014, p. 510) – a move towards a re-professionalisation that was closer to governmental values and priorities.

Since 2010, government policy has seen the debate reinvigorated. Of particular note is the impact of Ben Goldacre's (2013) paper: *Building Evidence into Education*. Goldacre was commissioned by the former Secretary of State for Education Michael Gove to examine the role of evidence in the education sector. Goldacre is a British physician and academic who has written about 'Bad Science'. He draws parallels between evidence-based practice in the medical profession and education arguing 'that the education profession is still far from evidence based, despite the range of programmes developed during the 1990s and 2000s designed to mobilise knowledge within the profession' (NFER, 2014, p. v). He favours an approach where RCTs and other forms of experimental research are a key foundation of a research-based education profession. A number of policy documents emphasise this standpoint (see DfE, 2013a, b). Goldacre's views continue to capture the mindset of many politicians and policy makers. RCTs and experimental designs are considered the gold standard in research and evaluation. These research designs have become all but synonymous with evidence-based practice; they define what counts as 'rigorous' research and how evidence-based practice should be implemented.

BERA-RSA Inquiry

The publication of the Final Report (BERA-RSA, 2014) marked the end of an 18-month inquiry looking at the contribution research can make to

> the development of teachers' professional identity and practice, to the quality of teaching, to the broader project of school improvement and transformation, and, critically, to the outcomes for learners ... especially those for whom the education system does not currently 'deliver'.
>
> (p. 3)

The Report draws on a substantial domestic and international evidence base and presents a range of stakeholder views (classroom practitioners, school leaders, senior inspectors, local and national policy makers) about the evidence collected during the inquiry. The recommendations are jurisdiction-specific, recognising the distinctive practitioner and policy maker situations in England, Scotland, Wales and Northern Ireland; each facing different challenges and beginning from different starting points. In relation to vision and principles the Report makes the observation that

> *all* teachers and school and college leaders now have much greater access to data than was the case only a decade or so ago, and ... while many teachers are now much better at working with data, they typically do so from an institution-specific, rather than system-wide, perspective. Further, while this new confidence with data is to be welcomed, it is only one pillar of a broader research-rich culture.
>
> (p. 24)

The Report brings a broad, inclusive and collaborative definition to the term research and moves from an emphasis on evidence to a focus on action and makes the case for the development, across the UK,

> of self-improving education systems in which all teachers become research literate and many have frequent opportunities for engagement in research and enquiry. This requires that schools and colleges become research-rich environments in which to work. It also requires that teacher researchers and the wider research community work in partnership, rather than in separate and sometimes competing universes. Finally, it demands an end to the false dichotomy between HE and school-based approaches to initial teacher education.
>
> (p. 5)

This, as the Report states, 'is the essence of what ... educational professionals in the UK need to be able – and must be *enabled* – to do, whatever the national setting they work in and whatever the educational challenges and statutory frameworks they are required to address' (p. 4).[4] The BERA-RSA Inquiry is seen as marking an important step in the future development of the teaching profession in the United Kingdom.[5]

Geography education research as a field of study

In 2010, Lambert commented on the condition of geography education research as a field of study, emphasising there was more research being done than two decades previously. However, he also observed, comparatively speaking, it was also 'self-evident that geography education research [did] not easily measure up' (p. 84) and furthermore, 'this state of comparative weakness ... is not going to change any time soon' (ibid.). Butt (2015) gives a similar assessment of the state of research in geography education, commenting

> unfortunately [it] sits rather uneasily within the domain of educational research. It has not traditionally attracted much government funding council money, large scale research projects are unusual, with most research being produced as small-scale, practitioner-based, unfunded work.
>
> (Butt, 2015, p. 7)

In discussing the 'usefulness' of research Brooks (2015) observes that 'there is a gap between the work of educational researchers and the experience of practitioners [and] within the field ... this gap is arguably even wider' (p. 34).

Taking up Lambert's (2010) emphasis on the importance of 'making the most of what we have and the opportunities that may arise to strengthen what we have' (p. 84) attention is drawn to some international developments. Of particular note is the International Geographical Union Commission on Geographical Education (IGU-CGE, 2015) *International Declaration on Research in Geography Education,* which supports and promotes research in geography education in all nations and cross-nationally and encourages those in positions of influence at institutional, regional, national and international levels to consider the ways in which geography education research can be fostered, to the ultimate benefit of young people, teachers, schools and societies.

In the USA the *Road Map for 21st century Geography Education* articulates a strategic vision and research agenda to develop and grow the status and quality of classroom-based practice (see Bednarz et al., 2013). The report downplays the importance of practitioner research and focuses on 'what works' and developing research instruments that can be replicated in a variety of contexts. In other areas such as Turkey (see Demirci and Tuna, 2017), geography education is a more diverse area of scholarship with much new research in the field, using a variety of methodologies and approaches (although this trend may have been assuaged due to political events). China has seen the development of research active centres within universities and the reporting (publication) of research by Masters students. The nature of this research is focussed on extended study into the micro features of classroom practice around particular geographical topics, a stark contrast to the approach promoted in the USA. The approach, purpose and focus of research in geography education can therefore be influenced by local agendas.

Methodism in the field

In a recent publication by Butt (2015), which aims to support teachers who are undertaking research in geography education, Morgan describes much research in geography education as 'Methodist'. By this he means 'that much discussion of research in geography education is subject to an ideology which encourages an overly respectful and unnecessary attention to questions of method' (p. 145). Quite properly, he argues, teachers

> undertaking 'research' in geography education are keen to ensure that their research is rigorous and high quality. The problem is not identifying something worthwhile about their practice to research, but making sure that what they are doing is seen as research.
>
> (Morgan, 2015, p. 145)

He thinks 'that the effects of Methodism on geography education research are corrosive' (p. 146); it 'tends to encourage conformity and a narrow focus on the type of questions that can be asked and researched' (ibid.); it seeks to 'problem solve' rather than 'problem pose' (ibid.). His hope is that those who read *MasterClass in Geography Education: Transforming Teaching and Learning* (Butt, 2015) prior to undertaking research will be attentive to any signs of Methodism. But he is uneasy about the positioning of teacher research, whether by government policy or postgraduate (PGCE and Masters-level) courses and the writings of academics who unwittingly promote Methodism for the reasons outlined below.

The attraction of Methodism in geography education research is explained by Morgan in relation to the fact that it 'is a young field, with relatively low status within the academy' (p. 145) and "suffers from 'status anxiety'" about the products of its research' (ibid.). In addition, 'the field is populated by former schoolteachers and in universities is closely linked with teacher training' (ibid.). In consequence, 'it tends to follow trends in education as a whole' and 'has become closely geared to particular forms of practice' (ibid.). Further, 'it is generally agreed that the goal of such research is to improve outcomes or, more generally, improve the quality of teaching and learning in classrooms. The dominance ... of "evidence-based" practice ensures that there is a search for reliable and verifiable evidence based on "sound" methods' (ibid.).

Many of those who contributed to the recent BERA-RSA Inquiry into the Role of Research in Teacher Education 'were deeply concerned by the emergence of an environment, often narrowly data-driven, that appears to militate against teachers' engagement in more open forms of research and enquiry'

(BERA-RSA, 2014, p. 11). Morgan's discussion of Methodism both echoes and alerts us to this concern and like the Inquiry's Final Report seeks to encourage 'a broad and inclusive definition to the term 'research' (2014, p.5) and its purposes. It is also a wakeup call for the field.

Discussion

The idea that teachers ought to teach based on the best evidence available is intuitively appealing and is gaining increasing acceptance. It is a common sense idea that is likely to be viewed favourably by researchers, funders, practitioners, policy makers and parents alike. To request that, whenever feasible, teachers use the best research evidence about the likely benefits of an intervention is a sensible request that can be justified on both ethical and financial grounds. As Hammersley (2001) argues, however, the term evidence-based practice 'is a slogan whose rhetorical effect is to discredit opposition. After all, who would argue that practice should not be based on evidence? ... So there is an implication built into the phrase "evidence-based practice" that opposition to it can only be irrational ... In political terms, as a way of mobilising support, the use of such [an] opposition-excluding label is no doubt a highly effective rhetorical strategy' (p. 1).

One outcome of ongoing debate is that some advocates of an evidence-based approach in education now talk in a more meaningful way about the relationship between research, policy and practice, using notions such as 'evidence-informed' and 'evidence-influenced' practice. At face value such approaches do suggest a certain understanding of the complex ways in which research might inform policy and practice. However, they are at odds with the role that is ascribed to research by government policy. 'As a result, even more than before, we have a label that systematically obscures the grounds on which there might be reasonable disagreement with what is proposed' (ibid.).

Many questions have been raised about the appropriateness of the evidence-based approach for the field of education. Some have questioned the use of a biomedical approach (and the theoretical models underpinning it) as a framework that can simply be applied to any field of professional activity, including education, or whether it is a framework that brings with it a particular view of professional practice. Having said this, evidence-based medicine does 'take a more considered approach to the use of research evidence in medical practice, which is mainly due to the fact that evidence-based medicine was developed in the context of clinical problem solving ... research evidence is seen as one factor in a process of clinical decision making, rather than the only factor to drive clinical practice' (Biesta, 2007, p. 11).

In education the policy argument seems less nuanced: 'There seems to be an almost unanimous expectation that research can tell us "what works", that it can provide "sound evidence" about the likely effects of policy and practice, and "sound evidence of effectiveness" more generally' (Biesta, 2007, p. 12).

And 'central to evidence-based practice is the idea of *effective intervention*' (p. 7). Whether these expectations are justified ultimately depends on the ontological and epistemological assumptions one brings to the understanding of what research can achieve.

The ontological and epistemological assumption behind evidence-based practice promoted by the government is more or less positivistic (recognising that positivism takes many forms) and has a commitment to 'scientific methods' and causality as the best way of determining reliable knowledge to improve educational outcomes for all young people. Broadly speaking, positivism 'involves an ontology of an atomised, regular universe of facts in which regularity is taken as evidence of cause and effect, and where the real is reducible to experience' (Clegg, 2005, p. 420). 'This is manifested through an evidence hierarchy' (Petersen and Olsson, 2015, p. 1582) where one finds particular research designs favoured, in this case with randomised controlled trials and other types of experimental research design at the top. The consideration of evidence-based practice thus needs to start with an understanding of experimentation:

> By assigning experimental control conditions to an intervention and focusing on clear outcome measures, it is possible to make the argument that it is the intervention, not other causal factors, that is producing the desired effect. Careful experimental design can eliminate systematic bias and the ideal of randomisation allows for the calculation of the conditions under which it is safe ... to reject the null hypothesis that there is no difference between the control and experimental groups.
>
> (Clegg, 2005, p. 419)

Thus, experimental designs can produce regular events based on the *theoretical reasoning* that has gone into the design of the experiment and in interpreting the results. But when we are looking for an explanation that could allow us to understand the outcomes from a particular educational intervention, whether experimentally designed or action-researcher designed, we also have to be interested in the ways of scientifically conceptualising the underlying processes that produce the observed (empirical). But, the underlying assumptions of positivism operate only at the level of the empirical, and deny the reality of these underlying theoretical stipulations, 'referring to them merely as models or heuristics for understanding the really real of the empirical' (ibid., p. 420). In this way, the cultural work of experimentation remains concealed.

When explaining the outcomes from a particular educational intervention, therefore, we need to understand the relationship between the intervention and its effects, that is to say, how the intervention processes bring about certain effects. Effective interventions are those in which there is a secure relation between the intervention (as cause) and its outcomes or results (as effects). Here, 'it is important to note that "effectiveness" is an instrumental value: it refers to the quality of processes that bring about the effects' (Biesta, 2007, p. 7) but it does not say anything about the relationship itself. 'How do interventions work? How are links between actions and effects established?' (Biesta, 2010, p. 496). Evidence-based practice thus appears to rely on a separation between the means and ends of professional action: 'Evidence-based practice assumes that the ends of professional action are given, and that the only relevant (professional and research) questions to be asked are about the most effective and efficient ways of achieving those ends.' Teachers not only need to ask whether educational strategies or interventions are effective in themselves, they also always need to ask how they are effective and what they involve. And as Carr (1992) makes clear, the means teachers use 'contribute qualitatively to the very character of the goals which they produce' (p. 249).

These considerations raise questions about the appropriateness of the model of professional action and knowledge implied in evidence-based practice. What is needed is an acknowledgment of the fact that education is a moral practice, rather than a technical enterprise; it has multiple goals and its basis includes experience, judgement and local knowledge as well as research. Teaching is not homogeneous; it deals with difference and complexity: 'Professional action in education, as in many other professional fields always needs to take the normative dimension into consideration.' Teachers make judgments about the most appropriate course of action in specific circumstances. As Sanderson (2003) makes clear, 'the question for teachers is not simply "what works" but rather, more broadly it is, what is appropriate for whom in these circumstances' (p. 340). 'What works' crucially depends on judgments about what is educationally desirable. Evidence based practice has a top-down rationalistic view, incorporating the belief that policy goals and evidence have general relevance independently of context. It relies too heavily on empiricism and a narrow definition of evidence.

Conclusion

The chapter has highlighted the condition of the field of geography education research and the broader debate about evidence-based practice and 'the shifts in the power structures of educational policy that have occurred in England and many countries over the past 30 years as neoliberal governments have come into power' (Cochran-Smith, 2016, p. xii). The outcome in England has been described by Czerniawski (2015) as the almost seamless movement 'into a new era of school-centred, school-led or school-focused (take your pick) research' (p. 28). Czerniawski uses the word 'new' not just to emphasise the policy context and the movement of research (and teacher training and CPD) increasingly into schools, but that the tradition of teacher research itself, well established in particular theoretical and methodological traditions, is 'in danger of morphing into a form of instrumentalism far removed from the ideals it was intended to engender' (ibid.). What we are alerted to is how 'these neoliberal perspectives are becoming nearly imperceptible as ideology and are more likely to be understood as common sense' (Cochran-Smith, 2016, p. xii).

We hope some clarity has emerged about the terms of the argument. The idea of evidence is strongly associated with a particular view of science, which we have characterised as broadly positivist, and the way that evidence is understood is in practice being narrowed to a particular research methodology – RCTs and other forms of experimentation. In seeking to question the evidence-based practice agenda we recognise the problems with the instrumental rationality that underlies evidence-based practice. As Sanderson (2003) argues, 'by focusing on "formal" scientific and technical knowledge, [responses based on instrumental rationality] neglect the key role played in problem solving by "practical wisdom" and "informal" tacit knowledge. [And] by conceiving of rationality in terms of means to given ends, [responses based on instrumental rationality] neglect the ethical-moral dimension of problem solving' (p. 340). This is why the agenda of evidence-based practice is at least insufficient 'because judgment in education is not simply about what is possible (a factual judgment) but about what is educationally desirable (a value judgment)' (Biesta, 2007, p. 11).

At the same time, like Clegg (2005), we have sought to emphasise that 'arguments about evidence-based policy and practice are part of the sociopolitical realities of education' (p. 426). There is no simple evidence to practice relationship. In the current climate, however, the proponents of evidence-based practice propose an unproblematic relationship between research and practice, and also amongst policy, research and practice. At the same time, debates about 'evidence' are being used to reposition practitioner knowledge and to govern practice in particular ways. We do believe that there is considerable scope for improvement of the ways in which educational research and educational practice communicate and interact, as highlighted by the BERA-RSA Inquiry and Morgan's arguments about Methodism. Finally, a template of teacher-led research we do subscribe to is one in which 'teachers are the agents and source, and not the objects, of reform' (Winch et al., 2015, p. 207). This can only enhance the production and use of professional knowledge in educational practice.

Key readings

1   Elliott, J. (2001) 'Making evidence-based practice educational', *British Educational Research Journal*, 27 (5), 555–74. This article highlights the earlier debate about evidence-based practice in education. It draws attention to some of the assumptions that underpin what Elliott describes as an 'engineering model' of research and actionable knowledge and emphasises the importance of the relationship between educational aims and processes in informing educational practice. A major theme in the article is the need for an articulate educational theory to inform all educational research.

2   Goldacre, B. (2013) *Building Evidence into Education: The Goldacre Report*, London: Department for Education (DfE). The Report aims to promote a more evidence-based approach to practice in education, building on and

learning from the advances made in health and medicine that have accrued from such an approach. Goldacre is aware that, as a medical doctor, he is exhorting the education profession to change based upon the experiences of the medical profession. Whilst acknowledging that there are differences between medicine and education, he suggests that there are commonalities that mean an evidence-based approach is appropriate. It is an opportunity to read a government report that has been influential in recent education policy.

Notes

1 Over 700 schools took part in the intervention trials, co-ordinated through around 200 teaching school alliances. The scheme had two stages: a consultation to decide which interventions would be trialed, and a two-year programme of testing in schools. The research report was published in 2016 and is available at: https://www.gov.uk/government/publications/closing-the-gap-test-and-learn.
2 This is not to suggest that it is feasible or desirable that teachers continuously engage with and in research alongside their teaching duties and responsibilities.
3 Masters-level study is distinctive in that such programmes usually set out to develop teacher researchers to the point where they could conduct, write up and critique research and contribute to the wider knowledge base. The analysis of the Masters-level dissertations showed that over time the research undertaken by teachers has become increasingly framed in terms of particular forms of practice and finding ways of being more effective in delivering predetermined outcomes. Data (or evidence) seemed to be construed as a *post hoc* legitimisation of school improvement agendas rather than genuinely informing them. This highlighted not only an increasing utilitarianism within teachers continuing professional development through Masters study but significantly that teachers seemed not to recognise the 'invisible technologies' of government agendas.
4 Initial Teacher Education (ITE) is also an important area of consideration when discussing the relationship between research, policy and practice and teacher engagement in and with research. Historically, there has been close relationships between educational research and ITE provision. Over the past three decades ITE in England has become highly politicised, and 'positioned as an effective mechanism to transform teaching and teacher professionalism and steer change in schools' (Beauchamp et al, 2013: 7). Recent governments across the political spectrum have worked to control the content, location and quality of ITE, increasingly anchored in the centrality of practice and practical knowledge via the mechanisms of regulation and monitoring. The overall place of research in teacher learning has thus, arguably, diminished over time. It should be emphasised, however, that most university-led provision has maintained a commitment to combine perspectives from educational research with meeting the official requirements of the Teachers' Standards. Many of these programmes 'draw explicitly on practitioner enquiry or action research modes of learning and assessment for pre-service teachers' (ibid., p. 5). Despite the recent government emphasis on the importance of evidence based policy and practice (Goldacre, 2013; DfE, 2013) in England, the current direction of teacher education reform seems to place very limited emphasis on the use of research – of any kind. In consequence, the relationship between policy, research and practice is in flux. This situation has implications for the future contribution of research based professional knowledge in teacher preparation in England.

5 The Report emphasises that teachers might ordinarily engage with, and where appropriate, in research, but such engagement need not, and must not, become a burden on a profession that sometimes struggles with the weight of the various demands rightly or wrongly placed upon it.

References

Beauchamp, G., Clarke, L., Hulme, M., and Murray, J. (2013) *Research and Teacher Education: The BERA-RSA Inquiry. Policy and Practice within the United Kingdom*. Project Report, London: British Educational Research Association.

Bednarz, S.W., Heffron, S. and Huynh, N.T. (eds.) (2013) *A Road Map for 21st Century Geography Education: Geography Education Research* (A report from the Geography Education Research Committee of the Road Map for 21st Century Geography Education Project). Washington, DC: Association of American Geographers.

Biesta, G.J.J. (2007) Why 'what works' still won't work: evidence-based practice and the democratic deficit in educational research, *Educational Theory*, 57 (1), 1–22.

Biesta, G.J.J. (2010) 'Why 'what works' still won't work: from evidence-based education to value-based education', *Studies in Philosophy and Education*, 29 (5), 491–503.

British Education Research Association (BERA)-Royal Society of the Arts (RSA) (2014) *Research and the Teaching Profession: Building the Capacity for a Self-Improving Education System*. Final Report of the BERA-RSA Inquiry into the Role of Research in Teacher Education, BERA.

Brooks, C. (2015) 'Research and professional practice' in G. Butt (ed.) *MasterClass in Geography Education Transforming Teaching and Learning*, London: Bloomsbury, pp. 31–44.

Butt, G. (2015) Introduction, in G. Butt (ed.) *MasterClass in Geography Education Transforming Teaching and Learning*, London: Bloomsbury, pp. 3–14.

Carr, D. (1992) 'Practical enquiry, values and the problem of educational theory', *Oxford Review of Education*, 18 (3), 241–51.

Clegg, S. (2005) 'Evidence-based practice in educational research: a critical realist critique of systematic review', *British Journal of Sociology of Education*, 26 (3), 415–28.

Cochran-Smith, M. (2016) Foreword, in G. Beauchamp, L. Clarke, M. Hulme, M. Jephcote, A. Kennedy, G. Magennis, I. Menter, J. Muray, T. Mutton, T. O'Doherty and G. Poiser (The Teacher Education Group) *Teacher Education in Times of Change*, Bristol: Policy Press.

Czerniawski, G. (2015) Where are all the teachers? *Research Intelligence*, Spring 126, 29–30.

Demirci, A. and Tuna, F. (2017) 'Learning progressions in K12: a critical overview and prospects for the future', in O.M. Solari, M. Solem, M. and R. Boehm (eds.) *Learning Progressions in Geography Education: International Perspectives*, Cham, Switzerland: Springer.

DfE (2013a) *Research Priorities and Questions: Teachers and Teaching*, London: Department for Education.

DfE (2013b) *Analytical Review Executive Summary*, London: Department for Education.

DfE (2014) *Assessment, Curriculum and Qualifications: Research Priorities and Questions*, London: Department for Education.

Goldacre, B. (2013) *Building Evidence into Education*, Available at: http://media. education.gov.uk/assets/files/pdf/b/ben%20goldacre%20paper.pdf [Accessed 14 January 2016].

Hammersley, M. (2001) *Some Questions about Evidence-based Practice in Education*, Paper presented at the Symposium on 'Evidence-based practice in education' at the Annual Conference of the British Educational Research Association, University of Leeds, England, September 13–15, Available at: http://www.leeds.ac.uk/ educol/documents/00001819.htm [Accessed 14 January 2016].

Hillage J., Pearson R., Anderson A. and Tamkin P. (1998) *Excellence in Research on Schools*, Research Report RR74, Department for Education and Employment.

International Geographical Union Commission on Geographical Education (ICU-CGE) (2015) *International Declaration on Research*, Available at: http://www. igu-cge.org/charters.htm [Accessed 14 January 2016].

Lambert, D. (2010) 'Geography education research and why it matters', *International Research in Geographical and Environmental Education*, 19 (2), 83–6.

Morgan, J. (2015) Discussion to Part III, in G. Butt (ed.) *MasterClass in Geography Education Transforming Teaching and Learning*, London: Bloomsbury, pp. 145–7.

National Foundation for Educational Research (NFER) (2014) *Using Evidence in the Classroom: What Works and Why?* Slough: The National Foundation for Educational Research.

Nieveen, N. and Kuiper, W. (2012) 'Balancing curriculum freedom and regulation in the Netherlands', *European Educational Research Journal*, 11 (3), 357–68.

Oancea, A. (2014) 'Teachers' professional knowledge and state-funded teacher education: a (hi)story of critiques and silences', *Oxford Review of Education*, 40 (4), 97–519.

Ozga, J. (2004) From Research to Policy and Practice: Some Issues in Knowledge Transfer, *Briefing no. 31*, CES, University of Edinburgh.

Petersen, A. C. and Olsson, J. I. (2015) 'Calling evidence-based practice into question: acknowledging phronetic knowledge in social work', *British Journal of Social Work* 45, 1581–97.

Sanderson, I. (2003) 'Is it 'what works' that matters? Evaluation and evidence-based policy-making', *Research Papers in Education*, 28 (4), 331–45.

Stenhouse, L. (1981) 'What counts as educational research?', *British Journal of Educational Studies*, 29 (2), 103–13.

Tooley, J. with Darby, D. (1998) *Educational Research: A Critique*, London: Ofsted. Available at: http://www.ofsted.gov.uk/resources/educational-research-critique-tooley-report [Accessed 14 January, 2016].

Whitty, G. (2006) 'Education(al) research and education policy making: is conflict inevitable?', *British Educational Research Journal*, 32 (2), 159–76.

Winch, C., Oancea, A. and Orchard, J. (2015) 'The Contribution of Educational Research to teachers Professional Learning: Philosophical Understandings', *Oxford Review of Education*, 41(2), 202–16.

Acknowledgements

We are very grateful to the following individuals, groups and organisations for granting permission to reproduce material in the following chapters:

Chapter 2. The Geographical Association (GA) for *Figure 2.1*: Geography from 11–19 (Rawling, 2016). Jo Debens for *Figure 2.2*: GCSE aims: a version for pupils.

Chapter 4. Authors Peter Muller and Jan Nijma and the publishers John Wiley & Sons Ltd for permission to use *Figure 4.1*: The relationship between regional and systematic geography. American author Mark C Jones for permission to use the diagram in *Figure 4.3* showing its application to Southwest Asia & North Africa. Anke Uhlenwinkel for *Figure 4.4*: French *croquis* showing disparities in regional development, which was published as part of Jekel, T., Car, A., Strobl, J. & Griesebner, G. (eds.) GI_Forum 2013, Creating the GISociety.

Chapter 5. Figure 5.1: A curriculum map of earth science and physical geography in the National Curriculum, based on a document jointly produced by The Geographical Association, The Geological Society, The Earth Science Teachers' Association, The Royal Geographical Society and The Royal Meteorological Society and which was submitted to assist with the review of the National Curriculum for England (December 2011).

Chapter 7. The GA for *Figure 7.3*: Bennetts' diagram from Bennetts, T. (2005) 'The links between understanding, progression and assessment in the secondary geography curriculum', *Geography*, 90 (2), 152–70.

Chapter 8. The GA for *Figure 8.1*: Roberts (2003) Enquiry approach from Roberts, M. (2003) *Learning through Enquiry*, Sheffield: Geographical Association.

Chapter 10. The GA for *Figure 10.1*: Using the benchmark expectations in the assessment process (GA, 2014); *Figure 10.2*: Overview of how expectations of students might change over time (GA, 2014); *Figure 10.3*: Key Stage 3 unit: tectonic patterns and processes (GA AESIG, 2015) and *Figure 10.4*: Monitoring progress at different scales (GA, 2014).

Chapter 11. The GA for permission to use the Curriculum Making Model (no date). Also to the GA and and Royal Geographical Society with Institute of

British Geographers (RGS-IBG) as the model was used as part of teachers' professional development courses during the Action Plan for Geography.

Chapter 12. The RGS-IBG for permission to use Figure 12.4 from the original publication *Fieldwork Strategies.* Readers will find the schools section of the RGS website particularly helpful. Go to www.rgs.org/schools.

Chapter 13. Alec Couros of the University of Regina, Canada for permission to include *Figure 13.1a* and *Figure 13.1b.*

Chapter 14. Matthew Koehler and Punya Mishra, of Michigan State University, USA for permission to use the TPACK image from the original source http://tpack.org in *Figure 14.1.*

Chapter 16. Routledge for permission to include *Figure 16.1,* 'Approaches to values education' from Lambert, D. and Balderstone, D. (2000) *Learning to Teach Geography in the Secondary School,* London: RoutledgeFalmer, p. 293.

Chapter 18. The American Association of Geographers (http://www.aag.org/) for permission to reprint figure 1.4 the geographical plane from Hartshorne, Richard. (1939) *The Nature of Geography. A critical survey of current thought in the light of the past.* Association of American Geographers. p. 147. *Figure 18.1.* The GA for the figure from Vernon, E. (2016) 'The structure of knowledge: does theory matter?' *Geography,* 101 (2), p.102 Figure 18.2.

Index

Taylor & Francis eBooks

Helping you to choose the right eBooks for your Library

Add Routledge titles to your library's digital collection today. Taylor and Francis ebooks contains over 50,000 titles in the Humanities, Social Sciences, Behavioural Sciences, Built Environment and Law.

Choose from a range of subject packages or create your own!

Benefits for you
>> Free MARC records
>> COUNTER-compliant usage statistics
>> Flexible purchase and pricing options
>> All titles DRM-free.

REQUEST YOUR FREE INSTITUTIONAL TRIAL TODAY

Free Trials Available
We offer free trials to qualifying academic, corporate and government customers.

Benefits for your user
>> Off-site, anytime access via Athens or referring URL
>> Print or copy pages or chapters
>> Full content search
>> Bookmark, highlight and annotate text
>> Access to thousands of pages of quality research at the click of a button.

eCollections – Choose from over 30 subject eCollections, including:

Archaeology	Language Learning
Architecture	Law
Asian Studies	Literature
Business & Management	Media & Communication
Classical Studies	Middle East Studies
Construction	Music
Creative & Media Arts	Philosophy
Criminology & Criminal Justice	Planning
Economics	Politics
Education	Psychology & Mental Health
Energy	Religion
Engineering	Security
English Language & Linguistics	Social Work
Environment & Sustainability	Sociology
Geography	Sport
Health Studies	Theatre & Performance
History	Tourism, Hospitality & Events

For more information, pricing enquiries or to order a free trial, please contact your local sales team: www.tandfebooks.com/page/sales

 Routledge
Taylor & Francis Group

The home of
Routledge books

www.tandfebooks.com